HOSTILE INTENT

Other Titles of Interest from Potomac Books

The Castro Obsession: U.S. Covert Operations Against Cuba, 1959–1965
by Don Bohning

Intimate Ties, Bitter Struggles: The United States and Latin America Since 1945
by Alan McPherson

Spymaster: My Life in the CIA
by Ted Shackley with Richard A. Finney

HOSTILE INTENT

U.S. Covert Operations in Chile, 1964–1974

KRISTIAN GUSTAFSON

Potomac Books, Inc.
Washington, D.C.

Library of Congress Cataloging-in-Publication Data
Gustafson, Kristian, 1974–
Hostile intent : U.S. covert operations in Chile, 1964–1974 / Kristian Gustafson. — 1st ed.
p. cm.
Includes bibliographical references and index.
ISBN 978-1-59797-097-6 (hardcover : alk. paper)
1. United States. Central Intelligence Agency. 2. Espionage, American—Chile. 3. Subversive activities—Chile. 4. Chile—History—Coup d'état, 1973. 5. Allende Gossens, Salvador, 1908–1973. I. Title.
JK468.I6G87 2007
327.127308309′046—dc22

2007020814

Printed in the United States of America on acid-free paper that meets the American National Standards Institute Z39-48 Standard.

Potomac Books, Inc.
22841 Quicksilver Drive
Dulles, Virginia 20166

First Edition

10 9 8 7 6 5 4 3 2 1

Revolution is not a dinner party, not an essay, nor a painting, nor a piece of embroidery; it cannot be advanced softly, gradually, carefully, considerately, respectfully, politely, plainly and modestly.

—Mao Tse Tung

Not only are the men of democracies not naturally desirous of revolutions, but they are afraid of them.

—Alexis de Tocqueville,
Democracy in America

CONTENTS

ACKNOWLEDGMENTS

This book could not have been completed without the help of many individuals and institutions. In the United Kingdom, Professor Christopher Andrew at the University of Cambridge must be thanked for taking me on as a student. Further personal help came from Professor Peter Jackson at the University of Wales, Aberystwyth, and Professor Richard Aldrich at the University of Nottingham, while financial assistance came from both Downing College and the Faculty of History at the University of Cambridge. In the United States, immense help came from William D. Rogers at Arnold Porter LLB and Dr. Brian Latell at CSIS—without these two men there would be no interviews in this work. The President Lyndon B. Johnson Foundation funded the research conducted at the Presidential Library in Austin, Texas. Research in Chile would have been impossible without the help of Dr. Joaquín Fermandois at the Pontificia Universidad Católica de Chile and Dr. Cristián Pérez at the Centro de Estudios Públicos, Santiago. To my colleague Tanya Harmer I owe thanks for hours of discussion about archives, interviews, and life dealing with Chileans. Last, thanks for personal support must go to my family and especially to my wife, Christina, who makes me smile and laugh every day.

CHRONOLOGY

January 1961	The United States begins subsidizing Chile's Christian Democratic Party (PDC).
March 1961	Salvador Allende begins to deal with the KGB.
October 1963	The United States publishes the first National Intelligence Estimate (NIE) about Chile.
November 1963	John F. Kennedy is assassinated. Lyndon B. Johnson becomes president.
March 1964	The CIA begins its covert action program to prevent Allende's electoral victory in the 1964 presidential election.
Sept. 4, 1964	Eduardo Frei wins the Chilean presidential election.
May 1968	The U.S. government decides to initiate a covert operation to affect the 1969 congressional elections in Chile.
January 1969	The United States publishes the second NIE about Chile.
Jan. 20, 1969	Richard Milhous Nixon is inaugurated the thirty-seventh president of the United States.

March 1969	Chile holds congressional elections.
October 1969	Gen. Roberto Viaux leads *Tacnazo* revolt.
March 1970	The United States begins its spoiling operation against Allende.
July 1970	The United States issues National Security Study Memorandum 97 (NSSM 97).
August 1970	Track I begins.
Sept. 4, 1970	Allende wins a plurality in the Chilean presidential election.
Sept. 15, 1970	The NSC takes control of planning covert operations in Chile. Track II (Operation FU/BELT) begins.
Oct. 22, 1970	Gen. René Schneider is assassinated; he dies on October 25.
Oct. 24, 1970	Allende is confirmed as president of Chile; he is inaugurated on November 5.
November 1970	Raymond Warren replaces Henry Hecksher as COS in Santiago.
Nov. 5, 1970	NSSM 97 is revised.
Nov. 9, 1970	National Security Decision Memorandum 93 is issued.
Nov. 17, 1970	The United States begins a new covert action program in Chile and continues to fund *El Mercurio*.
January 1971	The United States authorizes support totaling $1.28 million for the PDC.
September 1971	Nathaniel Davis becomes the U.S. ambassador to Chile.

December 1971	Chileans stage the first major protest of the Allende government, the March of the Empty Pots.
January 1972	Gen. Augusto Pinochet becomes the army chief of staff. He later claims that this is when he begins plotting against Allende.
March 1972	The International Telephone and Telegraph (ITT) scandal breaks in Jack Anderson's syndicated column *The Washington Merry-Go-Round.*
June 1972	The United States publishes the third NIE about Chile.
Aug. 1972	Chilean strikes begin.
Nov. 1972	Allende calls his first emergency military cabinet.
May 1973	The Chilean navy begins coup plotting in earnest.
June 28, 1973	The Chilean army's Second Armored Regiment attempts a coup (El Tanquetazo) independently; it fails.
July 15, 1973	The "Committee of 15" admirals and generals decide to begin coup plotting.
Aug. 1973	Allende calls his second military cabinet. The CIA starts issuing periodic warnings of a coup.
Aug. 7, 1973	The Chilean navy reveals a communist mutiny plot.
Aug. 23, 1973	Gen. Carlos Prats resigns. Pinochet becomes army commander in chief and commits the army to the coup.
Sept. 7, 1973	The coup plot, as it actually unfolded, is completed and put into operation.
Sept. 8, 1973	The CIA receives its first hard intelligence on the coup.

Sept. 11, 1973	Allende is overthrown.
Jan. 23, 1974	The Chilean Junta issues decree law 1899, banning all political activity outright.
March 1974	The CIA stops funding the PDC.

INTRODUCTION: THE CIA IN CHILE

No matter what we do it will probably end up dismal.[1]

—Secretary of State William Rogers, commenting to Kissinger about Chile, September 14, 1970

On September 11, 1973, the Chilean army stormed into the presidential palace of the Republic of Chile, La Moneda, to overthrow the elected leader, Salvador Allende. This was *not* a palace coup, but a social upheaval of the first order, a shuddering spasm of violence and frustration and cruelty, an event that left hundreds of bodies in its path. The central act of the coup, the storming of La Moneda, was a well-planned attack, which proceeded almost perfectly. Yet it found the ultimate target of the coup, Allende, already dead by suicide. It is a testimony to the event's emotional power that, in our cruel world, it should still be considered important in the United States despite happening in such an isolated and distant land, so long ago. It makes more sense when one notes that the American government had, without a doubt, a direct interest—and perhaps a role—in what went on that day.

Pivotal to this drama are the actions of the Central Intelligence Agency (CIA) and the orders it received from a series of U.S. administrations. Over the course of more than ten years, the CIA produced propaganda, manipulated the press, funded opposition groups, dealt with coup plotters and rebellious army officers, funded strikes, and in many other ways made life difficult for Allende, a proud Marxist, the first to gain power via the ballot box during the Cold War era. Yet debates about the extent and intent of U.S. government action in Chile remain. Did the Richard Nixon administration, most notably, try to have Allende assassinated? Did the

CIA, acting under orders from the Oval Office, engineer the coup that resulted in Allende's death? Did the CIA choose and groom Gen. Augusto Pinochet, the coup leader whose dictatorial government subsequently executed hundreds, likely thousands, of political opponents over the course of its seventeen-year reign?

U.S. actions in Chile started the debate on the public acceptability of "covert action," that amorphous term that covers operations ranging from secret funding to assassination and other acts some say are scarcely short of war. In the 1960s and '70s, in the throes of the Cold War, the CIA and other U.S. government agencies operated in Chile to secure the interests of the United States against what it perceived to be an inroad of communism in the Americas. U.S. actions in Chile encompassed everything from benign propaganda to—perhaps—the plotting of a coup. But were the actions effective? Were they appropriate to the threat? Should the U.S. government engage in such measures against a democracy? And to what extent should the U.S. president be allowed to authorize covert actions without congressional consent? These critical questions, with implications for U.S. governance and the power of the president and the Congress, reverberate today.

The debate over covert action is not quiet or civil. Allende's death and the course of the vicious dictatorship that followed have caused a taking-of-sides on the issue that fits snugly into the polarization of the American political scene today: those on the left think the U.S. government bears ultimate responsibility for its criminal, imperialist behavior, and those on the right say the United States did nothing wrong. Like so much else in this world, the truth is somewhere in the middle of these perspectives. Yet in a world of political poles, to say so openly wins friends in neither camp, and so one is hard pressed to find anyone in popular or academic life who holds a position in the middle ground. Chile, more than many other topics, has been seized as evidence in a *political* argument: those who write about Allende's overthrow are inexorably pigeonholed as either left-wing or right-wing. Certainly, in the popular political culture of America and the West in general, the Chilean coup takes a prominent place among the litany of actions that are meant to confirm America's reputation as a modern agent of imperialism. The United States, it is argued, would ruthlessly and instinctively crush any communist or socialist government it possibly could, no matter how benign the state. Even in the post–Cold War era, governments of small states that challenge U.S. dominance in any region, and especially in Latin America, will be crushed before they can serve as David-versus-Goliath examples to their neighboring states. As far as this reputation applies to Chile, the belief that the United States engages in unbridled imperialist behavior is strong, despite the lack of any overwhelming evidence, and the means to disprove this belief must flow against a strong tide of popular misconception. As Nathaniel Davis, former American ambassador to Chile, said in his memoir, some people believe that "Allende *had* to succeed. Many were not ready to accept his failure, and they were particularly reluctant to accept the idea that Allende's tragedy has indigenous Chilean roots, even in part."[2]

But how can an event that took place more than a generation ago, and in another hemisphere, continue to be relevant to the modern politician, civil servant, or average citizen? The United States is engaged in a protracted war against unseen enemies around the world, and the use of covert action (an art practiced most often, but not exclusively, by the CIA) is important in this fight. Yet covert action has always been problematic for the United States. Most recently, it has been at the center of a serious diplomatic problem for the United States with its allies around the globe, especially those in the European Union such as Italy and Germany, who have gone so far as to issue arrest warrants for CIA officers they believe to be connected to covert action in the form of rendition (removal of a person from one nation to another without normal procedures of extradition) of suspected terrorists.[3] Perhaps less immediately, the authority to use covert action against U.S. enemies is a controversial point in the relationship between Congress and the president. As chief executive and commander in chief, the U.S. president has broad constitutional authority to engage in "little wars," "secret wars," and other actions short of the common definition of "war" in order to protect the United States and its citizens. The 1974 Hughes-Ryan Amendment to the Foreign Assistance Act states that the president must produce to Congress a finding that any authorized covert action is "important to the national security interests of the United States" before it can be funded.[4] This amendment is an indirect result of the public controversy over covert actions in Chile. Debates about the Hughes-Ryan Amendment (as well as its cousin, the Boland Amendment, enacted in the wake of the Iran-*contra* scandal) and about presidential authority over covert action still simmer, so what went on in Chile continues to be critical to our understanding of how the executive and Congress function and interact in the nation's defense today. Moreover, recent efforts by the Pentagon, apparently supported by President George W. Bush, have allowed the U.S. military to conduct covert action on its own accord in order to bypass established congressional oversight.[5] One can perhaps view this as an extension of the duel between Congress and the executive over the right to control covert action.

The events of September 11, 1973, are therefore not a matter of arcane historical debate or the private domain of foreign policy pundits. But likewise, they are not merely the preserve of those arguing the powers of the president versus the powers of Congress. Almost everyone alive at the time of the coup knows some version of the coup story, and many are likely to believe that the CIA arranged President Allende's downfall. Indeed, the story remained current long into the twenty-first century, with attempts by the Chilean government to bring Pinochet to justice ongoing up to the very point when the aged and ill Pinochet died of congestive heart failure on December 10, 2006. Moreover, those who would oppose the United States today, including Venezuela's Hugo Chavez as but one of many, frequently raise the specter of CIA action against them and invoke Allende's memory.[6] But the story—the mythology—about Chile, repeated in various forms for more than thirty years, is far too stark and simplistic to be accepted at face value. My hope here is to add color to what has become a debate remarkable for the use of black and white.

The point of this book is to better establish the facts of a particular series of covert actions initiated by the U.S. government and executed largely by the CIA in conjunction with the State Department and the Defense Intelligence Agency. It will not in general attempt to exonerate the United States for its past actions, and it will not try to apologize for the U.S. government; the reader may make his or her own judgments on the matters of morality and culpability. Further, this is *not* written with the assumption that all covert action is necessarily evil, wrong, or even always effective; rather it is a tool of statecraft used by all the major world powers, whose study is important for its future use. There are enough mistakes and errors in the history of U.S. foreign politics that one does not need to invent them to make a point, and so with Chile there is no need to invent greater errors where great errors already exist. Only with an open-minded examination can we identify the true lessons that need to be drawn. To paraphrase former Director of Central Intelligence (DCI) William Colby in his memoir *Honorable Men*, it is dangerous to make the CIA a scapegoat for all the evils of the world and of U.S. foreign policy; doing so creates a false image of the Agency that deprives the American nation of a useful and necessary tool in the international arena. If the CIA is to be a practical instrument of statecraft, those in government must understand what they can achieve with a carefully planned, long-term operation *in support* of some local leader or group, rather than simply *against* some perceived foe or danger.[7] U.S. leadership must understand that covert action is not the ultimate solution to intractable or embarrassing problems. The various operations conducted in Chile over the years support this concept amply.

To look at the events that occurred before and during Allende's presidency, therefore, is to study how the U.S. government deals with perceived threats to its national interests through its main arm of covert action, the CIA. We live in a postideological world, and we too easily forget the very real-life fears of our half-century-long confrontation with communism, a struggle that for much of that time was only a hair's breadth from violence. But this is a Cold War story, and what makes this story so curious and so interesting is the Cold War reality that the U.S. government could neither acquiesce in its confrontation with the USSR nor escalate, for "the former amounted to a loss in a campaign of the [Cold] War, with incalculable effects on the cohesion and vitality of the Western Alliance . . . [while] the latter strategy would have cracked completely the domestic popular basis that, with some fissures, held together so remarkably for almost half a century."[8] As long as East and West existed, they were fated to be in perpetual competition with one another, a competition neither could afford to lose. And yet, while this is very much a Cold War tale, it could very well have taken place since the collapse of the Berlin Wall. Even though Soviet communism has largely ceased as a threat, the United States continues to perceive subtle threats to its power. A look to tension between the United States and Venezuela, Cuba, Iran, and Afghanistan is sufficient evidence of this.

Before one begins to draw lessons from the history of U.S. operations in Chile, one must first understand more accurately what occurred. Accordingly, the very first priority of this work is to establish a coherent historical narrative of U.S. covert actions in Chile beginning in 1964, through the advent of the military dictatorship in September 1973, and into the new regime's first months in power. Most of the history written up to this point tends to deal with U.S. actions in Chile as events independent from one another, when in fact the events of September–October 1970, for instance, occurred as a direct consequence of programs initiated under Presidents John F. Kennedy and Lyndon Johnson in 1963. Proceeding chronologically, we can trace the initiation, growth, and maturity of U.S. covert actions in Chile and the political decisions that prompted them, from their inception prior to Johnson's presidency to their conclusion in early 1974. The focus will remain with the CIA's covert actions and the U.S. government's decision-making process. The specific aim of this is to draw out some of the lessons about the function and utility of covert action as a tool of statecraft. If this work can suggest something toward the theory of the employment of covert action or can raise questions about its application, then this is a beneficial addition to the current literature. We will of course have to look at aspects of Chile's internal political culture: this—not the U.S. government, Richard Nixon, Henry A. Kissinger, or the CIA—was the driving force behind the coup in Chile. Yet there is no room here, or any need, for these aspects of Chilean politics to be covered in lengthy detail, as they have been discussed in several more specialized books and here the reader is more interested in the extent of American involvement.[9] So where Chilean politics is dealt with, it is to serve as a counterpoint to American actions and involvement, or lack thereof.

Thanks to the declassification of U.S. government papers, U.S. intervention in Chile can be traced as far back as its origins under President Dwight Eisenhower. Under the leadership of President Johnson, secret interference in Chilean political affairs began in earnest during the 1964 presidential election in Chile. This period, the first in our chronology, is remarkable for the complex decision making that led to the initial involvement, a cooperative matter between the CIA, the Department of State, and the White House. It is interesting, moreover, because one sees the United States wed itself to the political center-left in Chile—a marriage it found difficult to dissolve long after it had ceased to be beneficial to either party. Yet this period, as with the period leading up to the 1970 election of Allende, is not widely known or understood, despite the (eminently examinable) pattern it sets for U.S. political aims in Latin America. These aims, and the means deployed to achieve them, cannot be separated from the actions executed while Allende was president of Chile. The foreign policy goals and the mechanisms the U.S. government used to achieve them are identical over the entire decade covered in this work. But the specific methods used in each case yielded different results as the domestic politics in Chile changed. As one can see with the 1964 presidential election and the 1969 congressional elections in Chile, the CIA was not always able to adjust its tactics to the subtle differences in the Chilean political scene in order to achieve its goals.

Among the greatest errors in the application of covert force, there are few better examples than the clumsy U.S. attempts to prevent Allende's election and inauguration in September–October 1970. Spearheaded by National Security Adviser Dr. Kissinger and spurred by an enraged and irrational President Nixon, the CIA—cut off from other government agencies in an operation it saw as pure madness—entered in Chile into what might be viewed as its most ill-fated operation since the Bay of Pigs. Though the fall of 1970 is the most heavily studied and cited period of U.S. action in Chile, documents released in the last five years allow a thorough re-evaluation of U.S. efforts. The notorious assassination of Chilean army commander in chief Gen. René Schneider, a product of U.S. machinations to avert an Allende government, can only now be placed in its proper context. In this action one can see the law of unintended consequences, as well as the troubles associated with unchecked ego in the determination of policy, bringing to mind Arthur Schlesinger's term "The Imperial Presidency."[10]

A more extensive examination of events during Allende's reign, from 1970 to 1973, reveals the deep and lively texture of Chile's political history and culture. The peaceful socialist who attempted to transform Chile's social landscape and thwart aggressive U.S. advances is not the same man who killed himself—with a gun gifted to him by Cuban leader Fidel Castro—as rebellious army troops, under the cover of air force jets, stormed almost unopposed into La Moneda. An energetic and charismatic public speaker, Allende captivated his audiences, both Chilean and foreign, with his earnest quest for justice, rejecting the economic tyranny of the "American Way" without embracing the Soviets' opposing physical tyranny. His was socialism "*con sabor a empanadas y vino tinto*"—socialism "with the taste of empanadas and red wine," an expression meant to show both the Chilean version's homegrown nature and its casual, easy progress.[11] Yet from the many sources available in both English and Spanish, there develops a picture not of a devoted democrat of Marxist inclination but rather a devoted Marxist working—if without sound political tactics—to convert Chile into a Marxist people's republic, which even if pursued through the ballot box would ultimately spell the end to liberal democracy in that country.[12] And while it is entirely correct to note that Allende rejected violence as a means to achieve his goals, it is equally necessary to doubt that he could restrain those members of his cabinet and his party who *did* embrace such violent means. In his three years in office, Allende alienated and stratified his population and lost control of his own ad hoc governing political party, the failed policies and provocations of which drove the country "into a cauldron of hatreds and tensions" to the point that the staunchly republican Chilean army took up arms against the president with the support of both the political right and the political center.[13] This is not to say that the government that followed Allende, that of Pinochet, was justifiable or a morally acceptable alternative. Rather, in the words of the scholar Mark Falcoff, "there is no reason to assume that the virtues of a vanished regime increase in direct proportion to the iniquities of its successor." [4]

The U.S. government's actions during this period are sometimes so different from what is often supposed that it does little good to leave them enshrined in myth. In the examination of this period, several prominent and controversial facts emerge: the evidence we have today suggests that the CIA *did not* attempt to organize a coup against Allende in 1973, even though it was not displeased to see the end of the Allende government; that the U.S. government (directed by President Nixon in a calmer mood) seems to have confined its activities to promoting Chile's opposition parties as a natural domestic check on Allende's plans; that U.S. knowledge of Pinochet and the coup was quite restricted until mere days or even hours before the army moved; and, digressing into the private sector, that U.S. corporate interest in Chile, in the form of the International Telephone and Telegraph Company (ITT) had very little direct influence on the determination of U.S. policy when it came to Chile.

Last in the narrative covered by this work is a narrow but important period, a period of about six months beginning the moment the Chilean military took power. In this critical period, various agencies of the U.S. government debated the way forward in an unfamiliar environment: namely, they had to deal with democratic parties that they had long supported but that suddenly stood in opposition to the emerging autocracy that their government supported. This dilemma, and the general U.S. reaction to the coup and Pinochet's emergence as the main power in Chile, provides an interesting coda to U.S. intervention in Chile, one that tells us much about the U.S. government's aims there.

When viewing events in Chile as a continuous campaign, a pattern emerges. From 1963 through to Allende's election on September 4, 1970, the main effort of American covert intervention in Chile was to maintain the democratic and constitutional order in Chile, an order that it was presumed would remain friendly and pro-American. While the U.S. government did seek to thwart Allende—an elected leader in a democratic state—it did so by relatively restricted methods. Indeed, this policy continued until the death of the Allende regime in September 1973, save for the short and disreputable coup attempts in September and October 1970. Once past the more controversial (but far too simplistic) issues of American guilt or innocence, the greater points about doctrine, decision making, and the overall utility of covert action can best be judged. Nothing we can do today can undo the mistakes of a generation past, but we can study those events to learn lessons for today and for the future.

REVIEW OF LITERATURE: NEW DOCUMENTS, NEW VIEW

Writing about intelligence is always a challenge. The most evident reason for this is the rather obvious fact that spies like to be secret about what they do—the agencies like to preserve their assets for future uses, governments want to keep their operations out of the public eye to preserve their proper diplomatic faces (or to prevent embarrassment), and the officers and agents do not like to talk about their experiences for personal and professional reasons, such as avoiding arrest for releasing secrets. When former intelligence officers write their memoirs, they either are too censored or circumspect (as in the memoir of the late DCI Richard Helms, *A Look over My Shoulder*) or are written to grind some personal axe (as in Peter Wright's *Spycatcher*, which accused the director of the British security service, MI5, of being a Soviet mole). Neither kind of memoir can be used as a sole source when discussing intelligence matters. But we cannot give up simply because the actual players refuse to speak up or refuse to speak calmly. Books on intelligence are important, as they are a part of the greater history of diplomacy and politics. The entire history of World War II is hollow if one forgets that the Allies could read all the German codes passed on their Enigma cipher machines, thus giving the Allies an incredible insight that might appear (as it did to Hitler) almost magical if one were not aware of the code breaking. As with the Enigma secret, intelligence sources eventually do come out into the open, but they are rarely complete on their own. As one cannot understand World War II without reading about Enigma, one cannot write a history of World War II with this information exclusively. All this is to say that it is impossible to comprehend the history of the Allende regime's fall without taking the CIA into account, but it is equally dangerous to write the history of the Allende regime based solely around the CIA's actions—to do so retrospectively grants the United States far more power than it actually ever had. Accordingly, what is produced here is not a history of the Allende regime, but an account of the CIA's actions in Chile in the context of those events. The aim of this book is to produce a better understanding of the secret part of the greater historical events in Chile during the Cold War.

Much literature about American covert activity in Chile from 1964 through to the early Pinochet years is available. In the period immediately following Allende's overthrow in September 1973, many books were written in a direct effort to condemn U.S. actions in Chile as entirely criminal in nature and execution. Very little was known at the time about what actions the Americans actually undertook, but this did not deter many pro-Allende authors. This was a period agitated not only by Allende's sad demise but also by the Nixon administration's excesses in Vietnam and in the Watergate scandal. The U.S. government at the time would have had, had it tried, a difficult time proving its bona fides with regards to its actions in Chile.

In the English-speaking world, few authors, most writing within the past fifteen years though some came earlier, have cut through the emotional politics of Allende's collapse to construct intelligent reviews of—to borrow one earlier author's title—*The Overthrow of Allende and the Politics of Chile.*[15] Few authors have had the qualifications or the data to write authoritatively on U.S. covert action in Chile. Those who have written interesting books on the topic, such as former U.S. ambassador to Chile Nathaniel Davis or former DCI William Colby, have highly recognizable biases. Beginning in 1999, however, the resources available on Chile grew immeasurably with the declassification and release of hundreds of thousands of U.S. government documents on CIA and State Department activities in Chile. The new government sources combine with the previous secondary literature to form a very accessible bibliographical base on which to construct a new interpretation of U.S. covert actions in Chile from 1964 to 1976. Ultimately, one must remember that the CIA's role in Chile (or in any other state around the world) is a politically heated topic, and there are few books that members from both political poles will accept unconditionally.

In the existing literature from Chile itself, the focus of study is neither on the U.S. intervention nor on the CIA's tactics but rather on the constitutional and political/tactical failures that caused Allende's government to collapse so completely.[16] Jorge Mario Eastman, a conservative, barely mentions American involvement in his book, and when he does, it is only to describe the inevitable American stance against a Marxist government in Chile, something agreed on even by socialist writer Joan E. Garcés.[17] The best of the new Chilean books on the topic, *Chile La Conjura* by Mónica González, likewise focuses on the progression of Chilean military plotting, with very few mentions at all of the CIA.[18] American intervention and pressure are, quite simply, not the paramount concerns. Overall, the books by Chilean authors stress the forceful and ultimately deciding role the Chilean armed forces played in the coup, after much discussion of the breakdown of the cohesion of the ruling Unidad Popular (UP) coalition.[19] The view that the Allende regime fell because of strings pulled in Washington seems almost nonexistent in Chilean publications since 1990.[20] The most recent writings out of Chile come from such public policy think tanks as the Center for Public Studies (Centro de Estudios Publicos, or

CEP) in Santiago and seem to demonstrate deeper understanding of Chile's particular place within the Cold War global battlefield.[21] Writing in the United States has predictably stressed the U.S. role in the coup and has remained even more concerned with the most sensational parts of the story. Perhaps the most notable example of this is Seymour Hersh's book *The Price of Power: Kissinger in the Nixon White House*, which propagates the common belief that the CIA aimed to assassinate Allende and was successful in overthrowing him. A successful *New York Times* reporter, Hersh made his name in journalism with his uncanny ability to brush aside the innumerable barriers of government secrecy to get the "straight dope" from inside sources. Yet his book tends toward conspiracy theory. Hersh alleges, based on the evidence of a clerk who handled some of the White House traffic on the matter, that "murder was one of the ways" that the CIA was directed to use to overthrow Allende.[22] In a subsequent chapter Hersh implies that the United States planned to assassinate Allende: "No document will ever be found, nor will there be an eye witness, to describe CIA plans . . . to murder Salvador Allende . . . [but] that the plans and pressures existed is confirmed by a senior member of the intelligence community" whose information, Hersh assures the reader, has been "unfailingly accurate."[23] Because it is quoted widely and despite its lack of proven sources, Hersh's book has become a machine to sustain misperceptions of American action in Chile.

But Hersh deserves a special place in history not only for his daring and provocative reporting but also for the results of that reporting. It was in part Hersh's articles (alongside those of fellow journalist Jack Anderson) that opened up to the public CIA covert action in Chile, thereby unleashing a spate of congressional hearings and inquiries about Chile that eventually led to some reform in the relations between Congress and the executive when it came to covert action.

The U.S. government first inaugurated the political partisanship rampant in debates about U.S. covert action in Chile. To understand the controversy that surrounds operations in Chile, one needs to remember the sparring between the president and Congress that marked the final months of the Nixon administration and much of the Ford administration. Chile became a focal point during this struggle. U.S. actions in Chile were never totally secret: between 1964 and 1973 representatives of the CIA discussed Chile with Congress members, their staffs, and congressional committees on forty occasions. On half of these occasions covert action was mentioned, and on many others the need for congressional funding approval was cited.[24] But the revelations about the CIA's relationship with ITT, published by Jack Anderson in 1972, sparked a new row between Congress and the president over the use or abuse of executive authority in an area that Congress as a whole thought was its own, or which committees such as the Senate Appropriations Committee reckoned ought to be theirs. This push was in part prompted by the fact that by the mid-1970s Congress had become a much more significant consumer of intelligence and wanted to have some say in how it was produced. But the primary trigger was concern about U.S. actions in Chile: one can directly link the congressional hearings of the mid-1970s to Anderson's revelations about ITT and Hersh's hints about the U.S. role in the September 11 coup that overthrew Allende. The reports produced from these hearings—the production of which independently formed a crisis of serious concern for the CIA—constitute a major cornerstone to any research on Chile.

The first of the two government documents available on Chile is the Senate report of April 1975 titled *Alleged Assassination Plots Involving Foreign Leaders*.[25] Dealing with several alleged American plots to assassinate leaders around the world, the report quotes widely from the CIA archives and submits a credible narrative of CIA and White House actions that were associated with General Schneider's death. This report exonerated the United States of responsibility for the murder. The second document, of wider scope and greater impact, was the *Staff Report of the Select Committee to Study Governmental Operations with Respect to Intelligence Activities: Covert Action in Chile, 1963–1973* and was commonly called the Church committee report.[26] Until quite recently, this report has been the primary source for all writing about Chile and the fall of the Allende government. Prompted in December 1974 by a *New York Times* story that detailed allegedly illegal activities undertaken by the CIA,[27] the Senate committee was formed under the chairmanship of Senator Frank Church, a Democrat from Idaho, to examine the allegations. It has remained the official word on the topic since its publication. Senator Barry Goldwater, a Republican member of the committee, publicly attacked the report for its partisan stance and free-flowing use of insinuation. As it was a staff report and not a committee report, members of the committee were not permitted to submit opposing views.[28] Both historian Mark Falcoff and Ambassador Nathaniel Davis support the view that the Church committee report, while containing useful information and apparent objectivity, "manages to convey at the same time the unmistakable impression" that all CIA activities were linked to coup plotting.[29] Yet one cannot dismiss this report entirely because it contains testimony from so many different players, given at a time much closer to events than any other source.

Highlighting the argument that Chile and the CIA's role there continues to be of concern to policymakers and the public in general, politically motivated releases of secret documents continued long after the scandals and crises of the second half of the 1970s. Specifically, the Chile Declassification Project by the Department of State has dramatically increased the public record as it applies to Chile. While Pinochet was the subject of legal wrangling and extradition orders throughout 1998, American president William J. Clinton ordered the release of all government documents that dealt with American intervention in Chile from the 1950s to the present. This was achieved with a massive declassification of documents from the Department of State, the CIA, the Department of Defense, the Department of Justice, and the National Archives between October 1999 and November 2000.[30] Thousands of documents dealing with Chile from the 1960s to the 1990s were declassified and compiled on a State Department website. All in all, over 40,500 documents—about 160,000 pages—are available to the general public.[31] While many of the documents have been censored, the excisions are not overwhelming and must be viewed as inescapable for documents pertaining to intelligence matters because the state has a duty to protect matters dealing with "tradecraft" (roughly defined as the art of spying) or the identity of officers, agents, or collaborators.

One of the first writers to make use of at least parts of this new archive was the British journalist Christopher Hitchens, who wrote articles for *Harper's Magazine* in February and March 2001.[32] A writer of remarkable journalistic style and power, Hitchens wrote with the express aim of having former National Security Adviser Henry Kissinger tried for crimes against humanity. Since then, other writers have tried to expand on this short work, to a good degree of success. Yet it is a controversial matter, and no book on Chile is published without much dispute and accusation, as illustrated when author Kenneth Maxwell and former Assistant Secretary of State William D. Rogers angrily jousted with each other in *Foreign Affairs* magazine in 2004.[33] Any discussion about Chile sparks debate, and not polite debate but heated arguments and often name calling. This is an emotional topic.

Two very recent books on Chile bear mention in detail here and will be covered more thoroughly throughout this book as their arguments diverge from my own. Perhaps the most popular book on Chile to emerge in the last fifteen years is Peter Kornbluh's *The Pinochet File*.[34] This text is based largely on the declassified documents of the aforementioned Chile Declassification Project, for whose continued release we largely owe to the ongoing efforts of Dr. Kornbluh and the National Security Archive program at George Washington University in Washington, D.C. Kornbluh dedicates two chapters to the period covered by this book, the first on Operation FU/Belt (covered in chapter four here) and the second on U.S. actions toward destabilization in Chile during the Allende presidency (roughly chapters 5, 6, and 7 here). The main criticism one might offer of Kornbluh's otherwise fine book is that he implicitly links *desire* to *action*. Actions taken in Chile that correspond to the desires of the realpolitik personalities in Washington are seen as the causation behind the events in Santiago. While this is certainly the case with the assassination of René Schneider in October 1970—dealt with in Kornbluh's first chapter—it is not necessarily true in the period of Allende's presidency, chapter 2 in *The Pinochet File*. This is an important book on Chile, yet at times it falls within the school of thought that wants to prove America's realpolitik aims and the subsequent actions of the CIA as the prime movers for all evil events in the developing world. Notably, as jacket comments on the book describe, Kornbluh aims at establishing the "smoking guns" that prove U.S. involvement as critical to the coup.[35] Because the book focuses so intently on the to and fro of U.S. documents, the domestic context is lost, and so the book seems to assume that the U.S. government's desires represented both the proximate cause (the straw that broke the camel's back) and ultimate cause (the rest of the straw) of the coup.[36] Every unfortunate event that occurred in Chile was the fault of the United States.

The second notable book on Chile to be mentioned herein is from Cambridge historian Jonathan Haslam: *The Nixon Administration and the Death of Allende's Chile*.[37] Appearing in late 2005, Haslam's slightly mistitled work focuses predominantly not on the Nixon administration but on the progress of Allende's campaign, election, and government. What justifies the mention of Nixon in the title are a limited number of assertions Haslam makes of that president's hand in the collapse of Allende's government. Like many previous works from other authors, Haslam offers little new evidence to prove the assertion of U.S. government support in the planning of the coup. While he presents some tantalizing nonattributed sources to indicate a secret link between Nixon and Kissinger to the coup plotters, he can offer only the theory that "the extraordinary degree of efficiency and ruthlessness" of the coup is "a notable feature . . . that always suggested special outside management," a not-so-subtle nod at the U.S. government (and a bit of a slight to the Chilean military's professionalism). That he suggests the coup was planned by some organization outside of the normal CIA chain of command—variously Gen.

Vernon Walters of the CIA and also members of the U.S. military assistance group in Chile—is especially notable and difficult to positively refute, outside of mentioning the lack of hard evidence to prove it in the first place. Nonetheless, these assertions form the minority of Haslam's book. He notes in his conclusion that, despite persistent U.S. involvement in Chile, the fall of the regime originated in its inability to maintain its own internal stability; that "domestic turmoil simply could not be insulated from the storms of the outer world"; and that this turmoil was a "direct consequence of UP policy"—though he still asserts that the U.S. government holds the bulk of the responsibility for the failure of Allende's government.[38] The detailed points of Haslam's arguments of American involvement will be dealt with through the book as they are chronologically appropriate and as they deviate from my own. What might be further noted about Haslam's book, as well as Kornbluh's, is that neither covers the whole sweep of what one might call "the Chilean campaign" (for reasons described later in this introduction) but rather they dwell on the more controversial episodes, so missing the full decadelong sweep of U.S. actions. This full survey, focused on U.S. plans and policies, is so far missing from the record.

One of the best recent books on Chile has been John Dinges's fine work *The Condor Years*. This thoroughly researched book stands as the benchmark for scholarship on the period after the 1973 coup and the Pinochet government in detail. It has excellent segments on would-be communist and socialist insurgent groups in Chile and the intelligence collected on them. While *The Condor Years* does not cover Allende's leadership, it does at least relieve the demand for scholarly work on the U.S. government's relationship with Pinochet. Since Dinges has, for the time being, cornered the market on the Pinochet government, I do not attempt here to overlap his research: little is said in this work of any events occurring after the 1973 coup and its immediate aftermath, except in the case where they shed light on the pre-coup actions and intentions of the CIA or the U.S. government as a whole.

THE CHILEAN CAMPAIGN

With more than thirty years of history passed, there is now a decent body of evidence on which one can construct a more coherent story about what went on in Chile through the 1960s and 1970s. The trend in writing about Chile so far has been to deal with particular incidents in isolation from the others—to look at the coup that toppled Allende, for instance, or to look at the assassination of General Schneider in October 1970, yet to do so without reference to the Unidad Popular election victory or Allende's previous electoral defeats. While this might produce more sensational books, it does little favor to the history of the events themselves, largely because it takes them out of their context. To understand U.S. action in Chile, it is important to view all of these events as a single decadelong campaign before examining the individual battles.

The study of U.S. actions in Chile—essentially a single campaign from 1963 to 1973—offers numerous opportunities for evaluating American doctrine (or lack thereof) when it comes to covert action. Several themes that arise over the course of the narrative bring this into clarity. First of all, study of this covert campaign mitigates the idea, popular in some circles, that the CIA is an all-powerful "dark force" that always acts above or outside the normal strictures of law and morality. In fact, it shows that the CIA is not that hawkish when viewed in comparison with the rest of the community of agencies and departments that make up the U.S. government: the demands and constraints of operating covertly, and the consequences of being caught, lend them a certain introspection when it comes to particularly aggressive programs. As a corollary to this point, the operations in Chile imply (as John le Carré, former intelligence officer and author of spy thrillers, suggested long ago) that covert action cannot solve all of a government's intractable problems. The secret world simply cannot make up for the failings of real-world diplomacy and normal interstate behavior, for it is implicitly bound by being secret and the strictures of secrecy prevents the CIA from applying force in sufficient measure to make good the worst of the failures of "normal" politics and diplomacy. One sees this as a negative lesson, for clearly President Nixon did not adhere to this belief, thinking that the failure of U.S. policy to stem the decades-long trend toward the Far Left in Chile—evident since at least the 1932 Chilean presidential election—could be reversed by a few men and some judiciously spent cash. The lesson one may draw from this is that covert action works best when it is least, that it cannot make conditions exist simply because one man wishes it to be so. The example of Chile shows, quite explicitly, that the state's power is limited when it comes to altering some other state's political economy. We may think the spies can go in and "save the day" when in fact they cannot. They may achieve the most when they have prevented the crisis from emerging in the first place.

It must be made clear to the reader that the U.S. government, as represented by several different administrations, absolutely sought to thwart Allende's government and plans. This fact is not questioned here. What is under debate is the method and reasoning that marked this opposition. However, contrary to many accounts, one *cannot* take for granted that the U.S. government was the driving force behind the coup that toppled Allende in 1973. While many authors have discussed the role of internal dissent and opposition to Allende in that president's downfall, most—including Haslam and Kornbluh, the two most recent English-language authors on the topic—play heavily on the U.S. government's role as the ultimate or proximate cause of the coup. The evidence presented herein will show that U.S. input and impact was less significant than many like to believe.

As for the organizational side of covert action, the Chile campaign demonstrates how harmonious interdepartmental relations are required for the success of covert action. Over the course of the ten years, it is simple to correlate periods of agreeable interdepartmental relations with successful operations, and conversely, those periods of disagreement or obstructionism with failures. This is likewise true of relations between the president and the Agency, and as the CIA's own history stated, "during Nixon's years in office, the relationship between the President and the CIA reached the lowest point in the Agency's history."[39] General Schneider's assassination stands at the extreme negative end of these relations, and the period 1971–1973 stands at a more positive—or perhaps just less negative—point on the spectrum.

More controversially, especially for those who agree with the concept of a strong executive, it becomes apparent with Chile that unfettered presidential authority to order covert action is not necessarily a good thing. Through the evidence presented by more than a decade of operations in Chile, it can be perceived that, despite the CIA's opposition, formalized approval processes for covert action *benefit* operations by imposing needed checks on the extent, proportionality, and morality of operations. Little-known and often ad hoc bodies at the cabinet and subcabinet level, such as the Special Review Group (SRG) and the 303 (later 40) Committee, have, since the Kennedy administration, taken it upon themselves to serve as a self-imposed check on covert action. Yet, with no legislated pathway for these processes and no congressional oversight, they were easily and quite legally bypassed by presidential fiat. While this benefited the Agency and the administration with speedy and streamlined approvals, it also allowed the ego or anger of a few individuals (in this case particularly, but not exclusively, President Nixon and his chief assistant, Henry Kissinger) to set a dangerous course for the CIA, despite that Agency's strongest recommendations. While members of the intelligence community such as Richard Helms complained seriously about the Hughes-Ryan Amendment and the general increase of congressional oversight in the aftermath of the 1975 Church committee investigations on Chile, the complaints are actually self-defeating.[40] Arguments that congressional oversight will block needed covert programs are belied by the fact that Congress will often stop operations that are superfluous or immoral—the latter a good thing unless one adheres to a radical realpolitik ideology that comprehends neither morality nor immorality in foreign policy as long as it is effective. But in the case of the former, even realpolitik must accept clear correlations: when, as with the case of Chile, these spurious and dangerous operations were allowed to proceed because of a lack of appropriate checks, they often resulted in abject disaster or more opaque and neutral, and therefore wasteful, results. Indirectly, Jack Anderson and Seymour Hersh—despite what many might think—might have helped to streamline the covert action process.

When viewed as a whole, these factors point to a secret world bound very much by the famous dictum of the Prussian officer and war theorist Carl von Clausewitz: "War is the continuation of politics by other means." The deductions drawn from this in the military field are copious: one goes to war for political reasons rationally determined by the government at the behest of the populace, and both trust the army (and so to chance, for war is always risky) to ensure an outcome beneficial to the state and to the people. But whereas Clausewitz's philosophy has made its impact on American military doctrine, as in Robert McNamara's "limited war theory," covert action remains so far heavily undertheorized—possibly much to the relief of many in the covert profession. Yet such a theory is clearly required, for the operations in Chile produced results neither beneficial to the state nor desired by the people. While the military can be guided by the utterly Clausewitz-inspired philosophy of Secretary of Defense Caspar Weinberger's "6-point doctrine," and its successor, the Powell Doctrine, no such guidance, however vague and unbinding, is there to steer the employment of covert means.[41] The result of this undertheorization is demonstrated in Chile, where the well-thought-out and planned covert actions were undermined by their foolish and haphazard cousins and where all the best intentions still led the United States down the garden path to association—either warranted or unwarranted—with the Western Hemisphere's single most reviled dictator.

1

THE CAMPAIGN BEGINS: CHILE'S 1964 PRESIDENTIAL ELECTION

Chile is important to the United States for a number of oft-stated reasons. It is a country with attitudes toward stable government and the rule of law much like those of the U.S., which cannot be said of many other countries in Latin America. It is obviously in our interest that this basic stability continue and that within its framework real economic and social development take place, making Chile a good example in Latin America for the success of democratic reforms. . . . It is to be hoped that through U.S. financial and technical assistance, and appropriate representation on specific issues, the government can be helped to retain the gains it has made . . . keeping to a minimum steps taken more for political than for sound economic reasons.[1]

—U.S. Embassy Santiago Assessment of Chile, February 1964

"From the viewpoint of U.S. interest, it would be better if any of the candidates other than Allende won the Chilean elections. Were Allende to win we could be faced with a pro-Soviet, anti-U.S. administration in one of the most important countries in the hemisphere."[2] So wrote the assistant secretary of state for the Bureau of Inter-American Affairs

(ARA), Roy Richard Rubottom Jr. in June 1958, reflecting a sentiment that dominated U.S. thinking about Latin America through the Cold War and that had its first expression in the U.S.-orchestrated overthrow of the socialist government of Jacobo Arbenz in Guatemala in 1954. But Guatemala was a minor player compared to Chile, and the intervention there was as much old-school imperialist Monroe Doctrine meddling as it was Cold War containment. Chile was bigger, much more economically significant, and viewed as a political weather vane for Latin America. Coming before the Cuban Revolution, the likelihood of an Allende electoral victory in Chile was the first serious Cold War challenge to the United States as it represented the threat of a high-profile pro-Soviet government *in the Americas*.

The shock of Allende's strong campaign in 1958—he was running neck-and neck with the conservative candidate—was doubly sharp because it was unexpected, at least to the Americans (most Chilean observers saw it coming). For the United States, Chile, prior to Allende's election in 1970, represented one of the *good* Latin American states, a true democracy with a strong record of civilian governance and peaceful handovers of presidential power, only twice broken since independence from Spain in 1818—a statistic that made Chile comparable to France or Germany in terms of political stability. After a revision in 1925, the Chilean constitution remained unchanged until after the 1973 coup.[3] Overall, Chile's history is one remarkably free of the *golpe de estado* (coup d'état) that fit within the North American stereotype of Latin America.[4] Chile's public officials were elected on mandates similar to those of their North American cousins: the president was elected for a six-year term and could sit two terms, although not hold them successively; deputies were elected for four-year terms and senators for eight-year terms. As U.S. ambassador to Chile Edward M. Korry described, Chile was

> the most stable, tested, freest democracy in South America. . . . Democracy in Chile meant exactly what it meant in the United States. Even more: it meant an unfettered press. It meant a multi-partied Congress. It meant an independent judiciary. It meant an apolitical army, an army that had never participated in politics.[5]

Certainly the "apolitical army" was an exaggeration or a misunderstanding of what was in effect a *very* political Chilean army, even if it was not a peer-competitor in the domestic political arena. In 1924, for example, the Chilean army overthrew Arturo Alessandri's government and, six months later, deposed the junta and restored Alessandri. Nonetheless, the United States considered Chile the one Latin American country that could be depended upon as a pro-West ally, largely because of its strong middle class (something entirely absent in most of the rest of the region) and burgeoning industrial/consumer economy.

Behind Chile's apparent economic success lurked a strong dependency on bulk resource exportation and a strong outflow of profit to foreign ownership. Essentially, the Chilean economy depended almost entirely on the export of copper. So, as with any resource-based economy, Chile's gross domestic product mirrored the rise and fall of copper prices on the global commodities market. Because war tended to drive up the prices of strategic metals, Chile had done quite well for itself between 1914 and 1945, though much of the profit still went to the largely American and European owners of the mines. This bred strong resentment toward foreign mine ownership and toward the Chilean agents of foreign owners. This resentment was reflected in the political system as the economy took a downturn in the 1950s. During the 1958 election campaign, the United States, for the first time since the 1879–84 War of the Pacific, had to pay close attention to Chile because from seemingly out of nowhere the Communist-Socialist popular front under Senator Allende had become poised—perhaps—for a win.[6] What was going on?

Chile had changed. While the nation had grown wealthy through the two world wars by selling copper and foodstuffs to the belligerents (Chile's large German population made them generally pro-Reich until quite late into the war), its population had stratified. Notably sophisticated upper and middle classes, upwardly mobile and educated, comprised about one-third of the population, with the remaining population existing in several distinct layers of working class and urban poor.[7] Historian Mark Falcoff argues that the Chilean socioeconomic stratification closely resembled that in the European and North American societies of the era, though the disparity in income distribution was much more severe in Chile. U.S. government officials later noted that despite Chile's wealth, real wages had been declining for half the population since 1950.[8] This social stratification and inequitable wealth distribution contributed to the rise of a number of Marxist parties such as the Socialists and the Communists.

The Chilean Communist Party (PCCh) was among the strongest communist parties in the West.[9] The majority within the U.S. government at the time was convinced that the Chilean party was directly "controlled by Moscow."[10] The Socialist Party (PS, a party overtly hostile to the Communists, yet by necessity often allied) could claim a thirty-seven-year history with impressive results both in and out of government, as the Chilean social-welfare system—and concomitant debt—indicated. Consciously copying the European model, Chile's Socialists began, in the 1930s, to form "popular fronts," the first of which, the Frente Popular, brought President Pedro Aguirre Cerdo (himself a low-key socialist) to power in 1938. This coalition, a mix of Communists, Socialists, Radicals, and other far-left parties, was under its initial leadership one of the most loyal to Moscow in the entire world.[11] Indeed, the decision to form this front was made at the Seventh Congress of the International Communist Movement, held in Moscow in 1935.[12] Suffice it to say that Chile was home to a strong strain of openly Marxist socialism/communism before the United States became interested in the state's domestic politics.

This movement of Chilean leftist parties ran in opposition to the country's long-established political culture. On the Right were, at various times, the Conservative and Liberal parties (which initially ran together in 1958 under the banner "Democratic Front" [FD]) and the National Party (PN). In the Center was the Radical Party (which, in 1962, also joined the Democratic Front), a collection of various socialists held together by a shared anti-clericalism and divided on the subject of cooperating with the Marxist Left.[13] All of these orthodox parties were historically very important in Chilean politics but saw some measure of their support drawn away to the Marxist popular fronts that emerged after 1935.[14] Likewise drawing support away from the center-right parties was the relatively new and center-left Partido Democrata Cristiána (Christian Democratic Party or PDC), which tended to support land reform, state influence in the economy, and "Christian communitarianism," a sort of free-market and Catholic interpretation of the social aspects of generic communism.[15] Prior to 1964 the Christian Democrats had not been involved in any government. Their chosen leader was Eduardo Frei Montalva, a charismatic, personally frugal, and hardworking senator from a prosperous immigrant family.

Despite all these active parties, the State Department's Intelligence and Research Bureau (INR) was quick to note that no more than 15 percent of the Chilean electorate belonged to a political party. A large majority of the noncommitted was "a floating mass of lower-class voters" who supported the candidate offering the greatest promise of improving their lot.[16] This voter base was potentially ripe for harvest by a keen popular front. The numerous American and Western officials who celebrated Chile's openness and democratic liberalism had much reason to be concerned by the nation's highly ideological political culture and the active participation of two large and well-led Marxist parties. Both of these factors played directly into the tension of the Cold War political climate and reasonable U.S. fears of Soviet-sponsored political inroads in the hemisphere.[17]

ALLENDE AND THE 1950S ELECTIONS

The 1958 presidential election was the second one in which Senator Allende ran. In 1952 Allende had been the candidate for a fringe socialist party and had received 5.5 percent of the vote. The socialists' poor showing in the 1952 presidential race left the United States apparently unimpressed by the threat of communism in Chile, but this changed in 1958. As the State Department noted in a character study of Allende, his defeat in 1952 "seems to have seriously disturbed him and to have reinforced his determination to win regardless of the methods used."[18] During the 1958 election Allende increased his appeal to the militant Marxist parties. Allende, head of the Popular Action Front (FRAP), was one of four candidates but notably represented all of the Marxist/socialist parties, which had been previously fractured. His principal opponents were Jorgé Alessandri Rodríguez, of the conservative Democratic Front, and Eduardo Frei Montalva of the PDC.[19]

Allende lost to Alessandri by only 3.3 percent—fewer than 32,000 votes. According to the Chilean constitution, if in an election no individual secures a majority, the two leading candidates are put to a combined session of Congress for a run-off vote. Long-standing tradition—but neither the letter nor spirit of the law—dictated that the candidate with the most votes in the general election be selected. The Chilean constitution was thus upheld as the Chilean Congress confirmed Alessandri as president in the required run-off vote.[20] Yet the vote was precariously close. For the first time—and owing in part to changing demographics and electoral laws that lowered the voting age and removed the literacy test for voting—the bulk of the Chilean working poor had exerted their significant but often latent electoral clout, and the United States paid attention.

The U.S. reaction to the 1958 election results was determined, if not yet panicked. Noting the narrowness of the conservative victory over the socialist front party, U.S. ambassador to Chile Walter Howe noted in a dispatch to Washington that Chile's political climate was likely to get worse, not better, for the United States. "We must recognize," the ambassador wrote, "that the political pendulum has swung as far to the right in Chile as it is likely to go, and that the return swing is likely to be evidenced in . . . the presidential election of 1964." Wanting more than increased support for the conservatives, Howe urged the U.S. government to get ahead of the swing back and support "the non-communist parties of the Chilean center and left."[21] His advice stands in contrast to the popular contemporary assumption that the United States would always support the conservatives as the main opposition to the Marxist Far Left, and in fact, the subsequent Democratic administrations of Kennedy and Johnson followed Howe's advice in their relations with Chile.

Chilean president Alessandri, while visiting President Eisenhower in February 1960, reiterated the suggestion of a broad-based anti-communist approach in Chile and noted that the Marxist Left had a sophisticated propaganda machine that regularly attacked the United States to the detriment of all the non-Marxist parties. President Alessandri "urged that . . . the U.S. conduct a vigorous campaign of counter-propaganda."[22] Eisenhower, while previously keen to overthrow the Guatemalan and Iranian governments, seems to have thought such low-threshold, pro-capitalist propaganda was inappropriate for Chile. According to the minutes of the conversation, Eisenhower "said jokingly he assumed that President Alessandri was not suggesting that the U.S. buy a newspaper in Santiago and turn it into an official U.S. propaganda organ."[23] While the United States eventually did buy a newspaper, *El Mercurio*, for the purpose of propaganda in 1970, this manuever was evidently unacceptable in 1960, and President Alessandri "laughed, and said that of course was not his intention."[24]

Nonetheless, the U.S. government began, sometime in 1961, to bolster its normal intelligence-gathering capability in Chile with a covert action arm. While CIA documents on these actions are not yet declassified, it is believed that the Agency began to establish assets in important centrist political parties, key unions, students groups, and peasant or tenant farmer organizations.[25] From former CIA officer David Atlee Phillips's memoir, we also know that at this point, in the late 1950s or early 1960s, the CIA began to establish the framework for what would become its most potent weapon in Chile, propaganda seeded within the popular media.[26]

THE ALLIANCE FOR PROGRESS

Although Kennedy beat Nixon to win the 1960 presidential election by only a thin margin, his rhetoric on taking office showed his determination to implement his own policy. Latin America played an important part in his inaugural address, an address otherwise famous for the stirring "ask not what your country can do for you" call to action. Addressing his comments to "our sister republics south of our border," Kennedy said,

> We offer a special pledge—to convert our good words into good deeds—in a new alliance for progress—to assist free men

> and free governments in casting off the chains of poverty. But this peaceful revolution of hope cannot become the prey of hostile powers. Let all our neighbors know that we shall join with them to oppose aggression or subversion anywhere in the Americas. And let every other power know that this Hemisphere intends to remain the master of its own house.[27]

As those in any political manifesto, Kennedy's words are densely packed with significance and indications of future policies. The last three lines of this passage are familiar to any student of politics since 1823: they are an unmistakable reiteration of the Monroe Doctrine, updated with a veiled threat against communism, that "aggressor" who might try to "subvert" the cause of freedom in the Americas. But whereas such a closing statement could have as easily come from the Eisenhower White House, the passage's opening sentiment most certainly would not have, for it states an understanding of, and sympathy for, those segments of society left behind by the course of statist capitalism (or pure kleptocracy) in the region.

The idea of social and economic support to Latin American democracies led to the creation, in March 1961, of the eponymous Alliance for Progress, an organization destined to be one of the greatest U.S. aid efforts ever conducted, which at $17 billion dwarfed even the Marshall Plan.[28] William D. Rogers, a Washington lawyer and later an assistant secretary of state for ARA under Nixon, served as deputy U.S. coordinator for the Alliance for Progress from 1961 until 1965. In a recent interview he noted, "There were a lot of people who were enthusiastic about [the alliance] at the time, regarding it as an enlightened chapter in American foreign policy towards Latin America, which was to move beyond old Cold War antipathies and to move towards positive development of the hemisphere." Rogers further said the program was "admittedly [designed] to counter the lure coming out of Havana."[29] Like the Marshall Plan, the Alliance for Progress was a reaction to the perceived aggressive intent of a pro-Moscow Marxist power. Nevertheless, Rogers believes that the alliance was not completely an aggressive countermeasure or a stopgap effort to contain Castro's still-lively revolution. Kennedy was wise and statesmanlike enough to realize that "for the U.S. to project that image [of positive development aid] was the best kind of antidote for the appeal of Fidel and Ché."[30]

Chile was to feature in the new Alliance for Progress, for at the time democracy was a rare system in Latin America. Particularly after the 1964 coup in Brazil, Rogers noted,

> democracies you could count on one hand: Chile, Costa Rica, Venezuela, and that was it. . . . In Latin America democracy was very much embattled at that time, so Chile was one of the few places where we felt that the concept of the Alliance for Progress had a chance of being realized in the near term. We ran a lot of programs in Chile for that very purpose, demonstratively.[31]

For the United States the 1964 Chilean presidential election existed in this greater hemispheric context. Holding up a non-Marxist model for Latin America required a shining example of democratic success. With the number of democracies in South America so sharply limited, if the Marxist front under a *Fidelista* such as Allende won the Chilean election, the president's alliance would have precious few chances to work its intended magic. Conversely, the alliance might give the impetus required for the victory of the pro-democracy party. The 1964 presidential election in Chile suddenly became a very important matter, as it was both the subject and requirement for the success of the Alliance for Progress.

That Chile was increasingly important is reflected by the production, in October 1963, of the first-ever National Intelligence Estimate (NIE) on Chile. Obviously concerned with the potentially negative outcome of the election, American policymakers had initiated the study to better inform the determination of a coordinated U.S. response, both overt and covert, to this threat of communism spreading out of isolated Cuba. The NIE echoed what many in the administration had said over the previous six years. The 1958 election results "raised apprehension that the 1964 presidential election might bring to power a government under strong Communist influence, if not control."[32] Policymakers viewed these results with some gravity, and responding to the NIE, a group of State Department officers echoed the "need to take the Allende campaign seriously."[33] Essentially, given the success of the recent Cuban Revolution, Chile became the most advantageous Western-hemispheric battlefield on which the United States could meet the Marxist challenge to capitalist-democratic ideals.[34]

Retrospective conceptions of Allende paint him as a pleasant and jovial "champagne socialist" along European lines, more democrat than despot. Was the reaction to him in the early 1960s unjustified, viewed through the eyes of unreasonably anti-communist Americans and made worse by Monroe Doctrine fears? It is likely that something more to Allende's stance spooked the Americans into action.

WHO'S AFRAID OF SALVADOR ALLENDE?

Dr. Salvador Allende Gossens was a recurring character in Chile's political dramas from the 1930s until his death. From a wealthy family, Allende entered politics while still in medical school and helped found the Chilean Socialist Party in 1933, the year he graduated.[35] Elected as a federal deputy in 1937, Allende served briefly as health minister in a (non-Marxist) Popular Front government in 1938. In 1943 he became secretary general of the Socialist Party, and by 1951 he was president of the Chilean Medical Society and vice president of the Chilean Senate.[36] During the early 1960s, revolutionary Cuba emerged as his party's main model, and Allende cultivated a close friendship with Fidel Castro, to whom he had been introduced shortly after the Cuban revolution in 1959. Allende played an important role in the forming of the Cuban-sponsored Latin American Solidarity Organization (LASO), which served as the political body behind Che Guevera's 1967 Bolivian campaign, and some new research suggests Allende was instrumental in having that expedition's survivors returned to Cuba.[37] Indeed, Allende's daughter Beatriz in 1970 married the Cuban diplomat (and intelligence officer) Luiz Fernández Oña, a former *Guevarista* and intimate of Castro.[38] In the merger of the Socialist and Communist parties each entity remained intact, but the combined party was cohesive enough to retain Allende as the presidential candidate over the course of three consecutive elections.

As noted by former CIA officer Phillips, the CIA had penetrated both the Chilean Communist and Socialist parties in the early 1950s and was thus capable of getting very detailed information about their leadership personalities and even finances.[39] Prior to the 1958 election, however, and despite accurate CIA reporting, few in the U.S. government ever heard the name Allende, and those who did were not unduly worried by the senator. Allende was just another socialist politician in another Latin American country. In the run-up to the 1964 election, though, Allende finally appeared as an ominous blip on the U.S. government's anti-Marxist radar screen. This is not to say that perceptions of Allende were entirely conditioned by anti-Marxist obsession or that the U.S. reaction to Allende was always hysterical in tone. Asked in 1963, as part of the NIE procedure, to give a sketch of Allende, the U.S. country team in Santiago, Chile, wrote,

> Allende is a chameleonic person. . . . Personally he is vain, quick tempered, easily offended, socially as well as politically ambitious, able turn on or off at will a considerable social charm. He is sensitive to charges [that] he would be dominated

> by Communists or that he would institute anti-democratic measures. Nevertheless were he to achieve power we think he could be led by events into being harsh and ruthless with his opponents but more likely use exile than prison or pardon. It is probable that he thinks in terms [of a] Marxist regime similar Castro's Cuba in its free-wheeling, relatively independent line but more sophisticated, cultured, without emotional excesses of a "tropical" country such as Cuba.[40]

Allende himself (who in the CIA's view did "not possess unusual intelligence") consciously used the rhetoric of Marxism within his party but nonetheless tried to maintain the external image of a democrat. His personal habits did little to discourage this impression. Allende was known for his conspicuous consumption, his lavish lifestyle, and his personal eccentricities. A former U.S. defense attaché in Santiago, Col. Paul Wimert, recounted his first meeting with Allende in the harbor at Valparaíso:

> This beautiful yacht . . . came gliding across the water to hook up to the wharf, and there was this gentleman in a white hat and a white cravat with a blue admiral's coat and white duck pants and shoes. He looked [like] one of the old wealthy people—the Vanderbilts of America—I couldn't believe he was Allende. . . . He was beautifully groomed, and of course his sailing ship was one of the nicest ones there. It didn't sit right that he was supposed to be a communist or socialist.[41]

Despite this image and Allende's periodic statements (often to American press representatives) that he was not a communist (he was always a member of the Socialist Party), as well as the widespread belief among Chileans (including many in the opposition) that he was basically a democratic socialist as opposed to a communist, the embassy staff believed that the "record [showed] he [had] collaborated with Communists for more than 15 years with no apparent difficulty" and that he was likely fully in league with Communist Party leader Luis Corvalán.[42] The State Department's INR added, Allende "has turned increasingly to the Communists as an instrument of victory and has risked becoming their tool."[43] Indeed, Allende might have believed himself to be a new breed of *Chilean* Marxist-socialist. He became agitated when he was accused of wanting to do away with Chilean democratic institutions and responded that he would actually *save* democracy by introducing "people's government": "The new social order will require new institutions. . . . We shall draft a new Constitution using the present Charter as a springboard."[44] Allende made a point of separating "bourgeois" democracy (of the American sort) from the "popular" democracy that the Marxist Unidad Popular (UP) offered.[45]

It is difficult to make out where Allende really stood. His assertions that he was not a communist are accurate in the sense that he belonged to the Socialist Party, a party often antagonistic to the Chilean Communist Party—the two parties never got along even when in coalition together.[46] It is also true that Allende opposed the hard-liners and militants within his own Socialist Party and that overtly he followed the electoral path to Marxist socialism. Yet the Unidad Popular was formed with the aim of deconstructing the "bourgeois" democratic state and implementing Marxist socialism in its place, and its members did not hide this fact.[47] So if one was unsure about the aim of the UP's electoral path, Allende provided a more concise explanation in his party platform: "The objective is total, scientific Marxist socialism."[48] Allende may have been a new-model Marxist (and even a rather dapper yachting connoisseur), but in using such language he confirmed, to any but those few American officials able or willing to differentiate between the various competing schools of orthodox communist, Castroite, Leninist, Maoist, or socialist thought, that he was indeed a Marxist and therefore an avenue of influence for Moscow. That the path he chose was electoral and democratic did not make him less dangerous but rather *more* dangerous, for his success could signal to the rest of Latin America that there was an alternative path to development, a road to socialism that was still a threat to the Western way of life but that the United States would find difficult to oppose for international and domestic political reasons.

"Allende the threat" was not taken for granted by U.S. officials. Many in the State Department and other parts of the government put significant thought into the question of what problem Allende may or may not have posed to the U.S. One particularly noteworthy discussion came from U.S. embassy first secretary Robert Hurwitch, who produced a lengthy and thoughtful letter about Allende's threat to America addressed directly to the national security adviser at the time, McGeorge Bundy. While suggesting that the Soviets would be likely, but not certain, to take advantage of a Marxist Chile to expand their presence in the Americas, Hurwitch was clear about the overall impact of an Allende victory:

> Dear Mac,
>
> I have had very much in mind your request for another

> opinion as to whether an Allende victory would be seriously detrimental to U.S. national security interests. . . . As a practical matter, whatever our assessment of the significance of an Allende victory, we may find our maneuverability the day after the election severely circumscribed. (I have often thought that the real tragedy for us of Castro's having embraced the Marxist, rather than our, world lay in the limitations now placed upon the flexibility of U.S. policy toward situations which superficially resemble that of Cuba.) Another "Castro" in the Hemisphere, particularly one who achieved power through the democratic process in a country where we have invested the highest rate of per capita assistance, would be awfully tough to handle from both the international and domestic standpoints. This would clearly be a case where one and one totaled much more than two and the consequences throughout the Hemisphere of a second Castro would be serious.[49]

That the issue of Chile was tied to the issue of Cuba was inescapable, as Hurwitch noted regretfully, but the U.S. debate over the prospect of a "second Castro" was considered dispassionately and within the context of hemispheric relations.

Hurwitch ultimately suggested quite simply, "An Allende victory would constitute a defeat for U.S. policy."[50] The practical examples of such a defeat were quickly identified: "If Allende wins and stays in power, we are in trouble," wrote Gordon Chase of the State Department, because Allende would "probably nationalize the copper mines, which in turn, might end the aid program because of the Hickenlooper amendment," which demanded aid be cut off to any state that nationalized U.S. property without recourse to a legal and transparent procedure for compensation. (Interestingly, Senator Borke Hickenlooper, the amendment's eponymous author, had derived inspiration from Harold S. Geneen, chief executive officer of the International Telephone and Telegraph Corporation [ITT], which was later a critical actor in Chile.)[51] The almost automatic invocation of Hickenlooper, and thus the cutoff of U.S. financial assistance, "could lead Chile to ask the Bloc for economic aid."[52] For the U.S. government in the 1960s all communist roads led to Moscow.

Even without reference to the Kremlin, the mere mention of the word "Cuba" caused numerous alarms to sound in a White House still occupied—for only a few more days—by the brothers Kennedy. It is likely that the CIA station in Santiago had a good idea of Allende's connections with foreign and domestic Marxist parties and with the Soviet Union itself. That the CIA was operating within the FRAP constituent parties is made clear by the security deletions in CIA documents about these parties. Detailed information about party strategies or personalities is followed by such deletions, probably—though not certainly—to obscure the CIA's source within these organizations.[53]

While it is unclear what precisely the CIA knew about Allende in 1963, new work by Professor Christopher Andrew and Vasili Mitrokhin shows that by this time Allende was indeed firmly in the Soviet camp. A KGB "Line PR" (the KGB branch in charge of political intelligence) officer from Buenos Aires, Svyatoslav Fyodorovich Kuznetsov (code name LEONID), made the Soviets' first contact with Allende in 1953. The KGB issued the appropriate code name LEADER to Allende, though the Chilean was not officially recruited as an agent nor did he ever take KGB payments. Systematic contact between Allende and the KGB was established in 1961, when relations were restored and the KGB set up a residency in a new trade mission. To the KGB Allende had "stated his willingness to co-operate on a confidential basis and provide any necessary assistance, since he considered himself a friend of the Soviet Union. He willingly shared political information."[54]

While this did not make Allende a "Soviet spy," it did, at least retrospectively, justify American fears that Allende was a pro-Soviet "agent of influence" in the Americas and thus had the potential to introduce another direct Soviet influence in the Americas, one that by the nature of geography would be harder to contain. One must keep in mind the very direct threat the United States and USSR each perceived the other to be and how real their mutual antagonism was throughout the Cold War. In the post–Cold War era it is easy to trivialize or dismiss this struggle as foolish ideological sparring, but at the time it was extraordinarily real, as the ultimate cost of "getting it wrong" was nuclear war. To the United States in the 1960s, political subversion of pro-Western democracies was seen as a direct challenge to U.S. security, allies, and civilization. The challenge for the United States—one not always met, as this study shows—was to oppose Soviet moves without forgetting the philosophy upon which their own democratic system was built.

As did their American counterparts, the KGB carefully analyzed the man in whom they placed a good degree of hope. Perhaps a comment on the judgment of both services, the similarities between the KGB and CIA assessment of Allende are perfectly eerie. The KGB noted, based on information from its contacts in the Communist Party, that Allende's "characteristic traits were arrogance, vanity, desire for glorification and a longing to be in the spotlight at any price. He was easily influenced by stronger and more determined personalities." Illustrating a distinction that would have been lost on most Americans, the KGB thought Allende to be "dangerously Maoist" and to have very bourgeois connections with Freemasonry. Making reference to not-so-secret information, Allende was further described as something of a womanizer; this is perhaps another oblique reference to his substantial personal charm.[55]

That international Marxist elements were supporting Allende was clear even outside the CIA. Presidential candidate Eduardo Frei reported to the U.S. ambassador that "large quantities of funds [around $1 million] for the Allende campaign had recently come in from Canada and that more were expected in the near future. [Political Attaché] Scott Fox had told him that he had not been able to track down the report but that the presumption was that the money had originated in Cuba."[56] Work in Soviet archives by Chilean-based researcher Olga Ulianova indeed shows Soviet aid to the Chilean Communist Party at a baseline of $50,000 per annum from 1960 to 1969 with spikes of up to $400,000.[57] Eventually, the sums of money passed to the PCCh were the highest in Latin America after Cuba.[58] Even without this knowledge (Phillips does not tell us what information his agents actually produced), many commented that Allende and his UP coalition were spending money at a rate far faster than could possibly be raised domestically.[59]

The rise of Allende and the strength of the Chilean Marxist coalitions helped prompt the Soviet Union to waive its normal aversion to operations in the American sphere of influence. After the sudden and unanticipated success in Cuba, the USSR no longer looked at Latin America as merely part of the American sphere but rather as an independent zone. Previously "out of bounds," Latin America now appeared as an enormous political arena that, if exploited properly, offered an opportunity to hurt the Americans.

For the first time, Latin American branches opened in the KGB and Foreign Ministry. The KGB branch was placed under the direction of KGB officer Nikolai Leonov, whose memoir offers substantial comments on Chile. The strategic vision of the KGB's Latin American branch was less direct or crude than many might think. Leonov proceeded on the assumption that the USSR was interested in Chile not because it would derive any necessary strategic or tactical benefit from a political victory in Chile but because *the United States would.* The USSR itself gained no particular advantage out of winning aside from winning, but such a "prestige" victory for the USSR, especially in the most capitalist (and most heavily U.S.-funded) Latin American country would be, as the Americans perceived as well, a tangible loss of face and influence for the United States.[60] The U.S. and the Soviet Union perceived their Chilean battleground within the same strategic paradigm.

Reporting from the U.S. embassy in 1964 described the chain of events resulting from a Marxist government in Chile and the impact they would have on the United States:

> Negative economic impact will be very great immediately and probably over short-term as well. Allende would probably try to expand activities and efforts of existing GOC institutions that directly involved in economy in effort compensate for lacks and lags in private sector. He will undoubtedly seek help from bloc and "unaligned" countries but conceivably might make unreasonable requests of USG [U.S. government] (e.g. low interest loan pay for expropriation copper companies and utilities) expecting turn down which he could use as ostensible justification Chilean public for turning [to] bloc. In general economic deterioration after Allende victory would tend [to] stimulate and be used [to] justify extreme internal measures toward full statist economic power as well as shift to excessive Chilean dependence [on] Communist bloc aid and trade.[61]

American statements to the effect that having Chile "go communist" would be a blow to U.S. prestige first and foremost showed the basic understanding of the great-power stakes shared by America's Soviet counterparts. Both East and West were on the same playing field. "In essence," said McGeorge Bundy to President Johnson, "the problem we face is that a very popular and attractive candidate, named Allende, who has thrown in his lot with the Communists, has more than a fighting chance to win."[62] That the United States had to do something to avert this was quite simply assumed. It was clear the Soviet Union was operating in Chile to ensure Marxist success, and from the contemporary American point of view the United States was required to thwart this enemy influence: Soviet money and influence were clearly going into Chile to undermine its democracy, so U.S. funding would have to go into Chile to frustrate that pernicious influence.

INITIATION OF THE 1964 OPERATION

In overt terms the determination to work against Allende had begun with President Kennedy's inauguration in 1961, largely through the Alliance for Progress. The idea of assisting the Christian Democrats was first brought forward in March 1962 by Ambassador Charles W. Cole and the then–special assistant to the president, Richard Goodwin. At this time covert action proposals needing review and approval went to the 5412 Special Group, a semi-official cabinet-level body that included the secretaries of state and defense, the director of central intelligence (DCI), the attorney general, the president's special assistant, and any other secretaries or directors who were concerned with the matter at hand. In this case the Special Group approved a program of "nonattributable" assistance to Eduardo Frei's Christian Democrats in April 1962 and again on August 30, 1963, with concurrent approval from the State Department's Latin American Policy Committee in January and June 1963. By the fall of 1963 the U.S. government had effectively decided to actively work against Allende's campaign in Chile. In late 1963 a subsidy of an unknown amount was given to the Democratic Front (then under the leadership of Radical Party boss Julio Durán Neumann). This one-time payment was not connected to any well-thought-out policy, though it was specifically requested by a member of the party to make up its $500,000 campaign shortfall.[63]

As one might perceive from the tone of CIA discussions regarding them, these payments were not part of a coordinated strategy but rather stopgap payments based on the recommendations of the embassy's country team. Kennedy's assassination in November 1963 brought a temporary halt to the measures to implement a coherent and high-level plan to be executed by the Agency. The transition to President Johnson was relatively seamless and had little impact on the developing program in Chile, although the White House's attitude behind the support to Chile changed somewhat. By mid-December 1963 the West Wing had absorbed the new administration, and the new staff continued with the business at hand.[64] McGeorge Bundy seems to have put Chile back on the agenda by writing to President Johnson on January 24 with the suggestion that the Special Group "might, at an early date, give consideration to the interests of the United States in the Chilean election which occurs in December, 1964." No one familiar with Latin American affairs, noted Bundy, "has any doubt as to the importance of the outcome of this election, not only in Chile but throughout the hemisphere," and covert action proposals for the election should therefore be dealt with promptly. Nothing further, however, was briefed to the president.[65]

The major problem the U.S. government faced in early 1964 was, who would America support to prevent an Allende victory? While the

Marxist far-left parties were united under the banner of the FRAP, the center and right-of-center parties—the PDC and the Democratic Front—both represented viable alternatives to a Marxist government and were running separately. Deciding which one to support was evidently the cause of much hand-wringing. The CIA's initial support to the PDC was aimed at getting the party into a broad-based non-Marxist coalition with the Radicals, previously Chile's largest single political party. Also, the CIA hoped the PDC, with U.S. support, would draw votes away from elements of soft-socialist/pro-clerical supporters of the FRAP in a way that the FD could not. U.S. funding for the PDC might have had prompting from President Kennedy directly, as former U.S. ambassador to Chile Edward Korry stated in an interview in Santiago in 1999: "It started probably in early '63 after President Kennedy met directly with Frei in the White House. It was a secret meeting. I believe it was in the spring of '63 . . . in that period."[66] But with Kennedy gone, this pro-PDC drive waned. Further the United States was unable to tell Frei that it was supporting him at all for fear that this very proud Chilean nationalist would react against it.

Asked by the Johnson administration to choose which party the United States should support, the CIA firmly backed the FD, despite Kennedy's pro-liberal and pro-Catholic sentiments, because the Christian Democratic Party would be less favorable and responsive to U.S. government policies than the Democratic Front and would likely to try to "establish relations with Iron Curtain countries, . . . endeavor to increase [Chile's] trade with the Soviet Bloc, and . . . not follow the United States lead in foreign policy with the same willingness as the present government."[67] The CIA's underlying reasoning was echoed by the State Department's assistant secretary for ARA, Thomas Mann, who suggested support should go only to the FD because Durán, being more pliable in economic matters (from the American viewpoint) than Frei, might be more ready to reinvest money in Chile and so improve the economy. Also, Durán's relatively left-leaning tendencies, more pronounced than those of the mainstream center-left of the PDC, "might draw further votes away from Allende." Some small measure of "support to the [PDC] should be continued because they too offer strong competition to Allende."[68]

Despite the Kennedys' drive for "progressive development aid" to back the Alliance for Progress in Latin America, the Agency and the State Department returned to the default position of supporting the reactionary right wing. It was no longer about the lofty idea of "progress" but the safe option of "stability"—an abandonment of reform in favor of the status quo. In February the CIA's chief of the Western Hemisphere Division

(C/WHD), J. C. King, submitted his recommendation to the Special Group to obtain approval for election support of the Democratic Front and a subsequent cutback in the subsidy to the Christian Democratic Party. Luckily for the PDC, however, the Special Group did not meet on March 5 as planned and failed to discuss Chile at its next meeting a week later.[69] As happened again in 1970, the Special Group dithered over which party the United States should support, and before a decision could be made, local politics forced America toward a more progressive policy with long-lasting effects on U.S.-Chilean interaction.

Chile, foreign political observers often noted, seemed to host nearly constant election campaigns. With presidential, congressional, municipal, and by-elections (special elections held in specific electoral districts to fill a vacancy left by an incumbent), some sort of campaigning was continually under way. In March 1964, as it happened, a deputy had died and left a vacancy to be filled by a by-election in his district of Curicó. Ralph W. Richardson, the ARA desk officer for Chile, noted that the Curicó by-election would serve as a good indicator of the relative strength of the parties leading up to the 1964 presidential race. Showing his almost-poetic hubris, Durán stated explicitly that the Curicó by-election would stand as a plebiscite for the ruling party, the Democratic Front, as well as his leadership of it.[70] This seemed a safe bet at first, noted historian Paul Sigmund, as Curicó was traditionally a rural conservative bastion.[71] The FRAP candidate in the election, however, was the son of a late and lamented Socialist deputy with great clout in Curicó, and he played the familial link to his immense advantage. On March 15, the FRAP candidate won the Curicó by-election with 39.5 percent of the vote; the next day, Durán resigned as the DF presidential candidate (though not from the presidential race itself). As the Democratic Front was a fragile coalition, the loss of Durán was fatal, and the party dissolved a short time thereafter. This was a high-impact event in the normally predictable Chilean political scene, and reaction in the United States was sufficiently dramatic to prompt the CIA's Desmond FitzGerald to write in a memorandum, "The most important thing is to keep people from panicking" in reaction to the DF's by-election loss to FRAP.[72]

While the FRAP victory vexed many in the U.S. government, some at the State Department (generally those of the pro-JFK persuasion who favored a pragmatic approach to Chile and backing the reformist Frei) saw the silver lining. One of these people was Richardson. Realizing the difficulty in running two horses against a very strong FRAP, Richardson believed that the best bet lay with a single, reformist candidate. The socialist parties had never taken more than 40 percent in any election in Chile, so if the center and rightist parties could be induced to support the PDC candidate, Frei, as the main non-Marxist candidate, then the election had a much better chance of producing the desired outcome. While noting that the PDC wouldn't be a shoo-in in the presidential election, Richardson commented on the positive impact Curicó had on the U.S. decision-making process: "I still cannot repress a feeling of satisfaction in seeing how quickly and cleanly our 'decision' to swing behind Frei was made for us. I really had wondered before Durán's disaster whether we were going to get any definite decision from the front office on which group we should help."[73] With the State Department and the CIA unable to force an executive decision on who should be supported—as was also the case in the 1970 election—the Americans nonetheless had a candidate thrust upon them.

While it is often assumed that the United States backed the PDC from JFK's inauguration onward, the record shows this not to be so. Kennedy—liberal and Catholic, like Frei—had an affinity for the Latin-American Christian Democrats, but sympathy had not been enough to swing the notably right-leaning Democrat White House and Kennedy's cabinet (which was not, like its president, conspicuously Catholic) into actually supporting them: the Alliance for Progress was to be run on political terms dictated from Washington, and those terms demanded a pliable, conservative government in La Moneda. This was especially so after Kennedy's death, when the more pragmatic LBJ took office and delegated his even less reform-minded staff to run the show. Only from the relatively late date of March 15, less than six months before the election, did the U.S. government—because it had no choice—truly commit to supporting Frei and the PDC. Some continued to think the loss of Durán was catastrophic, and as the embassy regretfully noted, "not without certain aptness has it been jested that the choice between Frei and Allende is between chaos and disaster."[74] Whatever the United States, despite occasional distrust of its now-chosen man, lost in time it made up with enthusiasm, and within a matter of days the situation changed dramatically: the proscription against "witting" (or overt) contact with the PDC was partially broken, and at the party's request incredible sums of money were sent to it from the United States. With no other choice to avert a Marxist government, the PDC suddenly became the Great Hope.

THE CIA ACTS

With focus thrust upon it, and determination accidentally imbued to the White House, the CIA acted with appropriate decisiveness in Chile.

Within a short time the implications of the Curicó defeat had been absorbed and processed by the Agency with the help of the State Department and the U.S. embassy in Santiago. On April 1, two weeks after the DF's defeat, the CIA submitted a comprehensive and lengthy memorandum to the Special Group titled "Support for the Chilean Presidential Election of 4 September 1964" which outlined the full plan for initial support to the PDC. The preamble to the memorandum was noteworthy and outlined the considerably different political scene in Chile after the Curicó by-election and the way the PDC approached American involvement thereafter. At the end of March a member of Frei's campaign team visited the U.S. embassy (whether the political section or the CIA is not stated) to present his candidate's campaign budget to the Americans. First he presented the campaign's current budget of U.S. $100,000 per month, which he claimed it met only with difficulty and which he did not think was sufficient anyway. Next, he presented the campaign's desired budget of over $300,000 per month. This monthly sum, he said, was needed to beat Allende. The Chilean coolly suggested that the U.S. government make up the difference, "which amount[ed] to one million dollars for the period [preceding] election time." The embassy and the CIA station reviewed the budgets, decided they seemed reasonable, and subsequently recommended that the Chilean's request for $1 million be granted as soon as possible.[75]

Giving money to the Christian Democrats, though, was not the end of the proposed U.S. program of covert support in Chile. "As a result of the [political] situation outlined above," the CIA memorandum to the Special Group continued, "it becomes necessary to take all possible action to assist Frei in his campaign." A battery of tactics that included the following was proposed:

- Prevent the Radical Party from formally endorsing Allende. "In the event the Radical Party declares for Allende, financial assistance will have to be provided to individual Radical leaders or groups capable of bringing Radical voters into the Frei camp."
- Convince (by bribes) the Conservative and Liberal parties to support Frei in a manner that would not damage his image as a reform candidate.
- Redirect the subsidy directly to the PDC, and convince Frei to reach a private agreement with the Radicals for their support in exchange for postelection patronage.

- Prevent the declaration of a third candidate (most likely Jorgé Prat, a conservative from a powerful political family) by bribery, and apply "pressure" to avert the splitting of the non-Marxist vote.
- Provide financial assistance to ancillary organizations, such as youth and student groups, peasant organizations, slum dwellers' associations, labor unions, and women's clubs, to bring their votes to Frei.
- Initiate "specialized propaganda operations, some of which will be black, to denigrate Allende."[76]

Altogether, and by the standards of the day, this seems a fairly restrained set of options considering the perceived problem. Indeed, it could be argued that this was standard American-style political wrangling, as its only sinister terms are the vaguely described "pressure" to be applied to keep other candidates from challenging Frei's dominance of the Center and Right. Further, the funding and lobbying aspects of the platform were not illegal under either Chilean or U.S. law. Nonetheless the plan outlined serious political interference with the electoral process in a democratic state, and the offhand inclusion of bribery as a means to achieve American ends suggests a dangerous undermining of the Chilean democratic system, which the Americans were supposedly protecting. To the Americans, however, bribery was merely a gentle inoculation to prevent the far worse anti-democratic disease of Marxism, a contagious disease with serious consequences should a "major Latin American nation . . . become the first country in the hemisphere to freely choose an avowed Marxist as its elected president."[77] A further option listed at the end of the memo underlines the gravity with which the CIA and the Special Group viewed the situation. Realizing that the first six options might not swing the required votes, the CIA was prepared, in the latter stages of the campaign, "to buy some votes outright if required."[78]

Notwithstanding the PDC's open and direct approach for requesting campaign funding, the Americans disagreed over whether to provide the funding in an overt fashion. Both the PDC and the U.S. government realized that, though it had not yet been stated explicitly, the revelation of wholesale U.S. funding to a Chilean political party would create an election disaster likely to result in massive political gains for Allende and the FRAP. Bribery and vote buying, viewed as far too obvious and too easily open to politically damaging exposure (though no mention is made of its potential immorality), were to be avoided if possible. Yet, because the point of American involvement in the campaign was to "obtain some essential leverage" over the PDC during its potential presidency, the CIA suggested that the money be passed in a manner that might "infer U.S. Government origin of the funds yet permit us plausible denial if necessary" by explicitly attributing the funds to nonofficial U.S. sources.[79] This was, FitzGerald apparently assured the Special Group, something the CIA could do. The embassy's political staff, in contrast, believed that the important matter was merely for Frei to win. The diplomats believed that the benefit of leverage over the PDC was dramatically outweighed by the risk of a leak from some nationalist in the PDC that would compromise the entire operation.

Upon considering the CIA and State Department viewpoints, the Special Group decided the PDC leaned a little too far left and thus required American influence. Accordingly, the Special Group authorized $750,000 (of the requested $1 million) in immediate funding to go to the PDC, in the semi-covert fashion outlined by the CIA. This decision was made, however, with the understanding that it did not "reflect the Embassy's position." The difference was not too great, however, and it seems that the CIA was able to accommodate the slightly skeptical Ambassador Cole. The day following the Special Group meeting the program outlined in "Support for the Chilean Presidential Election of 4 September 1964" was approved, and the new C/WHD, Desmond FitzGerald, announced in an attached memo that a solution to the slight difference of opinion between Ambassador Cole and the Santiago CIA station had been reached: the funds would be implicitly attributed to the United States *but there would be no hard evidence or proof of U.S. support.*[80] Whether this plan would be effective at deflecting realization of American funding remained to be seen.

After the Church committee investigations of 1975, the manner in which covert actions were approved changed dramatically. Within a day of approval by the successor to the Special Group, the president would have to issue a finding authorizing the operation as necessary for U.S. national security and then pass it to the House and Senate select committees on intelligence. This was not the case in 1964, a time when the covert action decision-making infrastructure was still free of bureaucratic hurdles or legal checks. The president might have been partially cognizant of the ongoing actions carried out in Chile, but this is by no means certain. President Johnson, never one to do much extra reading, chose not to read the still-classified "Intelligence Checklist" (now known as the "President's Daily Brief") from the DCI, as would later become customary, so unless he was informed directly by a staffer he might have remained in the dark with regard to the 1964 covert action program for Chile.[81]

Johnson was first informed about the program and the associated funding decision on or about May 13, 1964, when National Security Adviser Bundy forwarded to the president a memorandum, written by Assistant Secretary of State for ARA Mann to Secretary of State Dean Rusk, that outlined the entire U.S. program of actions in Chile, both covert and overt. To this memorandum Bundy appended a short note for the president that highlighted the salient points as he perceived them:

> We have a coordinated Government-wide program of action to strengthen [Allende's] opponent and support actions in Chile which will work to the advantage of those now in power. It is a highly fluid situation and one in which there may have to be further action as we get into the summer. I have been very much encouraged by the determination and unity which all Departments of the Government are showing on this one, and we will be watching it very closely, but I do think you ought to know about it yourself.[82]

The latter point—full cooperation of all the departments—is important. The success of this program hinged upon interdepartmental cooperation, as would be proved in later U.S. efforts in Chile.

It is notable that this entire program of covert actions (and tens of millions in overt funding) was proceeding possibly *without the knowledge or permission of the president* from his swearing in on November 22 1963 through to May 1964. Certainly, the system of security management in the National Security Council (NSC), as established by the National Security Act of 1948, was designed to allow swift responses by empowered staff acting within the conceptual framework previously established by the president. The chief executive is, after all, a fairly busy individual. Initially, it may seem surprising that such a delicate and seemingly important task, involving so much money funneled to a friendly democracy (an act, as historian and theorist Loch Johnson notes, more serious than operations in a repressive regime as it implied the tacit subversion of a fellow democracy), went forward without some small measure of presidential control—but there is an explanation. Johnson, by May 1964, had been acting as president for only five months and before that he was kept—at the request of JFK—almost totally in the dark about covert actions. Johnson had met on one occasion with DCI Allen Dulles in July 1960, when he was the vice presidential candidate, but neither Dulles nor his successor, John McCone, had made much effort to keep Johnson informed during the intervening years. Compared with the concerns of the Soviet Union, Eastern Europe, Cuba, and especially Vietnam, Chile was relatively secondary, so the fact that LBJ had not read about the matter until May, when real action was being planned, was not implausible. Nonetheless, by this time Johnson had long stopped reading the Agency's "Intelligence Checklist," as he preferred instead to let the Agency or the NSC take care of matters.[83] Accordingly, one can detect very little presidential input into the matter of supporting Frei after the Curicó by-election, both before and after this initial briefing.[84] The operation was, essentially, still operating under the control of the deceased Kennedy.

What JFK had started was impressive, as becomes clear in the rest of the memo Bundy forwarded to Johnson. In addition to the CIA's covert actions, the memorandum outlines the entire sweep of U.S. *overt* operations:

> ◆ Providing AID loans in CY 64 amounting to approximately $70 million. . . .
> ◆ 5) Organizing a political action and propaganda campaign through CIA contacts in coordination with or parallel to Frei's campaign. This includes voter registration drives, propaganda, person-to-person campaigning . . . and arrangements to provide some Italian Christian Democratic organizers to Frei as advisers. . . .
> ◆ 7) [Attempting] . . . to encourage [the Chileans'] rising awareness of the subversion which would take place under an Allende government.
> ◆ 8) Continuing USIA placement in Chile of un-attributed material, giving special care to low-keyed efforts which do not expose U.S. Government involvement.
> ◆ 9) Encouraging, through covert ties and private U.S. organizations, effective anti-Allende efforts by Chilean organizations including the Roman Catholic Church, trade union groups, and other influential bodies, such as the anti-clerical Masons.[85]

This was, indeed, a "full court press," with all aspects of the U.S. government directed to prevent Allende's election, without resort to bribery, vote buying, or "pressure."

Indeed, some observers were so impressed by the anti-Allende efforts of other U.S. government agencies that they assumed that they were

CIA fronts. Popular Chilean author Eduardo Labarca, in his book *Chile Invadido*, states quite firmly that the U.S. Information Service (USIS, the overseas arm of the U.S. Information Agency or USIA) was a CIA front organization. In its own internal records the CIA notes this accusation with some mirth and adds that it was not the case. CIA C/WHD William V. Broe wrote to the deputy director of plans, in explanation of his own activities, "The material disseminated [by us] does not duplicate USIA efforts, which in Chile are centered mainly in propaganda areas other than radio." While Labarca might have been correct in noting that the USIS was spreading pro-American propaganda, Broe wrote that the "USIA effort does not concentrate on disseminating a significant amount of anti-Communist material."[86] While Labarca points to some fairly unlikely patterns to support his theory—he argues, for example that any editorial from Santiago daily *El Mercurio* that finished with the letters O, W, or S was a plant from the CIA—he was correct in spotting the American hand behind the large pro-Frei propaganda drive in Chile, including (though his letter pattern is likely nonsense) editorials in major conservative papers such as *El Mercurio*.[87] Still, the Americans felt that the operation and all its millions were entirely sub rosa, to the point that Mann told his superior that the embassy staff "are attempting to insure that extraordinary caution is observed in this action campaign to conceal official U.S. government interest, and we have rejected several ideas which have seemed to entail undue risks or excessive American involvement."[88]

PLAYING POLITICS

Funding was not the sole action pursued by the U.S. government in Chile, and a large part of the CIA's mission was to directly influence the decisions of certain political parties. It is clear that, to this end, the CIA was involved in the internal affairs of some parties. A memorandum from the chief of the Western Hemisphere Division to the deputy director for plans in March 1968 discusses the renewal of funding for certain (unnamed) projects. It notes that for one of these projects the Agency had been providing funding to moderate elements within the Radical Party since 1963.[89] Though "we have worked with the same kind of collaborators within the party, the nature of our objectives, scope of involvement, and tactical use of such collaborators" changed along with the evolution in Chilean politics.

When funding had started, the Radicals were part of the center-right coalition in Congress that had supported Alessandri. This basis of support had evaporated when the Radical Julio Durán was defeated in the Curicó by-election. With Frei subsequently established as the United States' preferred candidate, CIA support drifted away from the increasingly left-wing Radicals. The CIA did not entirely abandon the Radicals, however, because Durán was able to thwart an attempt within his party (which the CIA had initially hoped would beat Allende) to endorse Allende directly. With this action the CIA—which had never come to the same opinion twice about the Radicals or Durán—realized that supporting Durán could still prove politically useful for the United States, and officers within the CIA's Western Hemisphere Division were happy to note that their funding had been "instrumental" in maintaining their preferred Radical candidate in the party's internal struggle.[90]

All along, the CIA and the country team could not determine whether Durán and the Radicals stole votes from the PDC or the FRAP, but with the Radical Party's attempt to align with the FRAP, vote stealing became a secondary concern to keeping the Radicals from supporting the FRAP directly. With the help of Frei, the PDC was thus enlisted to push money to Durán to keep him both in the race and friendly to Frei, for in the case of a slim electoral majority and a runoff contest between Frei and Allende, the hope would be for friendly Radical Party congressmen to vote for Frei as president. While the CIA could keep Durán in the race for president, they could not guarantee the postelection support of the Radical Party or the prevention of another Radical Party move to support Allende. Because of "ambassadorial restrictions against supporting Radicals, our equities in that party [are] quite diminished."[91] For the meantime, at least, this was not a major problem.

MORE MONEY

If the CIA could not influence every aspect of the Chilean political system, the U.S. government as a whole could at least throw a lot of money at the one party it could sway. On May 14, 1964, the Special Group considered a proposal to increase the funds available for covert use in the Chilean election and noted the CIA's opinion that "recent political developments and additional information" indicated that an additional $1,250,000 was needed for the program to defeat Allende. Almost all of these funds were to go to Frei to allow his party to "campaign at its full potential."[92] According to the minutes of the Special Group meeting during which this funding was approved, "the principle of financial flexibility" lay behind the new payment. "If, as the campaign develops, one segment [of the operation] needs additional support and another less, authority exists to shift the subsidy in the needed direction." We know that at this point LBJ had at least a cursory awareness of the ongoing proposal because Bundy informed the Special Group that "higher authority was aware of the seriousness of this election."[93]

Yet more money followed. The 303 Committee, established to review and coordinate sensitive national security affairs between the various departments while maintaining a good degree of information security, succeeded the Special Group June 2, 1964. The aim of the new committee was to cease the duplication of efforts by the various departments and to speed the sharing of information between departments that maintained their own intelligence-gathering capabilities. On July 23 the committee considered a proposal to provide "supplementary support for the Chilean presidential elections." In a July 21 memorandum to the 303 Committee, the Central Intelligence Agency reported that an additional $500,000 was needed for the program to defeat Allende, as this amount would permit Frei to "maintain the pace and rhythm of his campaign effort" and allow the CIA to meet any "last-minute contingencies." The 303 Committee's obvious question about why more money was required in addition to the U.S. $2 million already spent (an enormous sum even in a U.S. election, several people noted) was met with an apology from the CIA: Frei had miscalculated his finances, an error "attributable to the PDC's inexperience in organizing a campaign of this magnitude."[94] Apparently placated, NSC staffer Peter Jessup recommended approval of the suggested funding to Bundy on July 23, repeating the mantra: "We can't afford to lose this one, so I don't think there should be any economy shaving in this instance. We assume the Commies are pouring in dough; we have no proofs. They must assume we are pouring in dough; they have no proofs. Let's pour it on and in."[95] The funding was approved.

Further, an unnamed senior PDC supporter, apparently on the basis of conversations with various Americans, assumed that he had a tacit commitment for U.S. financial support. Although no formal commitment had been made to him and no deals were signed (the CIA, of course, was careful so that Chileans could not detect its hidden hand), the 303 Committee felt he "had made measurable contributions to the Frei campaign through his 'front' organization and that some allocation of funds should be made to defray his deficit of $395,000."[96] This was an enormous sum of money for an individual, especially in Chile in 1964. Indeed, State Department Ambassador-at-Large Llewellyn Thompson commented disapprovingly that it "seems a great deal," but he did not enter any caveat to the disbursement.[97] This incident indicates the seriousness with which the U.S. government viewed the elections but also, more important, how freely their money was injected into Chile.

A SENSE OF PROGRESS

If so much money was being thrown around in Chile, was it actually achieving the aim? Did it look as if Frei would actually beat Allende? By and large, the Santiago CIA station thought so: "In the Embassy's opinion almost every evidence and observation suggests that Senator Eduardo FREI should win the most votes in the national election on September 4, 1964 . . . [despite] FRAP charges that he is the candidate of the Church, the Right and the United States."[98] That CIA support—which was secret—might aid the FRAP was impossible, and so the CIA station concentrated instead on scientific polling—a function introduced to the non-Marxist Chilean political scene by the U.S. embassy country team, which shared it with Frei.[99] The U.S. embassy also met with local business leaders, who "all agreed with me that Frei [was the] likely winner. General feeling [was that] serious violence [was] unlikely and [the] GOC [was] well prepared to maintain order."[100]

There was, however, fear in the embassy and in the CIA station in particular. The CIA officers felt that all the money they were passing to the PDC was doing nothing to ameliorate the fact that the PDC was simply less well organized than the FRAP. It had become "convincingly evident that the communists [had] indeed been working hard for many years pointing toward this election. They [had] made notable inroads among the *campesinos* [peasants]" and other segments of the electorate that the PDC simply could not reach.[101] While most Chilean political observers were generally confident of a PDC win, "a certain tension is felt in middle and upper class circles as shown by such things as the greatly increased issuance of visitor's visas, plane and ship bookings and capital flight."[102]

Not totally dismissing the unscientific political prognostication of the locals, the CIA—haunted by the possibility of an Allende win and "another Cuba" on its watch—asked the Chilean army what it might do in the event of an Allende victory. The answer to this question was a resounding "nothing." Simply, the Chilean military was conditioned by a long tradition of "nondeliberation" and remained outside of politics, liable to act only if a party—any party—attempted to subvert the Chilean constitution. "If Allende should impatiently attempt to override Congress," the CIA station wrote to Washington, "the military would almost certainly intervene to preserve constitutional order. If he should too abruptly seek to impose his personal control on the military establishment, there might also be a reaction. Otherwise, the military and the *Carabineros* [the Chilean national police] would be likely to support the duly elected regime." Although the military had intervened in the government briefly in 1924 and 1935, in this case there simply was no great likelihood of extraconstitutional action: "Military intervention in politics can happen in Chile, though not without strong provocation."[103] Furthermore, this was no run-of-the-mill South American banana republic, and the White House was warned that "we should not confuse the Chile of 1964 with the Guatemala of 1954 unless we are prepared to physically occupy the country."[104] Luckily, this course of action did not seem too likely, as the polls were coming out in favor of Frei. An August 1964 sampling of the important areas of Santiago and Valparaíso showed Frei ahead by 20.2 percent over Allende in those cities.[105]

The station, however, was keen to stress that these were rough polling numbers, hard to translate into a prediction of the actual election outcome, and that the "important point" was that Frei looked like he was in for a simple majority and a solid mandate. Such a majority, the CIA noted hopefully,

> would mean that the election would not have to be thrown to Congress and therefore that the uncertainties surrounding that process, including the possibility of rioting, would be eliminated. Furthermore, with a clear majority Frei would not have to make any political deals with other parties. Forced to predict, however, we would give the following: Frei-53 percent; Allende-41 percent; Durán-6 percent.[106]

This was wonderful news for the White House. Nonetheless, as September 4, 1964, approached, there were, no doubt, more than a few white knuckles both in Washington and Santiago.

ELECTION DAY

Come the election day of September 4, the various parts of the Johnson administration involved in the Chilean operations closely monitored the official voting count in Chile. The Department of State received hourly updates from the embassy in Santiago, which in turn were forwarded to the White House.[107] Although the initial returns echoed the polls and put Frei into the lead quite early on, the final result was surprisingly decisive. With only slightly more than a tenth of the electorate not voting, Frei and the PDC received 56 percent of the vote; Allende and the FRAP received 39 percent; and Durán, center of such hand-wringing and worry in the Santiago station, finished third with just 9 percent of the vote—very close indeed to the CIA's polling numbers.

President Johnson addressed the importance of the Chilean election at a news conference on September 5. The election, he said, served as a reminder of the strength of democratic institutions throughout Latin America; it was a victory for democracy as well as a defeat for "those who are hostile to freedom."[108] The Santiago embassy staff was slightly more prosaic, commenting in a cable several days after the poll, "Midnight Wednesday mercifully brought to an end an election campaign which has been going on for longer than Embassy officers care to remember."[109]

EFFECTIVENESS AND RESULTS

The CIA was not shy about claiming the share of credit due it for the stunning win, the first clear majority vote in a Chilean election in twenty-two years, as DCI John McCone pointed out to the 303 Committee. The CIA was one of the "indispensable ingredients of Frei's success."[110] Frei, personally, praised the embassy for its role during the campaign and noted its staff's "discretion and cooperation" throughout his campaign.[111] The station likely agreed wholeheartedly and indicated to the 303 Committee their belief that Frei's chances of winning the election "would have been considerably more tenuous, and it is doubtful if his campaign would have progressed as well as it did without this covert U.S. Government support."[112] Ambassador Cole agreed, and the day after the election he reported that the combined effort of U.S. agencies "contributed significantly to the very satisfactory Frei victory on September 4."[113] Feeling, apparently, in a remarkably generous mood, McCone remarked that the voters "themselves . . . deserved some commendation."[114] It was, all around, a great day to be in the CIA. Whether it had been a good day for Chile was not debated. The potential long-term impacts of such a massive intervention were never considered in that forum.

Commenting on the matter almost forty years later, William D. Rogers gives a more reasoned and rational tone to the reaction, which also puts into perspective the supposed secrecy of the CIA's efforts:

> We saw [the election] in '64 as kind of an acid test. You know the old domino effect: we were terrified. I still remember the sense of relief in the Alliance that [Frei] won. He was our strong preference, so we put our money where our mouth was. But there wasn't any secret about it, about where our aid money

> was going. And I think it was applauded by most of the liberal side of the spectrum here in Washington.

He added, "It wasn't everything we could [have done to ensure Frei's victory]; we could have done a hell of a lot more. We were pretty restrained in what we really did. But there was no doubt in where we saw our interests lie." Rogers disagreed with the assessment that the CIA was a major factor in the Frei victory. Instead, he believes a combination of Frei's charismatic personality, the collapse of the Democratic Front after Curicó by-election, and the continued candidacy of a defeated Durán led to this notable majority.[115] Indeed, senior State Department official Ambassador John H. Crimmins echoed this opinion when he indicated in an interview that Bob Hurwitch, the embassy's first secretary, "believed that the [U.S.] efforts had had a *very* marginal effect."[116]

But U.S. efforts most certainly *had* an effect. Regardless of whether they actually assisted the Frei candidacy, almost universal suspicion arose in Chile that Frei was America's man. Within a few years of the election, Labarca remarked, "What is for certain is that during the government of President Frei, Washington preferentially helped, in its corrupt and imperialist labors, members of the Christian Democratic Party."[117] Habeas corpus or not, plausible deniability simply does not matter when everyone comes to believe that the supposedly unproved allegations are true. The United States had effectively, and with consent, undermined the credibility of the Frei government and the PDC by aligning too closely with them. This marks the significance of the 1964 election within the ten-year sweep of U.S. covert actions in Chile: the U.S. government (through its many departments and several administrations) showed in general an acceptance of the idea that the damage done to Chile by its intervention was less than the potential damage of an elected Marxist government. By giving its support to the Christian Democrats in 1964, the U.S. government also initiated what would become its ten-year acquaintance with the PDC, the party that was perceived as the U.S. government's own party, regardless of whether it was always, or ever, pro-American and of shared interests and goals.

The 1964 operation also seemed to confirm that the CIA was capable of swinging elections in the direction of a favored candidate. Certainly, this had been proved conclusively in the successful electoral intervention in Italy in 1948, one of the nascent CIA's first major covert operations, during which millions were funneled to Alcide De Gasperi's Christian Democratic Party to defeat the Communists—an operation to which CIA documents from 1964 consistently refer.[118] The CIA, therefore, thought it had more than one event by which to project its potential success at such covert actions, and after 1964 the Agency felt quite confident in the nature of its powers.

As the next two chapters will show, while some in the CIA might have been aware that their intervention was less decisive than it appeared, others in the administration felt that the CIA could be used to *avert* political developments they found unfavorable, whereas in reality the Agency could only delay those developments. That the U.S. government subsequently ignored the CIA's warning about those still-existing political currents shows that the Kennedy and Johnson administrations viewed covert action not as a long-term policy tool but as a "silver bullet" solution to intractable or uncomfortable foreign policy troubles. This is hardly the reality. The election of 1964 reinforces the theory that even simple covert actions in democracies have a negative impact that goes far beyond the apparently benevolent nature (in the eyes of those who order it) of their execution. At least in part, this is the law of unintended consequences: while the intervening power felt it was adding a small measure of assistance and making a change for the better, it in fact created an imbalance in the local political culture and unleashed resentments and political forces that it could not predict or control. Far from being a silver bullet, electoral interventions of this sort could only really delay the manifestation of a problem that continued to exist, that would still need to be dealt with at some point.

The final word on the significance of the 1964 election within the U.S. covert campaign in Chile can be given to Jorgé Alessandri, the ex-president who ran against Allende in 1970. Meeting a U.S. official several weeks after Frei's inauguration, the former president was noted as saying (in a curtly worded telegram to Washington),

> Chile was [an] over-politicized nation accelerating its plunge towards chaos ruin and inevitable military intervention. . . . [The] PDC [is the] incurably muddled inefficient cutting edge for eventual open Marxist takeover which only armed force could and should and would stop, however much he lamented blows to Chilean democratic tradition.
>
> Frei could not change stripes (he implied that he regarded Frei as a Chilean Kerensky) and therefore independents would oppose Frei to the end, running their own candidate in 1970 even if it assured victory of FRAP and put communists in GO[C]. At least such eventuality would trigger army intervention.

> He held USG largely responsible; not only for its direct actions, but for support it gave to such subversive organizations as ECLA [Economic Commission for Latin America] and FAO [Food and Agricultural Organization of the UN], for the imminent Chilean crisis. Intellectuals surrounding President Kennedy had meddled ruinously in Chile.[119]

Such a damning—and, as it turns out, shockingly accurate—appraisal of the results of U.S. involvement in Chile likely fell on deaf ears.

2

SUPPORTING THE MODERATES: THE 1969 CONGRESSIONAL ELECTION

All of us realize that war requires action. What is sometimes harder for us to realize is that peace and neutrality also require action.

—President Lyndon Johnson, Brenham, Texas, November 1939

After the 1964 presidential election, the first significant U.S. operation in Chile took place from mid-1968 to 1969: the manipulation of the Chilean congressional election of March 2, 1969. While the United States had, through the CIA, undertaken missions to influence the 1964 presidential elections and the subsequent congressional elections in 1965, no operation had been maintained with the explicit aim of preventing the dominance of the Marxist parties or electoral fronts in subsequent elections. What remained were low-key pro-Western propaganda or merely intelligence-gathering operations.

The United States discontinued active measures notwithstanding the fact that the political climate in Chile had not altered and, in fact, the chances of a Marxist victory had increased owing to notable changes in Chilean demographics and electoral law. Throughout 1968 and 1969 the U.S. goal in Chile remained stable if simple: keep the Marxists from power. The various U.S. government agencies responsible for Chile, however, were not able to adapt their policies in Chile to the growing radicalism of Chilean politics, and they could not in their minds easily abandon their old political allegiances to the increasingly left-leaning and anti-American Christian Democratic Party (PDC). Even worse, as Ambassador Edward M. Korry noted,

> our policy has been partially to blame for this state of affairs because we have over-emphasized economic support of Frei's program . . . in the mistaken assumption that economic performance would produce the political results we seek. [Frei] thinks the U.S. Ambassador should be providing more *political assistance.*[1]

The American operation to influence the 1969 election therefore reflects U.S. ambiguity and misunderstanding of Chilean politics. The efforts in the 1969 election were haphazard and progressed without clear executive direction—a fact perhaps compounded by the Johnson administration's handover of the White House to Nixon and Kissinger. Drifting along without significant executive-level input, both the ambassador (a State Department functionary) and CIA headquarters provided conflicting direction; neither side had a clear image of what strategic foreign policy goal it was pursuing. Furthermore, at critical points the CIA's political analysis was crucially flawed and misread the impact the Agency's measures would have on the Chilean political environment. In the case of the CIA's operations, perhaps, covert action was let down either because it was not supported by proper intelligence collection or because intelligence that was properly collected and analyzed was not properly disseminated. Likewise, disagreement between the chief of station (COS) and the ambassador highlighted the differing political predictions of the various American players. The ultimate result of the confused American action was to split the anti-Marxist vote and contribute to an electoral environment that *favored* Marxists in the period following the election. The hallmarks of the operation were a meandering mission, confused chain-of-command, and insufficient executive control.

If the benefits were so small, so undeterminable, why was the U.S. government willing to risk an operation in the first place? Covert action is, in the greater scheme of things, war undertaken without the knowledge of one of the participants, in the sense that it is a state's challenge to another state's sovereignty in order to achieve a political aim or desired concession. As one does not—or at least *should not*—initiate a war without some tangible goal, it stands that covert action should not be initiated without a campaign plan, without an express end state in mind. Was this war worth waging for the Americans? Did it have a goal? Examination of the evidence shows that the effort to influence the 1969 congressional election in Chile was likely a waste of time and effort, a procrastinating half-effort that compounded future troubles for American operations in Chile.

THE GENESIS OF THE OPERATION

The idea for the 1969 election operation apparently came from Ambassador Korry. Korry had approached the CIA station chief, Henry Heckshe
r, in late 1967 or early 1968 and asked him to request from the 303 Committee permission to undertake a "limited covert election operation aimed at Congressional elections."[2]

Chilean politics seemed fairly clear to the U.S. embassy team during this period. On the conservative right was Arturo Alessandri's National Party (PN). In the center was the governing PDC, surrogate Democrats in Latin America. On the far left were the constituent parties in the Popular Action Front (FRAP) and, wavering between them and the government, were the Radicals, formerly centrists like the PDC but now moving into the Communist-Socialist orbit. The CIA team at the embassy imagined it could use the congressional elections to stiffen the PDC's resolve to resist the Unidad Popular (UP), and at the same time it could promote moderate centrists within the Radical Party and any other leftist party that had more democratic tendencies.

In May 1968 the chief of the CIA's Western Hemisphere Division (C/WHD), William V. Broe, in a meeting with State Department representatives, formally suggested that the U.S. government attempt to influence the Chilean congressional elections of 1969 and by extension the presidential election of 1970. Broe believed that "these elections [were] all-important since their outcome [would] determine the nature of the party alliances that [would] be formed in connection with the presidential election of September 1970."[3] That Broe had to propose the start of such a program for this election is telling of U.S. Embassy Santiago's failure to sustain any covert mechanism to influence the Chilean political system in which it had such great interest after the 1965 elections. Generally, this failure resulted from a reduction in the size and number of U.S. covert operations as the 1960s drew to a close, a reduction that stemmed from budgetary concerns as well as the beginnings of more public scrutiny of the Agency:

> By the end of the decade, internal concern developed over the problem of exposure for large-scale operations. . . . Gradually,

> senior Agency personnel began to recognize the cumulative effect of long term subsidies to and associations with political parties, media, and agents overseas—a large presence invited attention and was vulnerable to exposure.[4]

This is not to say that the CIA had not maintained any assets in Chile—it is clear that they did—but that the level of commitment to covert action there had waned significantly from their effort in 1964.

In the case of Chile, the reduction in commitment originated from more than a concern of general risk or budgetary limitations. It was also the product of confusion about the general political situation. In the last presidential election the U.S. choice had been clear-cut: Only one non-Marxist party had any hope of beating the Socialist-Communist FRAP: the PDC. Deciding to subsidize the PDC heavily was easy for the Americans, as the PDC and their champion Eduardo Frei were viewed as much-loved political cousins to the American Democratic Party. Having cleared the major hurdle of the 1964 election, however, the PDC was left to its own devices under the trustworthy hands of President Frei. The United States assumed, perhaps because of the permanence of U.S. political institutions, that the PDC could be relied upon to remain a bulwark of the Democratic-style social reform that Kennedy and Johnson had favored. Politics evolved much faster in Chile than in the United States, however, and the PDC of 1968 did not resemble the PDC of even four years previously.

The embassy staff in Santiago was persistent, if anything, and decided that the PDC should be the focus of its plan regardless of the evidence that the party was moving to the left. An old soldiers' maxim asserts, "No plan survives first contact with the enemy," and in this case the maxim held true. Still, the PDC was the only party to which the United States could actually make an open approach, and the embassy did so sometime in 1968. The Christian Democrats, however, did not view of their relationship with the CIA as the latter did, and the CIA did not receive a favorable response. "[Station] overtures," wrote the chief of station (COS) Henry Hecksher, "have evoked no response suggesting PDC leadership's election planning encompasses [a] role on any terms [the station] would entertain."[5] The reasons for this had, for some time, been clear to many within the Chilean political environment, including President Frei himself. In January 1968 Ambassador Korry spoke at length with Frei about the PDC's drift to the left, and he noted, "High personalities in the PDC had argued . . . that some kind of broad popular movement [in conjunction with the Communist Party] was needed in Chile to assure the execution of PDC goals."[6] Essentially, the PDC had ceased to be the reliable pro-U.S. machine it had been in the past.

Indications of this shift came from PDC manifestos, which showed that the moderate reformist President Frei was in a struggle for control of his party mechanism with a group led by the FRAP-friendly Radomiro Tomic. Of all the Chilean politicians aside from Frei and Alessandri, the U.S. government and CIA had the most information on Tomic. For two years Tomic had been the Chilean ambassador to the United States and so had become quite well-known in Washington, both politically and personally. The CIA understood that Tomic was the representative of the new, vigorous left wing of the PDC called the Rebeldes (rebels), which was highly critical of Frei and which sought to move the party leftward, as that was where it saw the political feelings of the population in general.[7] The CIA's agents knew of Tomic's ambitions to lead a broad leftist front in the next election and dismissed his chances of doing so, for Tomic was "not trusted—let alone liked—by the other leftist parties . . . he envisions himself as leader of."[8] The Chilean Right—in this case represented by National Party founder Miguel Otero—believed that "Tomic was *very* close to what Allende was saying. Only a very slight difference. . . . I would say that Tomic would have been completely anti-American."[9] The CIA no doubt understood this fact, for the COS wrote that the rise of the Rebeldes wing within the PDC "casts into more striking relief fundamental incompatibility of [the station/U.S. government] role in support of PDC and PDC's dedicated travel of *via no capitalista*."[10] Yet, for some reason, the CIA could not move past the fact that the PDC was the only party that offered an alternative to a Communist-Socialist front in the coming elections. The CIA's conclusion, announced in a Directorate of Intelligence "Special Report," was that "in the absence of a strong Christian Democratic showing in the 1969 congressional elections, Chile probably will stumble along until a new administration—possibly with communist support—takes over in 1970."[11]

In March of that year a Board of National Estimates Special Memorandum titled "Chilean Problems and Frei's Prospects" stated that Frei was a lame-duck president who could not control his increasingly left-leaning party. In view of the conservative-dominated Senate's hostility toward the PDC, the estimate continued, "there appear[ed] to be little chance that [Frei] could secure passage of additional reform measures his [left-wing] opponents within the PDC [were] demanding." Further, "this could result in the Christian Democrats losing to the Communist-Socialist coalition in both the congressional and presidential elections."[12] In retrospect, we know the prediction was correct, but what about its premise: the need for a strong PDC?

The CIA considered two other non-Marxist parties, aside from the PDC, for support. The first and most interesting of these was the Radical Party (PR), which had been part of the right-wing coalition that had elected President Alessandri in the 1958 presidential race but that had been defeated by the PDC juggernaut in 1964. Yet, where the PDC had been left to its own devices, the CIA had maintained collaboration with the Radical Party and had been providing financial support to "moderate" elements within the party since 1964—apparently to no avail. In 1965 "the balance of power within the Radical Party shifted and the left wing came to dominate. . . . No possibility remained in the near future to recapture the party."[13] With perhaps little heed to warnings of "good money after bad," in July 1967 the 303 Committee approved a program to spend an unspecified amount of money "in an effort to discourage the movement of important elements of the Radical party toward a working alliance with the Communist party and Socialists."[14] This was a fool's errand as the party continued to move left and seek alliance with the FRAP. Nonetheless, in the debate about what to do with the Radical Party, the CIA decided to maintain "minimal" support for the PR in order to retain some influence within the party. This support had the potential to be a useful tool for the CIA, as the PR was entering into informal cooperation with the FRAP, meaning continued influence in the PR could either give the CIA information on the FRAP's plans or perhaps serve to cause some sort of vote-stealing split later on.[15] It is notable that the PR was the only party to receive U.S. funds between the two presidential elections; this perhaps serves to foreshadow CIA relations with the PDC through the congressional election to the presidency.

The second and more obvious party that the CIA considered was the National Party (PN), the right-of-center party that had elected the popular and very conservative President Alessandri in the 1958 election. As the 1969 congressional election approached, it appeared that Jorgé Alessandri would once again seek to represent this party in the crucial presidential election in 1970. The Santiago COS noted that the PN was basing its election strategy "exclusively . . . upon [Alessandri's] undeclared Presidential candidacy."[16] Nonetheless, the PN draws curiously little comment from the CIA in this period. For some reason, and despite the PN's high poll numbers and control of most of the not-inconsiderable right-of-center vote, CIA cables do not reflect consideration of this party as a universally suitable alternative to the PDC. Drawn by their concern over the Left, the embassy seemed to be ignoring the Right.

The plan to influence the election began to take shape in June 1968, before the parties selected their congressional candidates, in the fall of that year. "It was decided," stated the CIA in a brief to Viron Vaky, deputy assistant secretary of state for Inter-American Affairs, "that because the 1969 election might hold the key for 1970, an operation should be undertaken to help elect moderate candidates of the PR, PDC, and PN where it is decided, on the basis of hard information, that our support could be decisive."[17] The ambassador's election team had a massive job ahead of it; upward of 750 candidates would be competing for 180 congressional seats.[18]

Korry, himself a JFK appointee, was very clearly of the camp supporting the PDC, and his tactics reflected his trust that the party would continue in its reformist approach in a manner that would benefit U.S. (or Democratic?) interests. In view of the increasing leftward drift of the party, however, he felt that something had to be done to encourage the PDC to refrain from supporting the FRAP. Moreover, Korry perceived the general trend that politics in Chile were abandoning the center entirely, moving toward the extreme left and the ultraconservative, leaving no room for the gentle reformist. Korry's idea was apparently simple: the ambassador and his chosen staff would canvass the field of candidates from all the non-Marxist parties and would handpick a number of these candidates who appeared sufficiently moderate to suit American political interests. These candidates would be chosen with no consideration to their parent party, merely based on their own political merits and a rough system of triage: the chosen ones would be those moderates most likely to benefit from U.S. support. Despite the PDC's drift to the left, or the Radical Party's confirmed support of the FRAP, candidates from these parties stood a chance of being chosen for American support based on their own political views.

The program, however, was not entirely without guile. Support would continue for one potential splinter group from the Socialist Party (PS), the Popular Socialist Union (USP).[19] While it does not receive much attention—and cables and memos regarding the topic are heavily excised—support for the USP was considered of primary importance to the election program in the hopes that the USP candidates would draw votes away from the PS, splitting the left-wing vote and paving the way for the win of a PDC or PN candidate.[20] The U.S. Embassy Santiago staff believed the entire plan was sound and was timed to provide a good start on the project.

"By early planning, a country team setup, and personal direction from Ambassador Korry," wrote the COS, "significant results are possible."[21]

Discussion about the embryonic plan began at a meeting between the CIA and the State Department on May 24, 1968, and quickly seized on some of the tactical and political problems facing the country team and the embassy in the execution of the operation. As it appears, the country team was simply not positioned to provide all the information required by the ambassador's team to choose the candidates. Broe noted, "Our biggest trouble at the moment was lack of information." Indeed, the Agency was considering appealing to "its European and Latin newspaper contacts for information about political temperatures in the Chilean hinterland; the sort of information in other words that our Embassy could not readily produce."[22] Moreover, the CIA did not have any ability to ensure that parties chose moderates as their candidates in the first place; Santiago had already determined that this was impossible, for the system was too complex, and the station "lack[ed] sufficiently detailed intelligence to second-guess party decisions/deals." Further, the COS admitted that the station did not "have covert political muscle to impose its will."[23] In addition to lack of information and covert leverage, however, the State Department official present, one Mr. Sayer, brought up a serious issue of command and control: who would be choosing the candidates, and by what criteria? On being informed that the ambassador directing a team of CIA and embassy staff would make these decisions, Sayer posited that the principal difficulty "would be to get the Ambassador to be specific enough to give us a fair idea of exactly what he wanted to do and how we would go about it."[24]

While it is clear that the State Department was not entirely convinced by the plan—or by the "inadequate" quality of the CIA staff's work—it gave the CIA and the ambassador the benefit of the doubt and gave its endorsement for further planning by both agencies.[25] "The ARA agrees with the objectives of the proposal program," wrote State Department officer Covey T. Oliver. Oliver added that he thought the CIA's tactics were sound and that "the survival and health of [these democratic, reformist] forces is desirable and congenial to our interests."[26] The program was recommended to the assistant secretary of state for ARA with no reservations. Accordingly, the incomplete plan moved forward along the approval process and, with the basic support of all the agencies involved, was approved by the 303 Committee, with a budget of $350,000, on July 12, 1968.[27] On approval, the committee stated that the support given to moderate candidates would be made "in an effort to brake the leftward drift toward a popular front which threatens to engulf" the PDC and President Frei.[28] Nonetheless, "the 303 Committee would be just as satisfied if we were not involved in this election, even on a limited scale."[29] This was hardly a ringing endorsement of the plan, and the budget perhaps reflected this enthusiasm.

THE PLAN IN EXECUTION

Both the CIA and the State Department moved forward with the plan that had been agreed upon, but before long they were reading off different sheets of music. While the CIA had been relatively clear on what tactics it would use in the operation, the 303 Committee and the CIA, the CIA and State Department, and officials within the three groups diverged on their views of the mission's overall intent. As far as the State Department understood it, the object of the program was to

> promote the election in 1969 of the greatest possible number of moderate senators and deputies in order to maximize effective opposition to the popular front candidate in 1970 and to create a body of moderates who could act as a restraint on the policies of any popular front president, should one be elected.[30]

This diverges by a few degrees from what the 303 Committee stated in its approval note. Indeed, Broe in August 1968 told Vaky that the operation would be undertaken, quite sensibly, "because the 1969 election might hold the key for 1970."[31] The State Department, in its internal communications, added, "The rationale for this assistance, which is generally recognized as probably only the first installment, is that there is (perhaps) at stake the survival in Latin America of the sort of democratic reformism that President Frei represents."[32] This was closer to their position in the 303 Committee, but again faintly different.

While the 303 Committee talked about preventing the (short-term, tactical) collapse of Frei's hold over his party, the State Department discussed the (long-term, strategic) stability of Frei-style democratic reformism over all of Latin America. These views, while appearing different only in style, enthusiasm, and syntax of expression, are significant in that they show vastly different understandings of both the operation's scope and its overall intent. The discrepancy was caused by the executive's failure to send a mission statement telling everyone the operation's object. Thus, some thought the 1969 election mission was to be a precursor to the 1970 election mission, but as it developed this proved not to be the case.

And, as the plan moved into execution, the gap in understanding between all the organizations grew wider still.

The 303 Committee, as it stated when it approved the mission, was not entirely interested in supporting an operation for the congressional elections. This raises the question, who was pushing the mission onward? The answer, clearly, is Ambassador Korry, although it is perhaps doubtful that Korry understood what was going on. This doubt was felt by the COS in Santiago: "I suppose one can feel fairly comfortable about Ambassador Korry's judgment and lack of experience in Latin America, even though he certainly cannot qualify as an expert on Latin American affairs."[33] Moreover, because the selection mechanism was entirely in the ambassador's hands, any change in the administration and perhaps the introduction of a neophyte ambassador, had the potential to put the whole election mechanism into disarray. Left unanswered was the question about the nature and strength of the ambassador's political biases and how they might affect his choice of candidates.

Any doubt about the ambassador's qualifications or politics, however, is overshadowed by the question about the mission's overall focus. If the 303 Committee was disinterested in the operation and the ambassador was pushing it, who was there to bring the two constituent departments, the CIA and State, into concert on the operation's intent and aim? The answer might be "no one."

The 303 Committee received the first status report on the mission directly from a member of the election team on September 3, 1968. The report said little, and the committee was told that "the lack of spic-and-span picture at this time is largely due to the fact that particular candidates are not selected until November, and the campaign gets underway only later in December."[34] The first discouraging words to be uttered about the 1969 election program came only two weeks later. Though the full titles of the recipient and originator are partially deleted, it appears that someone in the United States wrote the memorandum to C/WHD Broe. A three-page document, it argued at length that the entire operation lacked focus, was likely to produce negligible results, and was potentially embarrassing for the United States. The author began by admitting that it was perhaps too late to do anything about the mission:

> I should like to go on record as having serious reservations about the basic concepts underlying the proposal. . . . By and large, the subsidies will go to individual candidates in the absence of any real indication of how they will use the funds,

> and without any control over the manner in which the funds are expended. . . . The mere insertion of funds to individual candidates does not assure us of any positive results.[35]

In addition to his concerns about the Chileans' mismanagement of U.S. funds, the memo's author raised doubt that all the candidates selected for support needed support. The CIA's early estimates of the PDC war chest indicated "that PDC's vigorous fund-raising drive yielded more than satisfactory results, (amounts as high as 2 million dollars have been mentioned). Come Nov 68, PDC campaign managers should be able [to] launch campaign without overpowering financial worries."[36] If money was not needed, then what could the United States gain from giving the candidates money, and small sums of it at that? It is clear that, unlike the PDC, the National Party, as one example, was perennially short of money, and Miguel Otero claimed that in 1969 the PN was "near bankruptcy."[37] One can argue that giving money to an organization flush with funding and, in any case, not sure to act in U.S. interests was a waste of resources. Funding to the relatively wealthy PDC seems odder still when support of another organization—the PN—that was more likely to act in U.S. interests and which *was* short of money, was restricted.

Last, the memo's author did not like the way the operation was being run from a tactical standpoint and thought it had a "more than normal flap potential." Simply, the author questioned the tactic of using priests as couriers: this method, he wrote, "seem[ed] to raise more security problems than it solve[ed],"[38] for many these unknown quantities were required to sponsor the many candidates necessary to make the operation effective, therefore inversely decreasing the operation's security. Otero was similarly skeptical of this tactic and said that some individuals bragged at the time that in their work for the CIA, in either receiving money or moving it to candidates, they did not see the funds move to an honest end. Rather, "they pocketed it."[39] The drafter of the CIA memorandum might have had similar suspicions and was thus not enthusiastic—indeed much less enthusiastic than the lukewarm, perhaps disinterested 303 Committee—about the operation. He concluded, "In sum the proposed project appears simple, both in conception and execution. I would maintain that is deceptively simple and that it will come back to haunt us sooner or later."[40] This not-so-resounding endorsement for the operation dramatically foreshadowed subsequent operations in Chile.

The dissenting memorandum appears not to have had any effect on the operation's progress, and as it proceeded, the conflicts and contradictions brought up by the plan continued to flourish. In mid-October, C/WHD Broe was given an internal CIA memorandum (likely from WHD, though this is not certain) that explained a State Department paper designed to brief the Nixon election team on the problems relating to Chile. The CIA was planning to review the paper on October 18 and either the deputy director of plans (DDP) or the director of central intelligence (DCI) wanted Western Hemisphere's views and consent on a few issues.

First, the drafter of this memorandum agreed with the State Department that the overall aim of U.S. policy toward Chile, both overt and covert, was "to keep both the Chilean Presidency and Congress free of Marxist control."[41] At the same time, however, the author disagreed on the congressional election operation's intent. State (and Broe) believed that the congressional mission would affect the 1970 presidential election, but the memo author, first disagreeing with the view that the Christian Democrats would control both houses of the Chilean Congress after the 1969 elections, posited that even "this would not substantially reduce the prospect of a FRAP victory in 1970 (40% FRAP/Radical vote vs. 60% remainder, which split)."[42]

Next, calling into question the PDC's suitability as the Americans' choice party in Chile and continued American support for it, the memorandum argued that the PDC's chance of victory in the 1970 election was more important than the outcome of the congressional elections. "The point will be made that [the 1969 election] strategy runs counter to U.S. objectives" and that this point needed to be made quite clear.[43] Nonetheless, the CIA was directed to continue to move money to the PDC, in hopes of fortifying that party's moderates, despite the fact that continued support for the Radical Party through the first years of the Frei presidency had not stopped that party from allying itself with the FRAP. This left the National Party as the only non-Marxist party not tainted with some association to the FRAP in the upcoming election, and Alessandri as the only candidate not urging some sort of alliance with the Popular Front.

This question on the problems of Chilean political alignments and U.S. funding also preoccupied the 303 Committee. What did they make of all this? "On the negative side . . . [Alessandri's] candidacy would split the democratic, anti-Marxist vote should it be a three-way presidential race in 1970 as now seems possible."[44] The increasingly pro-FRAP PDC would not be the problem in the 1970 election; rather, the conservative PN, the only remaining party not to have some designs for an alliance with the FRAP, would be the problem. Old habits die hard, and the United States had been supporting the PDC for a long time.

In preparation for Ambassador Korry's visit to Washington on November 20, 1968, for consultations with the White House and DCI Helms and C/WHD Broe, Broe sent a cable to Santiago outlining the briefing notes that he planned to go over with the ambassador. Broe began by pointing out that the 1969 election operation had not been designed to be more than a "minor" covert part of a total overt U.S. government diplomatic strategy aimed at preventing the rise of Marxist power in Chile. The operation was designed to support moderates from all the non-Marxist parties "in absence of a clear-cut choice [of presidential candidate] for 1970 which is the real test facing the U.S. in Chile." Developments in early August pointed out in the progress report, however, brought this strategy into question. The PDC was by that time under the control of Tomic to an indisputable degree, and furthermore the Radical Party, which had received U.S. support since 1967, had come to be considered "hostile [to U.S. interests] and in pursuit of an alliance with the FRAP." Conversely, Alessandri was by then clearly the PN's candidate for the 1970 election and was exerting influence on the party. Thus, Broe concluded that the "election program is now basically [PN]-oriented by virtue of both the preponderance of financial support we will provide . . . and the propaganda climate." More critically, however, he made one statement that seemed to suggest the unthinkable for Ambassador Korry: "We are building what might eventually become a pro-Alessandri machine for 1970." Worse, the cable did not suggest that this was a bad thing.[45]

To this point, it appears that none of the major players involved in the election operation—the ambassador, the State Department, the Santiago station, the C/WHD, and the 303 Committee—had a clear idea of the mission's overall aim. Was it to prevent a Marxist-dominated Congress or to prevent a Marxist president? Would this be achieved by the support of moderates, even those moderates who belonged to FRAP-associated parties? The station's rebuttal to the C/WHD's cable was not based on these questions but on questions of practicality. The station did not agree with Broe's logic, "particularly that our modest Ops machinery could either influence or significantly benefit possible Alessandri candidacy in 1970." This, the station argued, was because "both financially and in terms of number of persons involved [the mission] continues [to] be [a] minor part of total U.S. gov't package."[46] The operation was simply too small for the station to consider its scope as including the presidential election. The station's outlook, by force of resources, was distinctly short in view. However, as it filtered its way up the chain of command, the message became a bit diluted. Perhaps the 1969 election would not directly affect the outcome of the presidential election or perhaps, as it had been mentioned earlier, "the 1969 election might hold the key for 1970."[47] Regardless, Deputy Director of Plans Thomas Karamessines wrote to DCI Helms, "The program for 1969 was designed to be limited in scope and flexible in political terms, thus leaving all options open for the 1970 election."[48] The election operation changed color, if not shape, once again.

Ambassador Korry's input could not have helped the confusion about what was going on in Chile. It is unclear where Korry truly stood with regard to his support of the PDC and its leading contender, the left-leaning Tomic. The aforementioned Mr. Sayer of the State Department commented in May 1968 that "he felt he detected in Korry's correspondence and attitude hostil[ity] to former Ambassador Tomic," which would be expected considering Tomic's left-wing views.[49] The station perceived the opposite, however, and wrote later that year, "There is a difference in outlook between the Ambassador/Embassy and the Station, the former being inclined leftward towards the Christian Democrats and Tomic and the latter inclined right-of-centre towards the nationals and Alessandri." (This disagreement, the Station noted, did not impair its "fine relationship with Ambassador Korry.")[50] In the same month, "the Ambassador . . . made it abundantly clear that he lines up with President Frei and the Christian Democrats. . . . He gave the impression that Tomic is out and that a more moderate candidate . . . would rise as the party's candidate. . . . The ambassador took repeated swipes at Alessandri."[51] Korry apparently held this view even though the CIA had reported that the most likely presidential candidate for the PDC was Tomic, who had in August ushered in a new directorate composed primarily of Tomic supporters, which had in October formally adopted Tomic's political strategy of moving to the left.[52] In light of his earlier comments, and this information, the note that "Ambassador Korry has been skillfully trying to perpetuate Communist distrust for Tomic by making it appear as though the U.S. and Tomic have 'an understanding'"[53] takes on a more conspiratorial tone. Ambassador Korry might not have been honest in all of his dealings with the PDC and the CIA and was perhaps ensuring the continued preeminence of JFK's favorite party before a more hostile Republican president Nixon took office. Korry's 1998 remarks in an interview with the Santiago-based think tank Centro de Estudios Públicos make his reports at the time all the more curious. In 1998, when asked why the United States supported the PDC after it had clearly gone to the left under Tomic, Korry responded, "Why did we [support the PDC] at all? Because if we hadn't done it, the Democratic Congress would have been on my back in two seconds, as having reversed the Kennedy policy, taken it out." [4] Was Korry pressured by some part of the Johnson administration to support Tomic and the PDC? There is no evidence for this, for the 303 Committee seemed untroubled by Chile and even the State Department was unsure it should support Tomic. While all the contradictory information makes it unclear where Korry stood with regard to Tomic, it can be offered that the former was less than transparent in his dealings with the latter. What can be stated with certainty is that these conflicting expressions, from the man who was responsible for the direction of the U.S. government's election effort, did not contribute to the mission in a positive manner.

SELECTION OF CANDIDATES

Thus, with some conflict in aim among the main players in Chile the election operation pushed on. While the operation had been inaugurated in July, there was little to report until the beginning December, when the parties had finalized their candidate lists (a complex matter under the D'Hondt electoral system). While it had been thought, originally, that upward of forty candidates would be selected for support, the realities of the Radical Party's Marxist tendencies and concerns over some PDC members sharply limited the number of suitable candidates.[55] Thus, in the first week of December 1968, "in full recognition that the election program is a limited one *which cannot in any significant way be expected to affect the prospects for 1970*, . . . the Embassy/CIA election team approved ten candidates for support [italics added]."[56] Within two weeks an additional five candidates had been added to the list. These fifteen candidates were from all three "non-Marxist" parties, among which the United States included the FRAP-allied Radicals, as well as the PDC and the conservative National Party. While the number of candidates from each party has not been released, it is was recorded that these fifteen candidates were moderates for whom additional covert support could make the difference between election and defeat.[57]

Additional money was spent on propaganda to support the moderate candidates and in support of the dissident USP in a vote-stealing endeavor—indeed, the United States would ultimately provide the splinter USP with up to one-half of its campaign budget.[58] By December 26, the election team had spent roughly one-half of the approved total funding for the operation, or $175,000.[59] (This was, in an important foreshadow, the first information that Kissinger received on the topic of the U.S. operation in Chile. Also, at this point, the deputy director of plans, Karamessines, considered the election effort to have the highest chance of failure of all the CIA's covert operations at the time.)[60] The United States was unlikely to find any more candidates than the existing fifteen (who were spread among the 150 deputies and 30 of 50 Senate seats open for election) as the station election team was having a hard time keeping grips on the political upheavals in Chile, and in the PDC specifically. The COS apologized that his reporting was "bereft of all insight" for "a significant section of the spectrum of events no longer registers on our . . . radar screen. To substitute speculation where facts are unobtainable strikes us as dangerous practice."[61]

The station's fifteen candidates, trimmed down to twelve by February,[62] represented a small knot of moderate politicians within a much larger and very confusing political scene the Americans were grappling to understand. Through most of January and February 1969, little further traffic circulated between the Santiago station and Langley; it is impossible to determine whether the lack of reports reflects continued classification of these documents or an actual lull in communications. Informed speculation might indicate a drop of communications volume after the candidates had been chosen and the campaigns begun, but this can only remain speculation.

PROPAGANDA PRODUCTION

Throughout the entire period of political analysis and candidate evaluation the CIA was in fact carrying on an operation independent of the individual candidates, if united in general aim. This mission, directed at the production of propaganda for the station, was also the only operation undertaken by the CIA during this period that had any continuity with previous CIA actions in Chile. While the CIA had ceased to support any party but the Radicals in the period after the 1964 PDC victory, it had carried on in the production of certain propaganda, albeit at a low level. Several cables and memoranda show the existence of propaganda efforts covering "anti-Communist . . . activities, mainly in the form of wall posters, leaflet campaigns and other similar street actions" dating back to the 1967 fiscal year and before.[63] That this propaganda was considered important is made clear by developments through the 1969 election mission: by the end of 1968, the CIA was noting that propaganda rather than selective support had become the primary thrust of the election operation.[64]

The examination of this propaganda effort becomes interesting in light of the fact that it began as a separate effort but was soon rolled into the program of selective support. Of all its operations, the CIA holds its cards closest on its dealings with media and propaganda. For understandable reasons, the CIA does not want to be known for warping facts and sullying the truth, and further, it does not want its particular methods and mechanisms known. Thus, there are more deletions from those CIA cables dealing with propaganda than those dealing with, say, political analysis of parties or the methods of supporting candidates. Evidently, the CIA considers well-placed propaganda to have a significant force-multiplying effect on its target audience. Accordingly, propaganda took a major role in the 1969 election campaign that, as is noted, grew as the operation progressed. The propaganda mechanism developed for the 1968 fiscal year—which coincides with the beginning of the selective-support election mechanism—was a more sophisticated operation in organization, production, and scope.

If propaganda became an important aspect of the election operation, it still shared the uncertainty inherent in the greater mission. One can detect a slight confusion regarding the direct *intent* of the mission, and several different explanations of it are given in cables. Overall, one cable says, the aim of the CIA's propaganda efforts was to promote moderate politics among "the leadership class and the opinion molders."[65] Alternately, it was explained that the main thrust of the station's "broad spectrum propaganda is [a] plea to independent voter to exercise his vote. . . . Subsidiary function [is to] provide guidance to the uncommitted voter on how to choose among candidates the one best qualified to help steer Chile on [a] course of moderation, eschewing summons to class warfare which in long run [are] bound to lead to alteration of existing constitutional order."[66] Or one could believe the memo that asserted,

> The propaganda woven into the daily radio news casts is designed to influence those vocal groups—public and private—which play a role in the political process of the country. Over the long run and aiming particularly at the Congressional election of 1969 and the Presidential election of 1970, the purpose is to [one line deleted] . . . discourage an alliance of the democratic opposition to the Government with the FRAP.[67]

One might also take as the CIA's propaganda mission the statement from another part of that same memorandum:

> By promoting an anti-communist climate, the objective is to curb growing radical tendencies among the Chilean populace and, more specifically, to create tensions between the Government and the Soviet Bloc representation in Chile.[68]

Last, one might take the mission to be as stated later on in the operation, in February 1969: "A plea to [the] independent voter to exercise his vote and counteract [the] present state of lethargy (aggravated by distractions of [the] summer vacation period) and repugnance at Chile's party system as a whole."[69] This confusion of mission might have diffused the effectiveness and focus of the messages that the CIA was trying to disseminate, although some additional focus might have been given by the Soviet invasion of Czechoslovakia in late August 1968, which provided a touchstone for materials aimed at the doctrinaire Moscow- and Havana-oriented Communist and Socialist parties.

If the mission was slightly confused, however, this did not affect the crisp functioning of the propaganda mechanism itself, as opposed to the message. In March 1968, a full year before the election and months before the CIA's election mechanism was brought into action, the station in Santiago established a "propaganda workshop" aimed at disseminating station-produced propaganda through all mass media instruments.[70] This workshop, of unknown scale and cost, was needed to create the large amount of propaganda demanded by the station's media operations. Some cables show that a perhaps significant portion of the $350,000 earmarked for the propaganda operation went to "media operations."[71] We also know, however, that none of this money was expended until sometime after mid-August, meaning that the propaganda effort running until this time was operating on a much smaller budget.[72] Regardless, the propaganda machinery seems to have been very highly developed. One memorandum reported, "Agency-prepared news-items and editorials are inserted daily in the programs of [one word deleted] radio networks. These comprise some [specific number of] radio stations (of the 126 operating in Chile)." Further, this coverage reached the majority of the Chilean working class, which derived most of its information from the radio.[73] The station also directly sponsored some programs it felt were sufficiently anti-Marxist. In general, the CIA's propaganda attacked "the nature of communism, PCCh attempts to subvert and/or divide other parties . . . and implications of Czech invasion," which the station considered an exploitable example of Marxist aggression. Furthermore, it was thought that, as with the selective-support actions, the "propaganda benefits moderates in PDC, PR, and PN without stressing support for any one party." Yet, it was noted, "Propaganda must . . . be selective and sharp hitting rather than massive because of limited . . . funds."[74] The station believed it was handicapped by the election mechanism, which barred it from cooperating with any political party and left it with an absence of "non-affiliated political mechanisms to which propaganda can be attributed."[75] Some tailor-made propaganda, however, was produced for the usage of the chosen candidates.[76]

The number of articles the CIA successfully placed has been excised from pertinent memos, but the amount of money spent on the propaganda effort has been released. The sum is remarkably modest. In addition to the initial funding approval in April 1968,[77] an unknown increase was granted to bring the total to $16,780.[78] A parallel project, which supported "individual propaganda assets,"[79] received an increase to bring its total funds to the lofty heights of $8,050.[80] (The propaganda efforts were not reviewed by the 303 Committee, which by an unwritten rule judged only activities with budgets over $25,000.[81]) While it is difficult to determine precisely, this project was most likely supporting an individual or individuals, most likely known freelance journalists or correspondents who were placing propaganda onto a wire service for general usage. Numerous statements, describing the how and where the station's product was carried, back up this guess.[82]

A fairly clear picture of the CIA's propaganda mechanism emerges, though some conjecture is required. Desirous of producing a large-scale propaganda campaign, the CIA established the workshop to write articles and general editorial pieces for all three media (TV, print, and radio). Simultaneously, the Agency maintained several correspondents, editors, and freelance journalists as its own media "stringers." These assets were paid for by the two smaller operational funds. They would take the CIA media product (and, presumably, money) and place the pieces on a wire service for pickup by unwitting media outlets throughout Chile. Other such assets would place CIA editorials in editorial pages of papers and magazines or place them over the airwaves via radio (and to a much lesser extent, via TV). Still again, articles could be seeded into foreign journals or news services controlled by the CIA, with the knowledge that CIA media assets could pick up these stories with full credibility. The Agency could, it noted proudly, even seed American propaganda through Marxist press services, an operation technique that it thought added much credibility to its product.[83] William Broe noted in a cable that, because the CIA's propaganda product was "salted" into material from other sources and carried as straight news rather than rightist propaganda, "it does not usually draw any measurable or heated response."[84] One might wonder, then, what its purpose was.

CIA propaganda made it into the media in a widespread fashion, and we have CIA assurances that it was effective. Indeed, Miguel Otero's comments about the visibility of CIA propaganda show that it might have been fairly effective, if subtle. Otero noted, "I didn't really see anti-

Communist propaganda. That was made mostly through the TV, or the panels, or the radio, or people who were speaking in a forum or something like that. But that you would see on pamphlets or posters, against the communists . . . I don't recall. There might have been, but I don't recall that it was important."[85] Overt, over-the-top anti-Marxist poster campaigns or pamphlets would have been clumsy and transparently American, noted Labarca in his comments about the obviousness of American propaganda in the 1964 presidential campaign. Television, print, and especially radio placement of articles critical of the Marxists would have been much more effective in the Chilean context of an advanced media environment—though this did not stop the Americans from believing that they were better at producing "anti-Communist posters which darkly predict" the bleak results of a communist victory.[86] Regardless, close monitoring by the CIA team led it to congratulate itself for a job well done, as its material was "skillfully used and [compared] favorably with material deriving from the international news services with which the items are frequently interwoven."[87] The station was even able to produce in Washington "voluminous samples" of all the articles and broadcasts that it had originated.[88] As these same cables note, however, the true impact of this propaganda campaign can never be determined. Chile had no established polling organizations, the CIA itself could not conduct scientific polling and, most important, lacked information on public opinion outside of Santiago.[89] Thus the question is, was the best use of the money granted to the CIA for the congressional election mission propaganda?

ELECTION RESULTS AND PLANS FOR 1970

On March 2, 1969, the Chilean electorate went to the polls, and the result was, at least initially, pleasing to the CIA and those concerned in Washington. "According to initial reports," said a State Department memorandum, "the congressional election operation in Chile has been successfully executed." The report went on to state that ten of the twelve candidates supported had been elected, but most significant, the breakaway United Socialist Party, which the CIA had cleverly supported, polled 52,000 votes and had thus deprived the regular Socialist Party (PS) of about seven congressional seats, all of which were won by the PDC or the PN, save one to the Radicals.[90] Clearly the operation had achieved its aims, for, depending on one's methods of accounting, seventeen seats had been denied the Marxist parties.

Despite the increased left-leaning tendencies of the normally centrist Christian Democrats, many believed the election results were good news, and the congratulations were cabled from party to party. Ambassador Korry wrote to the DCI to thank him for the Santiago CIA officers' hard work. Korry congratulated the CIA and commented that this small operation had an outstanding effect on the political climate in Chile. The ambassador wrote,

> I would appreciate the 303 Committee being informed of my great appreciation for the excellent contributions to U.S. goals in Chile by the first rate contribution of the COS and his colleagues. . . . I am persuaded that we had a maximum impact in electoral terms for modest resources employed and that we benefited greatly from carefully selected multiplying-effect choices.[91]

Not everyone believed that those involved in the operation should celebrate its success. If the mission's stated aim had been to support a political climate of moderates for the 1970 election campaign or to act as a "break" on any popular front leader elected in 1970, then it was not as successful as some thought.[92] A document submitted to the 303 Committee noted that the CIA thought its operation had been limited—it did not spend its entire $350,000 budget[93]—and had achieved its limited objectives but could not be celebrated as a major victory over the forces of Marxism.[94] In the postelection wrap-up, even Korry was shocked into admitting that "the Chilean Right, born by a resurgent wind of Alessandrism, rose . . . to a strong vote that cut deeply into the strength of President Frei's Christian Democratic Party." While the PDC was received the most votes, Korry admitted, "the facts remain that it has suffered a grave defeat."[95] The 303 Committee, in a rare burst of attention to Chile, produced a direr verdict on the operation. The minutes of the meeting record,

> In the total picture, however, it should be realized that Chile's political moderates suffered a clear setback in the 2 March 1969 elections. What happened was a movement toward political polarization with the conservative right and the Marxist left coming out the greatest beneficiaries. In the present political climate the Communist-Socialist front would stand perhaps an even chance of victory for the presidency.[96]

This reality seems to have caught up with the ambassador. In his 1998 interview with the Centro de Éstudios Públicos, Korry had changed his opinion from his on-the-record celebration of the operation in a dramatic way. When asked to elaborate on the process and success of the election operation, Korry expressed doubt about the effectiveness of the operation overall:

> We did the minimal that would hurt and . . . targeted very specifically not . . . any one party, but . . . where possible a little amount of money would defeat a Unidad Popular candidate.
>
> So it went to all sorts of candidates of all persuasions, not many of them, it had a so-so effect, we never will know whether it had any effect. But some of the people we supported did get elected, some of the people we opposed did not get elected, and the total of that was minimal, because with a hundred, say a hundred and fifty thousand dollars to spread among twenty or thirty people, it can't be very much, not even in this country, and moreover not one candidate knew he got it. It was delivered by priests, I don't know who, by all sorts of people.[97]

Eight months of CIA work and close to a third of a million dollars thus was productive to a degree that no one could measure with any degree of certainty.[98] The congressional election operation mechanism, it turned out, was not maintained. When the COS in Santiago requested a budget renewal and permission to look for new contacts to affect the upcoming presidential election—itself now eight months away—he was rebuffed. A cable from Langley stated, "While we appreciate the reasons to project operational thinking and planning beyond March 2, 1969, it is felt that it would be best to wait for the results and the post-election assessment before taking any action which might imply [U.S. government?] commitment to a [deleted]-type undertaking in 1970." The COS was free to keep up his contacts but had no funding for further operations until a new operation mandate was given.[99]

TOO LITTLE TOO LATE?

When taken together, the propaganda effort and the assistance provided to moderate candidates offer an interesting if confusing image. What, precisely, was the American goal in both of these operations? What was the overarching *intent*? And what end was envisaged? The trouble with the 1969 operation is that there was no unifying political control over the effort. While the mission was important enough for the CIA to give it an "A" listing for "flap potential," the policymakers did not consider it to be at all important—and this despite one memorandum calling it a "deceptively simple" operation which "will come to haunt us sooner or later."[100] Yet this is not to say that the policymakers did not give it their proper attention. Quite to the contrary, they took bimonthly reports on the mission. Yet, there is no evidence that the U.S. executive gave any direction to the CIA or the State Department (and so to the ambassador) regarding what it hoped to get for the $350,000 it was willing to spend. One might say that the goal was "to keep the Marxists from power," but this does not fully qualify as a mission. While all parties implicitly understood that the ultimate goal was to keep the FRAP candidate from winning the 1970 presidential election—numerous documents cite this as the reason for starting the 1969 election operation—at no point did any higher authority explain how the smaller operation would link with the bigger intent. Ultimately, we see that the operation could not possibly help the process of the 1970 election to the U.S. end; it was simply too small and too restricted. This left each organization—primarily, in this case, the ambassador and Santiago station—to situate the mission as it felt best. In failing to provide direction, the 303 Committee, which was apparently (and appropriately) more concerned with affairs in Vietnam and the Soviet invasion of Czechoslovakia, dropped the ball. The result was eight months wasted in supporting a party—the PDC—that the CIA thought was becoming dangerously leftist, rather than in supporting the pro-American PN under Alessandri, who everyone but Ambassador Korry thought was the candidate most likely to win the upcoming presidential election. Had the executive promulgated a clear objective, a mission clearly attached to a greater U.S. foreign policy goal, the mission would either have been fully resourced and more successful or it would not have been carried out at all, for lack of any ability to alter circumstances.

Politics clearly affected the execution of the mission, though this is hardly surprising. The PDC had been a darling of JFK and the Democratic Party, and the Johnson administration was loath to give up on its old standby of non-Marxist reform. This despite the fact that the PDC was moving closer and closer to the communist left, while the favorite but lame-duck President Frei was unable to influence his party. The State Department continued with its policy of propping up the moderates, long after the moderates in Chile had gotten off the fence and chosen sides. No one, for some reason, was willing to support the only candidate that was actually pro-American, the nominally independent conservative Jorgé Alessandri. Meanwhile, the CIA, unable to push a coordinated agenda of what it wanted to do, and without a clear mandate or mission, was left by want of alternative running a small mission with a small aim, while bigger concerns were left unanswered. As Chilean historian Joaquín Fermandois has stated, "Korry insisted on very attentive observation (and intervention) in Chile, and the CIA assisted him discreetly, but the CIA still undertook operations that Korry believed were absurd. On the other hand, the State Department considered the threat minimal, and thought that Korry was living too much in the spirit of the 'Cold War.'"[101] This is a compelling description but is perhaps too simple a view of things. Korry was clearly, at this point, not working in a Cold War paradigm. More accurately, he was working in the paradigm of U.S. party politics. Throughout the mission he seemed reluctant to abandon the PDC, the Chilean avatar of the U.S. Democratic Party that was his home. This loyalty continued after it was clear that the PDC was not the pro-U.S. reformist organization it had previously been. Korry actually favored a party itself favoring an alliance with a Marxist, hardly the actions of a cold warrior as commonly depicted. Indeed, there needs to be a clear reappraisal of Korry's actions throughout his tenure as ambassador in light of his unwavering support for the PDC.

One may judge the wisdom of this operation by different standards. First, one might argue that it was too little too late. Support to a dozen candidates, most of whom were successful, might be considered a great success if one could judge for certain that they would have failed without the support. But with a maximum outlay of $30,000 per candidate, apparently rarely in cash, it is uncertain whether these funds really contributed to their success, especially to a party (the PDC) that already had a plentiful election coffer counted in the millions.[102] In retrospect, did these ten candidates make a difference? The other view one may take is that in its assistance to the congressional election, the CIA was "cutting off its nose to spite its face" in that it continued to focus on the PDC as the main alternative to the Communist-Socialist front and ignored the fact that in the upcoming presidential election the PDC candidate would most likely be inimical to U.S. interests if he won but, more important, that the continued strength of the PDC stripped support not from the Communist-Socialist bloc but from the only candidate likely to defeat that organization: Alessandri and his Partido National. Instead of supporting a Right versus Left campaign, the United States actually funded a Center versus Right fight.

The choice between these views requires one to judge the prescience of the CIA and State Department and their motives for support in the first place. The NSC's final report on the topic hinted at the realization that what the CIA actually achieved was minimal and showed an awareness of the erosion of moderate positions in Chilean politics. The CIA's and State Department's misinterpretation of the political change in Chile, which missed this erosion of the middle ground, was the critical failure of the U.S. effort overall. Though it took some time, the CIA clearly understood that that the PDC had drifted left and that the party mechanism was in the hands of pro-Marxists. Likewise, the Agency knew that the PN, through the nominally independent Alessandri, was the party most likely to defeat the FRAP in any upcoming election. So electing moderates to Congress made sense in the short term but not in the long term. By favoring the increasingly marginalized middle ground, the United States was stealing potential support from the one party able to achieve the longer-term goal of keeping a Marxist president from office, the PN. In view of the political climate and direction of the time, the better choice would have been to provide strong support to the most reliable party for the United States in the long term, the PN. Old party loyalties, and an ambassador who could not bury his bias, prevented this from happening.

3

LAST-MINUTE SCRAMBLE: TRACK I EFFORTS TO AVERT AN ALLENDE PRESIDENCY

> *Sr. Allende is a Marxist Socialist but his best organized backers are Moscow-Line Communists. Sr. Allende pays tribute, or lip-service, to constitutional democratic methods . . . but I cannot help being skeptical, and gloomy about the longer term. And it is very understandable that the Americans should be more gloomy still.*[1]
>
> —Mr. C. D. Wiggin, American Department, British Foreign Office, September 28, 1970

In 1964 America's perceived interests in Chile were very clear-cut. To prevent the ascension of a Marxist leader who could cause the United States economic damage and allow an unwanted Soviet influence in the Americas, the United States supported the Chilean Christian Democratic Party (PDC). With moderate, reformist policies and a trustworthy, pro-American reformist leader in the person of Eduardo Frei Montalva standing as the opposition to the Marxist Salvador Allende Gossens, the choice was obvious.

By 1970, however, the political landscape had changed dramatically, though U.S. operations during the 1969 election show that the U.S. government as a whole did not realize this or at least was not able to deal with it. By the time of the 1970 Chilean presidential election, the Republican Nixon administration had been in office for more than a year and a half and so presided over the new phase of U.S. covert actions in Chile without interruption. The administration's initial, Kissinger-driven disinterest in Chile—perhaps a means to protect the president from what was rightly considered a secondary theater—was reversed with a fury by the end of Nixon's first year in the administration.

Kissinger's initial lack of enthusiasm seems to have been mirrored in the operational branches of the U.S. government. What becomes clear through analysis of the 1970 election operation is that the CIA station in Santiago was not prepared to become heavily involved in an operation as complex as the election operation in Italy in 1948. The station believed that it did not have the capacity to carry out another election operation and it further believed for political and moral reasons that it should not influence another election. The State Department's malaise was similarly founded on the facts that the United States could do very little in Chile to affect the political process and that the marginal assistance the United States could give ran the risk of creating a scandal that could produce far worse effects on U.S. relations with Latin America as a whole. Disinterest in another election operation was compounded by a conflict between the Santiago chief of station (COS), the famously belligerent Henry Hecksher, and his nominal boss, Ambassador Edward Korry, a man known to be "an opinionated, eccentric, odd-duck."[2] Hecksher, a man known for picking fights with the ambassador,[3] berated Korry for not being more active in thwarting Allende, while Korry held a contradictory mix of lingering loyalty to the PDC, fear of Jorgé Alessandri's authoritarian manner, resentful confidence in the latter's victory over the Popular Action Front (FRAP)/ Unidad Popular (UP), and an interest to stay aloof from Chilean politics altogether. The policy result of all these inputs was a half-hearted plan to spoil the election for the Marxist front while not supporting any single candidate against it, a plan that one CIA wag resentfully called "trying to beat somebody with nobody" and that ultimately failed.

The 303 Committee, renamed the 40 Committee according to National Security Decision Memorandum 40 of February 17, 1970, did not approve the CIA's ongoing, post–1969 elections operations until they were well into the execution phase, at which point an Allende victory seemed much more likely.[4] The Kissinger-led committee became gravely concerned about Allende's seeming lead and scrambled for last-minute solutions, which the CIA and ambassador, short on time, were unable to implement. The results of this scramble for the United States were embarrassing. Input from the president also came far too late in the game to truly influence events, and indeed Nixon managed only to amplify the CIA and State

Department's previous inaction. The president, in expressing his will to the actors in Chile, directed as much spite at the CIA as at Allende, and this certainly did not help matters. The episode showed that covert operations were a serious matter no matter how small they seemed and could have consequences beyond their limited scope and means.

The seriousness of Nixon's intervention in Chile can be explained in a theoretical, as well as apparent, way. University of Georgia professor Loch Johnson has explained that covert actions, as varied as they are in execution, can be divided into four "thresholds" that resemble Herman Kahn's famous "Escalation Ladder." The first threshold is standard security measures pursued by all states; the second represents noninvasive support, such as propaganda, within foreign nations; the third threshold, which Johnson calls "High Risk Options," encompasses funding (and sometimes arming) groups within democracies; and the fourth threshold, called "Extreme Options," deals with any direct violent action within another state.[5] Of interest in Johnson's adapted escalation ladder is that covert actions run against a democracy are by default more serious than those in any other type of state, as they implicitly excuse the interference in or subversion of the type of government that Western states explicitly condone and encourage. In Chile, American ambivalence, the president's enforced ignorance of operations, and the White House's refusal to take the sound advice of its policymaking and operational arms forced the CIA to jump from what Loch Johnson would call a modest intrusion into high-risk and, eventually, extreme covert operations.

If one can draw a lesson from the failed covert operations in 1969–70—for indeed they did fail—it is that in the world of covert operations, long-term planning, preparation, and firm executive guidance are needed to ensure a mission that is both successful and in line with national foreign policy goals.

THE NIE ON CHILE

The progression of U.S. covert operations in Chile can be charted with reasonable accuracy. On January 28, 1969, eight days after Nixon's inauguration, the U.S. Intelligence Board (which represented all intelligence agencies, including the CIA, in the production of National Intelligence Estimates) completed the second available National Intelligence Estimate (NIE) on Chile.[6] Probably the most significant document produced by the U.S. intelligence community about Chile, this twenty-page memorandum acted as the central text in CIA planning for operations in Chile, as it encapsulated all of the Agency's significant conclusions about that nation. As it was not superseded by any other major document until after Allende's election as president in September 1970, the NIE can be seen not only as the collected wisdom of the USIB about Chilean politics but also as the document most responsible for guiding the Agency's approach to actions in Chile. Moreover, in this NIE is a gem of accurate and reasonable analytical work; of all analysis by all major policymakers and intelligence professionals about Chile, the Chile NIE has proved (as confirmed by hindsight) to be the best reasoned and most prescient. For this reason one cannot understand American efforts to influence Chile's presidential election without making reference to this document.

When the NIE was written, the USIB did not have the results of the Chilean congressional vote to serve as a weather vane for future actions in Chile. Regardless, the results of the election, the NIE noted, were important but would not likely reflect the presidential election, which would involve mass voter attention and thus be more focused on national issues and especially national personalities. Accordingly, the NIE noted that the 1970 presidential election was likely to be a three-way race, with the FRAP/UP (probably under Allende) facing the PDC's left-wing candidate, Radomiro Tomic, and nominal independent (though National Party member) Jorgé Alessandri. The NIE continued, "In sum, the current odds are that there will be a three-man race, in 1970, in which no candidate will win a clear majority, and the final choice will be made by the Chilean congress [which will in our opinion choose] the candidate with the largest number of votes" from the election ballot. While cautious to avoid predictions, the NIE offered that at the time of writing the conservative forces in Chile appeared ready to make a strong showing in the presidential election "if the aging Alessandri were to campaign vigorously. His remarkable appeal cuts across class and party lines and also reaches a considerable number of independent voters." The likelihood of his victory, or that of any other party, was not speculated. Similarly, the "threat" posed by a FRAP victory in the presidential election was not commented upon.[7]

Regardless, the NIE noted, the Chilean security forces, and especially the Carabineros, held a strong dislike for the Communist and Socialist parties, the FRAP's dominant constituent parties. Since the mid-1960s, various sources had noted that many officers in the Chilean armed forces felt a keen threat from the Left. David Fox Scott of the British embassy in Chile noted in 1966, "There was real unrest in the army and to a much lesser extent, in the other armed services. Officers at the Colonel level felt . . . it might conceivably be advisable for the Services to step in to avert chaos."[8]

As one historian has noted, to assert that the Chilean armed forces were apolitical is to take an extreme interpretation of their historical role in Chile, which involved forays into politics in 1891, 1925, and 1932. It can be argued that the military in Chile was in fact hugely important in the formation of the state after the War of the Pacific and that thenceforward it considered itself the first line of defense of the national constitutional order.[9] The USIB seems to have shared this point of view, and at the time of the 1970 election, the board thought that the Chilean army did not yet perceive a threat and so would not act to prevent the inauguration of an "extreme leftist" and "Communist-supported" administration. In fact, rather than intervening, the NIE explained, the Chilean armed forces would "maintain a constant surveillance over it, particularly if it were led by Salvador Allende, and would plan to move against it only if they were convinced that Chilean institutions, especially their own, were threatened." The NIE offered that a Marxist front victory would surely move Chile toward alliance with the Soviet Union and world communism but that this move would be restrained by several factors, including

- nationalist sentiment that would be as anti-Soviet as it would be anti-American;
- a need to appeal at least partially to the opposing spectrum of the electorate in order to pass certain reforms;
- a concern that if the new government "tried to move too far and too fast, the Chilean security forces would unseat it"; and
- an apprehension (shared by the USSR) that moving too quickly toward "a full embrace of communism" would engender a counterreaction by Argentina, Peru, and/or the United States in support of the Chilean military, if not a direct invasion.[10]

By this point in the NIE, USIB came to the eerily prophetic conclusion that the Chilean armed forces would intervene before any Marxist government disassembled the state's democratic structures. Further, the document showed an awareness of where Chile sat on the scale of significance in the Cold War contest between the United States and Soviet Union: solidly in the periphery and beyond the immediate concern of the Soviets as a likely target of seduction. If the four restraining factors prevented too drastic a move by the UP, what was the outlook for a putative president from either the PDC or PN? A new PDC administration in Chile would be under increased public pressure to take a strongly nationalist tone, and any of the three potential new presidents would certainly "stake out a more independent line" with regard to the United States. Likewise, the next Chilean administration, all parties included, would "continue Chile's traditional policies supporting non-intervention, the protection of national sovereignty, and the sanctity of treaties." Of the candidates, Alessandri was likely to be the most pro-American in his outlook, although nationalism and international independence would restrain him from relations too close with the United States, even if to a lesser degree than those factors would restrain the other potential presidents. As for a new Chilean president's possibly negative impact on U.S. interests, the NIE stated that the most sensitive U.S. interest in Chile, copper, would be liable to varying severities of nationalization no matter which party—from the Left, Center, or Right—took power, as such concerns were in Chile based in nationalism, not economic or even party-political grounds.[11]

The big question remains: whom did the USIB think would win the election in 1970? On this issue, the board was quite restrained in its comments. First, the NIE noted that, were the election held that day, former President Alessandri would likely come out on top. But this conclusion did not take into account a unified opposition from the Left. In the previous three elections, the traditional Chilean centrist and rightist parties had faced the FRAP, an ad hoc coalition of leftist parties specific to each election. A later intelligence brief on Latin America commented on this phenomenon:

> In most countries the extreme left, composed as it is of disparate groups, will remain a troublesome problem, but more as a source of agitation and pressure than an immediate threat to any government. Only in Chile does there seem to be a possibility that extreme leftist groups might come to power through elections in the near future. This would depend on whether various groups including Socialists and Communists could form a successful coalition for the September 1970 presidential election.[12]

The NIE had hope that the coalition would not be effective this time around because the traditional parties that joined together to form the FRAP for each election—the Socialist Party, the Communist Party, and four other small parties, including parts of the Radical Party—were in a state of mutual antipathy preceding the election. Should the coalition, by chance, overcome its troubles (and at this point the NIE offered no comment on the history of the FRAP, including its coalescence in similar conditions over three previous elections), the USIB believed that "their candidate would be a strong contender" who would "benefit from the likely continuation of the general trend to the left" in Chilean politics.[13] In an unwitting commentary on the U.S. propaganda machine, the NIE noted that the Chilean Communist Party had not been "greatly damaged" by its defense of the Soviet occupation of Czechoslovakia and that fear of communist dictatorship did not register in the Chilean political consciousness.[14]

All in all, the estimate does not provide a terribly surprising consensus view of politics in Chile. But it is a commonplace in the U.S. intelligence community for one to read the dissenting footnotes of an NIE as avidly as the main text. In the footnotes lies the opinion of any particular intelligence agency that disagrees with the consensus view of the multiagency board. In this particular case, the NIE offers only one footnote, from the State Department, which is revealing in how it describes State's continued belief in the PDC's reliability and strength within the Chilean political system. The note was filed by Mr. Thomas L. Hughes, director of Intelligence and Research (INR) at the State Department, who "believe[d] that the Estimate overstate[d] . . . the Christian Democratic Party's predicament in the forthcoming elections." The footnote further asserted that the PDC, "especially in its reformist but moderate elements, is stronger than the Estimate suggests." While this might be taken as something of an optimistic view of the political situation in Chile, it at least complemented this appraisal with a sound appreciation of the political trends. "The long-run direction is toward reform," explained the INR footnote and "even radicalism from the conventional point of view." What is remarkable is that INR did not perceive this movement toward radicalism as a problem, as it thought the dissatisfaction among the conservatives in Chile was "counterbalanced . . . by favorable political reaction of elements that [had] benefited" from Frei's earlier reforms.[15] In light of this footnote, the State Department's continued opposition to any cover action in favor of the National Party, or against the Unidad Popular, makes more sense.

THE DIFFICULT FIGURE OF RICHARD NIXON

If the USIB, under the leadership of the director of central intelligence (DCI), had put much effort and analytical skill into the production of the NIE on Chile, did the effort have any effect? Is it likely that the document, or any information produced from this document, was ever considered by the nation's chief decision maker, President Richard Nixon?

These questions, and the more general question about the relationship between the Agency and the president, became highly significant after the Nixon's election victory in 1968. Beginning even before Nixon's inauguration, the interaction between the president-elect and the Agency was different from that seen under any other administration, in large part because Nixon held stronger credentials in foreign policy than almost any other president before or since and his national security adviser, Henry Kissinger, was viewed as a prestigious academic theorist on the same topic. Arguably, the Nixon and Kissinger team was one of the most successful in U.S. diplomatic history. DCI Richard Helms noted the powerful dynamic between the pair: "Nixon was the architect, and Kissinger the construction manager" of a new vision for the world.[16] Notably, the team eventually achieved the established of U.S. relations with China, the first arms control agreement with the USSR, and the U.S. withdrawal from Vietnam. Yet, since Nixon's resignation, the pair have been dogged with criticism, much of it at least partially justified, for the realpolitik they brought to the White House and the methods they used to implement their often Manichean view of the world.

Neither Kissinger nor Nixon liked the State Department, and both sought to centralize the execution of foreign policy in the White House itself, at the expense of the department that was constitutionally entrusted with the task. The desire to take this responsibility originated in part from Nixon and Kissinger's perception of State's political leanings. In a private meeting with President Augusto Pinochet's foreign minister, Patricio Carvajal, Kissinger said, "The State Department is made up of people who have a vocation for the ministry. Because there are not enough churches for them, they went into the Department of State."[17] He was suggesting to his Chilean counterpart that those in the State Department based their actions primarily on a higher sense of morality, rather than on politically defined national self-interest—to a hardcore realpolitik theorist like Kissinger, there could be no worse sin. Nixon chose William P. Rogers as secretary of state because Rogers would "brook no nonsense" from "the little boys" of Foggy Bottom and, oddly, because he knew little about foreign policy.[18] Roger's naiveté would help Nixon and Kissinger keep foreign policy and security affairs firmly in the White House, where the much-maligned savants of the State Department could not, in Nixon's view, act on their soft and nonsensical view of how foreign policy should be conducted.

With the State Department out in the cold, briefing the president was the job of Kissinger alone. "Kissinger's determination to monopolize all contact with the new president" caused troubles, noted a recent CIA study on the briefings of incoming presidents. The study further noted that Kissinger "did not want to give Nixon anything he and his National Security Council staff had not had time to mull over," and thus the president's adviser effectively cut off Nixon from the director of central intelligence too.[19] If the president did not like and trust the State Department, it is certain that he also did not like the CIA. Based on his exposure to them while in the vice president's office, and through government in general, he thought that CIA officers, similar to their colleagues in the State Department, were "Ivy-League liberals" who had consistently opposed his political aims. Even worse, Nixon, a man from a working-class background and a non-Ivy-League education, which he was able to complete only thanks to scholarships, believed the foreign policy establishment's opposition to his policies was a reflection of its opposition to him personally.[20] Nixon distrusted everyone. As Helms commented elsewhere, the president thought that "the State Department was just a bunch of pin-striped, cocktail-drinking diplomats, that the Agency couldn't come up with a winning action in Vietnam, that the Interior Department was a bunch of 'pinkos,' it just went on and on."[21] This jaundiced view of the departments of government—on whom the president relied to execute some of his more controversial diktats—proved significant over the subsequent years. In regard to operations in Chile, it was decisive.

The roots of Nixon's distrust of the CIA were simple: he felt the CIA had cost him the 1960 election by leaking information of the "missile gap" to the Democrats.[22] Yet, upon entering office, Nixon chose, after strong recommendations from President Johnson, to keep Helms as DCI. Working to secure this initial favor, Helms sought to accommodate the new president's particular habits by making changes to the intelligence products presented to the president. Despite this effort, after a short while the relationship soured. As the CIA noted in a recent study, "During Nixon's years in office, the relationship between the President and the CIA reached the lowest point in the Agency's history."[23] One senior CIA analyst recalled, in a letter to historian Christopher Andrew, "Nixon seemed more interested in the CIA for covert action than for intelligence analysis. Why not? Covert action was an extension of administration policy, while analysis often showed policy to be unwise."[24]

The adverse relationship between the White House and the CIA lay with Nixon and Kissinger's seemingly very similar personalities. Both had a tendency to think in terms of conspiracy theory, and both viewed world conflict as a duel between forces of good and evil. Because of the urgency of this duel, they sought to secure victory as quickly as possible. As one historian has put it:

> They were risk-takers contemptuous of the slow-moving foreign policy bureaucracy, they enjoyed secrecy, surprise and power-plays, and they harbored a cynical attitude toward democracy. Both had large egos but were insecure and always on the look-out for enemies, real and imagined. Their unorthodox outlooks made them well suited to undertake innovative foreign policy, but each brought out the worst in the other.[25]

Their latent paranoia and distrust of others drew Nixon and Kissinger toward back channels—as in their back-channel discussions with Soviet ambassador Anatoly Dobrynin—as a smoother way of conducting business, presumably out of sight of their enemies. The drive to use these back channels extended, as is described below, even to their dealings with the CIA. Nixon's speechwriter, William Safire, noted in his memoir, "Intrigue was second nature to [Nixon]," and biographer Stephen Ambrose noted that Nixon and Kissinger "shared a love of eavesdropping on others . . . of secrecy, of surprises, of conspiracy."[26] As Andrew noted, men with personalities of this type do not handle intelligence agencies well; "they lack a sense of proportion in their grasp of the relationship between the secret and the non-secret worlds."[27] As will be seen with regard to the CIA in Chile, this lack of proportion led first to disinterest and then to pernicious maneuvers that ignored the best council of those departments mandated to provide advice, guidance, and intelligence in matters of foreign policy.

THINKING AHEAD TO SEPTEMBER 1970

It would be incorrect to state that no thought was given to Chile's presidential race until after the 1969 congressional election. At the end of September 1968, the Western Hemisphere Division started "to assess the political prospects and contingencies in Chile over the next year or so, and the outlook for U.S.-Chilean relations."[28] By this time in the congressional contest it was clear that the candidates were maneuvering for more than congressional seats: they were also setting up their parties for the presidential contest. The CIA's efforts to influence the presidential election thus maintained continuity with the operations surrounding the congressional election. This is not surprising, considering the short time between the elections, as well as the amount of time and money invested in the "infrastructure" of the CIA's various propaganda and contact mechanisms. For the Agency, all of the operations carried out in Chile from 1964 through to 1970 were part of a continuum designed to reduce Marxist influence, not individual operations isolated from one another. Accordingly, following the completion of the congressional election mission, the CIA kept running the propaganda establishments devised for that election. In addition, and more significant, the station intended "to maintain its contacts [with the various political parties] and—to the extent compatible with operational security—capitalize on the good will it [had] created through [name deleted] especially in the National Party circles but by no means confined to that party."[29] The station required, until a 303 (or later, 40) Committee mandate was secured, sufficient funding (from WHD operational funds) so that it could maintain this covert infrastructure in Chile; if the station was directed to involve itself in the 1970 elections its basic covert structures would be "absolutely indispensable."[30]

The station was initially doubtful of "the advisability of actions which imply a [U.S. government] commitment to a [deleted—Italy?]-type undertaking in 1970." The station reminded the chief of the Western Hemisphere Division (C/WHD), William V. Broe, that the Santiago chief of station would be in Langley shortly to discuss operations in Chile and urged headquarters not to again leave affairs in Chile "to last-minute improvisations."[31] While the specifics of the next mission were not its to determine, the station was keen to see that its previous efforts were not wasted.

The White House did not turn its attention to Chile until the following month, on April 15, 1969.[32] At that time, during a regular briefing on covert intelligence gathering in Latin America, the 303 Committee was made aware of the results of the Chilean congressional elections and was briefed on the initial breakdown of the upcoming presidential contest. Though individuals within the CIA and contacts within Chile urged the committee to authorize prompt action, "The members decided that [Jorgé] Alessandri's prospects are reasonably good but decided no immediate steps [were] necessary since the presidential candidates [were] not yet formally declared."[33] The committee would review the subject again in March 1970, after the formal declaration of candidates. Echoing Santiago COS Hecksher and perhaps his knowledge of the CIA's election operation in Italy in 1948 (Helms cites that successful pro–Christian Democrat operation several times in his autobiography),[34] DCI Helms "observed that a great deal of preliminary work [was] necessary, and CIA [had] learned through experience that an election operation [would] not be effective unless an early enough start [was] made."[35] Essentially, the 303 Committee—wrapped up with affairs in Vietnam and Eastern Europe—had deferred consideration of Chile until eleven months hence. Until then, the CIA and State Department would decide without executive input what interests the United States should pursue in Chile. By contrast, while Cuban intelligence "trusted in the fact that Salvador could win" but thought "it was very difficult to predict his victory," Cuban intelligence (and Fidel Castro personally) immediately put full effort into helping Allende.[36]

Despite Hecksher's urging that positive measures be taken with regard to the presidential race and that the CIA's contacts in the Chilean political parties be cultivated, the CIA and State Department reached a far less interventionist consensus. Clues toward this point appear not long after the congressional contest. On March 11 the ambassador told Hecksher that under no circumstances would he allow the station to interfere with the PDC Convention (to choose their new presidential candidate) that was scheduled for mid-1969.[37] The following week the station sent a cable to WHD saying that it did *not* require a mandate for any further covert action, as the operations it was maintaining "represent, essentially, bread and butter general purpose propaganda assets and are not at this time mechanisms supporting any particular party, candidate, or election activity." Earlier enthusiasm for contact with the PN had evaporated. As propaganda activities were nonpartisan, they did not require approval by the 303 Committee and could simply be lumped in with the rest of the 1970 fiscal-year request when it was submitted.[38]

Along with these cables were several studies of the breakdown in the campaign. The first of these, succinctly titled "The Chilean Vote in Recent Years and Its Meaning for the Candidacy of Former President Jorgé Alessandri," seemed to make a case for U.S. support of Alessandri. An officer within WHD commented that, while Alessandri seemed to be the favorite to win the election and while many believed his victory to be a forgone conclusion, hard voting data showed that he was likely to be bested by the FRAP if it nominated Allende as its presidential candidate.[39] The station disagreed and continued to favor the aged former president.[40] Perhaps because the CIA considered Alessandri to be the sure winner, the station or WHD as a whole felt little urgency to begin influencing the election, which in any case was still over a year away.

As time progressed, it seemed that the CIA and the State Department had less and less interest in acting as a partisan of any particular candidate. In June, members of the station met with the Chilean national who was running CIA propaganda efforts in Santiago to explain to him how the station would be running the next phase of its covert operations: "The salient objective [of the station's election mission] is to exacerbate contradictions within leftist camp, while eschewing all partisan involvement (specifically support of Alessandri)."[41] Likewise, in July 1969 the CIA prepared a document, which it sent to the State Department, to sum up a conversation between Hecksher and Korry. In it, the COS was quoted as saying that under no circumstances would he "carry out any political action not approved by the U.S. Government and the Ambassador, and that the Station did not wish to become involved in making policy." Hecksher was saying—and he reiterated this several times in the document—that all the station's political contacts were in accordance with State policy.[42]

The CIA, despite the COS's advice and regardless of fear of a FRAP victory, was avoiding involvement in the election, and indeed was eschewing all political contact with the FRAP's strongest opponent, Alessandri. What was happening? The explanation for the American reticence to support Alessandri offers an interesting and unexpected insight into the political thinking of the U.S. government at the end of the 1960s.

WHY THE UNITED STATES OPTED NOT TO SUPPORT THE PN

Some who criticize U.S. foreign policy believe that the United States—and so the CIA—will automatically oppose any form of Marxist government, especially in countries within the Western Hemisphere, and will support the most unsavory characters if they seem likely to thwart a potential communist or socialist president. This argument is implicit, and often explicit, in the works of such theorists as Gabriel Smirnow, William Robinson, and the more conspiracy-minded Noam Chomsky.[43] If this argument is correct, then why did the United States refuse to support Alessandri, the charismatic, popular, and generally pro-U.S. leader of the PN? This salient question cuts through many preconceptions about U.S. behavior in Chile and offers a new insight into CIA and State Department thinking on intervention in democracies. The answer to this question may also reveal the curious thinking of the Chilean story's most enigmatic protagonist, Ambassador Korry.

Even before the congressional election, it was clear that Ambassador Korry was no fan of the conservative Right in Chile. "The Ambassador did not directly state his strategy for the period preceding the presidential elections," wrote Hecksher, but "he made it abundantly clear that he lines up with President Frei and the Christian Democrats." The ambassador, Hecksher added, "took repeated swipes at Alessandri."[44] The ambassador's pro-Kennedy leaning was not the only reason he refused to support Alessandri: the embassy considered Alessandri a "strong favorite" to win without any U.S. intervention at all, despite the Directorate of Intelligence analysis to the contrary.[45] Indeed, "short of the death of Alessandri, or some such decisive event, [Korry did] not expect the left to win the election, despite the force of an Allende candidacy."[46] Why support a man who was bound to win?

This was not the end of the logic that denied Alessandri support. Even if the United States was inclined to help him and if he had needed the money, "it would be difficult [to] regard program assets as [a] force which could significantly increase" his strength as a candidate because Alessandri and his party were sympathetic to those who rejected "the rapidity, if not the direction, of necessary economic and social change in Chile."[47] All the money in the world would not help him win the votes of people who demanded the land reform that his party refused to consider. This logic is similar to that that underlay comments made by the CIA after the Italian operation in 1948, in that support for Alessandri endangered the development of a nonradicalized democratic system.[48] Alessandri's effect on the Chile's democratic system was apparently a strong concern, beyond the land reform issue. As one think piece from the station stated, "the name of our game is Democracy." Unfortunately, Alessandri had made it "abundantly clear that he regards both political parties and the Congress" as anachronisms that no longer served the country's interests and that he might move to eliminate. The CIA put some weight on the argument that an Alessandri victory meant an eventual military or authoritarian government, either under the control of Alessandri himself or, if the army moved against Alessandri for his authoritarian motives, under leftist influence. The later possibility represented a backdoor route to power for the Communists, who would support an army move against Alessandri as being "pro-democratic."[49] Also, one might speculate that the CIA did not want to find itself the subject of accusations that it had thrust into power yet another authoritarian leader in Latin America. An authoritarian government would be fine if it were elected on its own merits, but the CIA saw no need to court the troubles associated with the "imperialist" action of helping Alessandri into office.

The CIA's fear of being tied to authoritarian governments highlights a greater concern for both the country team and the ambassador, what a modern politician might call the "optics" of supporting Alessandri. According to certain State Department officials, everyone *expected* the United

States to support the right-wing candidate and therefore U.S. involvement in Alessandri's campaign would be ripe for discovery and disclosure. The concern of one State Department official was intensified "because of two underlying factors: one is the sensitivity to CIA in Chile now and another is the assumption in Chile that in the election the U.S. would be pro-Alesssandri."[50] This position was confirmed in an internal State Department memorandum in which "Ambassador Korry explained that he feels an Alessandri victory would be bad for U.S. interests, as he sees it bringing on a military government, and thus, to help Alessandri come to power is not in the ideal interest of the United States."[51] The State Department's INR went on at length in the debate over the morality of involvement in the election. One INR officer, James R. Gardner, explained,

> The practice or custom of intervening in other peoples elections is becoming raddled and of increasingly dubious long-run value. So it is in Chile. . . .
>
> We have been covertly intervening in the Chilean political process for some eight years now in an effort to weaken left forces. The left has maintained its strength notwithstanding, and promises to continue to do so. At some point the Chileans are going to have to be left to their own devices. . . .
>
> The assertion is made that a UP victory could well produce a Castro-like government in Chile. We are unsure of the soundness of this assertion. . . .
>
> There is throughout Latin America a growing sensitivity . . . to allegations of CIA intervention in Latin affairs. This sensitivity is especially acute in Chile. . . . The costs to us, were the proposed operation exposed, would be so high both in Chile and elsewhere that we nonetheless are unconvinced that the marginal advantages that we might gain are worth the potential price.[52]

Many of the factors widely perceived as central to American strategic thinking in the Cold War are questioned in this memorandum: the propriety and effectiveness of intervening in elections, fear about the threat of another communist country in the Americas (which in turn questions the *threat* of communist Cuba in the first place), and the retrograde effect of American meddling in hemispheric politics. This last point is the most subtle: while it might appear that something was achieved by a covert action, in the long run *any* hint of CIA intervention, plausibly deniable or not, was going to produce much more trouble than could be averted in a single operation. The likelihood of being exposed was high, and the cost of exposure even higher.

Another State Department memorandum—a briefing paper written for the secretary of state before his discussions with the CIA—sharpened the point and supplemented it with U.S. domestic politics. Initially, the paper noted that, short of direct military force, the United States had no ability to prevent Allende from achieving his political objectives (if he won) and that "too much of the discussion of options seems to assume that the preventative actions being considered will [work] against Allende, when in fact they will not."[53] In fact, a "blown" U.S. covert operation would very much *aid* Allende's plans. This effect would not be limited to Chile alone but would also be transferable on Latin America as a whole:

> The governments of most of the rest of the hemisphere are negatively disposed toward Allende, but are inhibited now against expressing their negative disposition not so much by lack of United States leadership, as by the pervading non-interventionist philosophy of the region, concern over the possibility of appearing to be satellites of the United States. . . . Their position will be strengthened not by overt United States hostility to Allende, but rather by failures of Allende's programs [and] United States avoidance of the scapegoat and foreign diversion role.[54]

U.S. interventions in Cuba, Guatemala, and the Dominican Republic still resonated in Latin America, the memo noted, and there was no need to encourage this simmering hostility toward U.S. diplomacy with further interventions of dubious value.

Ambassador Viron P. Vaky, then–National Security Council assistant to Kissinger on Latin America, added to this argument when he discussed in a recent interview the costs of a blown operation versus the cost of an Allende government:

> If the operation were blown, well, that worried a lot of people including me, very much so. There was a lot of argument as to whether Allende becoming president would incite leftist trends in other countries. Would there be connections, Allende meeting leftists elsewhere to help them? There was a lot of debate about this. But I think the fear that if we were responsible and

> our hands showed in an intervention, then that would be a problem and that was a pretty strong argument against [intervention] accepted by most.[55]

There was domestic political justification for a cautious stance as well. "Chile is not now a large internal political issue in the United States," wrote a State Department official, "and the predominant reaction thus far here is in favor of a correct, hands-off posture,"[56] a posture that the U.S. government should mimic. The State Department, throughout this period, urged for the minimal influence possible in the Chilean presidential election.

KORRY WEIGHS IN

In this effort, however, the State Department was not the main decision maker on the Chilean policy but was rather the chief adviser. The role of leader was squarely with Ambassador Korry, who added his own, more practical, insight to that of the State Department. Korry did not consider himself a career diplomat: he had been a successful journalist in private life, until he was appointed by President Kennedy as ambassador to Ethiopia in 1963. President Johnson subsequently appointed him ambassador to Chile, an appointment in turn renewed—perhaps unusually—by Nixon upon his election as president. Beyond his feeling of independence from the State Department's internal political mandates, he was more hawkish than many in State about the threat of an Allende government. He remarked, "it would be very imprudent to act as if an Allende government would be anything but another Castro government, and one should assume that at a minimum the Allende government would act in this style."[57] This left it to the reader to decide the implications of "another Castro government," as neither the CIA station nor the CIA's WHD had assessed the potential impact of an Allende government.[58]

To counter the moral arguments of such men as James Gardner, the ambassador argued during a meeting in September 1969, "We cannot get anyone elected, because we do not have the ability to do so." Korry further speculated (accurately) that as the election approached, "business interests" would increase the pressure to stage a "midnight effort" to prevent an Allende victory. The ambassador's next point is revealing: he believed that "if an Allende victory appears certain, [President] Frei should [the "sh" in "should" is stricken by hand and replaced with a "w" to spell "would"] act on his own to have the armed forces intervene. [Korry] thought the military would take the initiative in this action" and proposed so to Frei.[59] Does Korry's original "should" reflect his wishful thinking?

Regardless, to all these arguments one must add the age-old bureaucratic prerogative of "looking after number one," or protecting oneself from recrimination when things go wrong. In discussions with State Department officials, "Korry said that he would not be unhappy if we did nothing, but if Allende were to win, in the end, how would we answer the question about what effort we made to prevent this?"[60]

Thus the guiding intellect behind the CIA's actions in Chile, Ambassador Korry believed first of all that Alessandri would win the election. Further he believed Alessandri's victory would be dangerous, as it would usher in a military government. In any case, Korry also believed that the United States could not truly influence the victory of any party in the election. And he believed that in the case that Allende won the election, Frei and the army would intervene to prevent his taking office—a thought reinforced by a lone station report that noted a "surprisingly large number of key officers [were] prepared to entertain extra-constitutional moves" (among those officers was the little-known Gen. Augusto Pinochet).[61] Korry considered a Frei intervention against Allende more palatable than an Alessandri victory on the grounds that, in any subsequent elections called after a military intervention, Frei would be permitted to run again. As had been clearly stated on many occasions, Frei was Korry's preferred candidate even if the Chilean constitution prevented Frei from serving two back-to-back terms as president.

Although Alessandri was to be the biggest beneficiary of the U.S. propaganda campaign against the UP, the United States thought it best not to support him outright because the PDC would become upset should American support move to the PN and because most everyone in Chile expected the United States to support Alessandri. So Korry's motivations to not support any party in the election did not necessarily parallel the State Department's or the Inter-American Affairs Bureau's intelligence: the ambassador did not want to support any particular candidate because he had convinced himself that Frei would not allow a Marxist government on the off chance that the UP did win the election.

THE CONSENSUS

The result of the internal debates on what to do in the run-up to the 1970 election was thus one that argued for the application of a minimal influence on the poll. Noting in September 1969 that "in the pre-election negotiations which characterize the Chilean political scene, the Marxists are experiencing difficulty in forming the FRAP alliance which has represented them in past elections,"[62] C/WHD Broe decided it seemed logical to act to prevent the coalition. The American strategy, then, from September 1969 was to prevent the formation of a popular front representing the Left in Chile. This was a direct continuation of efforts surrounding the 1969 congressional elections, which the CIA station reported as succeeding "very well in sowing suspicion between the PR and the Communists."[63] The concept was that if the CIA was successful in sowing suspicion, the race would be chiefly between the Alessandristas and the PDC, and thus the election to choose the new president of the Republic would be perfectly unadulterated and democratic. The State Department had trouble agreeing with any proposal to influence the Chilean election at all and assumed that such an operation would actually see Tomic and Alessandri splitting the vote and thus inadvertently helping Allende.[64] After an intense and especially lengthy debate, however, State decided to go along with the CIA's proposal to carry out this spoiling operation only as late as March 1970, immediately before the 40 Committee's planned review of Chilean operations, even though such an operation had been ongoing on for some months already.[65] As one memo states,

> [the] Santiago Station and Ambassador Korry have agreed on a hands-off policy with regard to the Chilean presidential election. Political action is confined to attacking the FRAP and no support is contemplated to any presidential candidate. The Station will resist any requests for support from the right in Chile and it believes that Tomic, who is still trying to gain the support of non-Allende leftists, will not seek U.S. Government support. Ambassador Korry, however, is committed to the PDC and it is conceivable that, should Tomic's position vis-à-vis leftist support become more moderate, he will seek to support Tomic's candidacy. The Station has no mechanism which could render covert support to Tomic *and has stressed the desirability of permitting Chilean voters to choose their president without outside assistance* [italics added].[66]

Or, as cryptically summarized by Ambassador Korry, "thus we are left with the minimal action taken to minimize the minimal possibility."[67] Assistant Secretary of State John Crimmins described the U.S. role somewhat more concisely as one of "assisting unwillingly and collaterally in an Alessandri candidacy and hampering a Popular Unity and continuing to cause dissension on the left."[68]

It at first appears that before the 40 Committee submission in March 1970, all parties involved had, at length, come to a consensus on what should and could be done in Chile. This, however, was not completely accurate. A cable sent at the end of December 1969 hints at some of the festering disagreement between Hecksher and Ambassador Korry. In the cable, the station reports that the ambassador accused the CIA of undertaking "gratuitous" covert actions and intelligence gathering aimed at "setting the stage for major shift . . . from abstention to involvement in 1970 elections"—and this despite Korry's apparent consideration of support for Tomic. The COS assured the ambassador that the station had not and would not go around his back and that it would endeavor to continue working with him "in perfect tandem." This correspondence was apparently motivated by the ambassador's request that the station curtail its reporting back to CIA headquarters, "since no . . . action in Chile [is] contemplated, information [requirements are] minimal." Enforcing his point, the station reported, the ambassador (who had a "propensity to overestimate [his] own role") was apparently planning to visit President Frei and let him know that Chile was "truly free and independent" of U.S. influence in its electoral system.

Yet the station's disapproval of Korry's approach (and Hecksher's dislike of Korry) was lurking not far from the surface. One ranking member of the station had "voiced concern over [his] role in Chile and [was] casting about for ideas on how to keep [himself] usefully occupied" in the enforced inactivity over the elections. He likewise suggested that "HQs consider stimulating SNIE in answer to question whether and to what extent vital United States interests in Western Hemisphere are liable to be damaged by [an Allende] victory in 1970."[69] This was an interesting request because for at least the previous year the CIA had been operating without the 40 Committee's approval or consideration, despite CIA requests, and so at no point had the White House officially expressed its foreign policy aims in Chile; instead they had been essentially determined by the ambassador. Further, no one had defined in writing the impact of an Allende government on U.S. interests. Might the suggestion of a Special Estimate have been aimed at gathering support for the station's view over the ambassador's? Perhaps, but it was too late in any case. In retrospect, CIA officer Ted Shackley, who replaced Broe as C/WHD in May 1972, believed that this disagreement between the COS and the ambassador, which at times became quite acrimonious, "was another case of America having the wrong team on the playing field" and was ultimately responsible for the mission's failure.[70]

THE GOVERNMENT ACTS

When the covert-action authorization committee—that is, the 40 Committee—met again in March 1970, it decided, based on the CIA–State Department consensus developed through 1969, that the United States should not support *any* of the three presidential candidates.[71] Rather than support one candidate, the 40 Committee upheld the various State Department position papers and recommended the continuation of the "spoiling campaign" against Allende, which encompassed activities designed to highlight the danger of a UP government and Allende as president, without actively supporting either of the two opposition candidates.

One Chilean senator, Pedro Ibanez (the son of a former Chilean president) appealed directly to the U.S. government on behalf of Alessandri, while the former was in Washington in March 1970, openly raising campaign funds for the latter. Ibanez requested U.S. assistance and financial support for the Alessandri campaign "because the Communist candidate must be beaten." The vice president's office, to which Ibanez made the request, rejected the offer as dangerous; if the United States gave money to Alessandri, it would be put "in a position of taking all the political risks of supporting Alessandri without any of the intended benefits."[72]

Indeed few within the American government were keen on heavily influencing the election at all, and the State Department was still publicly "as a whole . . . against" any support at all.[73] In its decision, the 40 Committee ignored a warning from Henry Schlaudeman, the DCM at the embassy, that "there is a real danger that the non-Marxist forces will sharply divide the electorate that provided [the PDC] the margin of victory . . . in 1964."[74] Regardless, the 40 Committee believed it would be possible to "beat somebody with nobody" and subsequently ratified the country team's decision to carry out only a spoiling campaign of propaganda—with the caveat that, following a review in April, "the Ambassador and the CIA Station Chief might recommend additional action, possibly even including direct support to one candidate."[75] The 40 Committee authorized less than $500,000 for the operation.[76] A total of $425,000 of the original half million authorized was eventually spent.[77] Even using the most conservative figures, this sum is one-tenth the amount spent during Frei's election in 1964. Perhaps more significant, it was actually less than the amount the Soviet Union put into Chile in the same time frame. In 1970 the Soviets contributed $400,000, with a further "personal subsidy" of $50,000, to Allende, as well as $18,000 to keep a left-wing senator from running against Allende. With a further $100,000 from the Soviets to the Chilean Communist Party, the United States was firmly outspent.[78] When one takes into account the additional and significant support by the Cubans (which Cuban intelligence officer Carlos Chain called "powerful"), it is clear that the Socialist bloc had taken advantage of the somnolent and overconfident Americans.[79] It is hard to tell from the available record whether the Americans were aware of the precise size and nature of the Soviet money going to Allende and the UP. One can say, based on David Atlee Phillips's memoir, that through its contacts in the Communist Party (PCCh) the CIA was at least aware that the Soviets were providing tangible assistance to the PCCh.

At no point did the U.S. decision to continue the covert action campaign in Chile go before the Senate Select Intelligence Committee. The Chilean campaign was considered a routine covert operation and so below the concern of the Senate committee. Because of this lack of congressional control, Kissinger was able to use the 40 Committee's informal interdepartmental structure as a locus for ensuring executive control over American covert operations. The informal, and so perhaps undemocratic, nature of this organization within the NSC is quite clear. The 40 Committee, like the 303 Committee before it, contained representatives from the Departments of State and Defense and from the CIA, as well as the attorney general and national security adviser. Kissinger, the "assistant to the president on national security affairs," was ex officio the chair of the committee. Critically, however, the 40 Committee was not established as an official cabinet- or subcabinet-level body and was therefore not subject to direct oversight by Congress, despite its relatively great decision-making power.

Kissinger, though he often used the 40 Committee to throw around executive power, knew the limits of his own expertise: during the early days of the 1970 election he was happy to go along with his advisers' suggestions, as he knew little about Latin America and viewed it as an international backwater. A few small vignettes demonstrated Kissinger's disinterest clearly: for example, when a Chilean minister from Frei's cabinet accused Kissinger of knowing nothing about South America, Kissinger responded, "No, and I don't care."[80] As a further example of the low relevance Kissinger assigned to Latin America in world affairs, he once snidely (if wittily) referred to Chile as "a dagger pointed at the heart of Antarctica."[81] This attitude kept consideration of covert action in Chile out of 40 Committee deliberations for a long time and subsequently allowed the president only the barest amount of information about ongoing U.S. activities. Meanwhile, back in Chile, the Allende campaign gained support and staged surprisingly well-attended rallies and speeches.

Allende's percentage of support in the polls grew steadily while Alessandri's stalled.

NATIONAL SECURITY STUDY MEMORANDUM 97

As Allende's popularity rose, so did the controversy in American government circles concerning U.S. actions in Chile. First, it was becoming evident that the "spoiling campaign" was achieving little. In a cable on June 18, 1970, Ambassador Korry reported,

> The trend lines for the past month: continued decline of Alessandri, stagnation of Tomic and gathering strength of Allende. . . . Unless altered, these trends could well culminate in the election of Allende as President. . . . It is clear that a good deal more in excess of [deleted] according to our calculations will be required to make this effort [successful].[82]

The anti-communist tone of the CIA station reports was also increasing with more sharply worded cables, which warned that Chile could become "another Cuba" and produce "a major setback for the U.S. and a corresponding victory for the USSR."[83] The policy of not assisting any particular candidate, a policy championed by the Bureau of Inter-American Affairs (ARA) at the State Department, also came into question. Vaky of the NSC argued on June 26, "Perhaps we should aid Tomic to at least come in second."[84] His suggestion was rejected out of hand, for reasons not fully explained.

Korry, too, began to change his tune as it appeared more and more likely that, contrary to months of the ambassador's assurances, Alessandri would lose the election. There was already, not long after the 40 Committee consideration of covert action in Chile, "some feeling in the Embassy, apparently fully shared by the Ambassador, that if by the middle of May it looked as if Allende might maneuver a victory, we would be well advised to move into a posture of all-out support for Alessandri."[85] This feeling only grew, and shortly after Vaky wrote his memo regarding Tomic, Korry began to argue for unspecified "increased U.S. government activity" in the election. As long as Korry thought Alessandri was going to win, he was happy to agree with the State Department's noninterventionist stance, but as he became "increasingly apprehensive that the leftists . . . [would] be elected President," he requested more money and the ability to produce more partisan propaganda.[86] While the specifics of the action Korry proposed are excised, one can guess that the plan was similar to that approved by the 40 Committee later in August: probes within the Chilean Congress and the army to determine the likelihood of extraconstitutional actions as well as ramped-up anti-UP spoiling actions. Upon receiving Korry's proposal, State reacted negatively and highlighted "the risks in eventually embarking on this course" and urged that it was "especially important that you ensure that no [repeat] no member of the embassy either [took] action or [made] any sounding outside the embassy until the 40 Committee" could review the action.[87]

As Korry's proposals for increased action went to the 40 Committee, the State Department's Bureau of Inter-American Affairs signaled that it was "not prepared to defend the Ambassador's proposal." ARA might have supported the proposal had it believed the CIA assurances that the operations would be secure.[88] As for the increasing worry by the United States about a Soviet inroad in Chile, INR's Wymberley Coerr dismissed it outright: "To equate an Allende victory with 'a Castro-type dictatorship' assigns insufficient weight to Chile's profound differences from Cuba."[89] John Crimmins of ARA put it another way:

> This was the approach of the August, early September [State Department] response of NSSM 97: we could live with him; the election of Allende would not be the end of the world. We were going to suffer no major defeats if he were elected. We would strongly prefer that we would not suffer the costs that his election would entail, but those costs were not so high that dramatic action had to be taken.[90]

Despite the State Department's reservations, the 40 Committee provided the embassy country team permission, in July 1970, to begin a more aggressive operational program, but this did not achieve much on the ground. While the details are not available, it is clear that the Department of State continued to oppose these actions, so aggressively it would appear that Korry felt he could not carry on:

> Because of the wide gap between your views and those expounded by me, I have instructed (without further explanation) [one word deleted] to hold in abeyance the implementation of the 40 Committee decision pending further consultation with you. I have done so because of my conviction that for such a delicate operation to be executed most efficiently there must be a modicum of mutual confidence. . . . I have

> concluded that I cannot implement a policy that has aroused such strongly expressed opposition after the Committee of 40 has taken its decision.[91]

Korry's anger was expressed, over six pages, to Secretary of State Rogers, in a cable in which he tried to justify his more aggressive proposal to a body that wanted nothing to do with influencing the elections in the first place. Korry tried to counter all of the State Department arguments and added a final point on the supremacy of the executive in the American system of government:

> Having assumed that our President and all his advisors would wish to oppose . . . a communist candidate . . . because it would be harmful to the interests of the U.S., we had, I sincerely believed, no other choice than to "have done something." Indeed, I would be derelict if I did not do something once I assumed that to be the view of my President and my Govt.[92]

The problem, as became clear after September 4, was that the president's will on this matter had *not* been clearly articulated to anyone. Of interest is the fact that this is one of the first instances in which Secretary of State Rogers appears in the record; his opinions on the affair, which was dominated by Kissinger, were otherwise conspicuously absent. Might it be that, in his search for positive direction from above, Korry was going over the head of the assistant secretary of state for ARA? Perhaps he thought that Rogers, a Nixon loyalist, might intercede on his behalf to secure a preferential decision directly from the president.

The root of this Korry versus State argument, in which the former was supported by the CIA, was the differing view between the two camps as to the threat Allende's presidency posed. The State Department view, in short, was that Allende would not oppose the United States and would not destabilize the Chilean democratic process. The opposing view, shared by the CIA and the ambassador, made it largely intact into the second NIE on Chile published on July 30, 1970. This view, that an Allende victory would mean the gradual imposition of a classic Marxist-Leninist regime in Chile, "occasioned considerable disagreement within the Washington community."[93]

National Security Study Memorandum 97 (NSSM 97), published on July 24, 1970 (though produced and reviewed over the course of several days by the Interdepartmental Group), grudgingly gave ground to the State

Department view that Allende's election was not the end of the world but still found justification for the stronger views of the CIA, the NSC, and Ambassador Korry. NSSM 97 asserted that with Allende's victory "the world military balance of power would not be significantly altered." It *would*, however, be the first time in the Cold War that a Marxist government would come to power by electoral means and, regardless of its electoral path, would seek "the suppression of free elections."[94] This would be a dramatic turn of events in Latin America and "the political and psychological costs would be considerable."[95]

Keeping in mind the different theater of operations, the wording of NSSM 97 is closely parallel to discussions held twenty years previously about intervention in Italy, during which the CIA had explained that should Italy elect a communist government,

> such a development would have a demoralizing effect throughout Western Europe, the Mediterranean, the Middle East. In particular, it would greatly facilitate Communist penetration in France, Spain and North Africa. . . . Italy [itself], however, is of relatively little direct value to the United States.[96]

Since events in Chile—as in Italy years before—would effect the surrounding nations and the region in general, what was at stake was more significant than simply domestic politics in a distant country. This regional significance demanded that the United States act. Thus, NSSM 97 urged that the embassy country team in Santiago carry on with a more activist program to seek the prevention of an Allende victory, and Rogers, under the weight of Kissinger's reiterated decision, deferred, stating in cable to Ambassador Korry, "The Department recognizes the 40 Committee decision transmitted to you through [deleted] as binding and as authorizing execution of Phase 1" of a more activist program.[97] From this point onward the State Department, except for the independent-minded Ambassador Korry, was effectively minimized in decision-making on Chile.[98]

The NSC's supremacy in forming policy for the Chilean elections brought a more decisive and unitary tone to policy formation—though by no means did it end the interagency wrangling. Starting with the prompt from NSSM 97 the NSC began in mid-August, to act on the assumption—now embarrassingly obvious to those at the embassy in Santiago—that Allende would win a plurality on September 4, the election day. At this point no plotting or conspiracy with Chileans had been authorized, despite the suggestion of such in NSSM 97. On August 11 Korry submitted an assessment of the situation in Chile but prefaced it with the warning that "the prohibitions imposed by the [State] dept on this emb [deleted] make my following comments of dubious value since they do not encompass firm knowledge of the thinking of key men [in Chile]."[99] As late as August 31, 1970, the CIA requested (from the 40 Committee) permission to begin collecting "the political intelligence required to plan and to implement a political action program" in the event of an Allende victory or plurality at the polls.[100] The restrictions under which the CIA had agreed to work had forced it to abandon many of its contacts within the Chilean political parties. Now that the Agency was being ordered to carry out more extreme political action, it found itself helpless, without solid contacts.

Even so, the 40 Committee believed that operations in Chile were getting back on track. The (in the committee's opinion) pernicious and vacillating input of the State Department was successfully minimized, and Ambassador Korry—exercising his tenuous independence from the mainstream State Department—was requesting permission to let the CIA agents collect vital intelligence. The consensus lasted no longer than a few short days, owing to certain assertions of NSSM 97, which presented four options for American action if Allende was elected, based on the supposition that he would win a plurality of the vote and on a particular quirk of the Chilean constitution.[101] As mentioned earlier, under the Chilean constitution, if one candidate lacked a simple majority in the election the two leading candidates would be presented before a combined session of the Chilean Congress for a runoff vote. Historically, however, Congress had simply confirmed the candidate with the plurality. The possible vote was already scheduled, according to the Chilean constitution, for seven weeks after the popular election, October 24, 1970. The first option listed in NSSM 97 was to leave Chile to its own devices, but this option was dismissed out of hand. The second option, also immediately rejected, was to continue the anti-Allende spoiling campaign into the post-election/preratification phase. Third, the "study document" recommended that the United States seek to influence the Chilean Congress to elect Alessandri instead of Allende. The fourth option was to foment a military uprising to prevent Allende from coming to power.

TRACK I BEGINS

Shortly after NSSM 97 was written, U.S. government officials began to make reference to "Phase 2" (not to be confused with "Track II," discussed later), that is, the plan for the period between the vote on September 4 and the congressional ratification vote on October 24. While the United

States had considered how to deal with this period for a short while, "up to now, the Ambassador and [CIA] Station have been under explicit instructions *not* to discuss or explore such an operation with any Chilean asset."[102]

Following the decision to engage in Phase 2 operations (essentially, the more active program to follow "Phase 1," or the spoiling efforts started the previous year), Ambassador Korry began a series of meetings with key Chilean politicians, while CIA operatives quickly initiated relationships with members of the Chilean military. Korry had already gathered much information in the meantime. Indeed, the key communiqué leading to Phase 2 was sent by Ambassador Korry on August 11, 1970. In this document, Korry outlined what would come to be known as the "Rube Goldberg" ploy, or the "Frei reelection gambit." Its complicated string of moves and evolutions aimed at a simple outcome earned it its name, a humorous reference to absurd mechanical creations of the popular wartime cartoonist Reuben Goldberg.[103] Simply, it played on a technicality in Chilean law that forbade the president from serving two *consecutive* terms. If there were even the shortest interregnum, a president would be able to sit again.[104] Korry described it thus:

> [Name deleted] came uninvited to the residence Sunday Aug 9 to speculate *inter alia* on this hypothetical situation. He noted that if Alessandri were elected by congress, the old man could keep his electoral pledge to respect the first majority by refusing to accept the presidency (Alessandri has always said he would not seek to govern without effective support and such renunciation would also be consistent with his view.) If Alessandri refused the congressional will, then, according to [President of the Senate] Pablo, new elections would have to be called with the President of the Senate acting as interim president. Frei would be a candidate in the new election and would surely win an overwhelming majority.[105]

For this political legerdemain to work, however, it required the input of the military. Without the stability the military could provide in the face of UP resistance, Frei could not move. Unfortunately, Frei would not approach the military on his own (Korry now considered him "a chicken," though he had earlier suggested that Frei would take the initiative in such an unconstitutional move), and the Chilean military wanted Ambassador Korry to make the approach to the president for it. Korry would not do this; he now thought that Frei would refuse.[106]

Thus the United States was left with the fourth option NSSM 97 outlined: a military coup. On this matter Korry was equally adamant: "If Allende is inaugurated by constitutional process, it is the CT [country team] estimate that it is highly unlikely that the conditions or motivations for a military overthrow of Allende will prevail."[107] The ARA already opposed to what it considered too much U.S. intervention, concurred with Korry and railed at the idea of a coup:

> There is little substantial prospect that the Chilean armed forces would attempt to overthrow Allende, even with U.S. stimulation, and there is no way to judge whether the attempt would succeed if made. The risk that our hand would be exposed is real. Exposure in an unsuccessful coup would involve costs that would be prohibitively high in our relations in Chile, in the hemisphere, and elsewhere in the world. Even were the coup successful, exposure would involve costs only marginally less serious in those areas.[108]

While these internal debates were raging, the Chilean electoral process continued and, on September 4, 1970, came to its culmination. The polls closed, votes were counted, and the Chilean election commission announced the results. With almost three million votes cast, Allende had come out ahead by a less than 2 percent with 36.6 percent of the vote, or a 39,000-vote lead. Alessandri came out with 35.2 percent. Allende had won a plurality by the slimmest of margins.

Allende's victory was a surprise to many. Even Allende himself was surprised that he had won, according PDC official Gabriel Valdés.[109] Only at this point did that the Chilean public truly react to the possibility that it had elected a Marxist government in the Western Hemisphere. Some twelve thousand Chileans fled the country in September, and a further seventeen thousand fled in the first two weeks of October. With them, the émigrés took about $87 million in funds from the banks, thereby provoking a general run.[110] Frei was said to be despondent. In a bitter cable from Santiago, Ambassador Korry wrote, "There is a graveyard smell to Chile, the fumes of a democracy in decomposition. They stank in my nostrils in Czechoslovakia in 1948 and they are no less sickening here today."[111] Such messages whipped Washington into frenzy. Kissinger, himself furious over events in Chile, remarked that President Nixon "was beside himself."[112]

The 40 Committee convened on September 8, 1970, to discuss the events and what the United States could do. "In the lively discussion that followed," read the minutes of the meeting, "there was general agreement that more time to assess the situation was essential. It was also agreed that there was now little likelihood of success." DCI Helms added, "A military *Golpe* against Allende would have little chance of success unless undertaken soon. He stated that even then there was no positive assurance of success because of the apolitical history of the military in Chile."[113] The State Department, at this point secure in its role as the policy doves when it came to Chile, again urged, in a memo issued on the day of the 40 Committee meeting, that "no encouragement be given to any extra-constitutional steps that the Chilean security services may contemplate."[114] Nonetheless, the 40 Committee meeting ended with a call by Kissinger for "a cold-blooded assessment of

> 1. the pros and cons and problems and prospects involved should a Chilean military coup be organized now with U.S. assistance, and
> 2. the pros and cons and problems and prospects involved in organizing an effective future Chilean opposition to Allende.[115]

These pros, cons, problems, and prospects were to be delivered for the next 40 Committee meeting, scheduled for September 14, 1970. Quite easily, Korry dampened the prospects for a coup: on September 12 he wrote, "we are saying in this 'cold-blooded assessment' [that] opportunities for further significant U.S.G. [U.S. government] action with the Chilean military are nonexistent." Korry then reversed his statements from the previous year that the army would take the initiative with Frei to prevent the ascension of a Marxist government. The Chilean army, Korry wrote bitterly, is "a union of toy soldiers who need an order to move and that order can only come from Frei."[116]

The 40 Committee meeting of September 14 "covered at length and in some detail the changing panorama in Santiago and focused on the Frei re-election gambit." A cable sent to Korry following the meeting outlined that this "gambit," the Rube Goldberg plan, was the United States's "last, best hope" for securing the Chilean presidency from Allende's hands.[117] The 40 Committee voted to budget $250,000 for bribing Chilean congressmen to vote against Allende within the framework of the Rube Goldberg plot. As David Atlee Phillips commented in his memoir, this was a laughably small amount of money, given the number of congressional votes necessary to guarantee success. "With two hundred and fifty thousand you can rent a majority of congressmen in some banana republics. But it won't work in Chile—not even with twenty-five million bucks," Phillips commented to a fellow officer. [18] This prediction, made on September 18 in the distant CIA offices in Langley, was absolutely correct.

Not long after Phillips made this comment, Ambassador Korry admitted that the Rube Goldberg plan had only a slim chance of success. "President Frei's attitude is very clear to me: He is 100% opposed to Allende but he will not repeat not move unless (a) he is convinced he has a certainty of winning the fight and (b) he has a moral base to justify his struggle."[119] These conditions would not be met: "The political plan is much more tenuous and diffuse than Korry had originally indicated," wrote Vaky in a September 14 memorandum to Kissinger. With this statement Vaky hinted that few if any in the Chilean political arena were willing to undertake any extraconstitutional action.[120] In fact, as events in Chile progressed, it became apparent that the Rube Goldberg plan had no hope. The PDC would in the next few weeks negotiate "a decree of democratic guarantees," PDC votes would swing to Allende, and he would win the runoff on October 24.[121]

"*I find Korry's answer very unsatisfactory and I believe we are now in a most delicate and difficult position,*" wrote Vaky the day after the 40 Committee meeting.[122] A couple days earlier he had started to realize the ineffectiveness of American actions in Chile. In Vaky's "firm opinion: . . . (a) we don't really know enough about what's going on to make any reasonable judgements; the situation is too fluid, and (b) trying to cope with the situation by drawing up plans and considering them in committees is useless. Things move too fast . . . [and] Korry may not now be objective and may commit us to things we don't really want."[123] One can see the development of a plan in Vaky's head, a plan that would lead to much more serious dealings in Chile and eventually circumvent the normal chain of command for covert actions. "The troubles are these," reported Vaky in another memorandum to Kissinger:

> —State is timid and unsympathetic; it will provide neither the imaginative leadership nor the tight coordinated overview we need.
> —[the next three points are deleted]
> —There is neither enthusiasm nor consensus among agencies up here for doing any overall planning and thinking. Hence we tend to react to what happens in Santiago, and ideas about new things to mesh into the operation are neither forthcoming

> or—if they are—are implemented [in]adequately.
> —The 40 Committee does not have the time for this kind of close supervision, and the time-lag would make it impossible anyway.[124]

While Vaky goes on to recommend that some "expert" be sent to run the Phase 2 plan under the ambassador's guidance, a different setup emerges at the recommendation of Kissinger, who perhaps put more emphasis on Vaky's final but vague suggestion that Chilean operations would go better if State, the CIA, and the 40 Committee were all stripped of control over Chile, and "the White House gives . . . the directive."[125]

THE END OF TRACK I

So ended the first "track" of the U.S. government's efforts to prevent Allende's ascension to the presidency. As the CIA reported, a total of $153,000 was spent in this effort to prevent Allende's election by attempting to induce various Chilean groups, including the Christian Democratic Party, the armed forces, and a number of independent organizations and individuals, to use legislative or military means to thwart his election and inauguration.[126] Apparently there were few enough greedy and immoral Chilean congressmen on whom the paltry quarter million dollars of bribe money could be spent.

While "Track I"—as it would come to be known to a very few people—continued into 1971 and beyond, its essential purpose had already come to naught. There was no cataclysm or explosion, merely intense frustration at the White House—by Nixon and Kissinger, essentially—that the other players were not getting the necessary job done. After the failure of the Rube Goldberg plot and of the military and President Frei to intervene on behalf of a constitutional effort to prevent Allende's election by Congress, the ambassador and his staff could do little to influence events. The embassy had been telling the White House as much for several weeks: the embassy staff had no hope of preventing Allende's election because the Chilean electorate and political classes were tolerant of his victory. Anti-Allende efforts had begun far too late to work their subtle way to what the Americans viewed as success, and the decision not to support one of Allende's opponents was clearly a tactical mistake. All of these factors mattered little to Kissinger. He wished to achieve Nixon's vague aim of keeping Allende from power, and the State Department, the ambassador, and the CIA (through its normal channels) had proved unable to achieve anything toward this aim.

Under Track I, the American government sought to block Allende's election. Its actual efforts, however, did not extend past funding for anti-Allende propaganda and some rather ham-fisted efforts at influencing the Chilean Congress. Almost all of the government agencies involved, while opposed to an Allende government, did not think that it was possible to prevent his electoral victory or ratification as president. Only in the Kissinger-controlled NSC was there any true drive to actively prevent Allende's assumption of the presidency, and the NSC lacked the ability to influence events independent of the ambassador and CIA's Chilean country team. Ultimately, the American decision cycle during the period in question was too slow to affect fast-moving events: the United States was perpetually one move behind the political evolutions in Santiago. When the ambassador and the CIA were finally put into action, their efforts came too late to achieve a satisfactory outcome—a fact they fully realized at the time.

Regardless, the 40 Committee meeting of September 14 had been a watershed. At this meeting Kissinger and the NSC decided to seize direct control of events and to remove the cumbersome chain of the 40 Committee, State Department, and even the ambassador. On September 16, a memorandum titled "Genesis of Operation Fubelt" (or FU/Belt, to follow CIA code-naming practice of the period) was issued; this memo directed the CIA to begin operations to "prevent Allende coming to power."[127] From this decision the NSC initiated what was soon titled "Track II," or the secret effort to thwart Allende, an effort executed without the knowledge of the State Department, the 40 Committee, or the ambassador in Chile. Track II operated parallel to the ambassador's failing (or failed) Phase 2 efforts, which came to be called Track I by those who knew of both.

THE LOGIC OF FAILURE

The decisions and actions of the key U.S. players during the Chilean presidential election campaign, in retrospect, almost guaranteed no meaningful influence on Allende's election. First of all, the 40 Committee did not seriously consider Chilean covert action until the presidential campaign was well advanced. In the meantime, officers from the Department of State (for ideological reasons), as well as the ambassador (for practical reasons), decided to remain aloof from the elections, assuming the role of disinterested observer, working only to "spoil" the UP's campaign. Initially the CIA in Santiago went along with this plan of inaction, since the station presumed that Alessandri was going to win no matter what the United States did. As it dawned on the country team that Allende was as strong as ever, it realized the need for more positive activity. The State Department, however, kept dragging its heels and even tried to thwart Ambassador Korry's more active political action program of "modest intrusions" after the 40 Committee had ruled in his favor.

The decisions not to support Alessandri or Tomic and not to get involved in the election reflect the U.S. government's enlightenment after years of covert influence around the world and in Latin America. There is strong justification for the argument that the United States *should* have followed the State Department line and remained aloof. All parties initially agreed that should Allende be elected, he would not be, for the time being, a practical threat to U.S. influence in the region because the Chilean military, the electorate in general, and chilly relations with Chile's neighboring states would restrain him. An election expert could have pointed out the very high probability of a UP victory, in light of the party's consistently high poll results over numerous elections.

None of these facts, however, take into account the will of the U.S. president, Nixon, a man elected on a strong anti-communist platform. Had Kissinger and the 40 Committee kept Nixon better informed, his reaction likely would not have been as aggressive as it was. Nixon's actions after Allende's election were well within the legal arcs of his office and represent the ultimate authority of the U.S. government in foreign policy and its execution, especially in the realm of covert action. That Nixon did not express his intent in Chile until after Allende's election is surely the greatest fault of U.S. relations with Chile from 1964–74 because without any strategic guidance from the organs of government meant to provide such input, the CIA and the U.S. embassy in Santiago wasted their time, energy, and money on minor tactical operations that offered only the opportunity for exposure and embarrassment.

4

THE DANGEROUS SECOND TRACK: THE ASSASSINATION OF GENERAL SCHNEIDER

A communist-front electoral victory would present a subtle and difficult challenge to the armed forces. In this event, the reluctance of the officers to intervene in civilian political affairs could be overcome if they perceived a threat of revolutionary change in Chile's democratic constitutional system and believed the military institution was in jeopardy. Faced by this prospect and egged on by a broad spectrum of influential civilian political leaders, the Chilean officers are likely to overcome their scruples, inertia, and lack of cohesiveness on political issues and to unite to protect the status quo and their own institutional existence.[1]

—INR report on Chile, September 1968

Assured by his advisers that the Marxist Salvador Allende and his coalition would be defeated, as they had been in three previous elections, President Richard Nixon was caught entirely off guard when Allende won a plurality in the Chilean presidential election of September 1970. Undeterred, Nixon set out after September 15 to deliver a clear and forceful directive for CIA operations in Chile. In the following weeks, the CIA actively sought to foment a coup in Chile, and along with the U.S.

government, the Agency was unequivocal about its desire to see Allende kept from power. Near the end of this period, the commander of the Chilean armed forces, Gen. René Schneider, was killed in an alleged kidnap attempt.

Schneider's assassination is primary evidence used by critics of American intervention in Chile. Journalist Christopher Hitchens, for example, suggests that an American conspiracy to kill Schneider and start a coup in 1970 was continued into 1973, led to the death of Allende, and brought Gen. Augusto Pinochet to power.[2] *New York Times* journalist Seymour Hersh has asserted that "no document will ever be found . . . to describe CIA plans or White House directions to murder Salvador Allende" but points to the Schneider assassination as clear evidence that the Agency and Nixon were plotting Allende's death. "Why else would [the CIA] be there?" he asks.[3] Recently, National Security Archive scholar Peter Kornbluh contributed a more reasoned line of argument, which acknowledges a lack of direct U.S. participation but lends perhaps too much weight to allegations that the CIA produced the "coup climate" that led to Schneider's assassination. Kissinger suggested to his staff that "*we* set the limits of [political] diversity [italics added]" in Chile, which "at a minimum will either ensure [Allende's] failure . . . and at a maximum might lead to situations where his collapse or overthrow later may be more feasible."[4] But how much of this is Kissinger's hallmark bombast and arrogance? While the White House certainly had hostile intent against Allende, its ability to action this intent was substantially less real than supposed.

Recently released CIA documents provide evidence that is the basis for a more restrained interpretation. The new evidence on the Schneider assassination suggests that the CIA knew it had far less ability to affect events in Chile than it had previously thought. Moreover, the Agency learned that it could do little to steer or control the Chilean army, a professional, loyal, and fiercely nationalistic body. Indeed, the Chilean army would most certainly have disagreed with the suggestion that it needed American help to do anything at all. Certain proud Chilean army officers believed that they could, and should, prevent an Allende government with little American help. They acted on these patriotic urges with nearly disastrous political results, which, in their relative naïveté, they could never have predicted.

The CIA, in contrast, could and did foresee the negative results of the actions it nonetheless carried out. It should be made clear, despite the allegations of a few more extreme commentators, that the CIA did not directly plot Schneider's kidnapping and assassination, although the White House would not have been dismayed if the Agency had.[5] Most in the

Agency understood the potential ramifications of a high-profile assassination in Chile, where all sectors of the population would presume American complicity and the political reaction would be entirely unfavorable to the White House. Yet, under tremendous and unrelenting pressure from Nixon and Kissinger, the CIA acted against its best instincts. This resulted in a disaster whose completeness was mitigated only by the lack of the Agency's total exposure or compromise. Throughout, the CIA uselessly flogged its tactical utility on what was, operationally and strategically, a nugatory and counterproductive operation.

Without a doubt, General Schneider's assassination remains a blot on the U.S. record with Chile and Latin America in general. Though neither the CIA nor the White House sought explicitly to kill the general, his murder happened in association with the plots they were following and encouraging. The specific degree of U.S. responsibility for Schneider's murder can be left to the reader to determine. What we wish to view here, however, is the effectiveness of the U.S. actions in September and October 1970, and what this might tell us about the utility of covert action. The events of this period show clearly that covert action is not the ultimate problem solver that many, Nixon and Kissinger included, seemed to believe. Conducted to correct the failed efforts to prevent Allende's election, covert actions resulted not in a better but, in fact, a worse political situation for the United States: Allende was stronger and more securely established after the plot than before.

THE AUTUMN OF CRISIS

American actions against Allende's government occurred in what Kissinger called the "Autumn of Crises," September to November 1970.[6] By this time, Soviet missiles and technicians had been moved into Egypt. The rest of the Middle East was in chaos as Israeli attacks against its Arab neighbors increased daily, while Syria attacked its supposed ally, Jordan. In the beginning of September, a large Soviet flotilla arrived in Cienfuegos, Cuba. There was suspicion that the Soviets had designs on the Cuban harbor as a new submarine base. At a more global level, Washington was struggling to successfully continue the negotiations for the first Strategic Arms Limitation Treaty (SALT). The Soviet Union was still considered the major threat to American national security, and the bulk of the CIA's resources and personnel were without doubt aimed directly or indirectly at this apparently hostile foe.

In this framework of global power plays between the Soviet Union and the United States, the White House dealt with the election of a Marxist government in Chile. On September 15, 1970, President Nixon called Director of Central Intelligence (DCI) Richard Helms, Henry Kissinger, and Attorney General John Mitchell into the Oval Office to give executive direction for U.S. policy toward Chile and Allende. William Colby—then DDCI and later DCI—noted that "Nixon was furious" and convinced that an Allende presidency would ensure the spread of Castro's revolution to Chile and the rest of Latin America.[7] The president wanted to prevent Allende from being inaugurated at the beginning of November. The message Nixon delivered at the meeting reflected his anger. The oft-quoted and handwritten minutes taken by DCI Helms are revealing:

> One in 10 chance, perhaps, but save Chile:
> Worth Spending
> Not concerned risks involved
> No involvement of Embassy
> $10,000,000 available, more if necessary
> full-time job—best men we have
> game plan
> make the economy scream
> 48 hours plan of action.[8]

Helms, who clearly understood these statements, commented, "If I ever carried a marshal's baton in my knapsack out of the Oval Office, it was that day."[9] In this age before codified approval processes for or any legal requirement to inform Congress of covert action programs, the president's order was not checked.[10]

The extent of the president's constitutional responsibilities and rights regarding covert action demands some further explanation. While Congress has some constitutional authority that may grant it control of covert operations, this power (generally dealing with letters of marque and reprisal—essentially licensed privateering) seems arcane and has not been exercised since the War of 1812. Above this, the Constitution grants broad powers to the president when it comes to the conduct of foreign affairs. Where the Constitution fails to delineate some specific power, the spirit and letter of the Constitution demands that interpretations must be consistent with the presidential power over foreign affairs—and there is no specific grant of authority in the area of covert actions.

The U.S. Supreme Court has assisted in the interpretation of this legal grey area, noting that the president, not Congress, "has the better opportunity of knowing the conditions which prevail in foreign countries"—time is often a pressing concern and so the president needs to be able to act quickly, and thus without the restraint of Congress's permission.[11] The Court's opinion further supports the argument that the president alone has authority to initiate covert actions against a foreign power because Congress lacks the constitutional authority (over foreign affairs in general) to deliberate on such issues. Therefore, before the Hughes-Ryan Amendment of 1974 (which demands that the Congress be informed of covert actions in a timely fashion), the president was not outside his authority when he ordered specific covert action in Chile without Congress's explicit authorization. What is curious, however, is that the president ordered these operations to be conducted without informing the other branches of the executive. While not strictly illegal, this maneuver was unprecedented.

The administration moved quickly to implement the president's Chile directive, which was to be overseen by Kissinger and called "Track II," to differentiate it from diplomatic efforts. On the day after the order was issued, William V. Broe, the CIA's chief of the Western Hemisphere Division (C/WHD), circulated through the CIA the first memo derived from the new directive. The memo recapped the president's directive, indicated that the Departments of State and Defense were excluded from the planning (so removing the U.S. ambassador to Chile and his defense attaché from the loop), and confirmed the CIA's deputy director for plans (DDP), Thomas Karamessines, as the head of the overall project.[12]

The first Track II situation report was issued on September 17 and indicated that the command structure for the Chile operation had been established and that "units will operate under the cover of the [deleted] 40 Committee approval of September 14 for political action and the probing for military possibilities to thwart Allende."[13] Significant resources from all over the world were drafted to staff Track II. David Atlee Phillips, an old Chile hand, was in September 1970 acting as chief of station (COS) in Rio de Janeiro but was summarily drafted into the mission, on September 18, with the curt cable: "Report to HQ on next available flight. Tell station and embassy you will be serving on a promotion panel. Advise ETA and flight number." On arriving, Phillips found that he was in charge of the Track II task force. He was shocked to learn not only that the ambassador and secretary of state had not been informed of the plan but also that the plan had not even been cleared by the 40 Committee. "I had never known of a CIA covert action operation abroad being hidden from the American Ambassador," commented Phillips in his memoir, adding that he was disturbed to learn that this whole scheme was being launched directly by the president and his NSC advisers.[14] This was certainly a violation of long-standing CIA directives and regulations, especially the Agency's "good-neighbor policy" of working in harmony with State. While the removal of the other departments from the project was both extreme and unprecedented, Kissinger and White House chief of staff Gen. Alexander Haig viewed it as necessary to guard the operation's secrecy. Moreover—and this is important to remember—keeping actions secret from certain government agencies was at the time within the president's authority with regard to covert activities.[15] Until Nixon's presidency it appears simply that no one had ever thought it proper or necessary to conduct covert campaigns this way.

Simultaneous to Track II was the continuing efforts of the U.S. ambassador and his diplomatic staff, who were attempting to thwart Allende by manipulating Chilean congressmen and senators within the legal framework of the Chilean constitution. These efforts were considered Track I by the White House. Track I was a haphazard program conducted by only a few individuals, and the State Department, which believed that the CIA's warnings of an impending electoral defeat for the centrist parties were exaggerated, had decided to exclude the CIA from its planning and execution. The CIA, for its part, thought that the State Department did not have a clear understanding of Chile, its politics, and the nature of the Eastern bloc threat posed by a Marxist state in the Americas. Such disagreements between the CIA and State Department would be a hallmark of American operations in Chile and would continue until the overthrow of the Allende government in 1973.

In the aftermath of Allende's electoral success, however, matters were made very clear by the presidential directive: the CIA was to do what it needed to prevent an Allende administration. Helms later commented, while under interrogation by a Senate committee, that he did not believe that assassination was within the guidelines given to him by the president, "and I had made that clear to my fellows."[16] This may be so, but no memo has come to light that explicitly states that assassination was considered out of the question. With these marching orders, several non-official cover (NOC) officers were sent to Chile, starting on September 27, to begin false flag contacts—that is, contacts by American intelligence officers operating under third-party passports—with Chilean military personnel considered potentially hostile to a CIA approach or too dangerous for embassy-based CIA agents to meet directly.[17] With the assistance of the NOC officers (two of whom are identified by Peter Kornbluh as Anthony Sforza and Bruce MacMaster),[18] the CIA made twenty-one contacts with Chilean officers in both the military and Carabineros between October 5 and 20, 1970. When contacted by these CIA officers, "those Chileans who were inclined to stage a coup were given assurances of strong support at the highest levels of the U.S. government."[19] The wisdom and legality of this action, questionable today, was not disputed at the time by the limited circle of men in government aware of the plot.

In its attempts to find men who were in favor of a coup, the CIA came to quickly understand the nature of the problem. As many Chileans and Americans had noted, the Chilean military had a strongly constitutionalist nature, which its new commander in chief, Gen. René Schneider, championed.[20] It was written into the Chilean constitution that the army was a "non-deliberative body": it was not to engage in any policy formulation or political process at all, and this was a restriction that many senior officers took seriously.[21] In the event of a coup, Allende's supporters, though only a minority of the Chilean population, were expected to react, and this raised the possibility of mass protests, street violence, and even civil war. To thwart such violence and to secure a post-coup government, the military, acting as a whole, would need to rally behind the coup leaders. The officers of the Chilean armed forces were largely drawn from the middle class and as such were conservative and anti-Allende, but a CIA field assessment noted that their commander in chief "General Rene Schneider . . . [would] only agree to military intervention if forced to do so."[22] In May 1970, during the election campaign, Schneider had told the newspaper *El Mercurio* that the army would respect the constitutional process and make no move at intervention.[23] This "Schneider Doctrine" angered many of the more conservative officers in the military services, who viewed a communist government as a threat to the constitution rather than as a legitimate product of that constitution.[24] Thus the Chilean military's chief plotters had to convince Schneider to join the pro-interventionist camp. If the general persisted in his constitutionalist stance, he would be removed from his position, by some means, to allow the military to intervene against Allende's inauguration.

Circumstances were such that Schneider was the constitutionalist chief of a military increasingly in favor of military intervention. The outgoing president, Christian Democrat Eduardo Frei, had tried the patience of many conservative army officers, and plotting was rife within the military as a whole.[25] The first shock to Chile's long history of civil control of the military was the revolt of the Tacna and Yungay armored regiment (an insurrection ostensibly about pay for soldiers) on October 21, 1969, during which the regiment took control of its Santiago barracks, the main arsenal, the NCOs' school, and the main recruiting center.[26] In the aftermath of this so-called *tacnazo* rebellion—suppressed without loss of life after just three hours—several senior army field officers, accused of plotting a coup, had been removed from command.[27] Furthermore, a CIA intelligence memo of September 26, 1970, reported that a number of former Chilean army officers were attempting to infiltrate leftist groups, including the violent Movimiento de Izquierida Revolucionario (Movement of the Revolutionary Left or MIR), as *agents provacateurs* in the hopes of conducting terrorist acts that would compel an anti-communist crackdown by Frei and the army. Others were working in primarily civilian rightist groups that had the same aim. Of this prolific plotting, the CIA was able to report "President Frei [is] taking no direct part in planning but close supporters such as Perez [are] said to be acting in his name."[28] Was everyone in Chile plotting against Allende? The American ambassador in Chile, Edward Korry, doubted this, and on October 6, 1970, he sent a message to Undersecretary of State for Political Affairs U. Alexis Johnson with regard to coup plotting in the Chilean army. He outlined one particular plan related by an unwitting young Chilean officer to a CIA co-optee and concluded by saying:

> Less precise but equally lurid information has been reaching us from many quarters and it usually proves to be nothing more than wishful thinking. This report must be considered in the same vein. . . . I would prefer that we ceased to check out all such reports and to be totally surprised by whatever might develop in the armed forces. In the present circumstances it is a waste activity for all concerned. Hence I am instructing [the CIA station] to desist from the normal efforts to learn of possible military moves.[29]

Ambassador Korry concurred that the Chilean military would need to act as a whole to ensure the success of military intervention, but simultaneously he doubted that such coordinated action was possible at all: the desultory nature of the tacnazo rebellion and the army's firmly pro-government response to it seemed only to confirm this thought. Korry reported to Washington, a full month before the beginning of Track II, "An attempt to rob Allende of his triumph by, say, a General Viaux, who has a certain mystique within the army, would, in all likelihood, fail in a post-congressional decision period and be almost impossible post-inauguration."[30] By mentioning Viaux's name, Korry tried to exorcise the influence of the general—the center of coup speculation—from the plans of many in Washington.

General Roberto Viaux was a former Chilean army officer, forced to retire after speaking out against the government, who several days after retirement had led the tacnazo rebellion, thus earning almost cult status among Chilean junior officers, NCOs, and the junior ranks. Though viewed by many as a firebrand and a fool and though he was no longer in the military, the CIA assessment showed that he had "extensive support among noncoms and junior officers."[31] Led by a general who respected the constitutionality of the Allende government and without a serving general officer to centralize the plotting against the Communist Allende government, the servicemen of the Chilean military "look[ed] to General Viaux for inspiration."[32]

KORRY SIDELINED

Ignorant of the new Track II initiatives, Korry was demanding "Washington consultations, noting that *all* elements in the mission accept Allende's presidency as assured."[33] This was an accurate statement, as at all levels of the CIA thwarting Allende's inauguration was considered impossible; as one CIA officer said, "the idea of a military overthrow had not occurred to us as a feasible solution."[34] Six weeks is not a long time to begin with, but when one needs to ensure secrecy while attempting to infiltrate operatives and promote a coup, it becomes incredibly short. With almost no contacts at the beginning of the operation and with little knowledge of the key players, the CIA officers in the field considered Operation FU/belt, as Track II was officially titled, to be a "crash endeavor."[35] On a more alarming note, Korry warned both his own CIA team and the State Department that to attempt a coup with the climate and personnel at hand was to court a failure as massive and damaging to American interests as the Bay of Pigs.[36] This warning was ignored in Washington.

With Korry's influence sidelined by the new dictate, CIA's Western Hemisphere Division under Broe (reporting to Kissinger) was now directing planning against Allende, with Kissinger and the president creating much pressure for success. Congressional testimony during the Church Committee investigations shows that the Santiago station was not pleased by the pressure and that COS Henry Hecksher tried to minimize the impact of this "high-level interest" on the station's members:

> I had left no doubt in the minds of my colleagues and superiors that I did not consider any kind of intervention . . . desirable. And

> one of the reasons certainly for my last recall was to be read the riot act—which was done in a very pleasant, but very intelligible manner. Specifically, I was told at that time that the Agency was not too interested in continuously being told by me that certain proposals which had been made could not be executed, or would be counterproductive.[37]

Hecksher also apparently told Kissinger directly that "Viaux's circle had been infiltrated by the Chilean MIR," but either Kissinger or Nixon told Hecksher to proceed with a direct contact to Viaux.[38]

Given their orders, and with little time to accomplish the task assigned, the COS and DCOS (as opposed to the station as a whole) went against their better judgment and began communications with Viaux, as well as with two serving officers, Gen. Camilo Valenzuela, who commanded the Santiago garrison, and Adm. Ismael Huerta, commander at Valparaíso. Valenzuela and Huerta did not have anything close to definite plans and so for the time being were kept on the side. Viaux took the spotlight. As early as September 23, the CIA reported that Viaux "was in touch with active duty army officers who may or may not decide to move."[39] The CIA first contacted Viaux on October 5, and on October 9 an undercover officer met with Viaux to offer "moral, financial, and material support in behalf of an unidentified U.S. group."[40] A die had been cast. The CIA noted, however, that as a retired officer, Viaux could not lead a successful coup without the help of the regular army.

With the NOC officers established and operating in Chile and with the secret assistance of the Santiago military attaché, the CIA set out to determine what real support Viaux had within the army.[41] The answer came back in early October: "COS met with [one of the NOC officers] who said he had talked with General Viaux, and as a consequence is convinced that Viaux has no military support."[42] This was troubling to the station, which passed to its headquarters the opinion that Viaux was not only dangerous but likely to lead whatever forces he could muster into a premature action that would do the anti-Allende forces more harm than good. They decided, on their own accord (or at the urging of Ambassador Korry, who had learned of the connection, if not the full details of Track II),[43] to stop working with Viaux for the time being: "Santiago Station was advised to use whatever channel available to persuade Viaux to hold off his action until a more opportune moment. . . . Since a mini-coup (which is what Viaux is most likely to produce) would be counterproductive to our objective [name deleted] has been advised to do everything possible to prevent a Viaux move, at least for the time being."[44]

So, after only three or four days of contact with Viaux, the CIA had developed reservations about working with the man and had begun to look at General Valenzuela, the serving officer. While his plans were not at all solid, Valenzuela was at least in a position to command real troops in a coordinated action, and he was not (possibly) insane or megalomaniacal.[45] There was some indication that Valenzuela was involved in Viaux's planning, and so the CIA took the opportunity to contact him directly:

> [A CIA agent] will see Genl Camilo Valenzuela, if possible, on [date deleted] Oct and brief him along these lines. [CIA agent] will take opportunity to caution Valenzuela about precipitate moves by Genl Viaux (of which Valenzuela possibly cognizant).
> 3. [CIA false-flagger] who briefed COS evening [date del] Oct, promised attempt to contact Valenzuela [deleted]. . . . Will ask aforementioned to dissuade Viaux, without RPT without promising Viaux USG [U.S. government] support for any later move. (FYI: [COS] relieved to learn [CIA asset] not goading on Viaux, which [we] would view as height of folly).
> 4. Urge you do not convey impression that STA has sure fire method of halting, let alone triggering coup attempts.[46]

The CIA thought that it should avoid further contact with Viaux, a man the Agency could not control and who represented only danger and a blown operation. Perhaps more interesting, the fourth paragraph of the station's October cable to headquarters makes a point repeated often: the CIA officers on the ground were not puppet masters capable of fully controlling the Chilean officers they contacted. The message had already been passed (to Viaux among many) that the United States favored military intervention, but the CIA's Santiago operatives did not want to bear responsibility for the unfortunate results of a coup led by a man such as Viaux:

> If Viaux moves on his own and succeeds (which is a distinct possibility) then we face the unpleasant prospect that Viaux's junta will be an autocratic, nationalistic military government, which may not necessarily be pro-U.S. . . . Accordingly, Viaux should still be considered only as an opportunity of *last resort.*

> . . . A Viaux Government, though preferable to Allende, would be a tragedy for Chile and for the free world. A Viaux coup would only produce a massive bloodbath.[47]

A bloodbath led by an uncontrollable fool was not the mission's aim, as the CIA understood it. In short, the far-right wing was not attractive to the CIA or to the U.S. government. As far as the CIA saw it at the time, association with a dictatorial and bloodthirsty regime—and one not necessarily pro-American—would do very little to forward American efforts for increased influence in the region.

At this point it is important to note one thing that is taken for granted by the government officers writing these cables. To the modern reader, "military intervention" means a violent coup. In the case of Chile, however, what the CIA officers were looking for was, in the first instance, *not* an armed coup. Rather, they sought some type of parliamentary subterfuge, in which the military would declare a state of emergency (or some other such context) to seize temporary power, justifying the dissolution of the government in order to call new elections. Chileans called this a "white coup."[48] The obstacle to this was "that army not as yet set to move and that Schneider Doctrine still conditions it reflexes."[49] Moreover, the United States was not about to run a coup for the Chilean army. On October 6, Viaux approached the CIA and asked for weapons (maniacal-sounding and nonexistent "paralyzing gas grenades") to start an uprising.[50] The CIA in Santiago "turned down the proposal categorically," and reasoned that "[the U.S. government] would not provide arms if the *golpe* (coup) were to be made contingent on a favorable [U.S. government] reaction. [The U.S. government] insists that the decision to move must be a [Chilean] decision."[51] This does not mean that the CIA did not consider the possibility of a coup at this point, for there were routine exhortations on "seriousness of USG intent to attempt [to] deny [the] presidency to Allende."[52] The Agency wanted the Chileans to do it on their own, but found Viaux's plans "to be totally inadequate."[53]

Another problem with Viaux as a contact was his visibility as an anti-communist agitator. Having already led one military revolt, he was under constant scrutiny by the state security apparatus, and this made him dangerous as a CIA contact: "[It is] the Station's firm opinion that further contact with [name deleted] presents too great a risk potential and offers very little in return. Considering the way the [defense attaché Col. Paul Wimert]-Viaux relationship is unfolding we feel [the attaché's] contact not worth maintaining. . . . As we approach the 24th of October [Viaux] will just be too hot to handle."[54] To make matters worse, the CIA knew that Chilean Communist Party (PCCh) agents had their own contacts close to Viaux and his associates. It would be foolish of the Americans to offer Viaux continued support if the PCCh would later be able to disclose American activities.[55] Viaux was a disaster waiting to happen and had to be kept at a distance.

While the CIA wanted to keep Viaux at arm's length, the pressure on the Santiago station to come up with a solution to the Allende problem was massive, as attested by many of the men who worked in and around the project.[56] The problem from the CIA's perspective was that they could find no viable coup plotters. Viaux was clearly uncontrollable and probably even anti-American.[57] Valenzuela and Huerta had no plans, had no forces assembled, and were perhaps a bit scared of moving. But the White House was demanding a solution—a military solution—and, according to a October 7 cable from headquarters, "all other considerations [were] secondary."[58] The Santiago station responded to headquarters' cable with what can only be called a snide and cynical reply that is worth quoting at length:

> 1. Station has arrived at Viaux solution by process of elimination:
>
> a. Alto Mando (high command) solution cannot be achieved. . . .
>
> b. [Frei Solution] cannot be achieved. . . .
>
> c. Regimental commander solution. Station . . . lacks requisite leverage to pry loose most commanders from their instinctive obedience to Alto Mando directives. . . .
>
> 2. What can Viaux accomplish under optimum conditions? He can split armed forces. . . . Fencesitters will watch tide of battle before engaging themselves on either side. Carnage would be considerable and prolonged, i.e. civil war. Under best of circumstances, armed forces will break up and create unpredictable situation. . . .
>
> 5. Above not intended to be exhaustive enumeration of some of key factors that ought to have hearing on your final determination. You have asked us to provoke chaos in Chile. Thru Viaux solution we provide you with formula for chaos which [is] unlikely to be bloodless. To dissimulate U.S. involvement will clearly be impossible. Station team, as you know, has given most serious consideration to all plans suggested by HQs counterparts. We conclude that none of them stand even a

> remote chance of achieving [the U.S. government's] objective. Hence, Viaux gamble, despite high risk factors, may comment itself to you.[59]

In these three pages COS Hecksher made dramatically clear the problems he was facing in carrying out a near-impossible task that he was somehow supposed to construct from whole cloth. Summoning a coup in a country where no one was willing to start one was possible, but not if the United States wanted its own involvement to remain secret and certainly not if it wanted the action to be bloodless. As far as the Santiago station was concerned, Viaux was a dead end on all of these counts. Some days later Santiago sent another message to Langley: "After [deleted] debriefing, station would appreciate firm and realistic guidelines from headquarters on what objectives to pursue in further dealings with General Viaux."[60]

These comments from the Santiago station had achieved their intended aim. Following the cable a series of studies into the implications of supporting Viaux were initiated at CIA headquarters. The resulting papers—one titled "The Coup That Failed: The Effects on Allende and His Political Posture"—were not terribly optimistic.[61] The staff at Langley and the White House were slowly realizing that

> there is little climate in Chile to encourage or sustain a military move at this time, but General Viaux continues to try with his major problems apparently being (a) a sure way of containing the high command, especially General Schneider in the early hours of a coup attempt and (b) a method of controlling the pro-Allende mobs which very probably would swarm through downtown Santiago in the event of a coup attempt.[62]

The paper quoted here, like others, covered the basic problems involved in encouraging Allende's overthrow by the military and concluded that a Viaux-led coup would almost certainly result in American embarrassment and the strengthening of Allende's position. Hecksher, as well as Ambassador Korry, made clear that "Viaux did not have more than one chance in twenty—perhaps less—to launch a successful coup." With this information on hand, the 40 Committee, Kissinger included, came to the conclusion that "a coup climate does not presently exist. [Karamessines] noted that the highly unpredictable Gen. Viaux is the only individual seemingly ready to attempt a coup and expressed the view that his chances of mounting a successful one were slight. . . . [Kissinger] observed that there presently appeared to be little the U.S. can do to influence the Chilean situation one way or another. Those present concurred."[63]

The day the 40 Committee reached this conclusion, a directive to cut off plotting with Viaux was issued to the Santiago station:

> It was decided by those present that the Agency must get a message to Viaux warning him against precipitate action. In essence our message was to state: "We have reviewed your plans, and based on your information and ours, we come to the conclusion that your plans for a coup at this time cannot succeed. Failing, they may reduce your capabilities for the future. Preserve your assets. . . . The time will come when you with all your other friends can do something. You will continue to have our support."[64]

Many commentators have pointed out that this message did not truly end the Viaux plotting or, as Kissinger stated, Track II plotting entirely. Subsequent messages, however, shed some light on whether the plotting ceased at this point. One particular piece of evidence is a memorandum Kissinger wrote to the president on October 18, 1970. This lengthy memorandum starts, "It now appears certain that Allende will be elected President of Chile in the October 24 Congressional run-off elections. He will be inaugurated November 3."[65] This memo makes clear that Kissinger had by this time accepted the reality briefed to him by Ambassador Korry and many other individuals involved in Chile. Kissinger went on to say that because "our capacity to engineer Allende's overthrow quickly has been demonstrated to be sharply limited," the next step for the United States would be to formulate "a specific strategy to deal with an Allende government."[66] Thus, having ordered the end to U.S. involvement with the man the White House believed to be the only individual actively plotting a coup, Kissinger looked to planning a coherent policy for handling a communist government in Latin America.

A COUP PLOT MATERIALIZES

While the White House had finally decided to give up on Viaux and was cementing its new plans for Chile, Viaux's own plans were solidifying. By October 14, the CIA had learned that the Viaux group had decided that the best way to trigger a coup was to remove General Schneider, by kidnapping, from Chile.[67] If Schneider were kidnapped, the Chilean military could be more easily convinced that nationwide chaos was impending upon Allende's inauguration. To quell the burgeoning chaos, and so open the way—under Chilean constitutional law—for new elections that Frei could win, the military would have to assume power. The initial date for military coup, the CIA learned, was set for October 17 "between 0200–0700."[68]

Coincident with the White House decision to cease links with Viaux, a serving officer from the Chilean army approached the United States to request funds for a plan to kidnap Schneider. While the CIA assumed the officer was requesting the money for Viaux's plot, it decided to provide the individual with some funds to purchase weapons.[69] Later that day, another contact told the CIA that "[name deleted] believes that Viaux's attempt to kidnap Schneider will *not be made* [italics added] and now sees no possibility for anything to happen prior 24 October. . . . [The CIA case officer] reminded [his Chilean contact] that [the] U.S. stands ready to help with anything plotting elements may need. [The Chilean contact] replied 'what we need is not money but a general with b***s.'"[70]

The plotters did not have to look far for such a leader. A message sent from the Santiago Station on October 16 noted, "Coup rumblings within and outside the military have increased in recent days."[71] General Valenzuela, still unsure that a coup was necessary, arranged for a meeting with General Schneider on the evening of October 16–17 to attempt to convince the commander in chief that the military should intervene in the inauguration. Unfortunately, the "meeting . . . turned out [to be a] complete fiasco."[72] The following night Valenzuela, now determined to take direct action, sent a representative to meet with Colonel Wimert in a dark corner of Santiago. Valenzuela's representative requested three submachine guns and tear-gas grenades, which CIA headquarters authorized Santiago to give him even though the Agency was not sure why Valenzuela needed them (they were delivered at 2:00 a.m. on October 22).[73]

One cable from Langley makes it clear that those back in the United States were not entirely aware of the new evolutions in the plot to kidnap Schneider, as CIA headquarters had "several obvious questions:

> a. What happened between morning 17 October and evening 17 October to change [deleted] from despondency to measured optimism?
> b. Who, exactly, is involved in coup attempt?[74]

As it turned out, the plot was not significantly different from the one Viaux had planned, which had been disclosed to the CIA on October 19.

Schneider would be kidnapped as he left a stag party that evening. Once abducted, he would be flown to Argentina, and simultaneously, Frei would resign and leave the country. The cabinet would resign, and a junta led by an unnamed general would dissolve Congress. Valenzuela was at pains to state that the dissolution of Congress would be the military coup's only "unconstitutional" act.[75] Indeed, Valenzuela said that both "extreme leftists and rightist leadership will be . . . dispatched across [the] border" in the Carabinero sweeps to follow the coup.[76] Viaux himself might even have been a target for arrest in the coup's aftermath, as the military would use the kidnapping to "justify a move against leftist and rightist extremists [such as Viaux]."[77] It can be asserted with some certainty that Viaux's gang and those working for Valenzuela were in contact with each other, and perhaps the two groups were one and the same. Essentially, whether the CIA realized it or not, it could distance itself from Viaux only superficially, for it was still dealing with people linked to him.

The first attempt by the Valenzuela/Viaux group to kidnap Schneider failed as the team "became nervous due to inexperience."[78] A second attempt on the following night also failed, and the CIA assured Valenzuela that U.S. "support for anti-Allende action continues."[79] Valenzuela, for his part, assured the Americans that the Chilean military was still set to move. While assurances were being traded, the CIA concluded, "since Valenzuela's group is apparently having considerable difficulty executing even the first step of its coup plan, the prospects for a coup succeeding or even occurring before October 24 now appear remote."[80] It seemed there would be no kidnapping and no coup.

But events deviated from the anticipated script. Only five hours after the machine guns were delivered to the Valenzuela/Viaux group, a group of armed men ambushed General Schneider on his way to work. As he drew his sidearm, Schneider was shot by the attackers. He died on the operating table on October 25. His death marked the first political assassination in Chile in more than 130 years.[81] The shooting came just forty-eight hours before Allende was to be confirmed in a congressional vote and was not immediately followed by a coup. An intelligence summary produced in Langley on the morning of October 24 stated, "Yesterday General Viaux informed some of his followers that a military coup would be attempted during the early hours of 24 October. . . . It was agreed that given the short time span and the circumstances prevailing in Chile, a maximum effort has been achieved, and that now only Chileans themselves can manage a successful coup." But, the memo continued, "there has been thus far no indication that the conspirators intend to push on with their plans to overthrow the government."[82]

After the assassination, there was confusion, as well as a degree of hope, among the CIA officers in Santiago. They were not entirely sure who had launched the attack and whether it was a kidnapping attempt or an assassination attempt. They hoped that the assassination was the beginning of a move against Allende, but there was no evidence that such a move was going to occur.[83] The Chilean government imposed a state of emergency. Viaux was sent to prison, and his gang members surrendered, fled, or were arrested. The military and Carabineros were confined to barracks. Valenzuela was appointed Jefe de la Plaza for law and order, and Gen. Carlos Prats filled the position of the gravely injured Schneider. The Unidad Popular (UP) reacted immediately and there was tension that seemed to favor a coup, but Santiago remained quiet.[84]

Whatever the intended result of the kidnapping/assassination was, it ultimately increased the politicians' and most of the military's desire to ensure that the constitutional process for electing the next president was followed. Although Valenzuela was in a powerful position and free to act, the mood had changed so dramatically that he did not. On Saturday, October 24, Congress elected Allende as president of Chile. He received 153 votes in his favor and only 42 votes either against or abstaining.[85] The attempt to prevent Allende from taking power had failed.

AMERICAN INTENTIONS

While a military move against Allende was unlikely from the very start, Schneider's assassination guaranteed the collapse of American expectations. Despite the faint hope provided by the kidnapping plot, Schneider's death had not been in the U.S. government's interests.[86] Could the Unites States have prevented the assassination, and if so, did it make any efforts to do so?

What the Americans did and did not know about the assassination is evident in the message traffic immediately following the murder. A cable of October 22 relates that Viaux's gang was told that a coup attempt would be carried out on that same date and would be initiated by "something big" that would take place in the early morning hours. The cable speculated that "the assassination attempt on General Schneider, Commander-in-Chief of the Army . . . was very likely the 'something big' which the plotters hope to use to initiate their coup efforts."[87] The CIA's uncertainty about what would initiate the coup can be ascribed to its lack of contact with Viaux but also to a lack of intelligence-gathering assets. The CIA had started to pull out its NOC officers from Chile a week before the assassination, a move that does not reflect involvement in a coup plot. The Agency would surely have wanted to remain informed of what was going on in Chile had it been aware of the plot, and had it been actively plotting, the station would have needed to keep its NOC officers close to ensure control. Instead, the station officers were reducing their assets, a move that more closely reflects a recognition of failure and a sense that their extra NOC officers were irrelevant. A memo dated October 19, 1970, states, "[Co-optee] not at all sanguine re chances [of] perventing [*sic*] Allende from taking office and stressed [the] fact that abortive coup now could spell [an] end to any chance of success in future. . . . [The CIA officer] has done his work well and there are no further tasks for the false-flaggers at this time. He will be instructed [to] depart Santiago [deleted] October."[88] Moreover, as of October 21 the COS Hecksher had begun to develop post-inauguration asset-management plans.[89]

It is also evident that the CIA did not have absolute knowledge of the identities of Schneider's assassins. This indicates that the Agency was dealing with the leaders—first Viaux, then Valenzuela—and might not have known it was communicating with essentially the same group of plotters. Another cable, written on November 3, 1970, discussed Hecksher's review of the assassination and stated that one of the CIA's Chilean contacts "confirmed neither he nor [name of conspirator] [were] involved in Schneider assassination."[90] If the Chilean CIA station was still discussing who might or might not have been involved in the assassination and seeking confirmation from its Chilean contacts, it must not have had firm knowledge to begin with. One cable discusses the Santiago station's lack of sure knowledge:

> Station unaware if assassination was premeditated or whether it constituted [a] bungled abduction attempt. . . .We know that Gen. Valenzuela was involved [deleted]. We have reason for believing that Gen. Viaux and numerous associates fully clued in, but cannot prove or disprove that execution of [the] attempt against Schneider was entrusted to elements linked with Viaux. Important factor to bear in mind is that Armed Forces, and not retired officers or extreme rightists, set Schneider up for execution or abduction. . . . Before trying to anticipate further course of events station would like to await events of 23rd Oct which will obviously be decisive.[91]

The assassination took the station by surprise, and it was at first uncertain if the weapons it had provided to Valenzuela's groups were used for Schneider's death, a prospect viewed with some worry. The events the station had helped get rolling had gone wrong, and the officers were worried that the kidnap/murder plotters, if arrested, might implicate them. But who were the plotters? The CIA was unsure. The Agency eventually paid "hush money" to various members of the Valenzuela group in an effort to keep knowledge of CIA participation secret.[92]

So, were the American weapons used in the attempt to kidnap Schneider? The answer is a simple no, but this bears elaborating. One CIA cable from Chile, sent on October 29, hints at the confusion in Santiago in the assassination's aftermath, and the trouble the chaos caused the CIA station as it tried to determine what was going on. The message says that martial law made the officers' work difficult but that on October 28 they were "able to make first contact with [name deleted]. . . . [Deletion] stated that when [he] first heard of Schneider's assassination on radio he was quite upset but has since been informed by [name deleted] that three machine guns and ammunition are still in [name deleted]'s home and [were] never given to anybody. . . . Also [name deleted] still has three tear-gas canisters and three masks."[93] Furthermore, a transcript of a telephone conversation between DDP Karamessines and then–Secretary of State Kissinger (he took up the position in September 1973) quotes the former as saying, "I made clear [to Congress] that the group that did the thing was not the group to which we gave the weapons."[94] It is clear, however, that the CIA weapons, as well as funding, had been given to one of the groups ultimately associated with the kidnapping plot. When this kidnapping turned into an unexpected murder, Colonel Wimert hastily set out to recover the money and the weapons. Wimert even had to beat a Chilean general to secure the return of the money. COS Hecksher quickly returned the funds to the United States, and the weapons were dumped into the harbor at Valparaíso.[95] In a relatively recent interview, somewhat confused by his apparent senility, Wimert lamented, "I liked Schneider, Schneider was a good friend. I hated seeing him shot."[96]

A CIA review of its own actions, undertaken in 1973, states, "Three submachine-guns were provided to three military officers who planned to use them in instigating an uprising by the Armed Forces. This program was conducted at the request of President Nixon with the understanding that it was not to become known to the State Department or other members of the 40 Committee."[97] Other comments, in the telephone transcripts provided by Dr. Kissinger, show that the decision to give the weapons to the Valenzuela team was an internal CIA decision based on general guidance from Nixon and not specifically approved by the Nixon administration. The order Nixon gave, says Kissinger, "was so broad that [the CIA] would be allowed to do anything under it." To this Gen. Brent Scowcroft, deputy assistant to the president for national security affairs, replied that it was indeed "a purely internal Agency decision."[98]

Assuming this is all true, was the order to assassinate Schneider given purposefully? The CIA and the White House did not want Schneider assassinated. They understood that the general's death would benefit Allende more than it would his opposition because it would rally "the army fully behind the flag of constitutionalism."[99] It would, the CIA was saying, re-affirm the Chilean army's narrow and non-political role within the constitution. The CIA trusted Valenzuela, but not Viaux, to carry out a kidnapping, and until the last minute, they attempted to keep Viaux from acting independently in any capacity.[100] Indeed, one message directly laughs at Viaux's exhortations that his group "did not like killing."[101] The CIA and Washington specifically did not want their weapons in the hands of the dangerous and uncontrollable Viaux.

Overall, one can say with certainty that the central thrust of Track II, like that of Track I and the Rube Goldberg plot, was an extremely haphazard, true last-chance plan. Colonel Wimert remarked that CIA resources seemed to be used without thought:

> The money wasn't guided. It was like a Christmas party—throwing some here, some there and some to some place else. There was no real . . . leadership from the Washington area. Everybody was going to do something, nobody did anything. Once Schneider got shot, everything stopped. Everybody got scared. It's terrible and the whole thing came to a screeching halt. . . . They gave me $250,000 to spend and I didn't spend any of it.[102]

That CIA resources were committed to such a haphazard plan shows the Agency's desperation to respond to the fierce pressures from the White House. It also reflects a certain negative contrast to the actions of 1964 or 1969. In those instances, long-term, strategic thinking was coupled with subtle operations, to good effect. Rather than operating on their own, covert actions in 1964 were used to bolster overt plans such as the Alliance for Progress. Thus they acted as a force multiplier for U.S. foreign policy goals. In October 1970, covert action was separated from any strategic thinking and uselessly sent charging into the brick wall of immovable Chilean public opinion. Even if these desperate charges had resulted in the prevention of Allende's inauguration as president, the result would still likely have represented a debacle for American foreign policy aims: a dictatorship or, worse, a civil war. One has to wonder whether Nixon and Kissinger actually thought out what they wanted in Chile and whether the effects of the medicine were worse than the symptoms of the disease they thought they were treating.

WHAT'S DONE IS DONE

Some practical questions still remain about Track II. Did Kissinger actually order an end to contact with Viaux? The evidence shows that this is the case. Did Kissinger intend Track II to end, as he has testified? A transcript of a telephone conversation on October 15 between Nixon and Kissinger supports the thesis that he did. During the conversation Kissinger stated, "I saw Karamessines today. That looks hopeless. I turned it off. Nothing could be worse than an abortive coup."[103] This statement reads as though it were definitive, but it was made at a time when the White House, the 40 Committee, the Track II staff, and the CIA thought that Viaux was the only available option. Another memo shows that Kissinger ended the Viaux operation while he urged that the pressure be kept on Allende "until such time as new marching orders are given."[104] Other telephone transcripts add further to the matter. During one conversation General Scowcroft told Kissinger, "No, we didn't do it. There was a lag between the two groups. They were trying to do the same thing—they were trying to kidnap Schneider."[105] It may be here that Scowcroft is suggesting that the Viaux group, whom the CIA had at first encouraged to act then later discouraged, were not the ones who shot Schneider. But his reference to "the two groups" indicates that the Track II group knew of the Valenzuela group as well, but either did not think they would move or had no connection with them in the first place. In another conversation a month later, Kissinger recalled to Scowcroft, "I thought he [Karamessines] was turning them both of them off at the time. . . . My frank opinion is . . . that I told them to turn everything off and they, wanting to make brownie points with Nixon, just turned off Valenzuela."[106] This conversation shows Kissinger's consistent suspicion of the CIA—an attitude hardly conducive to conducting effective operations. Still, none of this contradicts his assertion that he ended Track II.

Peter Kornbluh argues that Track II continued well past Allende's inauguration (perhaps, goes one inference, until September 11, 1973)—a logical conclusion given the White House's continuing interest in coup plots.[107] Regardless, although Kissinger kept an interest in coup plotting and the CIA kept pursuing last-minute plans, Kissinger, as he has testified, did mean to end Track II as it was originally envisioned. One cannot deny U.S. interest in stopping Allende, but one can deny the U.S. government's competence and ability to do so. Kissinger likely wanted Viaux stopped but not an end to all domestic plotting, which could pay off in the long run. One need not insist that Track II continued to exist to demonstrate the continued White House intent against Allende: Track II was a discrete operation that failed, while the U.S. government continued to hope for some deus ex machina plot onto which they could latch to prevent Allende's inauguration.

Essentially, Kissinger did not want to discourage any anti-Allende faction, and perhaps he need not have worried. What he should have considered, however, is the fact that foreign army officers are not light switches and cannot simply be "turned off." The CIA had spread the message that it was interested in a coup against Schneider and "all interested military parties [knew] our position."[108] Whether this made a tremendous difference is a matter of dispute, which depends on how one views the autonomy of the Chilean officers who, even with American support for a coup apparently withdrawn, continued to plot. The independent will of the Chilean plotters was clear from the moment that the CIA went to "turn off" the plotters: "Station false flag officer met with [Chilean] on [deleted] October and attempted to dissuade Viaux group from undertaking a coup. The group, however, had met on 16 October and decided to attempt a coup on 21 or 22 October." Coup plotting was not restricted to Viaux's group, for everywhere "coup plotting continues to flourish."[109] This correspondence paints a picture of a machine with lights that keep blinking to its inventor's bemusement despite its plug having been pulled from the wall. A cable from Santiago indicates that no one from the station shared "in planning [a] professionally executed military coup."[110] Indeed it was "pointedly stated" that a possible coup was a Chilean matter from that time forward. On a wry note, the cable offers the observation, "this whole operation [is] so unprofessional and insecure that, in [the] Chilean setting, it could stand a chance of succeeding." All that was required of the station was to assure the plotters that they would not be left without U.S. support if their coup succeeded. "This we have done."[111]

Viron Vaky recently criticized the argument that the United States had done nothing to encourage the group that assassinated Schneider. That no *direct* encouragement was given was

> technically correct. But was our concern so obviously expressed to Chileans—we were sending false flaggers, etc.—that we in fact did stir it? We did not plan it or run it, it was not Guatemala or Mossadeq in Iran, but we came very close to letting it be known that we would sure like it to happen.[112]

Kissinger was most likely happy to hear that the opposition plotting against Allende was going ahead, even if the reports he heard hinted little chance of success and provided only sketchy information.

As for Track II, no memoranda or cables were written under the title "Track II" after Allende's inauguration on November 3, 1970. The last mention of Track II in the CIA's documents is a report that the CIA's summary of Track II activity was delivered to the U.S. attorney general on December 2, 1970.[113] An enigmatic cable dated May 26, 1971, might provide an answer to the question of when Track II ended. The one-line message reads, "Project [deleted] termination approved effective June 30, 1971."[114] Could the deleted word be "FU/Belt"? Regardless, Track II, being aimed at preventing Allende from being inaugurated president, effectively ended when that aim failed.

Some evidence indicates that after October 15 not all new intelligence regarding the coup was sent to the U.S. executive.[115] Many have doubted Kissinger's and General Haig's testimony that they knew nothing about the plots against Schneider. Karamessines, after all, stated in the same investigation that he had kept the White House abreast of all developments, and a cable from his office to Santiago demands details of the plotting because "high level policy decisions in USG may become necessary."[116] On October 19 a message from CIA headquarters informed Santiago that "[we] feel we must be prepared [to] advise higher echelons of nature of new military leaders and their programs in event coup [is] attempted or even succeeds."[117] These documents are phrased in the conditional, e.g., "prepared to advise," not "advising," so there is some room for doubt. This doubt is also bolstered by the conversation between Karamessines and Kissinger, in which the CIA officer, describing his testimony to Congress, reports, "They asked me if I cleared everything with you. I said no, that you were too busy. They said did you know about the sending of three weapons. . . . I said not likely."[118]

Certainly, though, the CIA was keeping a tight wrap on knowledge of coup plotting. A cable the day following Schneider's assassination, released under C/WHD Broe's authority, instructs the Santiago station to keep the intelligence of the plots from the State Department staff and the chargé d'affaires: "Do not REPEAT do not advise chargé [likely Schlaudeman, the DCM] of impending coup possibility. Should it occur, COS [deleted] should appear surprised and stonewall any and all queries. 2. FYI: Understand that Korry [is] departing for Santiago [the] night [of] 19 October. Para 1 instruction applies to ambassador as well as chargé."[119] Regardless of this State Department cutoff, information continued to reach CIA headquarters, and thus Broe and Karamessines. Broe and Karamessines testified that they met with Kissinger during this period. Assuming this testimony is accurate—and suitably mitigated by the conflicting evidence above—one might submit that Kissinger and the White House were aware of the coup plotting, were happy to see it go ahead independently, but at the same time had no control over events. Furthermore, the surprise that the CIA had over the assassination seems to indicate that the White House neither planned nor intended Schneider's *assassination.* Whether or not this is a distinction without a difference is for the reader to decide. What is beyond debate is that the U.S. government, despite a lack of any operational control, was inextricably linked with the plot, to its eternal shame.

Should Schneider's assassination be considered simply another event in the continuum of U.S. operations in the Chilean campaign or an aberration? At the beginning of his presidency Nixon decided to back off of operations in Latin America, and accordingly, Assistant Secretary for Inter-American Affairs Charles Meyer leaked that the United States "has stopped thinking that we have the duty to aid in impeding every anti-democratic threat."[120] But everyone thought Alessandri would win, and when he did not, the reality of Allende's anti-U.S. rhetoric belied Nixon's original policy of benign neglect. The decision to seek a violent overthrow of Allende can be credited to the president alone and its implementation can be credited to Kissinger, although many others were witting. Did Nixon's decision drive the escalation of violence that eventually consumed Chile in 1973? Likely it did, but the process also had inertia and direction of its own. What the violence that followed Nixon's decision most certainly did is convince the State Department, the CIA, and even the National Security Council and the president that it was infinitely difficult, and of dubious profit, to violently and negatively manipulate a foreign state's politics. In other words, the law of unintended consequences applied to the U.S. government also; any attempt to influence chaotic systems results in unpredictable outcomes.

In Chile the Americans learned that the power of the state operates on a significantly different level than the power of individual actors. As Lawrence

Freedman described it, power is a relative concept and therefore exists only when it is recognized by others. Unrecognized, as in the case of U.S. covert action to avert Allende's inauguration, it may simply not exist. Control of independent and willful human beings must therefore involve an explicit exercise of power, something the Americans were unwilling to do. And what is perhaps most critical to the argument, the more chaotic or complex a social system one is attempting to control—in this case a diverse group of willful Chileans all following different agendas—the more difficult that system is to control.[121]

So, for all their banks and investments, nuclear missiles and aircraft carriers, the Americans were unable to influence Frei, Schneider, and Viaux to so much as alter the "X" on an election ballot. Though sincere in their fear of an irreversible Marxist regime in Chile, the political unacceptability of the use of outright force, seen in the world's reaction to Schneider's assassination, sharply limited the exercise of American power. Ultimately, the assassination dramatically changed the course of U.S. intervention in Chile toward a policy of intense interest but more limited intervention.

5

WATCHING HISTORY UNFOLD: DEALING WITH PRESIDENT ALLENDE

> *The election of Allende as President of Chile poses for us one of the most serious challenges ever faced in this hemisphere. Your decision as to what to do about it may be the most historic and difficult foreign affairs decision you will have to make this year, for what happens in Chile over the next six to twelve months will have ramifications that will go far beyond just U.S.-Chilean relations . . . [They might] affect our own conception of what our role in the world is.*[1]
>
> —Henry A. Kissinger to President Richard Nixon, November 6, 1970

When it became clear that efforts to prevent Allende's election and inauguration had failed, the U.S. government as a whole began planning for something that it had always considered as unlikely as it was undesirable: a Marxist government brought to power by electoral means within the Western Hemisphere. Even the relatively disinterested Canadian Department of External Affairs believed Allende's election was "the most important political event in [Latin America], since the emergence of Castro, with wide political implications."[2] As CIA officer Jack Devine stated in an interview, everyone in the CIA understood Allende's victory and his government to be a significant challenge to U.S. authority in the hemisphere and a defeat in the overall East-West confrontation:

> Everyone saw it as menacing, how menacing might have been the issue. Nobody was looking and saying "oh, this is just another friendly democratic party and nothing is going to happen here." I do not remember too many people in responsible positions being un-concerned. How concerned and what they were prepared to do about it, well, honest people could disagree. But there were not a lot of people running around saying "God Bless Allende! This is a new democratic reform movement just the type they need in Latin America!" This simply did not happen.[3]

Precisely what the United States was going to do about this new government, however, was unclear. At no point had any contingency plans been prepared for Allende's election as president. Yet Chile was not, as various parts of the U.S. government now realized, "another Cuba"—at least not so far. Allende himself passed a message on November 4 to Charles Meyer at the Department of State's Bureau of Inter-American Affairs (ARA) that said Chile would never allow its soil to be used by any power hostile to the United States. Allende further wrote that the Unidad Popular (UP) would never attempt to export its political system to neighboring countries and added slyly that this was impossible since "to export the UP, the Chilean Way, one would first have to export *democracy*."[4]

Allende's sincerity, if not his sly humor, is uncertain. Recent evidence shows that Allende's government provided sanctuary to diverse rebel groups, including the Bolivian group Ejército de Liberación Nacional (ELN) and the Argentine groups Partido Revolucionario de los Trabajadores (PRT) and Ejército Revolucionario del Pueblo (ERP). These groups, along with Peru's Tupamaros, made use of weapons produced by Movimiento de Izquierda Revolucionario (MIR) in weapons factories the Allende government was aware of but did not allow the security services to raid.[5] The violence-prone MIR (itself an offshoot of Allende's own Socialist Party [PS]) was close to power—literally. Its members had been brought into the Grupo de Amigos Personales (GAP) to be Allende's bodyguards and security detail, and so it was given a sheen of legitimacy.

The level of support Chile gave to the ERP, the ELN, and others is debatable, and it is also uncertain how much control Allende had over the UP. If Allende eschewed a violent path to socialism—as the Chilean Communist Party (PCCh), most of the Radicals, and parts of the Socialist Party did—how much authority was held by his cabinet members, such as José Tohá González or Carlos Altamirano Orrego, who, like the Socialist Party general secretary and the majority elected to the Central Committee, "believed that armed conflict was inevitable"?[6] Altamirano had once said, "Civil war in Chile is inevitable and the role of the Left was to prepare for armed insurrection." These are hardly soothing words.[7] It was clear, however, that Allende wanted to minimize these potential indications of revolutionary Marxist fervor and to convey a sense that he was firmly in control of the quarrelsome UP coalition. He tried to make it clear that he was not a clear and present danger to American interests in the Southern Cone.

In part, international opinion forced the U.S. government to recognize a UP-governed Chile as a fait accompli. The jubilation at Allende's victory was vocal and public in many countries allied with the United States and even among large segments of the U.S. population. To openly threaten Allende was therefore politically risky. The fact that Allende had been elected fairly trumped high-level U.S. opinion, shared by Allende himself,[8] that the ballot box was merely "a tactical necessity" on the route to a Marxist "popular democratic" state. To openly and aggressively undermine a popular (though one must remember his narrow plurality), apparently reformist, and *elected* leader would court a diplomatic debacle for the United States on par with, if not worse than, the Bay of Pigs invasion or the 1965 U.S. intervention in the Dominican Republic, both seen as imperialist reversals of Roosevelt's Good Neighbor policy and both great sources of anger and discomfort for many Latin American leaders. The decision-making organs of the U.S. government realized they could not afford another such political disaster and created a detailed policy for dealing with Allende's government that took this understanding as its baseline.

Several other factors reinforced the U.S. inclination to tread softly with Allende. First, the United States was convinced that Allende's economic policies would lead to the destruction of the Chilean economy and so would either unintentionally invite a reaction by the Chilean army or, if the army would not move, would cause Allende at least to suffer defeat in the next presidential election. Thus, the United States realized that Allende was constrained by the same democratic structures of the Chilean constitution that had so frustrated its earlier coup attempts. The "constitutionalist" Chilean military would act to protect the existing political order as much from Allende as for Allende. Second, although the UP could convert Chile into an authoritarian or Marxist state before the next election, the United States had time to plan for this eventuality. In the meantime the U.S. government needed only to refrain from openly aggressive actions that might bolster Allende's position. "Cool and correct" became the new watchwords, and supporting, not circumventing, Chilean democratic institutions became the main U.S. tactic. Third, the uncontrolled disasters of Track I and Track II had forced Kissinger, Nixon, and most of the cabinet into a more circumspect appreciation of their ability to affect Chilean affairs. In the words of Deputy Assistant to the President for National Security Affairs Alexander Haig, "The intelligence community failed to sharply assess the full implications of the political trends in Chile or, perhaps more seriously, having assessed them with some accuracy, they permitted policy preconceptions to flavor their final assessments and their proposals for remedial action in the covert area."[9] Accordingly, CIA operations during the subsequent Allende government—well planned and quietly executed—proved much more effective than the morbid comic-opera of Operation FU/Belt.

The mistakes of 1970 facilitated a return to the relatively harmonious interdepartmental planning of the National Security Council (NSC), State Department, CIA, and embassy staff, which in turn contributed to the more hands-off approach to Allende. Beginning with a new presidential directive, the behavior of the U.S. government toward Chile after November 3, 1970, was much more restrained, aimed at (as they perceived it) the maintenance of the Chilean constitutional structure and Chile's public institutions against the political program of Allende and various branches of the UP coalition. American officers, with the full knowledge of their government, supported opposition parties and media outlets, attempted to sow dissent in the UP coalition, and gathered intelligence from the military. For its part, the U.S. government refused to extend further credit to a bankrupt Chilean government that had already defaulted on most of its loans.

The current weight of evidence indicates that from Allende's election to his downfall in 1973, no branch of the U.S. government engaged in coup plotting with the Chilean armed forces or any other domestic political body. The lessons learned from the pre-inauguration period remained in the U.S. government's and specifically the CIA's awareness throughout the three years of Allende's presidency. Evidence from multiple sources suggests that the CIA operated well within the limits of its authority and firmly under the orders of the policymaking branches of the government from November 1970 to September 1973.

DEBATES AND DISCUSSIONS

After Allende's inauguration on November 3, the U.S. government moved quickly to implement a new policy toward Chile. Little time was wasted in adjusting the pre-inauguration NSC discussion paper about Chile, NSSM 97, to address the new Marxist government in that country. An executive order on October 29 had the NSC revising NSSM 97 in anticipation of a meeting with the president scheduled for November 5, 1970.[10] The document endured no major changes at that time: It still set out four options for American policy toward Chile; the options had simply been changed to reflect Allende's election as president. The first two options presented could be viewed as one and essentially suggested that the United States maintain an outwardly correct posture, refrain from initiatives that Allende could use to his advantage, and at the same time, quietly limit Allende's freedom of action.[11] Option C called for the United States to act correctly in a diplomatic sense but make clear its opposition to the emergence of a communist government in South America and act outwardly to restrain Chilean diplomatic and political freedom. The last option called for an openly hostile posture toward Chile.[12]

To appreciate the choice of these options one must understand the U.S. government's assessment of the Allende regime. The preamble to the options paper outlined U.S. beliefs, and the paper itself (accurately) predicted the course the Allende government would follow. Allende's goals, the paper stated, would be "(a) To bring all significant economic activity under state operation . . . (b) to gain control over the security and armed forces; and (c) to dominate public information media."[13] The initial plan of operations against Chile was predicated on this estimate of Allende's actions. Overall, NSSM 97 is a remarkably lucid and well-argued assessment of the policy options for Chile, and the document served as the basis for the subsequent presidential decision of November 5.

The discussion of NSSM 97 in the White House cabinet office was lively and direct. Present were all the major cabinet officers, as well as Kissinger, Vice President Gerald Ford, and President Nixon. Kissinger knew that the hard-line approach followed through October had backfired on the Americans, yet he hoped this would not scare the NSC members from opposing Allende. Kissinger unsuccessfully tried to move the NSC meeting so the president could have more time to study the options papers, and he told staffer H. R. Haldeman, "Chile could end up being the worst failure in our administration—'our Cuba' by 1972."[14] Perhaps to ensure the president's meaningful, and slightly calmer, input where it had been lacking before, Kissinger sent Nixon a note prior to the meeting—quoted at length at the beginning of this chapter—which reminded Nixon of the extreme importance which he must assign to Chile. It was, he noted, "the most historic and difficult foreign affairs decision you will have to make this year," and so demanded immediate action:

> Contrary to your usual practice of not making a decision at NSC meetings, it is essential that you make it crystal clear where you stand on this issue at today's meeting. If all concerned do not understand that you want Allende opposed as strongly as we can, the result will be a steady drift toward the *modus vivendi* approach.[15]

Nixon seems to have followed this advice. He told the assembled policymakers,

> If Chile moves as we expect and is able to get away with it—our public posture is important here—it gives courage to others who are sitting on the fence in Latin America. Let's not think about what the really democratic countries in Latin America say: the game is in Brazil and Argentina. We could have moves under the surface which bring over time the same thing.[16]

Discussion about the Chilean threat to national interests and security led, as during Track II, to discussion about how to bring about Allende's downfall. Examining NSSM 97, Kissinger noted that the four options listed "basically . . . amount[ed] to two choices: (1) seek a *modus vivendi* with the Allende Government, or (2) adopt a posture of overt and frank hostility."[17] Kissinger said that the first choice offered a chance for Allende to consolidate his position and then operate against U.S. interests directly, while the second choice would strengthen Allende's appeal to anti-U.S. nationalism. Kissinger—clearly the driving force at this meeting and ably backed by the president—went on to offer a third option: "adopt what is in fact a hostile posture but not from an overt stance, that is, . . . move in hostility from a low-key posture."[18] In Nixon's elaboration on this option he integrated the themes of the threat to American interests and the proper course to pursue:

> No impression should be permitted in Latin America that they can get away with this, that it's safe to go this way. All over the

> world it's too much the fashion to kick us around. We are not sensitive but our reactions must be coldly proper. We cannot fail to show our displeasure. We can't put up with "Give Americans hell but pray they don't go away." . . . We must be proper on the surface with Allende, but otherwise we will be tough. He is not going to change; only self-interest will affect him.[19]

In this quote we see a classically Nixonian "realist" view of foreign policy, which reflects Nixon's continuing focus on "credibility," the political quality that commentator Paul Berman has described as "the ability to frighten people out of their wits."[20] At the same time, this quote shows that Nixon realized that an openly hostile position toward Chile would be counterproductive. As Kissinger told the author, "Once Allende was in office, and once the coup efforts had failed, I thought it was a better strategy to prepare for the next election. Anything else might make it easier for Allende to consolidate himself."[21]

Nixon's displeasure and hot-headedness tempered by Kissinger's astute sense of the situation in Chile produced the guidance for the new U.S. policy that emerged from the November 5 cabinet meeting. On November 9, 1970, the instructions produced during the cabinet discussion were incorporated into National Security Decision Memorandum 93 (NSDM 93), titled "Policy Towards Chile." NSDM 93 ordered that "within the context of a publicly cool and correct posture toward Chile" the United States was to pursue various courses of action, including ensuring that the surrounding nations of Latin America were aware of U.S. opposition to a communist state on the continent, excluding additional financing guarantees to U.S. firms operating in Chile, and "bring[ing] maximum feasible influence to bear in international financial institutions to limit credit . . . to Chile." Additionally, NSDM 93 stressed that the United States would make no new bilateral aid commitments with Chile and that those that existed should be delayed or reduced. A covert action plan to overthrow or assassinate Allende is not mentioned, although the various U.S. agencies are directed to "consider specific policy issues within the framework of this general posture."[22]

The policy set forth by NSDM 93 was predicated on the belief "that while the Allende government will vigorously pursue its Marxist goals, the economic and political difficulties facing it will place significant obstacles in its path . . . and overt hostile actions initiated by the United States would work to [Allende's] political advantage."[23] The belief that any hostile action would benefit Allende was even communicated privately to the British political staff: "[The U.S.] assessment was that Allende was going to establish a Marxist authoritarian state. . . . The Americans themselves had done a lot of soul-searching. They did not want to enable Allende to use the U.S. as a foreign devil to rally popular support."[24] Furthermore, the State Department urged that "a realistic assessment of U.S. capability to influence the situation there [be made]. . . . U.S. overt and covert capabilities to force the course of events positively in our favor, short of the use of armed force, are marginal at best . . . and could be seriously counterproductive."[25] Senior Deputy Assistant Secretary for ARA John Crimmins gave a more direct definition of the State Department's view of Allende's likelihood of success and the best posture for the United States to take:

> We said, in effect, this is not going to be nice for us but it is not the end of the world. We should not take heroic measures in response to an Allende victory, because that will only reinforce him. We would not do him any favors, we would certainly not approve new OPIC [Overseas Private Investment Corporation] guarantees, or EXIM [Export-Import] bank lending, nor would we do anything but oppose IDB [Inter-American Development Bank] and World Bank lending to him. We always thought we would make it to the next election. We thought that in NSSM-97 and throughout, that Allende would fall flat on his face one way or the other, that he could not rule, the economy would run out of control. If he were able to stay until the end of his term, Frei—who we looked to again—would come in as his successor.[26]

This was not an overly aggressive, thoughtless posture, but rather one designed to maximize American input on the fate of their economic assets and political position in the region.

An accurate summation of what the Americans believed they could achieve in Chile is made in a subsequent NSC options paper later in the same month: "Although events in Chile will be determined principally by internal Chilean forces and therefore U.S. influence can have only a marginal effect, the skilful exercise of our influence could be an important factor in complicating Allende's task."[27] Furthermore, many in the U.S. government did not view the president's choice of option C and the CIA's subsequent action plan to be final. "The program appears in general to be well-conceived," noted Assistant Secretary of State for ARA Charles Meyer, "but raises certain questions that should be kept under continuing review. The effect of interaction between the various elements of the proposed program is particularly important."[28] Unlike during Track II, after Allende's election the tone was set for meaningful interagency cooperation in Chile. Perhaps more significant, the plan of action was coordinated and multilevel, a strategic vision supplemented by specific tactical goals. This was a plan that was firmly grounded in the realities of U.S. power: economic levers, of which the United States had many, very subtly assisted by covert action in Chile meant to bolster existing trends or to support important domestic players.

SOCIAL UNREST

The planning and execution of U.S. government operations in Chile happened within the deteriorating social and economic conditions of Chile under the Allende government, which can be described only as ineffective. As predicted by many in the United States and in Chile, the various Marxist parties that made up the UP engaged in endless internecine struggles that caused inattention and disagreement that in turn caused unsuccessful management of the government. Various political components of the UP—most notably MIR—began illegal land seizures against the wishes of the UP government. Indeed, as Paul Sigmund has explained, while most of the extreme Right had either fled or been imprisoned after the Schneider assassination, "dissident sectors of the extreme left continued to insist that only violence could overthrow bourgeois institutions."[29] One extreme Left party, the Organized Vanguard of the People (VOP) assassinated Edmundo Perez Zujovic, President Frei's former interior minister, in June 1971. Such actions by dissident leftist groups contributed to a growing sense of physical insecurity in Chile.

In terms of economic security, after an initial honeymoon period with Allende, when large amounts of foreign reserve were spent boosting the wages of public employees (whose numbers were increasing owing to a rapid nationalization process), the population began to grow dissatisfied with the UP's management of the economy. The first major protests began on December 1, 1971, with the thirty-thousand-woman March of the Empty Pots.[30] As a direct consequence of the march, the opposition-controlled Congress successfully impeached the first of many UP ministers, Interior Minister José Tohá.

Other factors of luck and policy also added to the Allende government's troubles. Infighting and incoherency in the UP coalition, rudderless economic policy, a drop in copper prices and agricultural production, massive inflation, and vigorous opposition caused Chile's economic and social fabrics to disintegrate almost simultaneously. By August 1973, for instance, Chile had only $3 million in foreign reserves (a drop of over $350 million from 1970) and inflation was officially running at 300 percent but was in reality at an incredible 500 percent.[31] The Chilean currency, the *escudo*, was in 1970 pegged at twelve to the dollar; by 1973 it was traded on the blackmarket for twenty-eight hundred to one.[32]

Even the early, less severe symptoms of economic collapse clearly affected the Chilean population and especially the middle class. Beginning in mid-1972 a series of violent and protracted strikes slowly destabilized the UP government. The first of these began on August 21 and was led by the nation's independent shopkeepers.[33] Several weeks of wildcat strikes and street violence followed and continued until the police closed off downtown Santiago after a two-day running street fight between the youth arms of the rival political parties MIR and Patria y Libertad.

While efficient Carabinero action brought this violence to an end, the police were unable to control subsequent events.[34] Sparked by a government initiative to nationalize transport in the southern provinces, the nation's truckers (mostly owners of only two or three trucks) went on strike beginning October 9, 1972. A wide range of professional and small labor unions soon joined the truckers. The strike went on for three weeks, until November 5, and was estimated to have cost Chile as much as $200 million in lost production. More important, it forced Allende's cabinet to resign and brought military officers into the cabinet on November 2, 1972. The Chilean population was generally quite tolerant of its politicians, and these strikes were its last resort, its only means of combating Chile's economic deterioration under Allende. As one Chilean historian commented, "After only twelve months in office and despite its electoral success, the UP was weak and divided . . . the government had virtually lost its capacity for taking decisions."[35] As covert action works best when it is reinforcing existing trends, the U.S. government's operations in Chile found warm seas in which to swim.

A NEW MANDATE

Before dealing with the development of the CIA's operations plans in Chile, it is helpful to analyze the State Department's role, namely as administrator of financial action against Allende's government, as outlined in NSDM 93. On issuing NSDM 93, the U.S. government had decided to throw its economic weight against Allende. The United States has been fiercely attacked for its economic policy against Chile at this time, which has been dubbed the "invisible blockade" and is commonly viewed as economic imperialism.[36] Regardless, not every aspect of the American economic policy toward Allende was aimed at his ouster: the Americans maintained large economic interests in Chile and sought favorable concessions out of the UP government for their protection.

As far as the State Department was concerned, the best U.S.-Chilean interactions were not antagonistic, but rather saw the UP government remain within the strictures of international financial and banking law. A cable from U.S. Embassy Santiago to the State Department with regard to debt payments outlines this belief:

> We should not assume that Allende's realization of his dependence on the West means that there is no limit to our ability to push GOC [the Chilean government] toward more reasonable and forthcoming positions. . . . Our pressures for concessions will be effective only as long as GOC believes there is a chance for at least marginally beneficial relations with USG. In fact we have not closed off that hope and have kept relations in low-key correctness. [This has] probably contributed to [the GOC] decision to pay Braden installment [of their international debt].[37]

The economic destabilization of the Allende government was controversial and the main means of its execution were not covert. This subject has been adequately covered in several articles on the subject of U.S. economic pressure,[38] and Jonathan Haslam writes about the topic with great detail in his recent book on Chile.[39] Likewise, the World Bank and the International Bank for Reconstruction and Development (IBRD), as well as other, private banks, have testified extensively to U.S. legislative bodies on the topic of American economic destabilization in Chile and the invisible blockade policy.[40]

The Church committee report, for its part, seems to allege that the U.S. government caused the Chilean economy's collapse.[41] This is a dramatic overstatement. The invisible blockade, while a compelling theory on the surface, simply did not exist in the manner suggested by the term "blockade," and the term "invisible" seems tenuous also. While the United States attempted to exert pressure to convince the IDB and the World Bank to cut off funding to Chile, the evidence indicates that these multilateral institutions independently made their decisions based on the "underlying weakness in the Chilean economy" that Allende inherited and exacerbated.[42]

As Haslam points out in his book, Allende cared little about economics and paid little attention to the economic consequences of his programs. While in government he delegated ways and means to his ministers and economic advisers. Indeed, not until he was elected president did he actually initiate detailed economic planning. Once in power, he seemed to ignore or diminish the importance of the economic imbalances created by his hastily produced program. As one of Allende's economists boasted in 1971, "What interests us is to transform society and the economy and we are prepared to face the risks entailed in taking this road. . . . We know that certain incompatibilities are going to be produced, and we are prepared to face them. Because our interest, I repeat, our interest, is in constructing the new economy." The entire management of the economy under Allende was, as Haslam puts it, "a triumph for voluntarism over an understanding of the market."[43]

World Bank and IDB lending, however, was but a minority of Chile's foreign funds. The majority came from private overseas banks, most in the United States. Accordingly, the basic question is this: what had a greater effect, U.S. government policy or Chile's credit rating? Many of the major banks continued their credits to Chile until the country declared a unilateral moratorium on debt payments at the end of 1971.[44] Furthermore, many banks cut off service to Chile after the state nationalized its Chilean branches without compensation. To make matters worse for Chile, the price of copper dropped 23 percent in 1971, affecting the ability of Chile to import goods by substantially eroding their available foreign exchange. At the same time domestic food production dropped and thus increased foodstuffs imports were necessary.[45]

All along, Allende seemed to fully expect the cessation of American credits. In fact, in the newspaper *El Siglo*, in October 1971, he was quoted as saying, "If the U.S. closes credit to us, we will seek other lines of credit in other countries where this is possible. . . . We do not imagine that the U.S. will oppose other countries lending us money."[46] And so it occurred: when American credit dried up, Allende's Chile actually received *more* credits from Latin America, Australia, Canada, Japan, Europe, and the Eastern bloc. By 1973 Chile had $574 million in available credits, an increase of 185 percent over those available when Allende was sworn in as president.[47] The UP was discouraged to find, though, that much of this credit was tied to purchases in the creditor countries, and unfortunately there was no economically viable substitute for U.S. machinery, replacement parts, and technology. Most of the credits from the Eastern bloc subsequently went unused.[48] Furthermore, many of the European creditors, like the United States, withdrew their credits once the UP government set out to nationalize their Chilean business ventures.[49]

Crimmins spoke to the author of the view of the U.S. economic relationship with Allende's Chile that prevailed in the State Department:

> By the time I left in 1973 we had come to the point where we were talking to the Chilean government about getting some of the specific bilateral agreements like compensation for expropriation out of the way. We did not vote them any more new credits—we kept humanitarian stuff, as I remember—but no one had any problem opposing new IDB or World Bank lending, that kind of thing.[50]

Simply, there seems to be little in the U.S. economic behavior affecting Chile that was not covered by American law. The U.S. Hickenlooper Amendment stipulated that any state that nationalized American property without a fair process of compensation was no longer eligible for U.S. government aid. The amendment was invoked even in Peru, when President Juan Velasco Alvarado nationalized the International Petroleum Company, although the State Department softened the blow in favor of Alvarado's pro-American "reformist" government.[51] Chile, in contrast with Peru, not only expropriated American assets without compensation but also based its entire economic campaign on the deconstruction of foreign investment and American economic influence in the country. Allende himself wrote, "The central objective of the UP is to replace the present economic structure and to end the power of monopoly capitalism . . . in order to begin the construction of socialism."[52] Yet, even after this comment, the United States *did not* invoke Hickenlooper, which was considered too aggressive a maneuver for Nixon's "cool and correct" approach to Chile.

As taxing as the Chilean debt payment schedule was, the decision to stop repayments could have served only to ensure the reduction of Chile's private-sector credit rating. As one pair of authors has written, "Surely, the UP, given its ideology, could not have been surprised that the Nixon administration was determined to use its economic strength to cut off bilateral and multilateral aid."[53] This raised the question that cuts to the core of the modern economic system: Can the United States be criticized for not continuing loans to a nation that not only defaulted on existing loans but also actively and publicly opposed American involvement in its economy? As President Nixon said in his State of the World address in February 1971, the U.S. government was "prepared to have the kind of relationship with the Chilean Government that it is prepared to have with us."[54] As Allende was keen to remove the tentacles of American capital from his country, President Nixon was happy to oblige him, through the familiar levers of global U.S. economic regulation. "Chile of course is interested in obtaining loans from international organizations," said the president in a televised interview, and "where we have a vote and I indicated that wherever we had a vote—where Chile was involved—that unless there were strong considerations on the other side that we would vote against them."[55]

Peter Kornbluh points out that the White House moved to replace an IDB chairman who "was deemed not sufficiently malleable," but even if this was solely connected to Chile (which is not certain at all), it seems to have occurred through the use of formal and informal controls that U.S. had—and still has—over the world's major financial bodies.[56] For better or worse, the United States had (and will likely still have for some time) the world's largest economy, contributed the largest amount to the funding of these bodies, and so demanded a large say in the function of these bodies. Do U.S. economic measures in Chile after Allende's inauguration count as covert action simply because they happened outside of the public eye? Or should we view them as the normal (if petty and cruel) skulduggery of international diplomacy and finance? It would be interesting to learn how much actions in Chile drove U.S. economic policy in the IDB or IBRD at this time, but regardless it seems difficult to view U.S. economic actions as invisible or unpredictable, though they were certainly vindictive. In fact, such actions appear to be foreign policy efforts in their own right.

Ultimately, U.S. economic action in Chile may not have mattered. As was noted by the Senior Review Group in 1971, "continuing economic deterioration in Chile is not in question. Even the provision of major foreign credits could only affect the pace and degree of this process. Thus, the primary significance of the provision or non-provision of most credits would be political rather than economic."[57] One particularly detailed account of Allende's economic policies, by economist Ann Helwege, came to the following conclusion:

> The economic roots of Allende's problems also lay in the impossibility of a general increase in consumption without sustained copper earnings and commercial lending. Given the inherent instability of Allende's economic agenda, [American]

> sanctions added an important destabilizing element. Intervention through CIA covert operations, which hurt U.S. relations elsewhere in Latin America, was probably unnecessary to secure Allende's demise.[58]

Though the final sentence overestimates U.S. complicity in Allende's overthrow, the point is an important one in light of the popular perception of American efforts. Indeed, Helwege even overstates the level of American sanctions, for the United States continued, from 1970 to 1973, to disburse bilateral loans already agreed upon, and U.S. private banks even continued to extend some credit to Chile.[59] Likewise, the United States never imposed an embargo of spare parts or equipment to Chile and never prevented the shipping companies from carrying them. The Hickenlooper Amendment—the only provision that might realistically be viewed as an embargo or blockade—was never implemented.[60] Plans by the U.S.-based multinational International Telephone and Telegraph Corporation (ITT) to "unleash economic chaos" or Nixon's order to "make the economy scream" never left the concept stage because of the impossibility of implementing them.[61]

The economy did eventually scream but not as a result of U.S. government measures, which were largely political. The simple fact is that under the Allende government the economic situation deteriorated so dramatically that no Chilean company (of which there were fewer and fewer as Allende increasingly nationalized the economy) could afford further loans to finance imports. As Mark Falcoff wrote, the Chilean economy was so linked to the U.S. economy that the withdrawal of support on any level—especially political—was bound to have a significant impact. Having failed to prevent the triumph of Marxism in Chile at the cost of billions in aid and lost U.S. investments, the United States had no reason to ratify "its error by throwing good money after bad."[62]

MILITARY ASSISTANCE

Given this information on U.S. government and private lending, some commentators have pointed out that continued U.S. military aid to the Chilean military throughout Allende's presidency was a violation by the United States of its own policies.[63] Likewise, it is possible to assert that the continuation of the Military Assistance Program (MAP) and Foreign Military Sales (FMS) promoted military intervention into politics by the Chilean armed forces.[64] A review of the cable and memorandum traffic about MAP casts some doubt on these assertions.

MAP was one of the first topics broached by the Nixon administration subsequent to Allende's victory at the polls. In the initial frenzy after the election, it was tentatively decided to cancel MAP to Chile in order to prompt the Chilean army to act against Allende.[65] Because of the very transparency of this move, it was decided that "such action by the U.S. . . . would probably become known publicly and [be] interpreted by many both in and out of Chile as overt U.S. pressure upon the Chilean military to take the political situation into their own hands,"[66] and thus the decision was consequently reversed.

But public opinion was only part of the problem. The United States was dealing with a Marxist government, but the military, the branch of the Chilean government that could pose a threat to American national security, was still anti-communist and Western-oriented.[67] Accordingly, "the elimination of grant military aid, the low limits of MAP sales and the slashing of training funds . . . could only lead to the elimination of meaningful U.S. influence on the military."[68] The NSC's Viron Vaky wrote to Kissinger and asked him to continue MAP: "If we continue to suspend military aid it will appear we are punishing the military which is the last group in Chile we ought to punish."[69] At Ambassador Korry's urging, the United States decided to maintain MAP and associated military aid regardless of Allende's inauguration. After General Schneider's assassination, however, the ambassador was ordered to hold off telling the Chilean army about the restoration of MAP, as "it could be construed as [a] bonus for a job well done."[70] The United States remained very aware of the "optics" of arms sales to Chile, where American interests were so publicly challenged.

The change in U.S. posture after Allende's inauguration inevitably affected MAP and FMS. On November 6, during the NSDM 93 planning process, the Santiago station urged CIA headquarters to support continued MAP sales and training. The cable stated,

> Now more than ever, Chilean army needs [the] friendly open hand of U.S. The Army has U.S. equipment and doctrine. Supply system [is] U.S. oriented. [The Chilean] Army now feels it is alone without friends except for U.S. . . . If U.S. turns its back, Chilean Army will be "forced" to look elsewhere which it does not want to do.[71]

The U.S. government seems to have followed this advice. Adhering to NSDM 93, the United States decided to maintain the pre-election status of the U.S. Military Group of advisers in Chile and MAP and to refrain from discussing military support with the Allende government unless Chile raised the issue first. Furthermore, it was decided that the sale of tanks, air transports, and fighter jets to Chile would be delayed as long as possible but that no announcement would be made that these items would be embargoed.[72] This was a cautious first step, and at no point did the Allende government try to force the military to abandon this very overt U.S. military support.

Over the course of the subsequent three years, the United States extended over $30 million in credits for the purchase of military equipment, including $5 million in 1971, $10 million in 1972, and $12.4 million in 1973.[73] These credits were furnished after "agreement in principle with the GOC on the terms of the rescheduling of the amounts due" and were integrated into U.S. debt negotiations with Chile. An extensive "action memorandum" of February 1973 goes to some length to justify these FMS credits to Chile:

> The current Chilean Commanders-in-Chief and their staffs have so far successfully maintained the Chilean military's crucial non-partisan stance and its resistance to the governing leftist coalition's efforts to shift their source of military supplies and doctrinal orientation away from the U.S. The Chilean military leaders have resisted offers of Soviet military credits—reportedly up to $300 million . . . —and other forms of assistance including training.[74]

U.S. fears of a Chilean move toward Soviet weaponry were in part justified. In his memoir, Chilean diplomat Jorge Edwards reported on Gen. Carlos Prats's visit to Moscow in May 1973, during which Soviet defense minister Andrei Grechko made a direct approach on the matter.[75] Prats's own memoir reported that while he was predisposed to the idea of taking on Soviet arms, he felt that to purchase large quantities would so offend the sensibilities of the Chilean military that it might mutiny.[76] Chilean historian Joaquín Fermandois notes, "Nonetheless, Prats continued caressing the idea of buying arms from the Soviet Union" and even initiated a logistical support agreement with the Soviets.[77] One country or another was going to supply arms to the Chilean military, and as it stood the Chileans were happy with (and, because of FMS credits, could afford) U.S. weapons. The United States had little reason to encourage a switch to Soviet equipment, which a few quite high-ranking Chilean officers wanted and which were the only other arms available to an army deprived of U.S. supplies and without the cash to buy from the French, British, or other western nations.

When reviewing the course of MAP in Chile, one sees a U.S. attempt to use the program not as a tool to provoke a coup but rather as a means to keep the Chilean military from becoming a Soviet client. Allende had sworn never to allow the establishment of an anti-American force (i.e., the Soviets) on Chilean soil, but this did nothing to diminish the American fears that Chile would eventually become a Soviet client, at least in terms of armaments.[78] This would mean an intolerable Soviet encroachment into the American sphere and so pose a direct threat to American national security in the hemisphere. The advent of large amounts of Soviet equipment in Latin America might trigger a Chile-led arms race, especially against longtime enemies Argentina and Peru, both of which were at times U.S. allies.

From the American perspective, MAP was a passive attempt to prevent the UP's disarming or politicization of the Chilean army. Certainly the U.S. government held some hope that the Chilean military would prevent the UP from taking authoritarian control over Chile, and this motivated its continuation of funding. Some have thus viewed the program as a critical part of U.S. covert actions meant to topple Allende. Was it politically feasible, either in the United States or in its relations with allies in the Southern Cone, that the United States stop funding to the Chilean military? A funding stoppage stood the chance, from the latter perspective, of triggering a regional arms race and, from the former, of driving a friendly force into enemy arms. That the United States wanted to keep the Chilean army out of the Soviet orbit is hardly a revelation and not a link necessary to prove hostile intent against Allende.

A final note on military cooperation needs to be made on the planned visit to Chile of a U.S. aircraft carrier and its supporting naval group in September 1973. For many with a more conspiratorial view of U.S. relations with Allende's Chile, this planned visit is seen as sure proof that the United States had, at the very least, contingency plans to support the Pinochet coup with direct, armed force. While the carrier visit had some connection with American desires to bolster Allende's opposition, it had nothing to do with coup plotting, and in any case the carrier was never actually deployed to Valparaíso. Though the visit would have been part of the annual UNITAS naval exercise—a tour of South America which featured joint exercises with national navies along the way—which the U.S. Navy had been running since the end of the Second World War, there was considerable opposition to the Chilean leg of the 1973 UNITAS exercise. John Crimmins described how his office at the State Department—normally cautious about such things—endorsed the naval visit, to the NSC's shock:

> The Navy was keen to have an aircraft carrier visit [in 1973] and this was intended to maintain "military to military ties" as they said. As I remember, the embassy thought it would be all right for that purpose, and I thought it was alright, but Al Haig went ape, called me and was very upset that we were even contemplating this. I thought that [the carrier visit] would be a reassurance to the opposition of a U.S. presence, but Al Haig thought it would be a terrible mistake.[79]

The visit of the U.S. Navy to Valparaiso was thus, accordingly, cancelled on the NSC's orders. It was viewed, quite simply, as too provocative a gesture at a moment of extreme political instability in Chile. What was not cancelled, however, was the joint aspect of the exercise. Though the U.S. ships did not enter Chilean waters, the Chilean navy was meant to steam out to meet the U.S. Navy to conduct joint anti-submarine maneuvers. This they did on the morning of September 10, 1973, only to return the next day to begin the coup having used the UNITAS exercise as a handy excuse to mobilize for action. Despite General Haig's attempts to prevent a U.S. provocation against Allende's government, the tenuous connection of U.S. armed forces to the coup actions of the Chilean navy remains. There is no evidence that the U.S. Navy was aware they were being used as a figleaf for the naval side of the coup, but more declassified documents and research would need to be done to dismiss the significance of this particular connection.

POLITICAL ACTION

While the MAP program was ongoing, the CIA was engaging in political action against the UP directly. With a new mandate from NSDM 93, the CIA set about, in early November 1970, to produce a covert action plan for implementation in Chile, and by November 17, the Agency had submitted for approval this program. As described by Jack Devine and in various documents, two distinct operations were planned for the post-election period: covert action designed to bolster Allende's political and media opposition and a parallel intelligence-gathering operation aimed at the group most likely to stage a coup, the Chilean military. Though discrete from one another in operational terms, the two programs were pursued by the same group of CIA officers in U.S. Embassy Santiago—though now under the leadership of a new COS, Raymond Warren, who replaced Henry Hecksher in November 1970. Contemporary historians have argued that the overriding American goal of ridding Chile of Allende makes any separation between the two missions entirely artificial. Examination of the two missions shows them to be linked—but not by any desire for violence. Rather, the collection mission and the political action mission were connected because both conscientiously sought to weaken Allende's hold on power while they avoided the provocation of a coup or a repeat of the Viaux assassination plot.

The bulk of the CIA's efforts from November 1970 onward was dedicated to opposing Allende in the political sphere. Keyed to NSDM 93, the CIA's political action program was "directed at the Allende government, the non-Marxist opposition, the Chilean public . . . in an effort to maximize pressure on the Allende government to prevent its consolidation and to limit its ability to implement policies contrary to U.S. and hemispheric interests."[80] Jack Devine said, "The Russians, the Cubans were quite serious about trying to bring this country into their orbit. We were equally determined that was not going to happen."[81] In retrospect, Soviet and Cuban influence over Allende or the UP was overstated by Devine and others. Neither country thought that Allende had much chance of success nor that it could influence his program, but both were happy to support him in the meantime.

The first aim of the CIA's program was to take "political action to divide and weaken the Allende coalition . . . to create splits within and between coalition parties."[82] The plan also included providing financial support to the opposition parties, the Christian Democrat Party (PDC) and the National Party (PN). Concurrent with this political party funding was support for opposition media outlets that could "speak out against the Allende government."[83] Because of poor organization and a lack of private-sector funding (which was made difficult by UP control of banking and the nationalization of many companies), the main centrist and rightist parties had difficulty, after Allende's election, mounting an effective opposition to the UP.[84] Likewise, there was a threat that the UP would use the PDC's leadership review in early 1971 to attempt to gain control of the PDC through support of its left wing.[85]

The central aim of this CIA effort was "to keep the current political set in Chile from becoming irreversible."[86] To achieve this aim, the CIA would assist the opposition parties, almost entirely by funding, so that they might maintain their domination of Congress, the main obstacle to

Allende's goal of a fully Marxist economy and government. At best, the Americans hoped the opposition might achieve a two-thirds majority necessary in the Senate to impeach Allende.[87] The Agency would not attempt to rig elections, bribe candidates, or conduct any other "black" operation to ensure the success of these parties; it would merely pass funds to them. Ambassador Korry approved of this limited plan with some reluctance.[88] Korry's grudging assent may have been helped by improved relations with his new COS, Raymond Warren, who was certainly not as difficult a character as his predecessor Henry Hecksher.

Central to the political action program was the belief that Allende and the UP government would not allow democratic opposition against the government to continue for very long. While his government had been elected, Allende made it clear from the beginning that he had no interest in maintaining the political status quo and that if necessary he would seek methods to circumvent the intransigent, opposition-controlled Congress. As Henry Kissinger said, "I was convinced that he was trying to lead Chile into a Castro-like situation and I think all the evidence shows that. Was he strong enough to do this? That I cannot judge. But I was convinced that this is where he was heading."[89]

Indeed, Allende may not have been strong enough. The UP's lack of seats in Congress (the UP had twenty senators out of fifty in the upper house and sixty deputies out of 150 in the Chamber of Deputies) made it nearly impossible for the party to implement the legislation required to change the constitution of Congress or the judiciary and, in many cases, to enact budget legislation. Allende maneuvered around these difficulties—and around the Charter of Democratic Guarantees that he had signed to secure congressional approval—by using a series of legal loopholes he cleverly termed *resquicios legales*. These allowed him to *requisition* many private companies, banks, and estates (nationalization without a congressional vote violated the constitutional right to property). Meanwhile, he tried to pass a new constitution to create a unicameral Assembly of the People subordinate to the president and the politically appointed judiciary. In Jack Devine's view, the UP was

> basically trying to undermine democratic institutions. In the case of media they were cutting off access to print. They were intimidating the segment of the public that did not support them. I was on the Carrera Hotel looking down on the plaza during the March of the Women when the *MIRistas* arrived by truckloads, throwing rocks and bottles. This was not New York,

> Bloomberg and Ferrer, this was serious strategy: seizing of land, workers taking over factories. There was reason, a vivid reason to support the opposition, to fight this thing without a coup, to support the parties, to support their capacity for receiving funds.[90]

Without this support, the UP's opposition would be starved of funds and intimidated out of conducting any coherent opposition to the UP in Congress, despite the PDC and PN majority, and so allow the dismantling of Chilean democracy.

Once the U.S. government had approved the policy of supporting the political and media opposition to Allende, the CIA set out—after a short period of assuring themselves of the secrecy and security of their plan—to move very large sums of money to the PDC and PN. The first attempt at this program was made in time for the Chilean municipal elections of April 1971, on the basis that those elections "will be viewed as a plebiscite for the UP."[91] On January 28, 1971, the 40 Committee approved $1,240,000 "to cover ongoing administrative support to bolster Party infrastructure."[92] Additionally, the money was to be used to purchase favorable content on radio stations and newspapers to assist in publicizing the party's efforts.[93] Subsequent funds were voted to the PDC and PN for the congressional elections and by-elections and for ad hoc needs as requested. In total, $2.6 million was spent supporting the Christian Democrats, the National Party, and Radical Party splinters. Two-thirds of this total went to finance opposition campaigns in the 1972 by-elections and the congressional elections of March 1973.[94] Ted Shackley, chief of the Western Hemisphere Division (C/WHD) in 1972, felt that this support was nearly decisive because it helped to bring the opposition only "two votes short of the two-thirds majority in the Senate that would have permitted Allende's impeachment."[95] No one criticized the direct support of non-UP parties as they had the CIA campaign efforts during the presidential election.

A further sum, under a separate appropriation, went to subsidize the main opposition paper, *El Mercurio*.[96] The newspaper's preservation was doubly important to Nixon, who was a friend of its owner, Augustín Edwards, whose advice to Nixon was likely important in the formation of Track II.[97] As the major conservative paper and media crusader against Allende, *El Mercurio* had fought the president tooth and nail through the campaign, and Allende returned the favor by making public promises that he would "get" the paper. If the paper had fallen under Marxist control, the UP would have held editorial power over more than half of the printed press, as well as over twenty-four of twenty-eight radio stations and three of four television stations.[98] The initial UP effort against the paper took the form of attempted labor disputes to seize editorial control, followed by a forced increase in wages with a freeze on prices.[99] In October 1971, the UP government tried to seize effective control over *Papelera*, the only private pulp-and-paper company, in the hope of driving up *El Mercurio*'s prices to an intolerable degree. The Americans perceived this effort to force the paper under UP control as a major threat to freedom of the press.[100]

Despite journalist David Corn's recent arguments that "Allende had no evil designs on *El Mercurio*,"[101] U.S. support of the paper was justified, as the UP had used a similar set of tactics to cause the closure of the pro-Christian Democrat publishing house *Zig-Zag*.[102] Furthermore, it must be noted that *El Mercurio* was one of the most forthright media outlets in calling for increased military intervention in the Allende government, especially during Allende's two military cabinets in 1972 and 1973, when for instance the paper issued an editorial that argued that the military's "constitutionalist" stance required it to protect the constitution from the government's illegal measures: "Their spirit of loyalty to the Constitution should not be utilized in order that they remain inactive while the other principles . . . are violated."[103] The president, understandably, would have had a very direct interest in curbing *El Mercurio*'s editorial voice. But the paper operated in a free society, and calling for increased military control over a government that had independently formed a military cabinet to control public chaos was not beyond the bounds of normal press freedom.

None of this means, of course, that everyone in the U.S. government thought running its own paper in Chile was a great idea: a discussion paper in the NSC cast doubt on the wisdom or effectiveness of supporting *El Mercurio*. "I reluctantly conclude that we should go along with this," said one NSC functionary, citing the poor democratic precedent of buying the press, a move rejected outright by President Eisenhower more than a decade earlier, when the United States was practically invited to do so.[104] According to the Church committee report, a total of $1.7 million was given to *El Mercurio* to keep the paper afloat.[105] In total, one CIA memorandum reported, the 40 Committee authorized "financial support totaling $6,476,166 for Chilean political parties, media, and private sector organizations opposed to the Allende regime."[106] This was a massive amount of money, although, as will be seen later, not all of these appropriations were spent.

Meanwhile, the CIA worked to implement the second aspect of the political action program: creating dissent within the UP coalition. Noting severe friction between the Communists and Socialists—the two main parties in the UP—the CIA hoped to "continue programs designed to exacerbate mutual suspicions and frictions between PCCh/PS and PCCh/MIR, including both propaganda as well as [deleted] attribution pieces."[107] The CIA hoped that the Radical Party of the Left (PIR), then part of the governing UP coalition, might act as a dissident element within the UP and be used "to heighten tensions within the government coalition."[108] Though the methods the Agency used to create this split are deleted from the files (as is most information dealing with tradecraft), it is clear that the plan succeeded. In April 1972 the PIR left the UP coalition to work with the opposition. Though it was only a small party and the loss of PIR seats did not adversely affect the UP's power, it was a definite blow to government morale and some proof to the United States that its covert aid was working. Following its split from the UP, the PIR began to receive support funds from the United States along the same model as the Christian Democrats and National Party.[109]

The success of U.S. financial support, despite such clear victories as the PIR split, was debated by the differing agencies and individuals involved. The CIA and some parts of the State Department felt the support was a success for the full period of the program.[110] In 1972 the CIA issued a report stating that the funding helped the opposition to "maintain its vigor." The report went on to state,

> The continued vitality of the congressional and popular opposition to the UP testifies to the effectiveness with which the three parties have maintained their independence and their appeal. While the precise extent to which our assistance has contributed to this situation is of course unknowable, it seems clear that it has helped.[111]

However, after an abortive coup by a single army regiment on June 29, 1973, the CIA became skeptical of continuing support for the opposition parties. The Santiago station based its opinion against this support on political reality. First of all, the military had remained loyal to the government through the attempted coup, and this had not done anything to encourage the political opposition.[112] Furthermore, the opposition did not make any gains in the March congressional elections (though it had not lost ground) and the outlook for gains in future elections was poor. Even if the opposition did win, it was believed that a Frei presidency would not be that beneficial to the United States. It needed to pursue a new tactic.

Director of Central Intelligence William Colby,
left, with wife Barbara, receiving the
State Department's Distinguished Honor Award from
Secretary of State William P. Rogers in April 1972.
State Department

Deputy Undersecretary of State for Political Affairs
U. Alexis Johnson (right) being interviewed by an unidentified reporter in February 1970. *State Department*

Edward Korry taking the oath in 1967 as
U.S. ambassador to Chile. *State Department*

Charles Meyer being sworn in as assistant secretary of state for inter-American affairs, in February 1969. *State Department*

Street violence between the Marxist group MIR and its conservative opponents Patria y Libertad is broken up by tear gas during anti-government strikes in Santiago in the fall of 1972. *National Archives/CIA*

Troops patrol Santiago's streets on October 20, 1972, the tenth day of nationwide strikes against Allende's government. *National Archives/CIA*

Chilean dockworkers unload a tractor from an East German ship in January 1973, part of an Eastern Bloc solidarity consignment. With foreign reserves spent, Allende hoped these shipments might help replace Western goods Chile could no longer afford. *National Archives/CIA*

A crowd caught in a crossfire between loyalist and rebel troops outside La Moneda, the presidential palace, during an unsuccessful coup attempt in June 1973.
National Archives/CIA

A loyalist soldier takes up a position outside Government House during the abortive June 1973 uprising. *National Archives/CIA*

President Allende listening to a warning by leaders of the September 1973 coup that La Moneda would be attacked if he did not surrender. *National Archives/CIA*

Allende enters the palace courtyard with bodyguards on September 11, 1973, moments before air force jets struck the building with rockets and bombs. *National Archives/CIA*

Firefighters carry Allende's body from La Moneda.
National Archives/CIA

A recoilless rifle points toward the U.S. consulate as troops sweep through the area following Allende's overthrow.
National Archives/CIA

THE PRIVATE SECTOR

During the summer of 1972, members of the State Department and the administration began to suggest cautiously that the CIA support non-party and nongovernmental civic organizations in its campaigns against Allende. The impetus for this new tactic likely came from reporting about the civil opposition to the Allende government that became more and more effective through 1971. The greatest example of this opposition was the aforementioned December 1971 March of the Empty Pots, when thirty thousand (though some say fewer) women marched through Santiago shouting slogans such as "Listen to us Allende," "Chilean Women—Save Chile from Marxism," and "There is no Meat; there is no nothing."[113] This event provoked a surprisingly strong reaction from the government, which had the Carabineros prevent the protest from reaching the presidential palace, while the MIR mobilized busloads of supporters, mostly young males, to attack the march with clubs and bottles. In the June 1972 NIE titled "Chile: The Alternatives Facing the Allende Regime," the analysts wrote, "Unrelenting economic problems and sporadic outbursts of political violence have cut into the UP's popular support, provoked discontent among the traditionally apolitical security forces, and strengthened the hand of the political opposition generally."[114] In short, the actions of civil society and private sector organizations had a definite impact on the UP's ability to govern and yet were not at that time violent or coup-minded. It was becoming clear that a selection of private sector organizations could also be supported safely as part of the political action program.

Around the time the NIE was issued, State Department and CIA officials began meeting to discuss the feasibility of private-sector funding. The main justification for support, as far as the State Department saw it, was "to strengthen the ability of the named private sector organizations to contribute to the general opposition effort against the UP government."[115] Simultaneously, the support would prevent the total destruction of the private sector by the UP's nationalization drive and so maintain the private sector as a source of funds for the opposition political parties. This plan had potential problems. The PDC was philosophically dedicated to Christian Communitarianism and, being not entirely friendly to the private sector, could end up a target of its own activities, drawing force away from the desired attacks on Allende.[116] The other fear was that the funded organizations would begin working toward violence or plotting. On this count State and the Agency agreed that adventurous use of funds would result in the termination of funding to the organization. The State Department staff at Foggy Bottom passed on the recommendation to the NSC to begin a three-month trial period of funding to the private sector from August to September 1972.

When the 40 Committee heard the joint Agency–State Department proposal for private-sector funding, the agencies made clear that their proposal had little to do with coup plotting. Organizations they had selected for funding included labor groups, professional unions, and private-interest groups with sympathies for the opposition parties. Allende's desire to expropriate all businesses with a net worth more than $500,000 forced many small and medium-size business groups to organize *sindicales*, which Shackley considered perfect candidates for subsidy.[117] Essentially, the private sector had become politicized by the growing economic crisis in Chile and was becoming increasingly supportive of the political opposition to Allende. The proposal stated explicitly that "support and encouragement of the politically-oriented activities of the private sector would represent an operational adjunct to the main effort of direct support to the opposition political parties."[118] Yet, opposition from the ARA initially stalled the proposal in the 40 Committee.

John Crimmins and Charles Meyer argued against the proposal in a letter to the new U.S. ambassador in Santiago, Nathaniel Davis, who had assumed the post on September 30, 1971. They thought that private-sector funding would weaken the security of the political action operation and that leaks to certain groups would have far-reaching consequences. Concerned that the organizations receiving funding would misuse such funding, the two ARA men argued that all the caution in the world could not prevent some elements from using the belief of U.S. support as "the final determinant in a decision to go for a coup (e.g., 'the Americans know what we're about and, despite their pro forma cautions, are giving us the green light. They're putting up the money, aren't they?')."[119] A coup was not as much in U.S. interests at the time because it was unlikely to be successful, and even were it to succeed, the new government would have no international legitimacy and even might not be pro-U.S. Davis—a much more reasonable character than Korry—responded the day he received Crimmins and Meyer's memo. He noted that he shared the same concerns but that the CIA station had convinced him the fears were unfounded. He supported the program with the significant caveat that funding would be disbursed with CIA and State clearance "only when local conditions make further delay critical to survival."[120] A coup was not part of the plan, and with this assurance, Meyer gave his support.

Two weeks later, the agreed-upon proposal for funding found its way to the 40 Committee in an amended annex to the original proposal of

August 24. The new proposal stated that the elevated political temperature of strikes and street demonstrations made it advisable to delay implementation of the program until the crisis had subsided, likely by mid-October. This last point was viewed as a major concession to the State Department's sense of caution.[121] The lobbying of various State Department officials (as well as Kissinger) continued for some time, repeating the arguments for and against the support. Authorization for the private-sector funding was finally approved some four months after it was initially proposed, on October 26, 1972, on a trial basis from the end of October until the March 4, 1973, congressional election. The funding was not released for use until the beginning of January, so it is fairly clear that it did not go toward the first truckers' strike of September 1972—though a *New York Times* article from September 1974 asserts that the strike did receive funding meant to go to the press.[122]

The funding scheme was "designed fundamentally to strengthen the ability of these organizations . . . to contribute to the political strength of the opposition" in the forthcoming congressional election.[123] As briefed to the undersecretary of state for political affairs, U. Alexis Johnson, a significant side benefit to the support included "an improvement in the ability of these organizations to resist the government drive to weaken further the private sector, and the maintenance of private business, industry, and agriculture as a broad source of funds for the opposition political parties."[124] As it turned out, most of the funding went toward enfranchisement campaigns in support of the opposition.[125]

As political instability in Chile grew in 1973, the State Department, heeding the CIA's observation that "the private sector is becoming desperate," once again raised the proposition of supporting the private sector.[126] There was significant unwillingness from State to provide such support, and it was reported that Ambassador Davis and Assistant Secretary of State for ARA Jack B. Kubisch were reluctant to authorize support to the private sector "because this sector is working to promote military intervention."[127] Ambassador Davis was particularly fervent in his opposition. In a memorandum to Kissinger, NSC staffer William Jorden argued that the ambassador did not support the proposal:

> He believes this course of action could lead to *de facto* U.S. commitment to a coup. He thinks the chances of exposure are significant and that those Chileans who learn of what is happening, or even suspect it, will take it as a signal that we want a coup . . . [and] some military elements with whom they have

> contacts [may] be tempted into rash actions on the assumption that they would have quick and effective U.S. support.
>
> The Ambassador believes (correctly) that present U.S. policy is to keep the pressure on, but not to take action in overthrowing Allende. He believes the new proposal would move us toward the latter.[128]

The rest of Jorden's argument was as direct. Current operations were *not* to encourage a coup from any sector, but support for a coup was the direct implication of any support. The 40 Committee approved the proposal to fund the private sector during the last half of August but made all disbursements contingent on "the Ambassador's approval."[129]

Among other authors, Gabriel Kolko has suggested that these funds were used in "generously aiding the militant opposition," including the most significant opposition movement, the second truckers' strike of August 1973.[130] Luis Vitale quotes a contemporary source who said, "*se puede afirmar categóricamente que las huelgas . . . fueron financiadas por la CIA* [I can state categorically that the strikes . . . were financed by the CIA]."[131] Most CIA documents seem to refute this allegation. As Director of Central Intelligence (DCI) William Colby noted in a report to Kissinger a week after the coup, the short timespan and the ambassador's reluctance prevented the provision of this support to any civilian organization that the Agency thought was supporting a coup or insurrection:

> No support was provided to the private sector, whose initiative in launching and maintaining a series of crippling strikes was instrumental in provoking the military coup of 11 September 1973. Thus, while the Agency was instrumental in enabling opposition parties and media to survive and to maintain their dynamic resistance to the Allende regime, the CIA played no direct role in the events that led to the establishment of the new military government.[132]

After much discussion and despite the approval of significant funds, apparently no money of any consequence was passed to the component organizations of the Chilean private sector in 1973. National Party official Sergio Onofre Jarpa noted in interview that his party, which had received money from the CIA, had a "strike department which encompassed bankers, private employees, public employees, shopkeepers, truck owners";

therefore, it might be hard to distinguish between funding for the PN and funding for the truckers.[133] Jack Devine could not recall any funding given with the aim of supporting the truckers' strike.[134] Another U.S. official, however, noted that modest financial support went to some private-sector organizations independently assisting the strikers, indicating that the United States was indirectly supporting these strikes.[135]Additional conflicting evidence, however, points toward fairly large sums going to the various organizations involved in the strikes. Haslam cites Chilean press articles and other Chilean sources that point to large amounts being moved into Chile.[136] Many Chileans believed or assumed this money was from the CIA, though it is acknowledged that it might also have come from corporations such as ITT, which was acting independently, or from U.S. trade unions. Regardless of whether the sums of money were large or not and of whether funding was given directly to the truckers union, U.S. support would have had an effect on the strike. As one source puts it, "Money went a long way there. A couple of copy machines, etc., and a few thousand dollars did things." Yet this official carried on with the argument that the Agency's indirect funding was not a sine qua non of the strikes: "Would [the strikes] have gone forward without the agency? Of course! There was spontaneity about the truckers."[137]

Another document shows that while some funding went to organizations associated with the truckers' strike, the CIA viewed the whole situation with caution. While it wished to encourage disobedience to the Allende government, it did not want to encourage a situation in which public order was so threatened that it forced the military to support the government. "We would not encourage any large-scale confrontations, such as a general strike," wrote a Chile desk officer.[138] Historian Arturo Valenzuela described the trouble the CIA might have had in directing the course of the strikes or their resulting political ramifications:

> Acting out of fear of economic threats [the *gremios*, or independent business associations] moved to defend their basic economic interests. Because of the importance of trucking in the Chilean economy, the truckers' strike in particular dealt a serious blow to the government and served to rally other groups and associations who subsequently joined the movement to paralyze the economy. . . . Christian Democratic elements, as well as sectors of the National party who had a role in the organization of these groups . . . found that they acted increasingly on their own.[139]

The strikes started spontaneously as a result of small economic stakeholders who attempted to preserve what little they retained in the face of ongoing nationalizations and the deepening national financial crisis. Even their long-associated political parties had difficulty controlling the actions of the myriad *gremios* involved. So, while there is some conflict about what specific amount went to which private sector organizations at any given point in time, it would seem that the Agency was involved in the funding but was not the main motivator behind the crippling strikes of 1973. Assuming the CIA was involved, one sees the sort of operation by which the Agency felt it could best influence events: it was neither the ultimate nor proximate cause of the event, nor was it the driving force, yet it was able to amplify its effects in the direction it desired. Can we say that the CIA supported the private sector because the U.S. government felt it was the best way to produce a "coup climate"? Some within the Agency or the government might have assumed as much, but producing such a climate does not seem to have been the core mission of the overall covert action program, which at first sought to maintain the opposition to Allende's political program.

INTELLIGENCE ON THE ARMED FORCES

Those who believe the U.S. government encouraged or even planned the 1973 coup point to American contact with the Chilean military as evidence. The Church committee, for one, wrote, "U.S. officials in the years before 1973 may not have always succeeded in walking the thin line between monitoring indigenous coup plotting and actually stimulating it."[140] The CIA maintained contact with the Chilean military throughout the Allende administration, but the degree of that contact and the CIA's influence over the Chilean military is often overestimated.

The U.S. link to the Chilean military surely was a main topic of discussion among U.S. government officials as they were determining American policy toward the Marxist government in Chile; in fact, tucked into the text of NSDM 93 was the topic "the armed forces." The first paragraph of the section about the armed forces, which is heavily excised, does not appear to call for the assassination of or a coup against Allende. Simply, it states, "We are maintaining and where possible enlarging our contacts in the military. . . . We continue to provide intelligence [to key military officials] such as the background of the Cuban intelligence personnel who are arriving in Chile."[141] The U.S. role as stated in the document was one of intelligence gathering and dissemination.

The Santiago station initially sought, perhaps because of residual impressions from the Track II period, to produce a coup in Chile. This was not in the plan for the post-inauguration period, however, and this was made clear in a series of cables exchanged in November 1971. A cable of November 12 discussed the CIA chief of station's plans to gather intelligence on coup plotting within Chile. The three pages of the memo discussed the mechanics of initiating relations with coup plotters, learning about their plans, and perhaps influencing them by giving advice or suggesting techniques they had not considered. While COS Warren stated that the CIA should not lead or participate in any of these coups, he concluded that the CIA's mission was to "work consciously and deliberately in the direction of a coup" with fresh contacts in the Chilean military.[142]

C/WHD Broe responded to Warren's cable with absolute clarity: "We cannot accept your conclusion . . . nor can we authorize you to 'talk frankly about the mechanics of a coup' with key commanders, because the implications of that amount to the same."[143] Clearly, Warren had overestimated U.S. belligerency toward Allende. Broe, a man on very good terms with his colleagues in Foggy Bottom,[144] set the COS straight:

> The essential fact which must be kept in mind by all officers connected with the [deleted] program is that we do not have any authority to state, or even to imply, that [the U.S. government] favors a coup as a solution to the Chilean dilemma. If and when Station reporting indicates a favorable political atmosphere and a serious military intent to take action against the Allende government, it will become the responsibility of other [U.S. government] authorities to use this intelligence in reaching a policy decision. [deleted—the CIA] might or might not at that time request such a decision from [deleted—the U.S. government]. We just cannot say at this stage or seek advance advice on the basis of hypothesis. Policy does not work that way. . . . In sum, stay with history as it unfolds, don't make it.[145]

The CIA was going to operate strictly within the bounds of the interdepartmental framework of covert operations, and this quotation puts to rest the Church committee assertion, which referred to the same cables, that the CIA "realized that the U.S. government's desire to be in clandestine contact with military plotters . . . might well imply U.S. support for their future plans" and continued the contacts regardless.[146]

Within the current evidence, it seems that the CIA, in active consultation with the other interested branches of government, expressly stayed away from any coup plotting. As one officer stated, "The military was a collection task, a foreign intelligence collection task. Not 'how do you work with the military on developing a new government?' or 'how do you organize a coup there tomorrow?'"[147] Responding to a proposal from the Santiago Station in October 1972, CIA headquarters said,

> While HQs prepared [to] consider any specific detailed proposal, even if we believe it has merit would still have to consult with other interested agencies and secure their concurrence. FYI only, our present reading of other agency thinking is that any proposition that smacks of adventurism will be most difficult to sell.[148]

One particular incident in June 1973 demonstrates that the CIA did not cross the boundary from intelligence gathering to coup plotting, perhaps because the conspiracies developing within the Chilean military were so fractured. By 1973 inflation, breakdown of the UP coalition, and massive civic unrest caused by the trucker and miner strikes markedly increased the anti-Allende sentiment in Chile. The greatest symptom of this tension, as manifested within the military, was an attempted coup by low-level army officers—many of whom belonged to Patria y Libertad—on June 29, 1973. On that day Col. Roberto Souper and his junior officers led the Second Armored Battalion in surrounding La Moneda, the presidential palace in the center of Santiago. The battalion and Patria y Libertad attempted the revolt in the apparent hope that the rest of the military and the police would join. Instead, the bulk of the armed services came to the government's defense.[149] Interestingly, it was the *Tacna* Artillery Regiment that succeeded, after only three hours, in putting down the rebellion while inflicting some "needless deaths" on the hapless Second Armored Regiment.[150] This rebellion was quickly referred to as the Day of the Tanks or, in ironic reference to the history of those who suppressed it, *El Tanquetazo*.[151]

There is no evidence at the moment that the United States had advance knowledge of this failed coup attempt. Indeed, a CIA report of the same day stated, "At this time there is no available information to indicate that the attack by the Armored Regiment on the presidential palace was more than an isolated and uncoordinated effort by that unit."[152] Another document, designed to answer potential White House questions about CIA involvement in the abortive coup, asserted that the CIA had nothing to do with the events of June 29. The first question, "Did the Agency play any role whatever in supporting or encouraging the coup?" was answered with a terse "none." While admitting that the CIA had been in contact with some in the army who were plotting, the document said the Santiago station was not sure if any of these contacts were involved in the rebellion. Furthermore, the CIA document said that the Agency did nothing to support or encourage the attempted coup and that, when one of its contacts asked for help in developing arrest lists or in collecting names of potential co-conspirators, the CIA told the Chilean officer "that neither the Agency nor the U.S. Government was stimulating, encouraging or favoring a coup and that no information could be given to him."[153]

The UP press accused the U.S. government of sponsoring the attempted coup and went so far as to name Mr. Keith Wheelock as the CIA officer who had fomented the anti-Allende action through a Chilean intermediary, Manuel Fuentes, a member of the Patria y Libertad. The internal CIA discussion about this accusation discovered that "Wheelock left Chile in late 1969. He had contact with Fuentes . . . and passed him onto another embassy contact . . . but apparently dropped him as a contact in April 1970 when Fuentes became insistent in asking for USG financial support for anti-Allende purposes."[154] Jonathan Haslam adds to this debate by asserting that the U.S. military assistance group in Chile helped plot the rebellion and in doing so used—without the knowledge of anyone but a small circle in the Pentagon and, of course, Kissinger and Nixon—links with the Chilean army it had built up. Unfortunately, Haslam does not cite a source for this information, and so for the time being it must be accepted only as a possibility. Indeed, if true this allegation shows the difficulty of plotting a coup and the ultimate result when amateurs unaware of deeper political currents attempt a covert action. As is described later in this chapter, this rebellion did little to assist U.S. policy in Chile, at least in immediate consequence.

In its own review, the Agency concluded that the revolt, "an almost futile gesture of frustration by the action-oriented military officers, . . . was doomed to failure."[155] Haslam provides an excellent description of internal Chilean political events leading up to the rebellion, which had its roots in Patria y Libertad connections to disaffected junior officers.[156] But if, as he asserts, the U.S. Military Group, under the secret direction of Kissinger or the deputy DCI Gen. Vernon Walters was behind the plotting of the attempted coup, then it was working at cross-purposes to the main arm of covert action, the CIA, and this Byzantine expedient could not possibly serve U.S. interests as a whole; it would instead be a further example of how opaque and ill-considered tactical covert actions do little to further the government's strategic aims.[157] The CIA, ignorant as it was of some of the coup-plotting currents within the officer corp's lower ranks, concluded that the action had fostered a greater degree of unpredictability and instability in an already chaotic environment. The CIA, in this case, did not approve of chaos, which made events tricky to forecast and the results of Agency work more difficult to define.

THE RUSSIANS AND THE CUBANS

The CIA's work became ever more difficult as Allende's term progressed. On coming to power Allende had renewed diplomatic relations with Cuba. Fidel Castro toured Chile for a full month in November 1971 and, despite his misgivings about the *via Chilena*, offered significant support to Allende, including contributing to the construction of an efficient internal security agency for Chile.

Work by Chilean researcher Cristián Pérez shows that significant Cuban assistance was directed at the GAP, Allende's private security force, which was under the direction of Beatriz "Taty" Allende, soon-to-be wife of Cuban agent Fernández Oña. The GAP, in which Allende's own nephew served, underwent lengthy security and weapons training in Cuba and, on top of its guard duties, undertook certain security tasks for the UP.[158] Similarly, the Chilean equivalent of Scotland Yard, the Investigaciones, were "*absolutamente infiltrada por el marxistas*" (absolutely infiltrated by the Marxists) and turned into an effective counterespionage force with training by and direct assistance from the Cubans.[159] A Santiago station cable from November 1971 supports Pérez's research and identifies GAP's second section, Informacion y Chequeo, as being heavily supported and well armed by the Cubans (who also caused some dissent by favoring pro-Cuban Socialist Party members over the more extreme socialist splinter group MIR).[160] The Investigaciones were likewise converted into the UP government's tool and set to the task of political intelligence gathering and political action against the regime's opponents.[161] A substantial number of Cuban intelligence officers began operating in Chile, both under diplomatic cover and as "illegals."

Shortly after Allende's inauguration, the CIA began to find it difficult to gather intelligence in Chile. Jack Devine explained:

> [In] Chile and most other Latin American countries we owned the territory. By that I mean we were friendly with the host government, we worked together on anti-Communist, anti-Cuban operations. Here we were on the defensive, it was al-

> most a denied-area environment, in the sense that the security system was more concerned about us than the Cubans. I believe there was something like a thousand Cubans in Chile, I could be wrong, but they had a substantial presence. I have a lot of respect for the Cuban Intelligence, they were a lot more effective than the Russians, in the sense that they still had revolutionary fervor, they were prepared to make sacrifices, they spoke the languages, and they were prepared to mix it up with the *campesinos*. The Russians, well, it did not come as easy to them in dealing with the Chileans.[162]

But although the Russians might not have been as good at charming the Chileans, the *Mitrokhin Archive* confirms that the KGB was still active in Chile. According to LEADER's KGB file,

> in a cautious way Allende was made to understand the necessity of reorganising Chile's army and intelligence services. . . . The KGB devoted its attention to strengthening Allende's anti-American leanings. To this end, information obtained by the KGB Residency in Chile on the activities of American intelligence services was conveyed to Allende. Important and goal-directed operations were conducted according to this plan.[163]

Cuban and Soviet attention, moreover, was directed at the main target of U.S. intelligence gathering: the Chilean army. The Investigaciones were, by mid-1972, maintaining round-the-clock surveillance of the Chilean General Staff.[164] Thus CIA's Chilean operations, both supporting the opposition and gathering intelligence on the military, were far more difficult than operations in any other operating environment in the hemisphere. But more important, the increased Cuban presence only enforced American distrust of the Allende regime and strengthened the more hawkish members of the Nixon administration. Former assistant secretary of state for ARA, William D. Rogers, described how U.S. opinion of Allende changed as the United States became more aware of Cuban intelligence activities:

> My initial view [in 1970] was Allende was Allende, he was not Fidel redux, and we had to come to grips with him in his own terms. . . . I was proved wrong in the event because the Cubans got into Chile after the inauguration, in hordes. And it

> became much more, if you will, an extension of—with Allende, in the Chilean context—of Fidel than I had thought would be the case. I think I was surprised then and I am surprised now. . . . What remarkable influence the Cubans had in a sector of the coalition that supported Allende and on Allende himself.[165]

The natural question unanswered by Rogers's comment is when—and how much—this more negative impression of Cuban influence on Allende hardened the U.S. administration's outlook on Allende. The same CIA officers ran both the political action program and the intelligence-gathering mission against the military; thus, did they, perhaps, have difficulty abiding the rule barring discussion of a coup as Chile was evidently becoming a major Cold War battleground? Were the lines of this rule blurred by the increasing instability and violence in Santiago in the spring of 1973?

John Crimmins spoke of the trouble the State Department perceived with one particular CIA officer, Ted Shackley, when it came to staying away from coup plotting:

> We wanted the proper safeguards to be maintained. I had a real problem with Shackley, who I did not trust really. He had an interest in getting a Chilean involved who was, we were convinced, an extreme rightist and a dangerous activist. And we said "under no circumstances." Shackley was a bad actor, and I felt I had to keep careful tabs on him when he kept raising this Patria y Libertad group. I said to him, and the department agreed, "Under no circumstances are you to get involved with [Patria y Libertad]. Is there anything you do not understand about that?" There were times when we had to be more blunt.
>
> Shackley made us uneasy, and I think in this sort of situation where there were lots of subtle, or maybe, hedged-about circumstances, things that were not easy to deal with where we had to be careful, well, we were concerned that the Agency might be a little aggressive, especially during the Shackley period.[166]

It seems that Shackley, perhaps because of strong State Department pressure, did not succeed in his attempts to link the United States with the ultraright Patria y Libertad.[167] In his memoir, Shackley notes that some money did go to Patria y Libertad during the trucker strike, but "with the complete agreement of the Santiago Station and Ambassador Nathaniel Davis, it was agreed that this group was to be avoided like the plague."[168] But Shackley's admiring comments about the group's effectiveness in furthering the strike's impact and Crimmins's comments about Shackley's obduracy make it clear that Shackley did not so much "agree" with State as "submit" to its wishes.

State had such sway over the CIA's operations perhaps because it dominated Latin American policymaking at the time. As the British political section in Washington noted, "It is generally the case that policy on matters in which the president has a close interest (eg SALT, Europe, Indo-China) is made in the White House. In areas where the President has shown less interest (currently e.g. Africa, Latin America) policy is generally made in the State Department."[169] Unlike in October 1970, when Kissinger and Nixon were pushing the extreme options with apparently little concern for their implications, since November 1970 the State Department was calling the shots. Even Shackley agreed that "the level of coordination implied by this episode was the rule rather than the exception. . . . Gone was the compartmentation of Track II. Now all covert-action programs were fully discussed with the station, Ambassador Davis, and the Forty Committee."[170]

As CIA operations in Chile became more and more difficult, as Crimmins suggested, the desire to encourage the army into a coup remained among U.S. officers. But, as Crimmins further noted, daring men like Shackley were an exception to the otherwise reasonable men at Langley, such as the sensible and reliable William Broe. An undated CIA document likely from the first half of 1973, offered an assessment of U.S. options in Chile and noted that even supporting the PN was becoming untenable because the Nationalists, as well as some private-sector organizations, were "becoming increasingly prone to higher risk plans," which were not secure and over which the Agency had no influence. Perhaps reflecting Crimmins's opposition, the author of the document noted that operations in support of the PN "would almost certainly have to be undertaken without the concurrence of Ambassador Davis or the Department of State," and thus it was an option the CIA was not keen to undertake.[171] Not unusually, then, the CIA agreed with the State Department's restrictions and, like the drafter of this memo, Jack Devine, in no uncertain terms, refuted that coup scenarios ever evolved:

> You had an aggressive covert action designed to support the political dimension, then you had a collection task, as opposed

> to a covert action. There was no authority [to talk of a coup], and it was *gospel*. People can and do argue this, but from my vantage point, we had clear instructions not to foment or start coup planning with the military. Yes we supported truckers and other groups, but would that somehow lead to a clash, a coup, and so on? That is a question, but that is different than planning a coup. And it overestimates what you can do. It was more of a defensive game than an offensive game, trying to keep these institutions alive until the next election.[172]

Though many historians since have strongly disputed the point, many of Devine's arguments center on the presumption that it was necessary to support the opposition. All former U.S. government officers interviewed agreed that the outlook for continued democracy in Chile was grave, that support to the opposition was required, and that coup plotting with the army was rejected. "Yes, that is what I was convinced of," said Kissinger, adding, "It is absolutely absurd going around apologizing and defending your actions. . . . I am convinced it was necessary. All ideas of organizing a coup were rejected."[173] It must be noted that in this statement Kissinger is being specific: he is not denying that the United States opposed Allende or that the CIA ran covert actions in Chile but simply that the U.S. government attempted to organize a coup. Devine agreed with Kissinger: "The mission was to support and resist Allende's attempt to destroy the democratic institutions, the parties. I was comfortable with it and I remain comfortable with it today."[174]

Despite these statements rejecting a coup as a plan, in a memorandum to the State Department, William Colby, then-director of plans, described the situation with pragmatic clarity:

> The Santiago Station would not be working directly with the armed forces in an attempt to bring about a coup, nor would its support to the overall opposition forces have this as its objective. *Realistically, of course, a coup could result from increased opposition pressure on the Allende government* . . . [as] the broad consensus of the opposition appears to have the massive entrance of the military into the Allende government with real power as its present objective [italics added].[175]

That is, the U.S. government would not plan a coup, but still, a coup could result from U.S. covert action. The question that naturally follows, of course, is, how decisive was American support to the opposition in creating "pressure on the Allende government"? Was it an incremental addition to a natural and existing trend, as Devine suggests above? If this is so, its relative success as a covert action mission contrasts sharply with the October 1970 attempt to prevent Allende's inauguration, for which the reluctant CIA attempted to construct a coup out of thin air.

6

THE CIA AND ITT: THE AGENCY RESPONSE TO CORPORATE INTEREST

> *[John McCone] felt that there was already too much open talk in these circles which was filtering back to Chile. Even Frei had pointed out that publicized large-scale U.S. business support for his candidacy would be a kiss of death. On the basis of the risks and the apparent lack of security, he felt the U.S. "private sector" should not engage in political action in this Chilean election.*[1]
>
> —Minutes of a Special Review Group meeting, May 1964

In March 1972 famous Washington muckraker Jack Anderson published in his syndicated column, "The Washington Merry-Go-Round," a sensational allegation that the International Telephone and Telegraph Corporation (ITT) had constructed, in league with the CIA, a "bizarre plot to stop the 1970 election of leftist Chilean President Salvador Allende." As published in his later book, *The Anderson Papers*, Anderson alleged,

> The giant conglomerate was scheming to create financial chaos in Chile, to put pressure on the Chilean congress to keep Allende from power, and to organize a coup to take control of the government. Participating in the conspiracy were the CIA's clandestine services chief William V. Broe, and the ambassador to Chile, Edward Korry.[2]

These were serious accusations for two reasons: if they were true, the U.S. government was not only attempting to subvert a democracy but also doing so as the servant of corporate, not national, interest. The allegations had a seismic impact on a country growing increasingly disillusioned with the perceived opacity of foreign affairs and the war in Vietnam. As the editors of the *Washington Post* argued, "This is a charge so serious it is hard to see how anything less than a congressional investigation can dispose of it."[3]

The allegations, in fact, proved excellent fodder for the highly partisan Senate Foreign Relations Committee, chaired by Senator William J. Fulbright, which "asserted its paramount jurisdiction over intervention abroad" and voted to investigate.[4] The Senate committee's actions alone were sensational in that up to this point in the history of U.S. intelligence a congressional foreign relations committee had not exerted any influence over the CIA; rather congressional influence over the Agency was carried out by the House and Senate armed services committees and their military appropriations subcommittees. Perhaps sensing the history he might make, Fulbright wasted no time in letting loose one of his most ambitious and aggressive fellow senators and committee members, Senator Frank Church, an Idaho Democrat, by empowering him with the Subcommittee on Multinational Corporations. In time, Senator Church's investigations into ITT led both to the more serious Church committee investigation, which covered the full scope of the CIA's duties, and to a universal questioning of the Agency's policies and modalities. These investigations, in addition to inadvertently revealing many CIA methods and sources, brought an end to the older generation at Langley and to the laissez-faire attitude with which Congress traditionally provided oversight of its activities.[5] Moreover, they fueled the fire that was slowing burning under Nixon's presidency and that would eventually engulf him and the office of the president in general. Few would doubt that the errors of Nixon's presidency, and the scandal with which it ended, irrevocably changed the way Americans view the office of the president, and significantly eroded the trust they had historically given to that office as a matter of course.

If Anderson's accusations and evidence had such a great impact, one might assume that they were an accurate portrayal of the CIA's operations in Chile. In fact, as a careful analysis indicates, the ITT documents and Anderson's column contained far more sensation than fact. An appeal to recent document releases, as well as older congressional testimony, shows that the CIA and ITT did not in fact conspire to create economic chaos in Chile, nor did they combine to suborn the Chilean congress to any unconstitutional move against Allende. The ITT Corporation was not dictating programs to the CIA, and it does not seem that the corporation had the influence over the U.S. government that Anderson led the public to believe.

Yet Anderson's columns and subsequent book were not without their facts, and those facts remain extremely relevant when discussing the CIA and its covert actions of the 1970s. While the massive declassification undertaken over the last few years has made available the bulk of the State Department's, the CIA's, and the National Security Council's documents about Chile, there is little to give context or depth to these bureaucratic documents. So, unintentionally, the ITT documents released in 1972 by Anderson in his column and subsequent book provide insight into the CIA's functioning in one of its most debated and controversial operations—an intimate and well-informed view of CIA operations from *outside* the CIA. When viewed in parallel with declassified CIA and State Department papers, the ITT papers show a covert action policy *not* influenced by corporate interest but rather driven by an impatient chief executive. The CIA was no "rogue elephant," as U.S. Representative Otis Pike famously alleged.[6]

THE ITT CORPORATION

While it could be argued that multinational corporations and conglomerates have existed since the mists of economic antiquity, ITT stands as the prototypical modern, globalized corporation. Beginning as a small firm in the Virgin Islands, by 1970 it had grown—under the guidance of its mercurial president and chief executive, Harold Sydney Geneen—into the eighth-largest corporation in the United States, with about 450,000 employees in over sixty countries producing upwards of $7 billion in sales annually, with around $550 million in profits.[7] The corporation had always kept the majority of its assets outside of the United States, and it did this with a full realization of the potential profits—and losses—such a strategy held, for by doing so they avoided higher U.S. taxes and anti-trust restrictions, but stood to lose much should a subsidiary be nationalized or expropriated. To survive ITT had developed the resources and methods required to cajole, force, and manipulate policy in often Byzantine and brutal foreign political arenas, yet these tactics did not always suffice.

By 1970 ITT had lost two corporations when their host countries fell behind the iron curtain. The communist victory in China had cost ITT all its assets in the Shanghai Telephone and Electric companies, and Castro had seized the Cuban Telephone Co. from ITT, costing the conglomerate

$50.6 million, the largest loss ITT suffered before Chile elected Allende president. All in all, seven different communist regimes had by this time expropriated ITT property without compensation, and Geneen and the rest of his executives had a healthy fear of communist regimes. In Chile the fear was acute.

Since 1927 ITT had owned the Chilean Telephone Company (Chitelco), which by 1970 was valued at $153 million, and Allende's regime had marked communications infrastructure as one of the six areas of the economy targeted for rapid nationalization.[8] To smooth the operations of its foreign holdings (which in Chile also included hotels and telephone-directory companies), ITT had long maintained an office in Washington to lobby the U.S. government for beneficial policies. In 1964 this office had successfully pushed through the amendment on the U.S. Foreign Assistance Act now known as the Hickenlooper Amendment, which demanded that aid to any country that expropriated U.S. property be cut off. In 1970 ITT's Washington office, under the guidance of Vice President William R. Merriam, was set the task of preventing the expropriations of ITT assets in Chile.[9]

THE SCANDAL BREAKS

The news of ITT's collaboration with the CIA in Chile appeared, after the Anderson columns of March 21 and 22, 1972, in the pages of the *Washington Post* and several other papers across the United States. Director of Central Intelligence (DCI) Richard Helms considered the information in the Anderson columns so serious that he apparently tried to convince Anderson not to publish them, though admittedly such requests were fairly common in the era.[10] Not at first a front-page story, Anderson's "Washington Merry-Go-Round" column nevertheless caused a stir, especially so when the journalist released his source material to the government and the public. The accusations in his columns, backed by the documents, were stark and direct: ITT "dealt regularly with the Central Intelligence Agency" and the conglomerate and the Agency "were plotting together to create economic chaos in Chile."[11] To do this, ITT made "an offer to the White House to 'assist financially in sums up to seven figures.'" To ensure the forward movement of its schemes, Anderson asserts, ITT was assisted in Washington by William V. Broe, the CIA chief of Western Hemisphere Division, and apparently ITT men in Chile were included in the intimate details of Agency and embassy plotting in Santiago. Anderson added that the CIA as well as ITT was "pinning its waning hopes" on a plot developed by Chilean general Roberto Viaux.[12]

While some might have hoped to dismiss Anderson's column as idle anti-Agency gossip, the ITT memoranda released by the columnist seemed to entirely support his accusations. One of the most damning documents among Anderson's collection was a memorandum written on September 17, 1970, in which it is reported that on September 15, Ambassador Edward Korry received a message from the State Department giving him permission to do everything "short of a Dominican Republic-type action" to keep Allende from taking power. To this end, the memo continued, the Chilean army "has been assured full financial assistance by the U.S. military establishment."[13]

Anderson's article provided significant detail of the CIA's actions in Chile and discussed the CIA-ITT plan to support *El Mercurio*, the conservative and anti-Allende newspaper that was under threat from pro-Allende forces and which had even been threatened with closure and expropriation directly by one of Allende's lieutenants. But Anderson's accusations did not end with ITT's alleged links to covert action in Chile itself:

> ITT officials were in touch with William V. Broe, who was then director of the Latin American division of the CIA's Clandestine Services. They were plotting together to create economic chaos in Chile, hoping this would cause the Chilean army to pull a coup that would block Allende from coming to power.

Accordingly, "approaches continue to be made to select members of the Armed Forces in an attempt to have them lead some sort of uprising—no success to date."[14]

While the article gives some descriptive weight to some of these allegations (and many more column inches to independent ITT activities against Chile), they seem serious enough on their own—serious enough to act as a catalyst for a Senate investigation and to remain in the public mind for decades afterward. But while Anderson's column no doubt made good press, the question is, Was it accurate?

THE REALITY OF THE SCANDAL

To assess what the ITT memoranda actually say about CIA and U.S. government policy, one has to confirm their accuracy, and obtaining confirmation can be tricky when dealing with such scant information. The key questions in this assessment are, Did the two men reporting for ITT in Chile have any special knowledge of CIA actions, and if so, how detailed was that knowledge?

Historian Peter Kornbluh writes that ITT employee Bob Berrellez "repeatedly misled the Church subcommittee by denying any ITT contact with CIA officials in Chile."[15] Likewise, David Corn, in his book about CIA officer Ted Shackley, spends several pages expositing on the connection between Berrellez and his ITT colleague Hal Hendrix and the CIA station chief in Santiago, Henry Hecksher, as well as ITT's links in Washington to Shackley, Broe, and others at Langley.[16] But it is nearly impossible to cross-check Kornbluh's and Corn's accusations, which essentially imply that the CIA was working with, and at the behest of, a corporation. Most of the 1970 Santiago station personnel have passed away, and those who remain are not talking, at least on the record. While authors such as Kornbluh and Corn seem convinced of an ITT-CIA connection, none can offer any concrete proof of the connection and none can offer any explanation or give nuance to the connection's nature.

This leaves the inquisitive reader with only two rather indefinite ways of untying the knot—or at least confirming the solution provided by the two authors mentioned above—textual comparison and intuition. Likewise, the ITT-CIA link has two distinct parts: the connection in Washington and the connection in Santiago. Each part needs to be dealt with separately to be understood in context.

PART 1: WASHINGTON

During the congressional investigations of 1975, Senator Church, directing the investigating committee, concluded that in 1970 "U.S. Government policy prohibited covert CIA support to a single party or candidate, at the same time, the CIA provided advice to an American-based multinational corporation on how to furnish just such direct support."[17] This conclusion is based in large part on testimony that repeated allegations made by Anderson, who concluded "that ITT officials were in close touch with William V. Broe, who was then director of the Latin American division of the CIA's clandestine services. They were plotting together."[18] When Anderson's ITT memos are examined with reference to the CIA's own documents and more recent information, one can perceive a greater degree of nuance in the matter.

Cooperation between ITT and the CIA at the executive level had its origins in the Agency's "Old Boys Club," which included John McCone, a senior director of ITT who had previously been the DCI. Harold Geneen, ITT's CEO, using McCone's connections to his advantage, secured a meeting with President Nixon at the end of July 1970. Geneen's discussions with Nixon about the Alessandri campaign's finances and about Cuban funding for the Allende campaign persuaded the pliable president that channeling extra money to Alessandri's campaign was a matter for the CIA. In fact, a CIA memorandum following the meeting asked if "someone from [deleted] be willing to meet with [deleted] for a discussion on Chile?"[19]

Before his meeting with President Nixon, Geneen—a man called "a very *very* unpleasant freebooter . . . the kind of guy who thought Latin American governments should be manipulated and bought off" by senior State Department official John Crimmins[20]—met with Broe at the Sheraton-Carlton Hotel in Washington on July 16. During this meeting Geneen gave Broe a short history of ITT's involvement in Chile, which included the passage of funds from the conglomerate to the Christian Democratic Party (PDC) during the 1964 presidential election.[21] He went on to tell Broe that ITT wanted to pass funds to the Alessandri campaign during the 1970 election and hoped that the CIA might act either as a channel for funds or as adviser to ITT on the best way of channeling them itself. Broe, prepared by a WHD briefing memo, replied that the CIA "could not absorb the funds and serve as a funding channel" and had been advised "that the U.S. Government was not supporting any candidate but was most anxious that Allende not be elected." However, Broe promised Geneen that he would explore routes by which ITT could channel the funds by its own means.[22] He must also have assisted in getting Geneen his meeting with the president. Up to this point, the CIA was "highly impressed by ITT's professionalism," and the Santiago station expressed hopes that such professionalism would be maintained through the 1970 election. Always hoping for more corporate involvement in the presidential election campaign, the CIA had stepped outside the strict boundaries of the nonpartisan ruling of the 40 Committee to ensure the security of ITT's own funding channel to Alessandri.

The CIA move to support an outside organization like ITT was relatively bold, and the Agency's normal reticence to breach security protocol soon reasserted itself. "Since [deleted] 16 July meeting with Geneen [word deleted] we have determined," wrote Broe, "that the ITT election operation has not been closely held even within the company, contrary to what was I was led to believe."[23] To an Agency very heavily concerned with the repercussions of exposure of its operations in Chile, this lack of operational security must have caused much worrying. It seemed it did, as Broe's cable continues for another two pages discussing the nature and scope of the security compromise. Yet at this time, the CIA's Western Hemisphere Division concluded that ITT did not have information that could jeopardize the CIA's election operation, as "conversation with Geneen was limited to commenting on the integrity of the [word deleted] channel [already set up by ITT] and mild encouragement that ITT *et al* become involved in the election."[24] Still, Broe urged that the Santiago station limit its discussions with ITT's local representatives because if the CIA became heavily involved in the passage of funds from ITT/Chitelco to Alessandri's party, it risked both a breach of operational security as well as a breach of the nonpartisan stance in the election ordained from Washington. Neither option held consequences the Agency was happy to allow.[25]

Yet, within a short while, Broe was talking to E. J. Gerrity, ITT's senior vice president for public affairs, about CIA operations in Chile. What they discussed, however, vastly outshines the review of a funding channel in terms of seriousness: when they met on September 17, 1970, Allende had, two weeks earlier, won the presidential election with a slim plurality and awaited only the formality of the congressional confirmatory vote in October and an inauguration in November. The pressure on the White House from ITT was not small, and on September 12 Kissinger stated that he "had a call last night from McCone . . . [he] thinks it would be a catastrophe if we let [Chile] go."[26]

The CIA became more active in its discussions with ITT in the week following this call. In what can be viewed as phase 2 of the ITT revelations in the *Washington Post Merry-Go-Round*, Anderson disclosed the topic of these discussions: the CIA's attempt to convince ITT to participate in a plan to cause economic chaos in Chile that would force the army to prevent Allende's confirmation and inauguration. As quoted in Anderson's column, the memorandum seemed to reveal particularly sinister planning by the CIA. On September 29 Broe again met with Gerrity to present "suggestions based on recommendations from our representative on the scene and analysis in Washington."[27] This could mean that the Agency was taking orders from ITT, though this interpretation is eclipsed by Broe's suggestions. Gerrity wrote in a memo to Geneen,

> The idea presented, and with which I do not necessarily agree, is to apply economic pressure. . . . [Broe] indicated that certain steps were being taken but that he was looking for *additional help aimed at inducing economic collapse*. I discussed the suggestions with [ITT's VP of Latin American operations, Jack] Guilfoyle. He contacted a couple of companies who said they had been given advice which is directly contrary to the suggestions I received. [Italics added.][28]

Unfortunately, little in the CIA's files can corroborate the discussion between Gerrity and Broe, though its occurrence is not in doubt. In the CIA's own memoranda it is clear that they solicited the help of a corporation in the matter of wrecking the economy of another country, and this was a truly scandalous occurrence. Regardless of the CIA's intentions, ITT dismissed Broe's idea as unworkable and its own memoranda indicate that no move was made by the company to increase economic chaos in Chile because it had information "from other sources [that] indicates that there is a growing economic crisis in any case."[29] Whether or not the CIA carried on with the plan independently will be discussed later in this chapter.

PART 2: SANTIAGO

There is no doubt that the CIA, through C/WHD Broe, was in contact with the upper echelon of ITT in Washington. The nature of the ITT-CIA relationship in Chile, however, is perhaps a better indicator of whether the interaction can be considered a scandal. The first very clear implication of Anderson's allegations was ITT was working hand-in-hand with the CIA in Santiago as a sort of adjunct civilian operational arm of the ongoing covert actions in Chile's capital. Weighing the evidence makes clear that Hendrix and Berrellez had some contact with at least one CIA station officer, perhaps even Hecksher himself. Thus, the question needs to be more specific: Was CIA-ITT contact casual or secret, continuous or sporadic? Was it the case, as U.S. Ambassador Edward Korry reported, that some of the things going on around the embassy "were more appropriate to John Le Carré"?[30]

Agency documents suggest that the CIA-ITT relationship in Santiago was not longstanding. Before he went to speak with Geneen on July 16, 1970, Broe had been made prepared by WHD with a likely questions-and-answers memo. The last of the potential questions listed in the memorandum, "Are we currently in touch with ITT personnel in Chile?" is answered simply "no."[31]

The Agency's general policy, witnessed in Chile during the 1964 election, was to discourage private companies from getting involved in secret funding of political parties for fear that the companies were likely to be caught and exposed to general U.S. embarrassment. This policy was facing something of a reality check in 1970. Faced with a massive loss in funds in Chile, private U.S. corporations were making independent moves toward supporting the PDC and other parties. As the Santiago station reported to CIA headquarters, this was a trend the CIA would unlikely be able to stop:

> [We] doubt they can be dissuaded, coordinated or channelled. Approx 800 million dollars of investments are at stake. Also, most American corporations believe that the U.S. embassy has done nothing in the past and will do nothing in future to stave off disaster. Short of telling them what is being done, ref arguments would carry little weight.

"More doom and gloom," scribbled Broe in the cable margin.[32] Looking at the odds, the Agency must have decided it was in U.S. interest to assist the biggest of the corporations in as unobtrusive a way as possible. If the corporations could not be stopped, they could at least be shepherded. The July 16 meeting in Washington thus initiated the Agency-ITT relationship in Santiago, a relationship meant to prevent, via CIA guidance, a massive uproar that would occur should the ITT be caught passing funds.

Memoranda written in the days following the Broe-Gerrity meeting show that the CIA conducted a security review of a Chilean who could help ITT move funds to Alessandri discreetly. The Santiago station reported back to Langley that "with advice of our Chief of Station"[33] a local ITT representative had made contact with a member of Alessandri's entourage and had made an offer of $300,000, which had been accepted. "Station midwifery [was] neither mentioned nor implied [to the Alessandri contact]."[34] A subsequent review of the contact, written sometime after April 1972, revealed that only three or four individuals were witting to the ITT-Alessandri transaction. "None of these [deleted] individuals have ever been used operationally by the Agency," and "there is no indication that these individuals were aware of the advisory role played by the Agency in this funding."[35]

Thus, beginning in July 1970, the CIA station in Santiago met with ITT representatives in Santiago for the purpose of passing funds. These representatives were Berrellez and Hendrix, two former newspapermen who, as confirmed by ITT's papers, were the conglomerate's men in Chile at the time. A review of the ITT memoranda made public by Jack Anderson reveals a vast amount of intelligence reporting by Berrellez and Hendrix that hints they had access to the secret parts of the embassy, if not access to the CIA station itself.

In one of the first ITT documents released is a description of the Frei reelection gambit, information that is hardly scandalous and that certainly did not emerge from Agency sources. The gambit was a matter of public record and Alessandri's offer was actually placed in *El Mercurio*. A comment in the same memorandum, however, aroused significant furor in the United States when Anderson secured publication:

> Late Tuesday night (September 15) Ambassador Edward Korry finally received a message from State Department giving him the green light to move in the name of President Nixon. The message gave him maximum authority to do all possible—short of a Dominican Republic-type action—to keep Allende from office.[36]

Did any cable go to Santiago on September 15 giving a "green light"? One transcript of a call between Kissinger and Nixon shows that by September 12 the president and his adviser were interested in more aggressive action in Chile. In their conversation, Nixon asks the latter to "send a back channel to Korry" and for the CIA to get a man to Santiago to make "an appraisal of what the options are." This was necessary not because of any rift between Korry and the State Department—though Korry never had a strong or necessarily cordial relationship with his official State Department superiors—but because the president believed Korry was "a Kennedy Democrat" who "may have wanted to put us on the spot."[37] This statement might reflect some latent regret Nixon had for renewing Korry's political appointment as ambassador.

Two days after the Nixon-Kissinger phone call, on September 14, Secretary of State William P. Rogers counseled caution in Chile and told Kissinger, "I have been disturbed by Korry's telegrams. They sound frenetic and somewhat irrational. . . . I think we've got to be sure he acts with discretion."[38] We know that Rogers did not encourage the embassy to exploit its relationship with ITT; indeed, he urged caution and worried about what the "frenetic" Korry might do. The only cable sent by State to Korry on September 15 tells the ambassador to increase his contacts with the military to ensure the flow of information but reminds him, "Your role is thus a very delicate one and you will be required to walk a fine line. We do not want you to get out in front and we do not want to 'take over.'"[39] This is hardly a green light. Furthermore, it is unlikely that a green light for joint operations with ITT came from the embassy at all. As Ambassador Korry noted in an interview, he threw Berrellez and Hendrix "out of the Embassy. I gave everybody instructions to have nothing more to do with them."[40] Thus, the go-ahead must have come from Washington or somewhere, at least, outside of the Santiago station.

What further steals credibility from the assertion that ITT's information regarding the State Department's green light came directly from the embassy is a later paragraph in the same ITT memo:

> Ambassador Korry, before getting the go-signal from Foggy Bottom, clearly put his head on the block with his extremely strong messages to State. He also, to give him due credit, started to maneuver with the CD, the Radical and National parties and other Chileans—without State authorization—immediately after the election results were known. He has never let up on Frei, to the point of telling him to "put his pants on."[41]

Several indicators in the paragraph show its origins to be from a source outside the Santiago Station. In a statement written after the scandal was revealed, Korry points out that he met with President Frei only once after the election, for about thirty minutes, and at this meeting on September 12 at Viña del Mar he served only as translator to several other diplomats.[42] Otherwise, he had minimized all contact with the president or any other political party. That he stopped all meetings is corroborated by the September 12 telephone transcript, in which Kissinger informs the president about Korry's recent actions in Chile, including the fact that "Korry has stopped all appointments unless they come to him."[43] The "pants" comment is likely never to have been uttered.

None of this is meant to ignore the very real measures that the Nixon White House took to undermine the congressional vote to elect Allende. On this point again, however, the ITT cable has its facts and figures wrong. The first meeting to decide on a hard covert action in Chile occurred on September 15 when President Nixon called DCI Helms, Kissinger, and Attorney General John Mitchell into the Oval Office to give executive direction for U.S. action toward Allende. During this meeting the president launched Operation FU/Belt, otherwise known as Track II,[44] and thus also prompted memoranda on September 16 and 17 with "green light" potential. Thus the ITT cable is wrong in stating that Korry received the green light: From the start, Korry was not privy to Track II information. Furthermore, the first few telegrams sent to Santiago for Track II did not authorize any movement; instead they noted the president's desire "to prevent [Allende] from coming to power or unseat him" and requested a report on the feasibility of this project by September 18.[45]

So the question remains: Who was the source of the "green light"? One can largely dispense with the explanation given at the Senate investigation of ITT—that the source was an associate of President Frei—

although this does not automatically mean that the source came directly from the embassy or that the ITT men did not have contacts with, or report information from, Chilean sources.[46] Essentially, it seems, the ITT men made reference to generally true information that had been taken out of its original form by one or two removes.

Certainly, either Berrellez or Hendrix was the vehicle for ITT's funding to the Alessandri campaign, and the two worked with the Santiago station likely during that action alone. A CIA internal audit of contact with ITT throughout the Allende period notes, "ITT representatives [deleted] maintained close contact with the Santiago Station throughout the 1970 electoral campaign and consulted with the Station in ITT's proposals to support Alessandri."[47] They likely associated with station officers only with regard to funding Alessandri or perhaps as cutouts for information passed from the National Party (PN) about the reelection gambit. In their meetings with CIA officers, they would have gathered that a major operation was afoot, and perhaps a station member indicated the presence of a strong presidential directive. The inaccuracy and sparseness of their information overall, however, does not indicate full intimacy with the CIA plan, merely awareness of its existence.

Giving the details of an extremely secret operation to former reporters, however friendly and familiar, would have been an inexcusable breach of security for professional intelligence officers. While this conclusion that ITT was not given secret information by the CIA does not at first appear significant, it calls into question the Church committee's conclusions about the CIA-ITT relationship and, further, the conclusions drawn about more serious allegations against the CIA.

One possibility, at least, has not been explored in any context: Were Berrellez and Hendrix nonofficial cover agents? As one CIA officer described, "When I hear of a corporate man associated with a secret operation, the first thing that comes to my mind is NOC." According to this same officer, it is commonly understood that corporations that allow the CIA to operate NOC officers within their organizations are offered a quid pro quo: the corporations provide cover, while the CIA hands over intelligence that might benefit business. Such an NOC officer is a CIA employee bound by the same requirements of secrecy as any other officer under official cover.[48]

Since the CIA considered ITT to be particularly leaky, would NOC officers in its (apparent) employment hand over important and sensitive information? The garbled versions of real information repeated in the ITT memoranda might be a reflection of the downgraded political intelligence an NOC officer might pass on to his host company. But even if Berrellez and Hendrix were NOC officers, ITT would have had little input in or control over U.S. covert operations in Chile. If anything, were Berrellez and Hendrix NOC officers, the corporation was being used, if benignly, by the CIA. In any case, no hard evidence available at the moment suggests these men—whose names *also* appear frequently in the Agency's documents regarding Cuba—were actually employed by the CIA. While the NOC officer theory, which would account for the incredible entrée in the CIA these two ITT employees enjoyed, is compelling, it is currently unprovable, and if true it would do little to alter the facts of the CIA's interaction with the ITT Corporation.

THE VIAUX PLOT

The most controversial part of U.S. involvement in Chile's 1970 election was the assassination of Gen. René Schneider, the commander in chief of the Chilean army, on October, 22, 1970. On this topic too Anderson's columns draw conclusions greater than the sum of the information revealed in the CIA's and ITT's documents.

As discussed in chapter 4, former brigadier general Roberto Viaux was dismissed from the Chilean military after leading an aborted army revolt in October 1969. By early October 1970, Viaux had begun using his stature among junior officers to plot a coup against the newly elected Allende government. Knowledge of Viaux's plotting was widespread, and "rumors that he would trigger a coup on October 9 or October 10 were rampant in Chile and spilled over into Buenos Aires, Argentina," noted Hendrix in a cable to ITT on October 16, 1970.[49] The CIA's desperate scramble to comply with presidential directives had up to that point produced little of value, as almost all Agency and State Department officers had noted "the idea of a military overthrow had not occurred to us as a feasible solution."[50]

The ITT reporting on the Schneider assassination was relatively good, though frequently off in timing. Viaux was first mentioned in an ITT document on October 16, in a long situation report filed by Hal Hendrix for E. J. Gerrity back in Washington. Noting that rumors about Viaux's plotting were rife, Hendrix's report also mentioned that the general likely did not have sufficient support for a coup: "Viaux has been conferring with high-ranking and junior officers about taking some action to prevent Allende from becoming President. He has pledges of support from several, but unfortunately not from any key troop commanders, at least not to our knowledge."[51] This report fairly closely matches information cabled by the Santiago station to Langley: "COS met with [a false-flag officer] who said he had talked with General Viaux, and as a consequence is convinced that Viaux has no military support."[52] The CIA cable was sent six days before Hendrix's report.

As discussed in chapter 4, one of the most controversial aspects of the Schneider assassination was Kissinger's October 16 message to Viaux requesting that the coup be canceled. Kissinger's message was reworded by the CIA station and passed to Viaux by a false flag officer. Here we have a strong link between the CIA station and the ITT men in Chile. The ITT memo of October 16 states:

> It is a fact that word was passed to Viaux from Washington to hold back last week. It was felt that he was not adequately prepared, his timing was off, and he should "cool it" for a later, unspecified date. Emissaries pointed out to him that if he moved prematurely and lost, his defeat would be tantamount to a "Bay of Pigs in Chile." . . . Viaux was given oral assurances he would receive material assistance and support from the U.S. . . . [but] friends of Viaux subsequently reported Viaux was inclined to be a bit skeptical about only oral assurances.[53]

Strikingly similar to the CIA's cable, the ITT memorandum is sufficient to convince most readers of an intimate relation between the CIA and ITT in Santiago. The final sentence of the paragraph, however, and the time lag between the first CIA memorandum and the ITT memorandum indicate that the information was likely passed either through Chilean contacts or through a one-time chat with a sympathetic CIA official.

ITT saw clearly that the result of the assassination was not to be of benefit for those who opposed Allende's ratification as president. With Schneider out of the way, the army chief of staff, Gen. Carlos Prats, would be promoted to commander in chief of the army, and Prats (later assassinated in Argentina by Pinochet's dreaded National Intelligence Directorate [DINA]) was as firmly constitutionalist as General Schneider. As Hendrix commented to Gerrity,

> We will continue to monitor the situation. Whether it will develop into any military action remains to be seen, but at this stage it seems doubtful with General Prat [*sic*] now in command. . . . Prat supported Schneider in his attitude toward General Roberto Viaux, who had attempted to spark a military coup

> earlier. Prat does not like Viaux personally. As far as we can determine, Prat will display the same loyalty to Frei as Schneider did in the past.[54]

At the same time that the ITT men made this accurate prediction, the CIA continued to hope for an eleventh-hour coup.[55]

The information *not* mentioned in the ITT telegrams is also revealing. Gen. Camilo Valenzuela, allegedly a coconspirator with Viaux and one of the other men with whom the CIA was plotting, is not mentioned at all by ITT. This suggests that ITT was not fully aware of Track II. The information is cumulative: Hendrix and Berrellez certainly knew the CIA men in Chile and likely associated with them on occasion. They were not, however, part of the plot to overthrow Allende. Regardless, Anderson's columns about the fictitious ITT-CIA connection succeeded in revealing to the American public the CIA's covert operation against Allende.

THE SENATE INVESTIGATION OF ITT

The rumors started by Anderson's columns prompted a break in the unspoken agreement between the Agency and Congress whereby the CIA enjoyed relatively lax scrutiny from the combined legislative body. In the early 1970s, a congressional committee to oversee intelligence did not exist; this function was covered largely by the House and Senate armed services committees. As ITT began to appear in newspaper headlines across the country, however, the public, already angered by the Vietnam War and the excesses of the Nixon administration, seemed to push Congress toward a more zealous stance. In 1972 the Democratic senator from Idaho, Frank Church, set up a Subcommittee on Multinational Corporations of the powerful Senate Committee on Foreign Relations, to follow up disclosures of ITT's interventions in Chile and to investigate how big companies were influencing or forming foreign policy. "The multi-national corporation is a relatively new phenomenon," noted Church, apparently ignoring the likes of well-established companies like IBM, Ford, General Motors, and the United Fruit Company, and he suspected such corporations were unduly influencing government.[56] ITT's involvement in U.S. operations in Chile "is not a question of private or public morality. What concerns us here is a major issue of foreign policy for the United States," he said,[57] mirroring the *Washington Post* editorial comment that President Nixon "stands charged in what is purported to be an authentic ITT document, of personally approving an attempt [to keep Allende from power]."[58]

Apparently under pressure from the Nixon White House, Church agreed not to hold hearings on ITT until after the 1972 presidential election, though in September 1972 members of his staff started to conduct interviews with ITT employees, CIA officers, and other officials from the State Department and the NSC.[59] This put the CIA in an interesting position: it could keep its collective mouth shut, in which instance whatever was said in Anderson's *The Washington Merry-Go-Round* would go unchallenged, or it could explain the allegations, in which instance more secret operations would be revealed. The Agency, the DCI, and the administration as a whole thus faced a no-win situation.[60] The hearings commenced at the beginning of February 1973.

From the beginning of the hearings the subcommittee seemed most concerned with the "scheme to create economic chaos." Senators Church and Clifford Case, firing questions at John McCone, suggested that the memo from Berrellez and Hendrix was ITT policy, reflecting CIA policy and therefore U.S. government policy. McCone reacted first against the suggestion that ITT wanted economic chaos, for as a corporation it had a duty to stay in business, and that to create an economic crisis would undo its raison d'être. Answering in his capacity as a former DCI, McCone said,

> Now I understand that various ideas were generated at the staff levels of the CIA. They were never approved by Mr. Helms, never were submitted to [the 40 Committee] and, therefore, were not policy. This must be clearly understood; that is the difference between staff thinking and policy determination.[61]

Broe explained that the approach was based on the "thesis that additional deterioration in the economic situation" could influence Christian Democrat senators to vote against Allende, as was their right, but that the thesis quickly proved to be impracticable.[62] Charles Meyer, undersecretary of state for inter-American affairs (ARA), likewise offered the opinion that "one of the problems facing this distinguished committee . . . is the distinction between policy and examinations of feasibility." He continued:

> Mr. Broe . . . explored with Mr. Gerrity the action and reaction within Chile, which he clearly stated, of an advance of the economic deterioration which was going to occur anyway, as a potential effect on the congressional support or non-support

of Dr. Allende. He explored it, they brainstormed. Had it been adopted, it would have been a change in [the official] policy. It . . . disappeared.[63]

The Frei reelection gambit also received a degree of attention. Hendrix himself pointed out that this plan was common knowledge in Santiago and that references to it in ITT documents did nothing to show that the corporation was actively plotting with the CIA to manipulate the Chilean congress. The gambit was a domestic event that ITT had no role in instigating and no influence over at all and that in any case was perfectly legal, if perhaps untraditional, under the Chilean constitution. Broe added that the gambit was "of great interest at the time and we were all watching to see if there was any feasibility to it," but when the Agency realized the plot was impractical, ceased actions in support of it. It was merely an investigation into a natural event in domestic politics abandoned as easily as it was picked up.

As historian Mark Falcoff has explained, in an operational sense no coordinated ITT-CIA plan to bribe the Chilean congress or create a financial crisis ever existed.[64] There were, indeed, large bank withdrawals by the Chilean public following the election on September 4, but these were born of legitimate fears of Allende, his well-stated expropriation agenda, and his plan to drastically lower interest rates. In his testimony to Congress, Broe emphasized that the CIA hoped only to build on this existing trend,[65] and several others, including Berrellez, reported that neither the CIA nor any U.S. company ever closed or caused a run on a Chilean bank.[66]

As for ITT's reason for talking to the government in the first place, William Merriam, ITT's man in charge of the Washington office, commented that ITT's approaches to Nixon and Kissinger were "just to let anyone who would listen, in government, know that ITT stood to lose a bundle."[67] In most cases, as with ITT's initial contact to Viron Vaky at the NSC, the government disregarded the corporation's attempt to influence policy.[68]

The hearing testimony showed that the participants in the operations believed that, if their actions were questionable, they were still legal. Nonetheless, the Senate investigation into this matter—as well as other established matters such as the CIA's funding of Alessandri and of *El Mercurio*—was enough to provoke a reaction in Chile and gave the Allende government the excuse it required to expropriate ITT's Chilean holdings without compensation as retribution for the company's "imperialist actions."[69] It did not matter what had actually happened, only how it looked.

The matter of ITT's expropriation requires further comment. Allegations that ITT provoked its own expropriation through its efforts to block Allende, as Peter Kornbluh has asserted, ignore the reality of expropriations under Allende. By 1973 the Allende government had multiplied tenfold the number of the Chilean firms under government control, placing well over 90 percent of the Chilean gross domestic product in the government's hands.[70] It is doubtful that Allende would have left Chitelco, Chile's primary phone company, unnationalized, as communications firms were listed specifically in the Unidad Popular (UP) manifesto as targets of expropriation.[71] What the ITT scandal did, however, is provide the Allende government with an internationally recognized reason to expropriate the company, a reason that the United States could not bring to the Paris Club or any other organization for review and that alleviated the U.S. Overseas Private Investment Corporation (OPIC) from paying out on the ITT insurance policy. Ultimately, while Anderson might have saved the U.S. taxpayer $500 million, that same amount was lost to American investors.

THE ITT EVIDENCE

For all their lack of discretion in intelligence affairs, ITT's officers and directors had an appreciation of conditions in Chile, of international economics, and of the relations between the two. In the Church subcommittee investigations, testimony from several ITT officials, including board member and former DCI McCone, indicated that ITT predicted months before the CIA that Allende would win the election.[72] An examination of declassified documents shows that neither the CIA nor the State Department had predicted an Allende victory until July or August 1970, less than a month before the election.[73] In a recent interview John Crimmins argued that ARA realized Allende had a *chance* for victory all along but was not sufficiently moved by the prospect to back any significant covert action. Such covert action, if it had failed, might have had negative long-term effects on U.S. diplomacy in Latin America, and this outweighed the negative aspects of a six-year Allende presidency.[74] The ITT board of governors, in contrast, at their monthly meeting in June 1970, expressed a unanimous belief that Allende would indeed triumph.[75] When McCone informed DCI Helms about this verdict, Helms indicated that the opinion was not supported by the 40 Committee. Allende's narrow victory justified ITT's initial fears, while it highlighted the general failure of the U.S. intelligence establishment in Chile, including the Bureau of Intelligence and Research (INR) and the CIA, to adequately weigh the chance of Allende's victory at the polls.

ITT also did not fully share the belief that an Allende government would immediately produce the total communist dictatorship that the CIA, as well as Korry, initially predicted. While acknowledging the lack of action by the Chilean army after Schneider's assassination, ITT concluded,

> The election of Allende by congress pulled the plug [*sic*] from under the anaemic Chilean economy. Without help from Washington, Allende will be forced to turn to the communists and Moscow. The Russians don't want another Tito on their hands. In order to fortify their hold, the communists will have to start tampering with the congress, the trade unions and the military. This will invite some serious troubles for the communists.[76]

This was indeed an accurate prediction. During a recent interview, a former Santiago station CIA officer, present in the capital when the Chilean armed forces overthrew the president, explained his appreciation of the military's motivation for overthrowing the Allende government and noted that the army believed that the institution of the army "outranked the constitution and the president and the democratic process—for the good of the institution they had to take the coup plotting out of the dark."[77] This quote represents thought popular several years after the Allende election. While, three years before Allende's overthrow, ITT was predicting an eventual coup before a Marxist state could be established, the CIA (if not the calmer State Department) continued to shrilly predict the rapid progression of communist oppression.

The ITT scandal itself offers valuable insight on the CIA's tactical thinking in Chile. "The Station has no mechanism which could render covert support to Tomic," read one CIA document, "*and has stressed the desirability of permitting Chilean voters to choose their president without outside assistance* [italics added]."[78] Yet, at the same time, the CIA was relatively quick to "encourage" (in the CIA's words) ITT to contribute funds to the Alessandri and PN campaigns in the election. Why the discrepancy? While no clear explanation is in the papers, it is likely that the CIA's arguments are sincere and reflect the belief in *its own* ability to affect the outcome of the election. Nevertheless, all along the CIA had been dismissive of Alessandri's and the PN's appeals for money because it did not believe that the U.S. government should finance Alessandri's campaign, a duty best carried out by members of the local business community, whom the CIA believed were too apathetic overall. To the CIA, the local business community included ITT's majority-owned Chitelco phone company. Part of the problem, which CIA planning did not factor in, was that Chitelco, trying desperately to avoid expropriation (a clear promise of Allende), *could not be seen* to pass money to the PN or the opposition press. Thus, it was a death-or-glory scenario for ITT: sit idle and let a victorious Allende expropriate Chitelco or move to prevent an Allende victory by covert passage of funds, which if discovered would help an Allende victory and speed expropriation. From ITT's perspective it made perfect sense to accept the CIA's help, and from the CIA side it made sense to keep the corporation from getting itself into trouble—trouble that would affect the entire anti-Allende effort—only for something it was going to do regardless of CIA help, which amounted to little more than advice on people the company could contact.[79]

ITT's cables also reveal who in the government apparatus dealing with Chile was for or against supporting Alessandri and even who was in favor of blocking Allende at all. The Kissinger-Nixon telephone transcript from September 12 adds some support to the theory that Ambassador Korry and ARA were less than sanguine about trying to block Allende. In the September 12 conversation, Kissinger states, "Latin America Bureau at State is against doing anything."[80] This statement first dismisses that Korry told Frei "to put his pants on" as alleged in the Hendrix report and second shows how the State Department and the ambassador were in agreement that Chile should be left largely to its own devices. It adds weight to the argument that the origin of the CIA's Track II operation lay firmly with "Nixon's aberrational and hysterical decision" in favor of an extreme covert action and against the wait-and-see approach counseled by the State Department and, less stridently, by the CIA.[81]

Recent comments by many of the players involved offer fairly blithe verdicts on the effect of the Church subcommittee investigation. Vaky said, "I think it just stirred things up but I do not think it was taken seriously. It was not taken seriously by Henry [Kissinger]. It just fed people's anxieties." Continuing, Vaky noted,

> I do not think it bothered Henry. Henry was just worried about Cold War and balance of power, those sorts of things. Nixon may have been, because . . . people supporting him were having their interests cut, [and] this probably fed his alarm, but even in this case I think the real concern is how [Chile] fit into the whole Cold War picture.

He later added, "what really disturbed the president and [Kissinger] and the government in general was, Where does this fit into the strategic balance of power, the bipolar world?"[82]

Corporate influence was not a consideration. Kissinger, speaking for himself, noted, "You have to see all of this in the Vietnam context. Opponents of Vietnam were trying to prove that this was a criminal government, and that everything it did all over the world was covert. Covert operations did not have a dirty name in those days; they were highly classified but were perceived as daring. So, I do not believe I focused on ITT."[83] Peter G. Peterson, Nixon's aide for international economic affairs, gave further corroboration of this opinion to the Subcommittee on Multinational Corporations when he stated that he did not take the ITT program seriously and that "if one reads what actually came out of [the January 1972 NSC review] . . . there is certainly no relationship that I can see between the recommendations of ITT and the administration's decision" on economic policy in Chile.[84]

Nixon's comments, however, might still be viewed as a little disingenuous: the ITT scandal and subsequent Senate hearings undoubtedly had people in the White House and the CIA quite concerned. On the most basic level, the hearings finished off Nixon's "cool and correct" approach to the Chile problem, and (as the CIA thought from the beginning) the exposure of ITT's involvement gave Allende the public justification to attack the United States, "whose preferred arms [against Latin American independence] were the CIA and U.S. economic integration in Latin America."[85] The "cool and correct" approach was meant to avoid giving Allende an attacking point that might allow him to strengthen his hold on power. ITT gave this tool to Allende in spades; as the Chilean president later declared, while the United States did not attack Chile with open hostility or arms, it was "on the contrary a sinuous, subterranean, always oblique attack, but one not therefore less harmful for Chile."[86] Even better, the ITT scandal showed how the United States exploited its economic tools to subdue Latin America. It was the perfect propaganda tool for Allende. And it was propaganda that the United States could not prevent Allende from using, regardless of its actual level of involvement with ITT.

The scandal had serious domestic political ramifications as well. The Subcommittee on Multinational Corporations hearings were only a precursor to the much more serious Church committee investigations of 1975. Certainly in the long run, the ITT scandal led to a sea change in the way that the CIA operated and the manner in which oversight was conducted. The old, easy way of running business in Langley and, more important, the 40 Committee were coming to an end. This was probably to the long-run benefit of the Agency, as the hearings emphasized the need for a more prescribed cycle of covert action authorization to be established and followed.

Clearly such an authorization cycle was not in place from September 4 to October 26, 1970, during which time the CIA rushed—under a legal but amoral presidential edict—to find *any* method, short of assassination, to stop Allende's inauguration. And because the panic to stop Allende proved detrimental to U.S. and Agency interests in the long run and, if successful, would have been of doubtful benefit in the short run, it is hard to see why such fast and loose operations were believed to be worthwhile in the first place. The ITT documents, regardless of their sometimes flimsy facts, revealed a CIA operation that many in the United States were unwilling to accept at the time or any time since, i.e., tampering with the constitutional process of a foreign democracy. In this sense, the ITT scandal, for all its hyperbole, marks the watershed in the public perception of intelligence that began in the early 1970s and largely persists to this day.

7

THE CAMPAIGN ENDS: THE FALL OF THE ALLENDE GOVERNMENT

I am not the president of all Chileans. I am not a hypocrite who says so.

—President Salvador Allende, reflecting on his limited mandate, at a Public Rally, January 17, 1971

Estas son mis últimas palabras y tengo la certeza de que mi sacrificio no sera en vano, tengo la certeza de que, por los menos, sera una leccíon moral que castigará la felonía, la cobardía y la traición.[1]

—President Salvador Allende, *Last Words*, September 11, 1973

When Allende's government was overthrown on September 11, 1973, many in both Chile and America believed that the Americans had been the crucial ingredient in, and perhaps the actual instigators of, the coup. This belief was the product of faulty logical reasoning: because of the U.S. government's posture against the Allende government, his demise *must* have been orchestrated by the U.S. government. Indeed, this correlation is not all that far-fetched, at least on the surface, for it is clear that the U.S. government, as led by Richard Nixon and Henry Kissinger, sought to thwart Allende's and the Unidad Popular's political trajectory. Both were also happy to see the end of Allende. All these circumstances—plus liberal amounts of supposition and conspiracy theory—seemed sure proof of American complicity, and this belief has gone unchallenged since the coup.

Authors such as William Robinson in his book *Promoting Polyarchy* and coauthors James Petras and Morris H. Morley in their book *The United States and Chile: Imperialism and the Overthrow of the Allende Government* espouse the belief that the United States "guided Pinochet and his cohorts in their takeover" or was responsible for "orchestrating the 1973 overthrow."[2] Robinson and others further contend that the U.S. destabilized the Chilean government through an "invisible blockade," which made the coup inevitable.[3] The U.S. government has done little to dispel this belief, which is still widespread today, and indeed, the main source for these books is the partisan and purposefully ambiguous Church committee report, from which many authors have taken the few facts known about the 1973 coup and merely insinuated or extrapolated American complicity and responsibility for Allende's ouster.

One needs to look no further than Christopher Hitchens's article "The Case against Henry Kissinger, Part 2" to see the weakness of the U.S. complicity argument. Hitchens quotes an American naval attaché—"Chile's coup d'état was nearly perfect"—to "prove" American involvement in the coup. He assumes that because the coup was well executed the United States was complicit in it.[4] Most Chileans, military officers especially, find this inference insulting.

The record seems to indicate something different from the widely accepted conspiracy theory. Not only was the CIA not involved in the coup, the evidence suggests, but the Agency also failed in its intelligence collection task in Chile. So studiously did the CIA seek to avoid appearing as though it was promoting a coup that it failed, because of the lack of contact with the military that this discretion demanded, to accurately predict its occurrence. Likewise, the CIA was not aware of the nature of the new military government and it did not have any contact with Chilean general and junta president Augusto Pinochet.

Thus, a careful look at the U.S. files on Chile points to a less sensational and certainly more confused conclusion. The evidence indicates that the CIA had only peripheral input into the coup that killed Allende on September 11, 1973. While the CIA certainly acted to support opposition groups, it was not the main agent of the coup and indeed lacked sufficient grip on the levers of power within Chile to affect the course or result of the building political pressure on Allende. The CIA, in short, had much less power to alter events in Chile than many, then and since, have supposed. Far from being able to steer events in the direction it desired, the CIA was limited, by caution and by aim, to observing and occasionally bolstering trends of domestic origin.

MORE SOCIAL UNREST

While the concerned U.S. government officers seemed sure of their program of action in Chile, the situation in that country was becoming less and less predictable as Allende's government progressed toward its third year. To break the truckers' strike, the Chilean president had been forced to make a controversial decision and, on October 25, 1972, called senior armed forces officers into an emergency national security cabinet led by the army commander in chief, Gen. Carlos Prats. The truckers returned to work in November, and the atmosphere in Chile cooled significantly as the summer approached.

Nonetheless, the long-term effects of the military cabinet were negative, as described by Paul Sigmund: "It accelerated the politicization of the military and undermined the position of those like Prats who favored the maintenance of constitutionalism and civilian rule."[5] Certainly the entry of the generals into cabinet helped to increase the polarization rampant in Chilean politics. From the Left, the generals were viewed as enemies within the citadel who were blocking the Unidad Popular program (by failing to override the judiciary, or the Contraloría, when it contradicted the government). From the Right, the generals were seen as lending legitimacy to a government that was acting in an illegal fashion.[6] The armed forces, the traditionally neutral arbiters of Chilean political life, were now coming under great pressure from both sides of the political spectrum.

The government's loss of control of the people was evident on the streets of Santiago and even in Chile's neighboring states. It became increasingly obvious that Cuban security agents were operating in the country, and that Allende's government was supporting, however indirectly, the insurgency in Bolivia.[7] As noted in chapter 5, the Allende regime had provided open support for the Bolivian rebel group Ejército de Liberación Nacional (ELN), the Argentine Partido Revolucionario de los Trabajadores (PRT), and Ejército Revolucionario del Pueblo (ERP). These, along with Peru's Tupamaros and other revolutionary groups, benefited from safe haven in Chile and weapons made in illegal but tolerated Movimiento de Izquierda Revolucionario (MIR) factories.[8] Further, the CIA had collected ample evidence of large "street brigades" of pro-UP youth armed with Cuban weapons (brought in via the Grupo de Amigos Personales [GAP], which was staffed by many MIR members)[9] and was aware of right-wing groups creating similar youth gangs.[10] The UP government was unwilling to curtail MIR's activities, and some parts of the government even encouraged the group's excesses.[11]

Internal Chilean political deterioration mirrored the country's deterioration in economic security. Another set of strikes began in late July 1973, this time encompassing such diverse groups as engineers, doctors, peasants, and laborers.[12] As described by the Rettig Commission—Chile's post-dictatorship National Commission on Truth and Reconciliation—opposition to Allende from within the UP itself was pushing for the "armed path," while the political opposition, in Congress and in the form of civil organizations, was following a policy of "ungovernability" to force the UP to negotiate, postpone, or give up aspects of its social charter.[13] As these two forces collided, the result was total chaos. Miguel Otero, founder of the National Party (PN) and staunch anti-UP activist, commented that in Chile "from July until September [1973] you knew when you were going out of your house but you didn't know if you were going to be able to come back! There were riots everywhere, disturbances, and so on. Nobody worked."[14]

Contributing to the chaos was a steep decline in quality of life. The UP's breakneck land-redistribution program was a disaster in which undercapitalized and inefficient small estates or cooperatives replaced the *latifundios*—the large Chilean estates, many of them in the same families for centuries—that were themselves never very efficient to begin with. While land redistribution had begun under the Frei government with American assistance, Allende sped the process past any pace to which the farms could adapt, and this process was made worse by the UP's price controls, which removed any incentive for increased production or investment.[15] Thus food was in short supply. Chile, a net exporter in 1969, was by 1972 importing foodstuffs totaling $280 million, money that needed to be spent but ought not to have been.[16] As the British embassy in Santiago reported to Whitehall, "President Allende may claim that the Chilean Way to Socialism got off to a good start in 1971 with a series of major measures. . . . In reality the situation in every field is becoming increasingly difficult."[17]

The Chilean government's situation became so unstable that on August 6, 1973, Allende formed his second emergency military cabinet, bringing the commanders in chief of the four services into key portfolios. Generals and ministers resigned as quickly as they could be brought into government. Street violence was an everyday fact.[18] As Director of Central Intelligence (DCI) William Colby reported to the White House, it was "increasingly apparent that three years of political polarization had strained the fabric of Chilean society to the breaking point."[19] In *Small Earthquake in Chile*, Sir Alistair Horne quotes locals, by late 1972, saying, "civil war in Chile is inevitable."[20] Ex-president Frei was reported to have said that the choice left for Chile was between "military dictatorship and a dictatorship of the proletariat."[21]

Even worse, for Allende, when it came to the crisis, none of his partners in the socialist world were prepared—past limited intelligence support and light arms—to back *El Compañero Presidente* because of either disagreements over ideology (with Castro) or lack of funds (the Soviet Union). "It was just a question of time," said Jack Devine. Reporting from "the Communists—some of our best reporting came from the Communist Party—showed that they had a pretty good fix on Allende and his durability. The KGB at the time, they knew they had backed a bad horse" and no further help would be extended.[22] Indeed, Soviet Premier Yuri Andropov, contradicting the Soviet's activist policy developed in the mid-1960s, wrote, "Latin America is a sphere of special U.S. interests. The U.S. has permitted us to act in Poland and Czechoslovakia. We must remember this. Our policy in Latin America must be cautious."[23]

Internally, also, Allende was facing a grave situation, with a dangerous vote on August 22 in the Chamber of Deputies, the "sense of the House" resolution, which declared his government essentially unconstitutional. This was an important psychological landmark for those military officers who wanted a patina of legitimacy to their forthcoming actions. That same day Allende's latest military crisis cabinet resigned after protests and demonstrations from middle-ranking officers. Fast after this was a very dangerous crisis among the naval chain of command. Chile was in the midst of certain political crisis. As historian Arturo Valenzuela wrote, "The whole political system had been reduced to the president and a few trusted colleagues, moving from crisis to crisis, minute to minute, twenty-four hours a day, attempting to cajole and convince others to postpone what now seemed inevitable."[24] According to the Rettig Commission,

> the 1973 crisis may be generally described as one of sharp polarization in the political positions of the civil sphere into two sides—government and opposition. Neither side was able (and probably did not want) to arrive at a compromise with the other, and there were sectors on both sides that believed armed confrontation was preferable to any sort of negotiation.[25]

THE COUP DECISION

By the time of the September 1973 coup, many in Chile expected some form of *golpe d'estado*. Yet it would be inaccurate to say that plotting had been ongoing for any length of time or that the military looked at the task with relish. The military, and the army especially, had been, from before Allende's election through to mid-1973, a general adherent to the constitutionalist school, which forbid its entrance into politics. Political events—such as the military cabinet of 1972 and its successors—and perceived threats against the military institution eroded this stance.

While MIR did not carry out armed actions during the Allende presidency, it was widely known that its members had been training for them and importing, producing, and stockpiling weapons throughout in anticipation of a fascist coup. MIR central committee chief Miguel Enríquez had also publicly called for soldiers' disobedience in the case of a coup.[26] More seriously from the Chilean army perspective, MIR actively tried to recruit cells within the armed forces. On August 7, 1973, Chilean naval intelligence announced that it had discovered an MIR plot to start a lower-deck mutiny among sailors at Valparaíso and Talcahuano. Socialist senator Carlos Altamirano and Movimiento de Acción Popular Unitaria (MAPU) deputy Oscar Garretón were also publicly implicated in the coup; this directly tarnished the government's legitimacy in the military's eyes. Many on the Left implicated in the plot openly acknowledged their moves, noting that theirs was the only responsible reply to the open plotting of many navy officers.[27]

As described in chapter 5, the most important event on the road to the coup was *El Tanquetazo* on June 29, 1973. While some of the Agency's analysts believed that the military's own resolution of this crisis had reduced the chance that it could subsequently launch a successful coup—that the incident had reinforced its preference of sticking with Allende until the 1976 elections—this was in fact not the case. Jack Devine offered the Agency's retrospective appreciation of *El Tanquetazo* and the rest of the threats to the military:

> The military went back to their senior people and they decided that there had been a breakdown in discipline among the junior members of the institution, and for the good of the institution—which outranked the constitution and the president and the democratic process—they had to take the coup plotting out of the dark. They began coup plotting in earnest.[28]

The analysts at Langley were not the only ones to miss the implications of this event or of the military's general view of the breakdown of social and political order. A July 25 cable the station (possibly via Devine) affirmed the view. Further the cable noted that Gen. César Ruíz of the air force and Adm. Raúl Montero of the navy "seem ready to move against the government" and affirmed "that they cannot and will not move until the army is ready to participate in force"—they did not believe it was in the revolt's aftermath.[29]

Yet a recent revelation by Chilean reporter and author Mónica González seems to show that, at least in part, it was the *tanquetazo* and general street violence that galvanized the general staff in their individual and collective determination to act against Allende. According to a document uncovered by González, on July 1, 1973 "the Committee of 15," a group of senior admirals and generals, sat down together and decided that they would have to act to prevent Allende from destroying the country. Pinochet was amongst their number.[30] The memorandum produced by the group stated clearly the position they were in: the current government's economic situation kept the armed forces from re-equipping themselves properly, all the while it seemed that Peru and Bolivia were becoming more aggressive towards Chile. The armed foces were being infiltrated by Marxists and de-professionalized by the government. The economy was falling apart and the country would soon be unable to feed itself.[31]

That they had to do something to right these problems was certain, but what was equally certain was that remaining in Allende's government did nothing to help. The military was caught in the middle: hated for supporting the government and hated for blocking the government's progress to socialism. And martial pride also played a role. Hundreds of housewives, both rich and poor, angry at food shortages and convinced that the UP was going to turn primary education into Marxist indoctrination, threw chicken feed at parading soldiers and cadets in front of La Moneda. "We felt vilified and cornered; the people were calling us cowards," recalled air force commander Gen. Gustavo Leigh Guzmán,[32] who had, in mid-August, taken over as air force commander in chief after the public resignation of General Ruíz and who had made it quite clear on taking command that the air force would offer little public support to the government.[33] General Prats, army commander in chief and member of Allende's cabinet, was also feeling extreme pressure from both the Left and Right in Chile. On August 21, 1973, a large number of army officers' wives gathered at Prats's home to demand his resignation. Some argue that this was the straw that broke the camel's back, for on August 22, 1973, General Prats, under severe pressure from the rest of the officer corps, resigned from Allende's military national security cabinet, as did his two greatest supporters, Gen. Mario Sepulveda Squella of the Santiago Garrison and Gen. Guillermo Pickering of the military academy. These resignations removed the last bastion of constitutionalism from the military—the last officers who, like the late General Schneider, adhered to a strict interpretation of the constitution and the military's role within it. The uncontroversial General Pinochet, who had been the Chilean army chief of staff since January 1972, became the army commander in chief upon Prats's resignation.

A Defense Intelligence Agency (DIA) report written after the coup reported these resignations as the most important contributing factors to the coup's success "because [they] effectively freed Army plotters to join with the other two services and the *Carabineros*."[34] Certainly, it was at this point that the generals and admirals of the Committee of 15 gained complete control over the military, and so at this point the coup could move ahead, assured of sufficient ability to apply the necessary force as a united whole.[35] But to ascribe the beginnings of coup plotting to any particular event is probably pointless. U.S. ambassador Nathaniel Davis wrote in his memoir that during his time in Chile the military did not rush to begin coup plotting, but did so only reluctantly and then without alacrity:

> They went to see Allende again and again, mostly through their commanders-in-chief, but sometimes collegially, and asked the President to reconsider his policies and control the extremists. They squirmed, temporized, and looked for ways out, and it was a reluctant, uncertain, inconclusive process. . . . [The passage] from planning to talk to discussion and action was made slowly. It was late—only days before the coup—when the armed forces moved collectively beyond the point of no return.[36]

For certain, all of these stages on the road to the coup were domestically driven and resulted in domestic plotting only. In none of the text, in not one of the CIA documents, can one find reference to American involvement, passive or active, in coup plotting.

Regardless, if one cannot identify the specific genesis of coup plotting, one can at least, as Davis wrote, find the moment that the *Alto Mando* was at last irrevocably committed. This point of no return was the naval chain of command crisis, during which Allende tried to influence the supposedly nonpolitical appointment of the navy commander in chief in his favor. The lead-up to this crisis mimics the crisis within the army. The incumbent navy commander in chief, Adm. Raúl Montero, had been under increasingly vocal pressure to resign from his second in command,

Adm. José Toribio Merino, as well as from the commander of the Chilean marines, Adm. Sergio Huidobro. Allende went to great lengths, politically and legally, to prevent Montero from resigning, as he likely knew that Merino was one of the chief plotters against him.[37] Yet Montero, nearly breaking down from the stress, was eventually allowed to resign. Allende found himself unable to promote any loyal naval officer above the more senior Merino, so the latter was allowed to take command. As a result, with Merino in charge, the navy, the most conservative service and so the most anti-Allende, secured the interservice coordination that had been lacking in previous coup plots or attempts, and word of the plans for the coup spread rapidly through the Chilean military.

THE COUP

Recent evidence shows that the decision to stage the coup was made on Friday, September 7, after the support of two Carabinero generals had been secured (though the lead plotter among the Carabineros, César Mendoza Durán, signed the official declaration only after Pinochet did).[38] The declaration supporting the coup—pushed by the very bellicose General Leigh of the air force and General Pinochet of the army—was signed on September 9.[39] Ambassador Davis, in a recent interview with the National Security Archive at George Washington University, stated that the final decision was made at this meeting, which took place in General Pinochet's house.[40]

Events moved quickly from this point onward, outside of the view of the U.S. embassy, if Davis is to be believed. Internal security plans developed by the services (the navy had Operation Seaweed, the air force Operation Thunder, and the army Operation Dawn) were converted into the three aspects of the coup plot and put into action with the Chilean armed forces' customary efficiency and professionalism.[41] On the morning of September 11, at about 5:00 a.m., the order went out from the army's communication center:

> ASUMIR INTENDENCIAS Y GOBERNACIONES DE INMEDIATO Y OCUPAR COMA EFECTIVAMENTE, PROVINCIAS Y ÁREAS JURISDICCIONAL . . . ACTIVAR CAJSIS PTO. ATTE.[42]

With great rapidity, all services moved to secure the main population centers in Chile. The navy, returning unexpectedly from exercises at sea, seized, without resistance, Valparaíso before 7:00 a.m. Alerted to the coup by about 6:00 a.m., Allende raced to La Moneda in a haphazard convoy, secured by heavily armed members of his GAP bodyguard. He arrived about 7:20 a.m. but had only an hour to prepare his political and military defense before the palace was first abandoned by its Carabinero guard, then surrounded by the tanks of the infamous Second Armored Regiment. By 8:50 a.m. Chile's second city, Concepción, was secured by the military.[43]

Because the military had captured most of the Santiago radio stations before 7:00 a.m., Allende's last public words went out to portions of Chile only on Radio Agricultura and Radio Magallanes at around 9:10 a.m. His call to resist the army was followed by a few, but not many, Chileans.

By about this time too, La Moneda had been seized. Hundreds of soldiers surrounded the palace, which was defended only by fifty GAPs and about forty Carabineros who had sided with their president. The remaining Carabineros left before long, after Allende told them they could go as long as they left their weapons.[44] Small groups of Allende loyalists, scattered about Santiago, fought it out with the army for a few hours that morning, but none held out very long. Severe shooting broke out between the GAP and the surrounding soldiers after 9:00 a.m., but no serious attack was made on the palace. Allende refused repeated calls to surrender. At 11:52 a.m., two Chilean air force Hawker Hunter jets began a straffing run, firing nineteen rockets that set La Moneda on fire.[45] Surviving the twenty-minute attack, twenty or so GAP fighters, as well as Allende himself, returned fire with rifles and bazookas. At 1:15 p.m., faced with inevitable defeat, Allende ordered his supporters to surrender and leave La Moneda and told everyone he would be the last to go.[46]

In the midst of this evacuation, Allende was found dead. Some writers, even one as recent as Peter Kornbluh, describe the fall of La Moneda in ambiguous terms that suggest that Pinochet had Allende murdered, though it is now widely accepted that the president died by suicide.[47] By 2:00 p.m. government troops had secured La Moneda, and aside from some limited fighting elsewhere in the country, the coup was complete. The coup, from the first troop movements to the death of Allende, took less than twelve hours.

KNOWING PINOCHET

It is often erroneously supposed that because the United States supported Pinochet after he became dictator of Chile that the United States also supported his coup from the start. Gabriel Kolko, for one, asserts quite assuredly that the CIA "did everything from maintaining constant contact with the coup plotters, whom it encouraged in every way . . . to drawing up arrest lists and the key targets to take when the coup began."[48] Extending this argument, Pinochet, as the coup leader, should have been a well-known figure to the CIA's station officers in Santiago. Yet the evidence suggests that he was not. Even taking into account the generally accepted fact that Pinochet was late in joining the plotters, evidence suggests that the CIA had little knowledge of and less contact with the man who emerged as the leader of the post-coup junta, a man supposedly chosen by the CIA.[49]

Through routine intelligence gathering after Allende's inauguration, the CIA had identified Pinochet as a notable character within the Chilean army leadership. Pinochet, who replaced Camilo Valenzuela as *Jefe de la Plaza* and Santiago Garrison commander in early 1971, had held the command and war academy posts required of those destined for senior flag rank.[50] The CIA felt that he was a "narrow-gauge military man . . . who clearly enjoyed [the] feeling of being important."[51] A September 1971 CIA cable listed Pinochet as one of the main officers "*strongly opposed to [the] present regime* [emphasis added by hand in original]," yet while he would favor a coup he "would want to close [his] eyes to events."[52] Nevertheless, the CIA noted that Pinochet avoided making any provocative statements and that he was "cautious and quiet on political matters," though he did have notable family contacts with the conservative National Party. Overall, the assessment in 1971 was very similar to the one made two years later: "[We] assess subject as person who could possibly be neutralized by conspiratorial group but who would not lead any coup."[53]

The next step in Pinochet's evolution from unknown army general to integral anti-*Allendista* happened in 1972, undoubtedly as a result of the worsening of the domestic situation in Chile. It had come to the CIA's attention that the junior officers of the Chilean forces had increased their coup plotting in defiance of the high command's compliance with Allende's policies. Pinochet, the CIA noted, though "previously [a] strict constitutionalist," was now "harboring second thoughts" about getting involved in the coup plots.[54] He apparently felt that Allende would have to be forced to step down or be eliminated. Another short cable suggests that Pinochet might have been involved with the "coup preparations of General Alfredo Canales Márquez, Army Chief-of-Staff."[55] At this point, however, Pinochet was not touted as the coup leader, but merely as "Prats's Man" and a loyal soldier. A follow-on cable reads, "Pinochet's changing attitude [might] reflect Prats' new posture. Some officers have recently commented Canales was ahead of his time, that Prats will lead eventual coup."[56] According to the CIA, Pinochet was a follower—a yes-man—not a leader.

It appears clear that Pinochet did not rate as a likely coup leader to anyone who even noticed him in the first place. Henry Kissinger recently said, "We did not know Pinochet, and when he [became the army chief of staff], we thought he might be someone favorable to Allende."[57] Kissinger's statement is consistent with the reporting in the CIA's and DIA's files. On May 2, 1973, Santiago reported to CIA headquarters some information regarding the coup that they had recently received: the CIA contact in the Chilean army had reported that plotting was well advanced, that these plans had the input or support of most of the influential generals, and that "Allende would not last another 30 days in office." More important, however, is what the Chilean contact said about Pinochet: "Pinochet will not be a stumbling block to the coup plans."[58] From this we can glean that the CIA's contact perceived Pinochet as being outside the plotting circles, and this impression was reinforced when the general, along with Prats, led the soldiers that put down El Tanquetazo.[59] In the aftermath of that uprising, CIA intelligence on certain mid-ranking coup plotters showed that the conspirators favored the next most senior officer, Gen. Manuel Torres, over Pinochet as a leader because they considered Pinochet an "[un]suitable replacement" for Prats given the atmosphere surrounding the developing coup.[60] Simply, no one knew the intentions of the famously inscrutable General Pinochet. As late as August 24, 1973, the DIA asserted, "Pinochet lacks the prestige and influence that Prats enjoyed and is unlikely to *wield the authority and control* of his predecessor over the services [italics added]."[61] It seems many considered Pinochet to be a "grey man," not a natural leader, an uninspired military technocrat finding his way to the top by hard work and loyalty, not by insight.

Perhaps Pinochet was consciously misdirecting all observers, both Chilean and American, as he determined his course of action in the brewing chaos. Even the defense attaché in Santiago, whose significant contacts within the military were often exploited by the CIA, expressed to David Atlee Phillips the belief that "it was highly unlikely that the Army would move against Allende so long as the top leadership such as Generals Prats, Pinochet, Sepulveda, [Orlando] Urbina, Pickering and [Hermán] Brady remained firm in support of the constitutional regime."[62] A slightly earlier report does not rank Pinochet alongside the firm constitutionalists, but neither does it list him among the five army generals joining five others from each service in coup plotting, either because this group's full composition was unknown to the CIA or because Pinochet was uninvolved.[63]

Confirming the former, the DIA reported on August 31 that Pinochet "is trying to diffuse the current tension." The report continued,

> He has set aside his earlier request for the resignation of army generals and intends to stage a series of intensive arms raids against extremists. The general also plans to take action against striking truck owners. He may adopt a stronger position toward the government to convince Allende to ease tension by making concessions to the political opposition.[64]

Whether this was sincere and Pinochet had not yet joined in the plotting or whether he was camouflaging his real intentions behind a screen of loyal staff work remains unknown. Pro-Pinochet historian James R. Whelan supports (with some evidence) the official line that Pinochet began plotting as soon as he was promoted to army chief of staff in January 1972.[65] In her book *Soldiers in a Narrow Land*, historian-journalist Mary Helen Spooner writes that Pinochet was not made witting of the coup plot until September 8, when Gen. Sergio Arellano Stark asked him to assent to the plan.[66]

Regardless, it seems clear that the U.S. intelligence community did not have a good read of the man most people believe it handpicked for Chilean leadership. Said Jack Devine, "I do not remember the Pinochet role at all. Pinochet was not considered a very strong military leader . . . which is very interesting."[67] Backing this assertion, Spooner argues persuasively, using evidence from exiled Chilean army officers involved in the coup, that Pinochet was the least involved of all Chilean flag officers eventually implicated in the coup plot.[68]

Reporting based on interviews with Chilean army officers has shown that Pinochet, if he was not the coup's instigator, might have been responsible for its violent nature. John Dinges suggests that Pinochet, once he became involved in plotting, took charge and transformed the plan from a *golpe blanco* into "a unique historic project to physically eliminate all possibility of another Allende in the future."[69] Some of Pinochet's later bravado could have stemmed from a visit he made to Panama in 1972, during which junior U.S. army officers told him their private belief that the United States "will support [a] coup against Allende 'with whatever means necessary' when the time comes."[70] Whether this was the official line of the United States or the opinion of the young officers, would Pinochet, a proud and self-assured senior officer from a military with a longstanding independent tradition, have been swayed by the musings of American majors and colonels?

That Pinochet was so severely underestimated by almost all observers and pundits, Chilean and American, is critical to understanding the coup. It not only speaks to the nature of the man and the coup but also to the CIA's involvement (or lack thereof) in the coup as it gathered intelligence on the military.

INTELLIGENCE ON THE COUP PLOT

Just as U.S. complicity with Pinochet specifically is assumed, it is sometimes assumed, as discussed in chapter 6, that the U.S. government commissioned the CIA to engineer a coup. This assumption, absent from more recent scholarship, is likely significantly overstated. Matters changed little for the CIA between the advent of the Allende government and its ouster, save for the increased difficulty in gathering intelligence in Chile because of the UP government's improved security structure.

As matters grew more serious for the Allende government by the end of 1972, representatives of the different American agencies—including the State Department, the Defense Department, the CIA, and the National Security Council (NSC)—gathered to discuss what the United States would do if it were asked to support a coup. One of the first points raised, as noted in the minutes of the meeting, was, "It is unlikely that the United States will be asked to help in preparing or delivering a coup." The various departments involved understood that the Chilean military had a strong, independent tradition and also that the plotters were likely to pursue extreme secrecy in planning for the coup. The meeting attendees discussed this point at length, and the minutes indicate they determined that positive U.S. involvement in a coup would have only the barest support within the United States and would not suit the international image the nation wished to project at the time. Moreover, "it would at most have only marginal influence on the course of events." The attendees went on to discuss the nature of the requests the United States might receive, the nature of a potential coup, and the core problem:

> On the basis of presently available evidence it would . . . seem that we would be well advised to hold ourselves back from specific commitments to Chileans who seek assurances on our attitude toward a new regime produced by a coup. If such commitments were to contribute to a decision to attempt a coup they would be too dangerous to give; if they would not contribute to such a decision they would be superfluous.[71]

This belief was born out in the farcical June 29 uprising. In an undated secret internal memorandum designed to answer potential legislative questions about U.S. involvement in the uprising, the author acknowledged a U.S. connection to some of the coup plotters but added that the Chilean contact only "provided this Agency with information on military matters and made no secret of his opposition to the Allende regime." He never requested any Agency support or assistance in planning a possible coup. On one occasion a CIA contact requested an "arrest list" to help round up key government officials in the event of a successful coup, but this request was denied. Overall, the Agency stressed, military contacts "were developed exclusively for intelligence purposes and have never received any encouragement with regard to coup plotting."[72] Perhaps having responded to requests for assistance from Valenzuela and, especially, Viaux, the United States realized that only an indigenous coup would be potentially desirable to American interests. Many in the United States believed that the UP government was inexorably sliding toward defeat in subsequent elections and that U.S. interests would be much better served by an elected successor regime than a regime produced by an armed coup.[73] Any failed coups in the meantime would bolster Allende's grip on power and allow him to rally political support around the external *gringo* influence.

It appears that until the very day of the coup, the CIA did not have a clear idea of the scope of contemporary coup plotting. In a cable of August 25, 1973, the Santiago station chief, Raymond Warren, described to Langley the station's contingency planning options over the coming few months. Warren boiled it down to four options: (a) do nothing; (b) continue on the present program as authorized by the 40 Committee; (c) plan a coup; or (d) slightly expand the current support to the opposition. Of these options, the COS opined, "The dynamics of the present situation point to either massive re-entrance of the armed forces into the government or an outright military coup. Until it becomes more clear which of these two outcomes, if either, will prevail, it is difficult to do realistic long-range planning."[74] Headquarters, in a reply two days later, agreed that no change to the current operations should be made, as the situation was too unpredictable.[75] Clearly, up to this point, the CIA was not involved in coup plotting and could barely keep abreast of the exponential growth of conspiracy against Allende. For the same reasons the CIA had no foreknowledge of Pinochet's involvement in the coup, it also had precious little intelligence about when and where the coup was going to happen.

According to Jack Devine, the CIA's lack of information about the coup was partly owing to its minimal connections to the Chilean military, as discussed in chapter 6. Devine rated the Agency's success in its intelligence-gathering mission against the military poorly:

> [Military] sources were few and not that forthcoming. The military, well, I would give it a "C." It was not like we were in bed with them at the planning/policy level. We knew what they were doing, we had advanced information about the coup, but that information did not come, *officially*, from the military, from a military officer. We did get the best report the day before—a very detailed report—from an officer. But to that time we were relying on civilians talking to their military friends.[76]

Thus, station preparation for the coup was necessarily minimal. Because the Chilean military's plotting at the senior level was rather guarded and the Agency had little contact with the plotters, the United States could do little but guess at what might happen. That a coup was going to take place was about the only sure knowledge—and one did not need to be a CIA operative to surmise this much.[77] As Ambassador Davis noted, "every correspondent, every foreign diplomat there" who came into contact with U.S. embassy staff passed on information about one plot or another. "The place was awash in rumors of one kind or another for months," he added.[78]

The DIA, via its defense attaché relationships, had better contact with the Chilean army generals than the CIA had. In May 1973, both the DIA and the CIA issued summaries that identified "discontent amongst field-grade officers," which had increased "steadily for some weeks. . . . Their leaders have been meeting this month to draw up tactical plans for a move against Allende." The summaries went on to note that the navy and air force were the most aggressive in this planning and to predict a coup before June 4.[79] One should note that despite their better connections to the military, the DIA also did not seem to have direct access to those plotting the coup, and still had to issue rough predictions instead of hard intelligence.

On August 3, 1973, the CIA gained intelligence that the PCCh had received warning of a coup attempt that would be carried out that week by "unnamed military leaders."[80] It is interesting to note, bolstering Devine's and Phillips's comments about the relative superiority of Agency reporting from sources from the PCCh, that this intelligence came not from CIA contacts in the military but through UP informants. The CIA comment at the end of this memorandum is deleted, unfortunately, so it is unclear whether the CIA had heard of these plans from other quarters. Regardless, no other CIA intelligence report about this potential coup exists.

On September 7, 1973, only four days before the coup, the attendees of a U.S. government interdepartmental meeting could not achieve a consensus on what was going to happen in Chile. While the CIA representative believed that a "creeping coup" might occur (in which Allende's military cabinet slowly took control), the State Department representative "felt that if circumstances continued to deteriorate an armed coup might be more likely."[81]

In retrospect, the initial indications of a solid coup climate emerged September 8, when the CIA reported that the Chilean navy planned to overthrow Allende on the early morning of September 10. The CIA thought that the navy would initiate the revolt by seizing control of a province (undoubtedly its home station of Valparaíso) and would then be joined by the air force and perhaps even the army. The air force commander in chief contacted General Pinochet, the new army commander in chief, and reported that Pinochet would "not oppose the navy's action."[82] The army, the CIA thought, *might* join the coup after the air force did, but its generals might not. This hearsay and speculation hardly constitutes hard evidence of a U.S.-organized coup with Pinochet as chosen man, not to mention a coordinated coup plot at all.

"The different military units were of a different frame of mind," said Devine. "The navy was gung-ho and the air force was not far behind them. But the army was slow coming to the coup table. Why? Because they had to do the street-work, and they did it but they also said they wanted the lion's share of control afterward."[83] Despite the fractured nature of the military's plotting and the disagreements between the services, which the CIA might have been aware of, it was certain that "President Allende [was] unquestionably confronted with the most serious threat from the Armed Forces to his continuance in office since his election."[84]

The CIA station's moment of awareness that a coup was on the way came from Allende personally, said Devine, likely recalling Allende's national address of September 4:

> I do not remember the date, but Allende had a radio broadcast a week to ten days before [the coup], I cannot remember exactly what it was I was looking for but, whatever it was, he did not deliver it. Whether it was giving the military even a greater role, or taking a harder line on them, and I thought well, he has

> just crossed the Rubicon. The tension in the city was high. [But] our analysts in Washington were still saying "no coup."[85]

Devine said that soon after this, on or about September 8, good reporting started to arrive from civilians connected with the military giving dates and times for the coup. These rumors and the report of September 8 notwithstanding, the first hard intelligence about the September 11 coup arrived only two days before the navy seized Valparaíso. The detail of the reports, and the extreme dispatch with which they arrived, keyed Devine to the possibility that many of the CIA's Chilean army contacts were using the United States as much as the United States was using them:

> Forty-eight hours before the coup, within near real time, a definitive report arrived that went into great detail. If you had doubts about the first two reports you should not have had any doubts about the third report that came from a very good [military] source. That was not a source that was reporting regularly. He had not provided a single report over the previous two years. The point was "Go tell the Americans that we are coming." Was it a controlled source? I cannot tell you. But my point is that it was not someone who would have been reporting that caliber of material all along and just added this other piece, because he would have been able to add other pieces before that.[86]

Regardless, the CIA had a detailed report (most probably) two days before the coup. Most serious reporting was arriving within a four or five day period. The CIA, up to the very last moment, was still skeptical that a coup was going to happen. And, as Devine added, several slight delays convinced the station officers that these coup plots were as illusory as the dozen others they had heard about over the past three years: "Well, they changed the day; we knew that. I was in the embassy the night before it was supposed to start, at seven (and it started at eight.) So at 07:25, "One more baseless report!" It was not as though everybody, including in Washington, was sitting there convinced that it would happen. [It] speaks to how well wired, how involved we were, in the planning."[87]

Both CIA and DIA intelligence reports of September 10 indicated that intelligence had been received and "that a coup attempt will be initiated on September 11. All three branches of the armed forces and the *Carabineros* are involved in this action."[88] Several days after the coup the

British political attaché in Washington cabled back to Whitehall the substance of a conversation with ARA's Jack Kubisch, who said the U.S. government

> did not know that the coup was going to take place when it did, the report they had received was one of many that they had had over the past few months that a coup was imminent and there was nothing to indicate that this one was any more reliable than the others.[89]

Sources reporting to DIA had similar difficulty in separating wheat from chaff in their coup information. A report filed at 1:10 a.m. on September 11 read,

> Navy plotters, perhaps heeding the call of Vice Adm Jose Merino to hold off, postponed a take-over of Valparaiso Province. . . . However, the plotters have allegedly informed the National Police that a new jump-off time has been set for today, possibly hoping this will evoke action from Allende. The defense attaché in Santiago reports that as of 0100 EDT the situation appears normal but that early this morning is apparently the planned time for a coup attempt.[90]

The DIA mused about the possibility that junior officers could force the high command to make "a show of force" at least against Allende, but apparently thought this possibility unlikely. The CIA, as Devine said, was still skeptical and noted that this attempt was supposed to have been undertaken on September 10 but had been delayed to improve the tactical situation. Station officers thought that Allende's planned national address on the afternoon of September 10 might be used "to announce some dramatic proposal such as the calling of a plebiscite which could again cause the plotters to hesitate."[91] Indeed, this was Allende's plan, though the speech, which was to be read on September 11, was never heard.

While there is a small chance that these skeptical messages are plotted misdirection crafted for posterity, it is more likely that U.S. intelligence about the coup plotters was minimal and that the analysis at Langley was off the mark. Devine made this argument clear:

> I do not think the analysts had a good feel. They overestimated the military, and the Agency, its analysts—not the operators,

> the analysts—felt that the military would never move against Allende. And that was even into the very late days before the coup came: "this is a constitutional government; the military feels bound by the constitution, and therefore they are never going to remove him."[92]

It also seems that the earliest *direct* contact with the coup plotters came as late as September 10, 1973, probably only hours after the message mentioned previously, when the CIA reported to Kissinger that a contact in the Chilean military met with a CIA agent to advise the United States that "early 11 September 1973 a significant part of the Chilean military planned to move to overthrow President Allende." The Chilean officer asked if the United States would provide support to the coup if the situation became "difficult." The agent, it is reported, responded by telling the Chilean officer, "the planned action against President Allende was a Chilean operation, and he [the CIA officer] could only promise that [deleted] question would promptly be made known to Washington."[93]

Even though the CIA learned of these coup efforts too late to affect them, there was continued interest within the CIA, especially among the Santiago station, to foster a coup in the national chaos of late August 1973. On the resignation of General Prats from the cabinet, the CIA in Chile believed that the Allende government was in such a shaky position that "significant events or pressures could affect its future." The time was ripe, the station urged, for the CIA to support a major move by the opposition (including the private sector) to force on the government an emergency military cabinet that would administer the country until stability was restored. There was a danger: "While this is probably the most realistic objective, it should be borne in mind that events may carry the armed forces beyond this point to that of a full military takeover."[94] Despite all the pressure to avoid direct connection to any coup plotter, the CIA would still have been happy had a coup occurred.

THE CIA TO SEPTEMBER 11

That the United States continued in its desire to see Allende fall is no great surprise, as its political aims had been clearly defined almost a decade before. Still, this does not mean that the U.S. intelligence community was working behind the back of the lawmakers in Washington to foment a coup. Reporting the station's plans in the weeks before the coup, DCI Colby assured Kissinger that "the Santiago Station would not be working directly with the armed forces in an attempt to bring about a coup nor would its support to the overall opposition forces have this as its objective."[95] Kissinger did not respond to this memorandum, probably because there was not sufficient time for a new directive before the coup was executed.

In his recent book on Chile, Jonathan Haslam has hinted that a secret link to the coup plotters—one that led exclusively to Nixon and Kissinger—did in fact exist, in the form of CIA deputy director Lt. Gen. Vernon "Bill" Walters and Hernández Westmoreland, son-in-law of U.S. general William Westmoreland. Haslam suggests, based on unattributed sources, that Walters and Westmoreland, working independently out of Santiago's Hotel Carrera, plotted the coup and coordinated the efforts of the Chilean military leadership.[96] On one hand, this assertion has a certain ring of truth to it, for even DCI Richard Helms noted that "Nixon thought of General Walters as his man in CIA and the only person who could be trusted to carry out his orders."[97] On the other hand, the notion of a two-man plot run by the CIA deputy director and the son-in-law of General Westmoreland, operating out of a hotel room, sounds like a harebrained recipe for folly, not the lead-up to the extremely efficient coup that occurred. If true, the Walters-Westmoreland plot presents an interesting challenge to the history of the coup, although it does not directly challenge the argument made here that the CIA station, Western Hemisphere Division, and Directorate of Plans seem to have been mostly in the dark with regards to coup plotting. While these two men, working out of their solitary hotel room, might have had some influence on events, it is unlikely they could have constructed the coup without the resources and personnel only the CIA possessed in Chile. Regardless, the Nixon-Kissinger/Walter-Westmoreland theory is not proven evidence, and it is difficult to detect any awareness of, and certainly no link to, this small cabal by the CIA station in Chile. The above memorandum from Colby—along with a significant amount of other hard evidence—shows that the CIA, up to the last moments of the Allende regime, were not involved in coup plotting and indeed were avoiding any move that might indicate to the Chileans that the Agency favored one any more than was already public knowledge.

U.S. actions to cut off funding to Allende's Chile can likewise not be related directly to the coup. Despite a continuing desire to see the Allende government's collapse, in the three years from the Chilean president's election to his death, the U.S. government carried out no action against the Chilean government that could not be justified within the norms of international banking or trade law and produced no policy with the direct intent of promoting a coup. As one U.S. government officer said,

> Whatever [the CIA] did with the military, collection had no impact on them moving. Yes, we were supporting all these different [political and civil] institutions, but only in a moment of bravado would someone have said we wanted a coup—and someone *may* have said something—but the only real cause here was Allende and his policies.[98]

Indeed, so careful was the CIA in avoiding the appearance of favoring a coup that it had trouble predicting the timing and nature of the coup that did occur. Dr. Kissinger recalled that he did not have any specific warning of the coup:

> [I was aware] there was a building crisis. This was a period when Watergate was cooking. I was being confirmed as Secretary of State, I had a lot of other things going on. I cannot say that I walked into [the White House] in the morning and knew first thing that there was a coup ongoing. There was a general coup climate, but there was not a specific consciousness of a coup.[99]

The State Department as a whole seems to have agreed with Kissinger's recent assertion. A document originating from Foggy Bottom on the very day of the coup shows that many in the department "doubted that there would be a military coup" but indicated the possibility of increased military power over government.[100]

If, as it appears, many in government did not have warning of the coup, then it can be argued that the Agency failed in its primary task of assisting policymakers with timely intelligence. Devine's "C" grade might be too generous, yet it speaks to the point of American complicity: If the United States could not predict it, how could it have plotted it? Haslam's Walters-Westmoreland link is one potential explanation, but one which currently cannot be taken as fact. If Kissinger and Nixon were plotting the coup—it is clear they certainly hoped for Allende's demise—and if their plot was being executed by Walters and Westmoreland, who was doing all the planning, contacts, and negotiations that gave the coup its "extraordinary degree of efficiency and ruthlessness"? It seems unlikely that these four men alone could be entirely responsible for the coup at the exclusion of domestic Chilean actors. If they had assistance from some official government body, that agency has kept remarkably quiet for over thirty years, a feat not even the CIA seems capable of achieving.

The policymakers' opinions on the coup are hardly a better indication of complicity. Kissinger went on to note, "We had no particular reason to be unhappy with [the coup]," but this cannot be interpreted to mean that the United States had a coup as its specific goal or worked at all to make a coup happen.[101] The last NIE written about Chile before the coup, issued in June 1973, noted, "The U.S. lacks powerful and reliable levers for influencing the outcome" of Chile's ongoing political crisis.[102] In his book *The Night Watch*, former CIA C/WHD David Atlee Phillips recounts the difficulty he had managing the CIA effort in Chile. On one hand, the CIA officers were expected to give the U.S. government proper warning of any attempted coup in Chile—something the station did not succeed fully in doing. On the other hand, it had been pointed out that in the (arguably inevitable) event of a coup in Chile, the CIA would be accused of complicity. It was ultimately ordered that discretion was to trump forewarning: the CIA wanted to keep its hands clean in a time when the agency was under increased scrutiny.[103] The result of this policy is what is described above: a difficult and ultimately unsuccessful attempt to gather information from the margins, on very secret coup plots, without leaving any impressions of favoring a coup.

The CIA's discretion did not pay off. The Church committee report imputes, without offering evidence to prove the allegation, that the CIA supported and *perhaps* even helped plot the coup. A review of the committee's documents sheds much needed light on the topic, reveals the report's partisan nature, and vindicates Falcoff's rejection of its rhetoric. Moreover, by looking at the documents one can determine the exact nature of the U.S. relationship with those who launched the coup in September 1973 in detail not achievable until the CIA, NSC, and State Department archives were declassified. They remove most of the doubt—doubt exploited by such works as Hersh's *The Price of Power*[104]—of the CIA's assertion that it had no connection to and barely any knowledge of the coup that ousted Allende. Some documents have yet to be declassified and the released files have suffered significant deletions, so there is still room for argument. Nonetheless, the weight of existing evidence sides with the CIA.

A post-coup CIA intelligence bulletin reported Pinochet's private comment that "he and his colleagues, as a matter of policy, had not given any hints to the U.S. as to their developing resolve to act."[105] Whether this policy was based on plausible deniability for a joint U.S.-Chilean effort, security for an indigenous effort, or simply out of nationalistic pride is unknown. Certainly, the Chilean military's amour propre would have been offended by the notion that it needed the United States to run the coup for it. Several days after the coup, the U.S. military attaché in Caracas was approached by his Chilean counterpart, Chilean army colonel Hernan Bejares González. Reporting on the meeting, the attaché noted that Colonel Bejares was "in good spirits and obviously pleased" that Allende had been overthrown. He delivered what the Defense Department believed was a message from the junta to the United States:

> We in Chile fully expect other nations and many individual political figures to deplore the coup and also try to link the U.S. with it or somehow blame the U.S. I feel the Junta would want me to emphasize in the strongest terms that this is purely a Chilean affair. [The Chilean military] as always welcome the friendship of the United States but we must and shall clean up this mess ourselves.[106]

The CIA was central in U.S. government operations in Chile, operations based on the policy of preventing the extinction of Chile's press and opposition parties, which were under a clear attack by more aggressive elements of Allende's government. The CIA did operate against Allende: the Agency sought to thwart what the U.S. president and many others saw as Allende's anti-democratic political goals. It did not, however, try to engineer Allende's death. Colby described the American efforts best, in a secret post-coup cable to Kissinger: "While the agency was instrumental in enabling opposition political parties and media to survive and to maintain their dynamic resistance to the Allende regime, the CIA played no direct role in the events which led to the establishment of the new military government."[107]

In the end, Allende's inability to lead, to manage his party, and so to manage his economy brought his end. "The real thing that brought Allende down was the economy—at the end of the day, a bankrupt economy," said Devine.[108] While some might dismiss this argument as economically determinist, it is less easily refuted than theories of active and aggressive U.S. complicity. Even the Soviets noted that the CIA was not the primary cause of the fall of the Allende regime. In a 2002 interview, the former head of the Latin American division of the Soviet Foreign Office, Yuri Pavlov, remarked that, although from his standpoint the CIA "had a lot to do with the coup," it was not the driving force. The main reason for Pinochet's takeover, he said, "was that Allende lost the support of the majority of the population." Worse, he "probably never had it."[109]

8

CODA: POST-COUP OPERATIONS

> *Finally, we are entering a stage of normality or consolidation where power will be exerted basically by civil organs, reserving constitutionally to the Armed Forces and security forces the role of supporting the foundations of law, order, and national security in their many modern forms.*
>
> —Gen. Augusto Pinochet, "Discurso de Chacarillas," June 9, 1977[1]

Allende's ouster was not an unwelcome event for the Americans. Despite this, the Americans' lack of full awareness of the coup makes it clear that the United States was not the coup's motive force. In most of the literature the story ends with the coup: Allende was out, Pinochet was in, and Chile settled down to seventeen years of dictatorship. Yet this conclusion is predicated on the assumption that the United States *was* complicit in the coup and that it sponsored Pinochet in it. Pinochet was in power, the mission in Chile was over; Q.E.D. But the story continues.

For almost a year after the coup the U.S. government, through the CIA, persisted in providing funds to the Christian Democrat Party (PDC) and other political organizations that had been opposed to Allende. The funds flowed even as it became apparent that the junta (increasingly controlled by Pinochet) was going to remain in absolute power for an extended time and suppress all political activity and that Allende's opposition, which initially welcomed the coup, would be the opposition once again. While the coup might seem the logical end to the long period of anticommunist covert action carried out in Chile, this oft-neglected fact—that the United States continued support for the political opposition in Chile for some months after the establishment of the junta government—lends a new perspective to U.S. thinking on Chile. Moreover, this residual operation provides numerous insights about the U.S. stance toward Chile in the preceding years and about the U.S. view towards noncommunist dictatorships.

THE PDC DILEMMA

One of the striking observations made by most of the people interviewed for this study was that the coup was not expected to be as violent—or as permanent—as it turned out to be. John Crimmins, who was stationed in Brasilia in September 1973, commented on the several thousand casualties in the first few days of the coup: "When the coup came, I was surprised it was so violent and appalled that it was so *hate filled.* It was more 'Central American' than I expected."[2] That violence was part of the greater surprise: the coup's permanency and ambition. Many, like Henry Kissinger, believed that the junta would reflect U.S. conceptions about Chile's democratic bent, that "as soon as they came in, once the coup had been made, they would return back to a democratic system in a measurable period of time."[3] There were no illusions, Crimmins said, that any of the Marxist parties would continue to exist in upcoming elections. Nonetheless, "no one had any thought that there would be the sort of dictatorship that we got. We thought a temporary government dominated by the military and then another election. Probably one that would be so confined that there would be disqualifications of certain parties, that kind of thing,"[4] added Crimmins. In chorus with his State Department colleague Crimmins, Jack Devine offered, "There was an assumption that the army was going to come in, stabilize things, and there was going to be an election a year later."[5]

This sense of the "Chilean" nature of the coup—that the coup was not launched because the army desired power but because it reluctantly but patriotically found it necessary because of President Allende's gross mismanagement—was held by most middle- and upper-class Chileans. It was beyond doubt that the coup vastly altered Chile's political landscape. The strong leftist trend that had won a significant portion of the vote in Chile since the 1930s would disappear. To the PDC, the National Party (PN), and the Radicals, the demise of these leftist-extremists was not necessarily unwelcome when viewed through the filter of the calamitous Allende years. The suspension of all political activity by the junta was necessary, the middle classes seemed to agree, to keep the country calm and to root out the Cubans, the Movimiento de Izquierda Revolucionario (MIR), and the alphabet soup of other leftist radical groups that threatened violence. Once these groups were dealt with, and after a brief period of benign military rule, a more-or-less pluralistic system would be restored:

> The moderate Christian Democrats (PDC) believe the military junta will remain in power for one to two years and hope to expand their influence. . . . Leaders of the PDC are concerned that the junta will try to remain in power longer, but they hope that support of the political parties will prompt the military to return to civil rule. Therefore, the PDC has avowed complete support of the government and is willing to accept suspension of party activities for the present.[6]

Accordingly, the major non-Marxist political parties saw it in their interests to bide their time, preserve their assets and credibility, and cautiously support the junta until they could officially reenter public politics. "The anti-Allende political parties so far are being kept at arm's length, but have announced their support for the Junta,"[7] noted Director of Central Intelligence William Colby. PDC President Patricio Aylwin encapsulated these ideas in a public statement made shortly after the coup:

> Precedent demonstrates that the Armed Forces and Carabineros do not seek power: their institutional traditions and the Republican history of our country inspires confidence that, once they have completed the tasks they undertook to avert the grave dangers of destruction and totalitarianism that threatened the Chilean nation, they will devolve power to the sovereign people who will decide freely and with sovereign power the destiny of the nation.[8]

Indeed, at the beginning of October the PDC dispatched a large delegation of senators and deputies to travel Latin America and Europe on a "truth tour" to outline the necessity of the coup and to justify the party's support of it.

The junta's rhetoric proved at first to coincide with the hopes of Aylwin and his party. Not ten days after the coup, the junta issued a statement to the effect that a "traditional democratic system of [government] will be re-established after 'national recuperation' has been achieved."[9] By early October General Pinochet told the Chileans that civilian government would be restored only after a "more or less long period."[10] The junta, which was reluctant to make promises, did not clearly define this period, but many, including the CIA, believed it would be one year.[11] This generally suited the PDC and PN, which hoped that the junta would take charge of the unpalatable task of cleansing their Marxist opponents from Chile.

The CIA reported that "Christian Democratic leaders are faced with a dilemma, however. . . . They hope to staff middle-level [junta] posts with their followers in an effort to moderate the government's policies, but they want to avoid being too closely identified with it."[12] This hesitancy was understandable in light of the (overestimated) figures reported to the PDC of five thousand to seven thousand deaths in the coup's first week.[13] Hoping at least to moderate the junta and to ensure it was well-positioned to transit into power as the junta relinquished control, the PDC sought a champion in the junta who might keep them in mind. Its choice was perhaps unfortunate, for the PDC "staked its hopes on Army Gen Pinochet, who has emerged as the most prestigious leader."[14]

Democracy was still very much on the PDC's mind. Like most Chileans, the Christian Democrats were shocked by the increasing number of casualties and the excesses of the all-powerful military. The party cautioned the junta in late October 1973 against imposing dictatorial measures or changing the constitution without a plebiscite. Like the CIA, the PDC had gravely underestimated the military's sense of righteous vengeance, and its comments did not impress the junta. The Santiago station reported, "The military government is annoyed with the stance of the Christian Democratic Party (PDC), despite the party's mild statement of support for the junta. The PDC has taken sharp exception to the dissolution of congress, where it had the largest representation."[15] The junta rebuffed the PDC deputies' attempts to curry favor, and on September 26 "recessed" all political parties (in addition to outlawing the Marxist parties) as a means of promoting "national unity."[16]

While almost all contemporaries believed that the coup was merely a short-term event designed to reintroduce democracy to Chile, it very quickly became clear that the junta had different ideas. As Mark Falcoff described, the hostility felt in the Chilean middle classes toward politics (for had not constant politicking resulted only in a communist government and economic collapse?) had infected the largely middle-class military. Having seen its prosperous and peaceable country destroyed with the acquiescence of the non-Marxist parties, the junta was not in a charitable mood toward *any* politician: "The junta blames *all* politicians for the conditions leading to the coup. They feel there was an excess of political demagoguery and that Chilean institutions had been over politicized [italics added],"[17] reported one CIA contact privy to a junta cabinet meeting.

The Chilean junta's political cynicism might have been part of the CIA's problem in making accurate predictions, both before and after the coup. Having been ordered to avoid prompting a coup on its own, the CIA had minimized its contacts with the army and had relied on political intelligence from the PDC and from scattered right-wing politicians and businessmen. Whatever right-wing individuals the CIA could contact were themselves kept in the dark by the insular military plotters as a matter of security or indeed might have been used by the plotters as carriers of disinformation. And Christian Democrats were, unfortunately for the CIA, not people the military plotters trusted: the military saw the PDC (its left wing specifically) as having been acquiescent to the Unidad Popular (UP) since the late 1960s.[18] Thus, through August and September 1973 the CIA did not have the best intelligence on the coup plot as it developed, and post-coup the CIA focused on the ongoing political machinations of a party that the junta planned to marginalize as much as any other party. But because the CIA did not have detailed intelligence, it soldiered on.

THE CIA AND FUNDING

As the immediate coup crisis subsided into something that could pass for normality in Chile, the CIA continued to share the PDC's assumption that the Christian Democrats' presence in Chile could benefit to U.S. interests there. As the PDC embarked on its Latin American "truth tour," the U.S. ambassador and the Santiago station immediately offered funding, based on 40 Committee spending approvals made before the coup.

This did not please Washington. A coup had not been figured into U.S. budget forecasting, and so after the coup Langley found itself with a series of projects and funds, authorized by a 40 Committee meeting of August 20, 1973, that many in Washington did not think were necessary in the post-coup situation. Ten days after the coup, apparently under pressure from the White House, Langley cabled the Santiago station to say that the August 20 approval was entirely irrelevant and that the station should suggest a new set of programs to be reviewed and perhaps approved. Langley expressed the belief that the CIA could not "justify [a] continuation of the level and type of subsidy support provided heretofore for opposition stance, but [saw] a continuing need for intelligence coverage and agent of influence capabilities in these areas."[19] Supporting the PDC "truth team" was conceded as a justifiable use of funds, but Langley "deeply regretted" that the Agency could not allow any disbursal of funds until a new 40 Committee decision.[20] Headquarters suggested that the ambassador appeal to the secretary of state, to go over the head of Jack Kubisch, the assistant secretary of state for Inter-American Affairs (ARA), who was a prime obstacle to further funding. The ambassador declined such a move and chose instead to try and "change Mr. Kubisch's mind."[21] Kubisch, however, continued to oppose the country team's proposals, though he did not give a reason for doing so, despite the submission of a formal request on October 4, 1973.[22]

In the month-long interim before a decision regarding Truth Tour funding was made, the CIA reported on the PDC's first national meeting since the coup. During the meeting the party members expressed their concern that the junta was not behaving democratically and decided that, while they would continue to express their unqualified support for the junta publicly, they would also move to curb government atrocities, executions, and imprisonments.[23]

At the end of November the Santiago station submitted a further request for support to two Radical Party splinters that "continue to function internally and are active in their efforts to expand their influence" despite the ban on political activity.[24] It seems that the CIA grew tired of waiting for 40 Committee approvals of new projects, and on November 20 headquarters cabled the Santiago station to say that "all political action projects [are] being submitted [to the president] for renewal now without waiting for 40 Committee action. . . . Projects will be amended as appropriate on basis of 40 Committee action."[25] Funding would continue at least until the end of the fiscal year.

The reasons for Kubisch's opposition to the CIA proposals became clear only in the last week of November. In discussions with 40 Committee members, Kubisch expressed the belief—an echo of earlier State Department reticence to conduct *any* covert action—that "political action should only be used as last resort for most compelling 'U.S. interest' reasons . . . [and he] kept raising the serious problem specter if [the] junta discovered we were funding PDC."[26] Still, the CIA did find support from ARA Deputy Assistant Secretary Henry Schlaudeman (who had been the deputy chief of mission in Santiago from 1969 to 1973). Schlaudeman argued on behalf of incoming U.S. ambassador to Chile David H. Popper (whose credentials were not presented until some time after the long-delayed U.S. recognition of the junta) that support to the PDC was necessary "on the grounds that [the United States] needed [the Christian Democrats'] future good will and abrupt termination of support would lead party leaders to believe we had used them during [the] Allende government and then dumped them as soon as military took over." Shlaudeman was apparently alone in suggesting that the PDC should at least be given a surge of funding to allow them a less sudden shift to private funds. Clearly, Langley reported, more persuasive arguments would be needed to win even this diminished subsidy.[27]

The CIA reacted negatively to the 40 Committee's and the White House's lethargy on the topic of continued political action in Chile. Writing at the end of November, David Atlee Phillips, now Chief of the Western Hemisphere Division (WHD), railed at the executive's languor at the critical post-coup juncture. His argument was persuasive and pragmatic; he believed that wasting carefully built political assets within Chile's still-functioning (if "recessed") party system would be a dangerous mistake:

> Since the coup d'etat of September 1973 and the assumption of power by military junta, the 40 Committee has vacillated on what subsidies, if any, should be given to the PDC to support its activities under the junta. These subsidies, however, appear to be necessary to maintain the PDC as a viable alternative party to the Communist and Socialist Parties should the junta relinquish power to civilian control under a new constitution. Since much of the financial base of support for the PDC was destroyed by the fiscal policies of the Allende regime, the PDC is heavily dependent on U.S. government funding if it is to compete effectively with the former UP Parties for support among middle and low income groups.[28]

By the end of December, fully three months after the first requests were submitted, the 40 Committee had granted no authorization to continue funding the PDC or to continue publication of an unnamed newspaper, which was likely *El Mercurio*. Using an argument similar to its justification for political action, the station asserted that a sudden ending to the CIA subsidy would cause a break with carefully nurtured propaganda assets that might later prove useful.[29] Without them, the station would be unable to "maintain our capability for influencing the Junta and molding Chilean public opinion."[30] Several station officers, feeling that "the sooner Pinochet departed power, the better," made personal remonstrations to Washington in favor of supporting continued covert action in Chile.[31]

Essentially, they felt to fail to continue their efforts post-coup was a waste of three years of political effort ostensibly aimed at preserving Chilean democracy from the clutches of dictatorship.

While the White House delayed and the station pleaded, the net was closing in on Chile's democratic parties. The station reported in late January that the junta sought to "broaden [its] political base . . . at the expense of the political parties."[32] This was put into effect with Decree Law 77 of October 13, 1973, which banned all Marxist parties. Decree Law 77 was followed four days later with no. 78, which declared "in recess all political parties and entities, groups, factions or movements of a political nature not included in Decree Law No. 77." Further, all of the political parties' properties were confiscated by the state.[33] Decree Law 1899 of January 23, 1974, prohibited parties from engaging in any political activity whatsoever.[34]

In view of the total abolition of political activity, as well as the continued curfews and surveillance by the newly formed Chilean central security agency, the DINA, when the 40 Committee finally met to consider the proposal for continued funding it was a moot point. The last piece of paperwork to mention the funding program came on March 1, 1974, from Ray Warren in Santiago to David Atlee Phillips in Langley:

> [Parties] were advised on [deleted] February that the changed political conditions in Chile make it impossible for us to continue to subsidize [deleted] and that we wish to divest ourselves of any responsibility for [deleted]. They were told that with the termination of this fiscal year, all subsidy support for [deleted] would cease. This news came as a shock and a disappointment.[35]

And with that, more than a decade of support and encouragement aimed at preserving Chile's political culture simply faded away with U.S. government inaction and the increasing authoritarian nature of the Pinochet junta.

The PDC simply never had the influence the CIA initially hoped it had. As for why the party was allowed to suffer such an unheralded end, the answer is unclear and the record of decisions entirely incomplete. Jack Devine argued that the reason was one of practicalities; he said that one should not seek "political motivation for not supporting the parties against Pinochet. [The U.S. government was] just sort of stuck with what they had, the Junta went on longer than we supposed, and Pinochet was *much* stronger and harsher in power than we had ever supposed."[36]

The permanence of the junta and of Pinochet's grip on the apparatus of government became clear to Henry Kissinger in "late November or December" 1973. He has argued that by that time U.S. options on Chile had been severely reduced by the realities of the situation. The United States had not sought a coup but one had occurred, and to subsequently move against the junta would have been folly: "One must judge it in relation to all the other things. We were willing to use our influence to improve the human rights situation, but we were not willing to take the step of overthrowing the junta. This is because the alternative was the Argentine situation: a civil war, an actual civil war."[37]

A civil war—one can assume that Kissinger was referring to the dirty war in Argentina—meant only more killing and would result in either a confirmed military junta or a new Marxist one. Thus, there was little point in initiating such a cruel set of events. Even had the United States desired, against all geopolitical reasoning, to rid Chile of the relatively friendly Pinochet government, it could do little in the short or even the long term: when faced with a personalized dictatorship, "there are only so many things you can do."[38] Political action with proscribed political parties would do little. Thus, funding ended because of a mixture of realpolitik recognition of the benefit of a noncommunist junta and the sheer inability to do anything about it anyway.

Whatever the reasons for ending U.S. support, the fact that the CIA was arguing in favor of continued funding for the PDC is a clear indication that the Agency did not expect the coup, had little to do with it, knew even less about the attitudes and positions of the junta that orchestrated it, and had not prepared contingencies for its occurrence. The Santiago station was, in short, slightly surprised, a reaction that the CIA generally tries to avoid for itself and its consumers. The CIA's support for the PDC is thus evidence against U.S. complicity in the Chilean coup of 1973 and serves as something of a criticism of its intelligence-gathering mission in the lead-up to the coup. Clearly after the coup the Agency had little knowledge of the junta's thoughts or plans and was still trying to figure out what the political fallout of the coup might be in the short and long term.

More specifically, the post-coup support indicates that the CIA generally does not seek "realist" means to its ends and that it generally supports any compliant dictator in the spirit of Franklin Roosevelt's reported comment on Nicaraguan dictator Anastasio Somoza: "He may be a son of a bitch, but he's our son of a bitch." Certainly, the Nixon administration treated Pinochet this way, at least for a short while after he took power, until both his and the Ford administrations began to cut off assistance and aid under heavy public pressure to do so. In this instance, neither the State Department nor the Agency followed the supposed traditional path of seeking a tractable warlord who could be trusted to keep a sharp eye out for American interests, "even if he lived on pillage and rapine," as political commentator Paul Berman described it.[39] Both in the months before the coup and in the months after the coup the CIA was more concerned with support to the center-left PDC and other centrist parties than it was with even the right-of-center PN—though the latter party did of course receive aid. One might surmise from this that the CIA was more directly concerned with its mission of supporting democratic organizations within the country, and as it became clear that the junta was going to be violent, authoritarian, and enduring, some felt that this mission was increasingly valid. This sense was ultimately disposed of by a combination of Kissinger and Nixon's realpolitik reasoning and the simple facts on the ground: the CIA, as throughout the entire campaign, had little ability to alter the state's fundamental political economy. It might have been able to keep a political party running for a few more months, but the Agency alone could not topple or halt a dictatorship whose greater sociopolitical context was three years in the making.

CONCLUSION: THE CHILEAN CAMPAIGN IN PERSPECTIVE

The history of US policy towards Latin America as a whole seems to be one constant swing of the pendulum between excesses: between studied indifference, ignorance and downright neglect and a kind of slushy romanticism . . . between paternalistic imperialism and reformist altruism.

—Alistair Horne, *Small Earthquake in Chile*

No matter what politics one professes, the violent overthrow of an elected government is always tragic; it means that somewhere, at some point, reasonable men and women made the conscious decision to put their sectarian or ideological interests above the welfare of the people and the nation. In Chile both the Right and the Left made this decision, a sad judgment compounded by a myriad of other sins of omission and commission. All of this led to the collapse of a prosperous economy, the destruction of the fabric of a vibrant and democratic state, and seventeen years of dictatorial rule. No rational human could fail to find this heartrending.

Despite this tragedy, Allende has become a martyr, perhaps unjustifiably so, while the United States has been cast as a villain. Through the remainder of the Cold War, the KGB helped build this image of "Allende the Martyr" to the cause of socialism, much to the discomfiture of the Pinochet government and its American allies.[1] The assumption of American guilt—aided by what Kissinger, in the climate of Vietnam and Watergate, has dismissively called the "bleeding press"[2]—pervaded the U.S. government itself. Men such as Congressman Michael Harrington assaulted U.S. actions in Chile as acts of "destabilization" and pointed menacingly at the specter of ITT's corporate interest. To this, former Ambassador to Chile Nathaniel Davis responded by noting that as time went on there was "progressively less Chilean institutional viability to 'destabilize.'"[3] But the damage had been done and no amount of rational defense (impossible to give in any case) would have undone the perception of unmitigated U.S. aggression.

Some may ask, quite rationally, could a man such as Allende in a country such as Chile ever have been a threat to the United States sufficiently serious to warrant the aggressive actions visited upon them? This well-meaning question ignores the threat perceived by many in the United States at the time, who saw (equally rationally) in the Soviet Union a stalwart challenge to the existence of the United States and its allies. The U.S. government as a whole viewed Chile not as a direct threat but "as part of a larger context of strategic relationships between the superpowers," said Davis in a interview with CNN. He added that the context in which the U.S. government viewed Chile was "that there was the Soviet Union and we were engaged in a world-wide confrontation. . . . Particularly in Chile, the communists [might] take over and then there would be a second nation in the hemisphere that was under communist control. That would be a problem to us."[4] The specific problem, as defined by another CIA officer, was that this might trigger a string of communist takeovers in Latin America, which would inevitably invite greater Soviet participation in a continent the communists had hitherto ignored.[5] More prosaically, reliance on Soviet arms by one nation might trigger the arms race in Latin America that the United States had historically sought to avert.

These important political drivers are quickly forgotten by the nation that won the Cold War and can hardly remember that a peer competitor challenged its existence. Thus, the political imperatives of the day are forgotten, eclipsed by the soul-searching of a calmer and more reflective era, coupled with an amplification of and sensitivity to the sins that were committed in pursuit of this forgotten national goal. As recently as 2003, U.S. Secretary of State Colin Powell apologized, noting in a public forum that "Chile in the 1970s, and what happened with Mr. Allende, it is not a part of U.S. history that we are proud of."[6] This statement ignores far too many of the domestic political and economic currents in Chile at the cost of American involvement. Too often, the Americans are assigned almost total agency in the collapse of Chile's democracy; they are given the sole and undivided blame. It must be acknowledged, absolutely, that the Chileans who overthrew the Allende government did not perceive it this way. Col. Paul Wimert recalls that, when he tried, in 1970, to disburse bribery money on behalf of the CIA, he was met by indignant reaction from his friends and contacts in the Chilean army. One officer put it starkly to Wimert: "Oh no no no. . . . You don't understand. . . . I love my country. I do this for my country not because of the United States. You keep the money, I don't want it." Wimert added that this "was typical of most Chilean officers."[7] Absurdly, those who argue that the United States played the decisive role in the Allende regime's collapse are unwitting adherents to the school of American exceptionalism and superpatriotism that they stridently criticize Kissinger and Nixon for.

Thankfully, scholarship and debate about Chile under Allende and Pinochet has grown more nuanced in recent years, especially in Chile. But if one chooses to focus on U.S. responsibility for the coup, one needs to separate causation from correlation. One could argue that the evidence to link hostile intent from Nixon and Kissinger (very clear in all instances) to the actions of the main executive arm, the CIA, is much more tenuous than many—Kenneth Maxwell, Peter Kornbluh, and Jonathan Haslam included—assert. Where the CIA acted against Allende, the evidence seems to show that its impact was far less significant than assumed. Undoubtedly, though, events did not proceed to script. The U.S. campaign—as many at the time perceived it—to preserve Chile's democracy ultimately failed but not in the manner the U.S. government thought it might. Democracy in Chile was ended by the very "constitutionalist" ally the United States sought to recruit, not by the creeping menace of socialism it feared.

But what is the significance of this failure? What can we learn from U.S. efforts to alter the internal politics of Chile? Are these lessons enduring or ephemeral? The late director of central intelligence (DCI), Richard Helms, in his posthumously published memoir, offered what he considered the most important lessons from Chile:

> There are three lessons to be relearned in respect to Chile and Tracks I and II. If a major covert action is to be undertaken, ample time must be allotted for preparation; if *any* secret U.S. contact is made with an individual or group thought to be planning a coup or revolution, it will be all but impossible to convince the plotters that this contact does not indicate U.S. support; and, finally, unless the fate of the nation is at stake, an intelligence service should try to avoid being saddled with the

> command, "do something, for Heaven's sake, do *anything*." When such hasty operations begin to come unstuck, the highest authority is likely to have forgotten its earlier command.[8]

These plainly stated lessons are certainly important, and they reflect the views of a man who led the intelligence community during a very trying time. The criticisms, though, focus on a very narrow band of time—fall 1970 and Schneider's assassination—and leave out the long periods of U.S. action both before and after the election of Allende.

The narrative of the full length of the U.S. covert campaign in Chile is instructive for many reasons. One can see that starting in the early 1960s, the United States sought to preserve democratic constitutional order in Chile (as the government perceived it) through support of centrist democratic parties and purposefully eschewed contact with extremist elements in its quest to find a suitable alternative to communist rule. The PDC, a wonderful simulacrum of the U.S. Democratic Party, seemed the perfect vehicle for America's Latin American ambitions, as initially directed by President John F. Kennedy. U.S. input in PDC's favor was mostly quiet, generally benign, and largely unnecessary. Success in the 1964 election, however, with the popular and generally effective President Eduardo Frei, confirmed ex post facto the wisdom of the decision to support the party.

Yet various sectors of the U.S. government remained uncertain about the wisdom of covert action, and this resistance, coupled with an administration that did not take Latin America seriously, led to a disastrous neglect of affairs in Chile. Through the 1969 election and the run-up to the 1970 presidential election, the Nixon administration ignored the CIA's pleas to support *someone* against the increasingly (or perhaps continuously) popular Allende; after all, if he was enough of a concern to warrant intervention in 1964, did he not remain so in 1970? We saw from Nixon after Allende's election an irrational reaction that ultimately resulted in General Schneider's death; by that time the president at least considered Chilean politics important in terms of U.S. interests. If this is the case, why was there no previous executive input on the matter? One is left with a choice: first, Chile's political structure was important to the United States, and so American inactivity was a mistake; or perhaps it was not important and the U.S. overreaction was unnecessary and damaging in the long run. Alternately, Chile's politics were important to the United States, but the dangers of intervention and the Good Neighbor policy of nonintervention outweighed the threat of a Marxist government there. Regardless of the choice, the results of the actions carried out point to a failure at the executive level of government and the damage was done.

Throughout the process, one can see a different side of the CIA than is normally portrayed in the popular media. Frequently depicted as hawkish and cruel, the Agency's own documents show that it was often one of the more circumspect of the agencies involved in Chile. Save for a few individuals, the Santiago station sought to avoid extreme measures and argued for gradual and low-key procedures to prevent a communist victory when most of the rest of the government was ignoring Chile. ITT's peripheral participation in Chile and its ultimate rejection by the CIA also tells a different story of the Agency's priorities than is often assumed. These factors show an executive agency of the state, one interested not in action for action's sake or in propping up big business, but rather in the efficient execution of properly determined state policy. Therein lays the trouble: in not all cases was the U.S. government policy fully or properly determined. Especially under Nixon, intelligence was ignored in favor of ill-thought and very kinetic "solutions" to "problems" often divorced from the state's concerns.

The story of the CIA in Chile from 1964 to 1976 is essentially also the story of the exercise of presidential authority over covert operations. Previous to the exposures of the Chilean operations through the revelations of the ITT scandal and through the subsequent Church committees, the covert action approval process, as seen in the 1964 and 1970 operations, was indeed a regular process but one not formalized by law or oversight—at least not laws or oversight that were taken overly seriously. National Security Decision Memorandum (NSDM) 40, issued in February 1970, was one effort to codify and streamline the process, though major concerns about what consisted of a "major" or "politically sensitive" covert operation requiring the approval of the eponymous 40 Committee and the attention of the president remained.[9] Even after the formation of the 40 Committee, the president could, and did, override and ignore the development and execution of a covert action. When this was done, as we saw in 1964 with Johnson (who basically ignored covert actions in Chile) or in 1970 with Nixon (who first ignored, then superseded the process), operations went wrong. When relatively smooth joint processes of approval were followed, with good direction from the executive, policy guidance from State, capabilities and resources from the Agency, and the local steering from a joint Agency-State country team with input from the ambassador, operations went well.

The Vietnam War forced American leaders to become aware of the limits of power—military power especially.[10] Chile seems to have had a similar effect in the secret world. When asked if the perceived failure of operations in Chile and the unprecedented revelations by DCI William Colby to the Church and Pike committees—so rued by Helms and others—had truly wrought a change on the conduct of covert action, former Assistant Secretary of State for Inter-American Affairs (ARA) William D. Rogers replied in the affirmative and noted that the impact was great even on the White House itself, where "there was a lot of feeling across the board that the United States had overstepped the bounds of propriety and that it was counterproductive in terms of the national interest and that we should not behave that way."[11] Such failures—for in this instance perception is reality—are truly problematic in a liberal democratic state. As former Secretary of State Caspar Weinberger stated, such failed operations exact a heavy price because "without accomplishing the goal for which we committed our forces . . . such policies might very well tear at the fabric of our society, endangering the single most critical element of a successful democracy: a strong consensus of support and agreement for our basic purposes."[12] As the 303 Committee noted in February 1969, "covert action proposals are to be supplemental to and in support of overt Government activities. There are to be no covert actions for the sake of having covert actions."[13] By pursuing "policies formed without a clear understanding of what we hope to achieve," the United States would only endanger its ability to intervene when it truly mattered, simply by eroding the trust of the public and those members of government who execute policy. Covert action, in short, is a resource wasted by ill-thought-out or overenthusiastic use. We see this exemplified by the fact that a decade of excellently planned covert actions have been forever tarred as criminal by the foolishly desperate plans and actions of October 1970.

If the United States committed grave mistakes in Chile, how should one view the entirety of the U.S. covert campaign? First, one must work on the belief that the U.S. intelligence agencies are neither superhuman nor innately evil—a belief that pervades much of the scholarship on U.S. secret intelligence and security writing, especially on the subject of Chile. Second, from that assumption, a look at the evidence amassed here shows, I believe, that the various organizations developing and executing state policy in the United States are organizations composed of fundamentally normal and moral people. While they seek a very partisan goal of success for their country and are pragmatic in this pursuit, they do not gain some sociopathic pleasure from undermining a state or inflicting suffering on any individual or group. Some, however, push normal morality to the wayside in this pursuit. CIA officer Ted Shackley has been identified as one of this sort of man, as has Harold Geneen of ITT. One correspondent has questioned the CIA's fundamental morality, noting that regardless of the Agency's successes or failures in Chile, it never questioned its own "arrogance in assuming that it had the right to work toward the destruction of a sovereign government."[14] But this misses the point. The CIA, like the Chilean military, is a nondeliberative body. It does not determine its own policy but rather executes only that policy determined by the president's legitimate authority. Nixon was elected with a strong anti-communist mandate, and so it is hardly surprising that he acted with firm anti-communist measures in his foreign policy once in office. Once given its orders, the CIA must move to implement them, even though they were given by a popularly elected president with the arrogance to assume that he had the right to meddle in the affairs of an elected and sovereign government. Through the period covered by this book, the actions carried out by the CIA did not infringe on U.S. laws, even when discussion moved to matters that were ultimately linked to an assassination—e.g., the kidnapping of Schneider. Only in the aftermath of the Chilean coup and revelations of U.S. involvement did Congress move to curb the executive's excesses when it came to covert action.

The lesson in this is clear: a codified approval process in covert action removes, at least partially, the danger of ego or immorality hijacking covert action for its own purposes, ensuring that it comprehends and submits to the policy's sovereignty. Thus, as much as the Church committee hearings were a lamentable and partisan inquisition against the CIA, their fundamental result has been a highly codified approval process for covert action, and so they have served a beneficial purpose to the state. The Hughes-Ryan Amendment, while viewed by some as a drag on the president's ability to engage in covert operations, at least ensures that the covert action in question serves some purpose within greater U.S. aims. Approval processes may seem cumbersome and unresponsive on the surface. The U.S. Defense Department has recently made efforts to conduct its own covert action outside of this process because it can be unresponsive and sluggish at times. Understanding, however, that covert action is best when it is most subtle, most effective when it is well thought out and planned, such temporary unresponsiveness should not be a major impediment.

Simply stated, covert action *is not* a replacement for failed or forgotten state actions required of a government; covert action *is* a single means within the normal array of means by which a government executes its duly determined policy. To rephrase using the Clausewitz quote mentioned in the introduction: covert action, like war, is the execution of state politics by other means. It is not the show-trial jury and summary executioner for some single self-styled judge hidden in the bowels (or head) of government. None of this is to ignore the U.S. president's rights and duties in the conduct of foreign affairs or in general safeguarding national security. Rather, it is a statement that takes into account the real effectiveness of covert action. But it also raises a serious question that further begs a theorization and codification of covert actions. If direct or covert actions are not war, then what are they?[15] Under whose authority do they fall? That a president could evade congressional authority over the waging of war by using covert forces under his executive authority seems unlikely, but it remains a distant possibility that requires our thought.

Great powers such as the United States will always undertake the actions required to protect their national self-interest, and because of this, intelligence agencies with covert action capabilities will always exist, just as armed forces will always exist. No environment or arena of human conflict, once entered, can ever safely be abandoned (almost all modern nations abjure the use of chemical and biological weapons, for instance, yet all soldiers carry respirator masks and protective suits and train for their usage), and so secret armies will continue to clash in the proverbial dim alleyways of the world. Nations will continue to prosper or fall because of them. So like the application of lethal force by national militaries, the use of intelligence agencies and of covert action is a matter far too complex to be left unstudied. If episodes such as the series of U.S. operations in Chile are left to the realm of mythology—that amorphous zone of assumption and fable—no lessons—or worse, the *wrong* lessons—will be learned. As the case of U.S. covert action in Chile shows, the lessons learned in U.S. operations are far too valuable to be abandoned in the favor of potboiler fables.

APPENDIX: GLOSSARY AND DRAMATIS PERSONAE

GLOSSARY

Ambassador-at-large: A special diplomatic envoy appointed by the president for specific assignments, primarily overseas. Presidents have usually appointed ambassadors-at-large to deal with specific foreign policy issues which have been frequently, but not always, spelled out in their commissions. They are usually referred to as "Ambassador."

Bureau of Intelligence and Research (INR): The State Department's intelligence analysis office.

Bureau of Inter-American Affairs (ARA): Bureau within the State Department that handles Latin American and Caribbean affairs.

Carabineros: Chile's uniformed national police. Not part of the armed forces, the Carabineros were nonetheless considered to be part of Chile's security services.

Chief of station (COS): The senior CIA officer in a U.S. embassy, who reports to both the ambassador and to CIA headquarters in Langley.

Chief of the Western Hemisphere Division (C/WHD): The lead CIA officer within the Western Hemisphere Division (WHD).

Chilean Communist Party (PCCh): The Partido Comunista de Chile was one of the two leading political parties (along with Allende's own Socialist Party) in the Unidad Popular (UP). Founded in 1922, they were loyal to Moscow and generally sought to avoid violence in the struggle to bring communism to Chile.

CIA station: The officers assigned to an embassy under official diplomatic cover.

Comisión Nacional para la Verdad y Reconciliación: The Chilean National Commission on Truth and Reconciliation, also known as the Rettig commission. President Patricio Aylwin established the commission, which was led by Senator Raúl Rettig, to investigate killings and disappearances during Pinochet's dictatorship. A report of its findings was published in February 1991.

Country team: The country team is the team of embassy staff, both CIA and State Department, assembled to help conduct any particular covert action in an embassy. The CIA officers working in the embassy are said to be under official cover, as they ostensibly hold diplomatic posts within the embassy.

Deputy director of plans (DDP): The CIA official charged with the execution of covert operations. At the time of the Chilean operation, the DDP was one of four line officers reporting directly to the DCI.

Director of central intelligence (DCI): The official charged with coordinating intelligence activities among and between the U.S. intelligence agencies; he also acts as the director of the CIA.

Directorate: The highest level of organizational structure within the CIA.

Directorate of Intelligence (DI): The directorate within the CIA charged with the production of finished (analyzed) intelligence from information collected by the Directorate of Plans.

Directorate of Plans (DP): The directorate within the CIA charged with the collection of information from human sources abroad, and with the conduct of covert operations. Under William Colby, its name was changed to the Directorate of Operations, to better reflect its actual task.

***El Mercurio*:** The oldest Spanish-language newspaper in the world and primary rightist newspaper in Chile. *El Mercurio* was the primary and most strident media critic of the Allende government.

False-flag officer: A CIA officer who operates falsely as an agent of another country to recruit potential agents hostile or sensitive to the idea of working for the United States. By extension of his method of operation, a false-flag officer is also a nonofficial cover (NOC) officer.

Foreign Military Sales (FMS): a program by which surplus U.S. military equipment was sold to allied or friendly nations at a reduced cost.

40 Committee: The executive committee responsible for reviewing and authorizing covert action programs. The 40 Committee replaced the 303 Committee in February 1970 with the issue of NSDM 40.

Frente Accion Popular (FRAP): The Popular Action Front, the Socialist-Communist front party that preceded the UP.

Grupo de Amigos Personales (GAP): Allende's personal security force.

***Jefe de la Plaza*:** Chief of the plaza, the general in charge of internal security in Chile.

Movimiento de Acción Popular Unitaria (MAPU): A small party formed by a "rebelde" section of militant PDC youth in May of 1969. They joined the UP front party in 1970 and remained in government until the coup.

Military Assistance Program (MAP): The U.S. government program by which military equipment and training were provided to armies in Latin America gratis.

El Movimiento de Izquierda Revolucionario (MIR): The Revolutionary Movement of the Left, an extreme left-wing political party and organization employed (unofficially) by the UP to enforce politically impossible measures, such as the occupation of privately owned firms, attacks on opposition press and political parties, and attacks on anti-government protests. MIR was the chief opponent of Patria y Libertad in the frequent street battles of late 1972 and 1973.

National Intelligence Directorate (DINA): Chile's central security agency, formed under Pinochet's junta.

National Intelligence Estimate (NIE): Written by the U.S. Intelligence Board, NIEs offer the intelligence community's assessment of particular national security issues, as directed by the president or DCI.

Nonofficial cover officer (NOC): A CIA officer operating outside of diplomatic cover, usually under corporate, professional, or press cover. An NOC may also operate as a false-flag officer.

Partido Democrata Cristiána (PDC): The Christian Democratic Party of Chile, a left-center party and the primary noncommunist party in Chile. The PDC was the main opposition to the Allende government.

Partido Izquierda Radical (PIR): The Radical Party of the Left, a non-Marxist member of the ruling UP coalition. PIR left the coalition in 1972, causing a significant ripple in the confidence of the government but not affecting its strength in Congress.

Partido Nacional (PN): National Party, a right-wing party in the minority of the opposition.

Partido Socialista (PS): The Chilean Socialist Party was one of the two major constituent parties of the UP. Salvador Allende was a member of the PS. More radical than the PCCh, there was a strong faction within the PS that was committed to violent revolution.

Patria y Libertad: Homeland and Liberty, an extreme right-wing organization that used violence and street gangs to oppose the UP government. Patria y Libertad's youth organization was MIR's chief opponent in the frequent street battles of late 1972 and 1973.

Senior Review Group (SRG): A cabinet-level group of CIA, National Security Council, and State Department officials charged with the review of security-related matters.

303 Committee: Committee established in June 1964 to review sensitive national security affairs and to coordinate action programs between executive departments. It had responsibility to provide political direction to covert actions overseas, and was the successor to the SRG and the predecessor of the 40 Committee.

Unidad Popular (UP): A united front of Marxist, socialist, and communist parties, formed in 1970 and headed by Salvador Allende and which comprised the left-wing segment of the Chilean political spectrum. The UP controlled the government of Chile only once, from 1970 to 1973.

U.S. Intelligence Board (USIB): Board representing all U.S. intelligence agencies in the production of National Intelligence Estimates (NIEs).

Western Hemisphere Division (WHD): The division within the Directorate of Plans that deals with covert operations and intelligence gathering within the Americas. To avoid confusing "WH" with White House, the name was subsequently changed, in 1974, to Latin American and Caribbean Division.

DRAMATIS PERSONAE

UNITED STATES

Tracy C. Barnes: Assistant deputy director of plans, 1964–June 1966.

William V. Broe: CIA chief of the Western Hemisphere Division (C/WHD), Directorate of Plans, from June 1965 to mid-1973.

Albert E. Carter: Deputy director of coordination for intelligence and research, Bureau of Intelligence and Research, Department of State, until December 1965.

Ray S. Cline: Deputy director of intelligence from April 1962 to 1966. From 1966 to 1969 special assistant to the DCI. Subsequently, Mr. Cline served as director of the Bureau of Intelligence and Research from October 1969 to November 1973.

William Colby: CIA special operations veteran. Colby pioneered the CIA's election operations in Italy in the 1950s. He was made executive director-comptroller of the CIA in 1971. Made deputy director of plans from March to August 1973, he was subsequently made DCI, in which post he remained until January 1976. With coauthor Peter Forbath, he has written a book about his career in the CIA, *Honorable Men*.

John H. Crimmins: Ambassador to the Dominican Republic from 1966 to 1969 and senior deputy assistant secretary for inter-American affairs from 1969 to 1973.

Nathaniel Davis: U.S. ambassador to Chile from October 1971 to October 1973.

Jack Devine: CIA officer, Santiago station from 1971 to 1973.

Desmond FitzGerald: Deputy chief of the Western Hemisphere Division for Cuban Affairs, Directorate of Plans, Central Intelligence Agency, until March 1964; chief of the Western Hemisphere Division March 1964-June 1965; deputy director for plans until July 1967.

Alexander Haig: Kissinger's military assistant from 1969 to 1970, deputy assistant to the president for national security affairs from 1970 to 1973, and White House chief of staff from 1973 to 1974.

Richard Helms: DCI under President Nixon, during Tracks I and II.

Henry Hecksher: Santiago COS from 1967 to November 1970. Hecksher had previously served at the CIA station in Vietnam.

Thomas Lowe Hughes: Director of the Bureau of Intelligence and Research from April 1963 to August 1969.

Robert Hurwitch: First secretary at U.S. Embassy Santiago from July to September 1964.

U. Alexis Johnson: Undersecretary of state for political affairs from February 1969 to February 1973. From February 1973 to February 1977, he served as State Department ambassador-at-large.

Thomas Karamessines: Assistant deputy director for plans from 1964 to 1967, then CIA deputy director for plans from July 1967 to

February 1973. Karamessines was made the head of the Chile Task Force, which executed Track II under the direct orders of the White House.

Henry Kissinger: Assistant to the president on national security affairs for President Nixon, de facto chairman of the NSC until November 1975, and secretary of state from September 1973 to January 1977.

Edward Korry: U.S. ambassador to Chile from October 1967 to October 1971.

Jack Kubisch: Assistant secretary of state for inter-American affairs from May 1973 to June 1974.

Charles Meyer: Assistant secretary of state for inter-American affairs from April 1969 to March 1973. Meyer represented the U.S. government at Allende's inauguration on November 3, 1970.

David Atlee Phillips: A veteran of CIA operations in Chile from the 1950s, he helped to run Track II in September–October 1970, though he was at the time COS in Rio de Janeiro. Phillips became C/WHD in June 1973. He has written a book about his CIA career titled *The Night Watch*.

David H. Popper: U.S. ambassador to Chile from February 1974 to May 1977.

William D. Rogers: Washington lawyer, head of the Alliance for Progress, and assistant secretary of state for inter-American affairs from October 1974 to June 1976.

William P. Rogers: Secretary of state under Nixon. President Ford replaced him with Henry Kissinger.

Henry W. Schlaudeman: State Department official. Schlaudeman was deputy chief of mission in Santiago from 1969 to 1973, when he became deputy assistant secretary for inter-American affairs.

Brent Scowcroft: Nixon's military assistant in 1973 and deputy assistant for national security affairs in 1974.

Ted Shackley: CIA officer, C/WHD from May 1972 to June 1973.

Viron P. Vaky: State Department, acting assistant secretary for inter-American affairs January to May 1969. From May 1969 to 1972 he was the NSC staff expert for Latin American affairs and adviser to Kissinger, though he was largely absent from this position after November 1970.

Lt. Gen. Vernon A. Walters: Deputy director of the CIA from May 1972.

Raymond Warren: CIA chief of station in Santiago who succeeded Henry Hecksher in November 1970. His tour as COS was his second tour in Chile, and he remained in place until after the coup.

Col. Paul J. Wimert Jr.: U.S. Army military attaché in Santiago from 1967 to 1971. A passionate equestrian, he had close relations with the equally horse-loving Chilean army and was seconded to the CIA during Track II to exploit these contacts.

CHILE

Salvador Allende Gossens: Presidential candidate for the FRAP coalition in 1964. President of the Chilean senate from 1966. Head of the Unidad Popular coalition that won the 1970 presidential election. He was overthrown in a coup on September 11, 1973.

Jorge Allesandri Rondriguez: President of Chile from 1958 to 1964, as member of the National Party. As an independent, Allesandri was the main candidate against Allende in the 1970 election.

Brig. Gen. Alfredo Cannales Márquez: Director of the War Academy after Allende's election. Cannales was involved in Allende's ouster.

Eduardo Frei Montalva: President of Chile from 1964 to 1970 and a leading figure in the PDC.

Adm. Ismael Huerta Díaz: Commander of the fleet at Valparaíso in 1970, he was an early coup plotter. He became minister of foreign affairs under the junta.

Gen. Gustavo Leigh Guzmán: Commander in chief of the Air Force, he was involved in the plot to overthrow Allende.

Gen. César Mendoza Durán: Director general of the Carabineros, he was involved in the plot to overthrow Allende.

José Tohá: Allende's interior minister. He was impeached in 1972.

Adm. José Toribio Merino Castro: Commander in chief of the navy, he was involved in the plot to overthrow Allende.

Gen. Carlos Prats González: Commander in chief of the Chilean army and minister of defense in Allende's first military cabinet. Under pressure from his chief staff officers, he resigned both positions on August 23, 1973. He was later assassinated in Argentina by the Chilean secret service.

Gen. René Schneider Chereau: Commander in chief of the Chilean army (*Jefe del Ejercito*) at the time of Allende's election. He was killed in a botched kidnap attempt on October 22, 1970.

Gen. Augusto Pinochet Ugarte: Senior staff officer in the Chilean army. *Jeffe de la Plaza* through the time of the strikes and civil unrest from August 1972. He replaced Prats as army commander in chief after the former's resignation on August 23, 1973, and held that position at the time of the coup. Subsequent to the coup, Pinochet became the president of the ruling junta and effectively the dictator of Chile.

Radomiro Tomic Romero: The PDC candidate for the presidential elections of 1970 and a former Chilean ambassador to Washington.

Gen. Camilo Valenzuela: Commander of the Santiago district at the time of Allende's election and inauguration. Involved in plotting the coup against Allende, he assumed the position of *Jefe de la Plaza* after the inauguration but resigned and fled after his role in the plotting surfaced.

Gen. Roberto Viaux Marambio: Chilean army officer who retired after leading the abortive *tacnazo* insurrection in 1969. He plotted the botched October 22, 1970, kidnapping of Gen. René Schneider and was subsequently arrested and exiled.

NOTES

INTRODUCTION: THE CIA IN CHILE

1. William P. Rogers and Henry A. Kissinger, telephone transcript, September 14, 1970, from the personal files of Dr. Kissinger (hereafter cited as Kissinger).
2. Nathaniel Davis, *The Last Two Years of Salvador Allende* (Ithaca, NY: Cornell University Press, 1988), x.
3. Stephen Grey and Don Van Natta, "Thirteen with the CIA Sought by Italy in a Kidnapping," *New York Times*, June 25, 2005; and Daniel Benjamin, "Rendition at Risk," *Slate*, February 5, 2007. Benjamin notes that the term "extraordinary" should be added only as a prefix when the country from which the rendition took place did not provide permission for the act to take place.
4. Matthew S. Pape, "Constitutional Covert Actions: A Force Multiplier for Preemption," *Military Review*, March–April 2004, 54.
5. Seymour M. Hersh, "The Coming Wars: What the Pentagon Can Now Do in Secret," *New Yorker*, January 24, 2005.
6. Reuters article, "Venezuela Ends Military Ties and Evicts Some U.S. Officers," as published in *New York Times*, April 25, 2005. See also Reuters article "The Chavez Victory," *New York Times*, August 20, 2004.
7. William Colby and Peter Forbath, *Honorable Men: My Life in the CIA* (New York: Simon & Schuster, 1978), 306.
8. Phillip K. Bobbitt, *The Shield of Achilles: War, Peace and the Course of History* (London: Allen Lane, 2002), 50.
9. For a more detailed view of the internal political situation in Chile under Salvador Allende, see Arturo Valenzuela, *The Breakdown of Democratic Regimes: Chile* (Baltimore: Johns Hopkins University Press, 1978) or the more recent book by Jonathan Haslam, *The Nixon Administration and the Death of Allende's Chile: A Case of Assisted Suicide* (New York: Verso, 2005). The latter is described in more detail as follows.
10. Arthur Schlesinger Jr., *The Imperial Presidency* (Boston: Houghton Mifflin, 1973).
11. This quotation is variously and widely used and repeated in several different versions in Allende's speeches.
12. Salvador Allende Gossens, *Chile's Road to Socialism*, ed. Joan E. Garces, trans. J. Darling (Baltimore: Penguin Books, 1973), 50.
13. James R. Whelan, *Out of the Ashes: Life, Death and Transfiguration of Democracy in Chile, 1833–1988* (Washington, DC: Regnery Gateway, 1989), 228.

14. Mark Falcoff, "Reviews," *Orbis* 21: 1 (1977): 386.
15. Paul Sigmund, *The Overthrow of Allende and the Politics of Chile 1964–1976* (Pittsburgh: University of Pittsburgh Press, 1977).
16. See Luis Vitale, et al., *Para Recuperar La Memoria Histórica: Frei, Allende y Pinochet* (Santiago: Ediciones ChileAmérica-CESOC, 1999), 184–190. This Chilean work limits its discussion of American involvement in Chile to citing published sources regarding the Schneider assassination in October 1970.
17. Jorge Mario Eastman, *De Allende y Pinochet al "milagro" chileno* (Santafé de Bogotá: Editorial Ariel, 1997), 56–57. See also Joan E. Garcés, *El Estado y los Problemas Tácticos En El Gobierno De Allende* (Madrid: Siglo XXI de España Editores, 1974), 127. In Spanish "*La necesidad de suprerar el Estado burgués.*"
18. Mónica González, *Chile La Conjura: Los Mil y un Dias Del Golpe* (Santiago: Ediciones B Grupo Zeta, 2000).
19. Andrea Ruiz-Esquide Figueroa, *Las Fuerzas Armadas Durante Los Gobiernos de Eduardo Frei y Salvador Allende* (Santiago: Centro de Estudios del Desarrollo, 1993), i.
20. Joaquín Fermandois, "Pawn or Player? Chile in the Cold War," *Éstudios Públicos* 72 (Spring 1998), 10.
21. Ibid.
22. Seymour Hersh, *The Price of Power: Kissinger in the Nixon White House* (New York: Summit Books, 1983), 259.
23. Ibid., 292.
24. John Prados, *Lost Crusader: The Secret Wars of CIA Director William Colby* (New York: Oxford University Press, 2003), 253.
25. Senate Select Committee to Study Governmental Operations with Respect to Intelligence Activities, *Alleged Assassination Plots Involving Foreign Leaders*, interim report, 94th Cong., 1st sess., November 1975, S. Rep. 94-495 (henceforth cited as Church Committee, *Alleged Assassination Plots*).
26. U.S. Congress. Senate. Select Committee to Study Governmental Operations with Respect to Intelligence Activities. *Covert Action in Chile, 1963–1973*. 94th Cong., 1st sess., 1975.
27. Pat M. Holt, *Secret Intelligence and Public Policy: A Dilemma of Democracy* (Washington, DC: Congressional Quarterly, 1995), 221
28. Barry Goldwater, "On 'Covert Action in Chile, 1963–1973': A Response to the Church Committee Report," *Inter-American Economic Affairs* 30: 1 (Summer 1976): 85–86.
29. Mark Falcoff, *Modern Chile 1970–1989: A Critical History* (London: Transaction Publishers, 1989), 236. See also Davis, *Last Two Years*, 319.
30. U.S. Department of State, press releases, October 8, 1999, June 30, 1999, November 13, 2000.
31. This page estimate is based on an unscientifically determined average of four pages per document.
32. Christopher Hitchens, "The Case against Henry Kissinger, Part 1: The Making of a War Criminal," *Harper's Magazine*, February 2001, 33.
33. William D. Rogers and Kenneth Maxwell, "Fleeing the Chilean Coup: The Debate over U.S. Complicity," *Foreign Affairs* 83: 1 (2004), 160–165.
34. Peter Kornbluh, *The Pinochet File: A Declassified Dossier on Atrocity and Accountability* (New York: New Press, 2003).
35. Ibid., jacket comment by Samantha Power.

36. Kenneth Maxwell, "The Other 9/11: The United States and Chile, 1973," *Foreign Affairs* 82: 6 (2003): 151.
37. Jonathan Haslam, *Nixon Administration and the Death of Allende's Chile: A Case of Assisted Suicide* (New York: Verso, 2005).
38. Ibid., 228.
39. John L. Helgerson, *Getting to Know the President: CIA Briefings of Presidential Candidates 1952–1992*, (Washington, DC: Center for the Study of Intelligence, CIA, 1996), ch. 7.
40. Richard Helms, *A Look over My Shoulder: A Life in the Central Intelligence Agency*, with William Hood (New York: Random House, 2003), 428–434.
41. The Weinberger Doctrine was inspired by the failure of U.S. arms in Vietnam, and more specifically by the death of 241 U.S. Marines in the Beirut bombing of October 1983. In essence, it called for U.S. combat troops to be used only when absolutely called for by clear-cut and achievable U.S. interests. In particular, the doctrine stated:

    1. The United States should not commit forces to combat overseas unless the particular engagement or occasion is deemed vital to our national interest or that of our allies.
    2. If we decide it is necessary to put combat troops into a given situation, we should do so wholeheartedly and with the clear intention of winning.
    3. If we do decide to commit forces to combat overseas, we should have clearly defined political and military objectives.
    4. The relationship between our objectives and the forces we have committed—their size, composition, and disposition—must be continually reassessed and adjusted if necessary.
    5. Before the United States commits combat forces abroad, there must be some reasonable assurance we will have the support of the American people and their elected representatives in Congress.
    6. The commitment of U.S. forces to combat should be a last resort.

    Adapted from Caspar W. Weinberger, "The Uses of Power," remarks presented to the National Press Club, Washington, DC, November 28, 1984. See Michael Handel, *Masters of War: Classical Strategic Thought* (London: Frank Cass, 1992), annex A.

CHAPTER 1: THE CAMPAIGN BEGINS

1. U.S. Embassy, Santiago, "Semi-Annual Politico-Economic Assessment—Chile," airgram to U.S. State Department, February 8, 1964, A-592, Box 2025, Pol 2-1 Joint Weekas Chile, RG 59, National Archives and Record Administration, College Park, MD (hereafter cited as NARA).
2. Roy Richard Rubottom Jr., memo to Deputy Undersecretary for Economic Affairs, June 18, 1958, in U.S. State Department, *Foreign Relations of the United States, 1958–60*, vol. 5, microfiche supplement, CI-6 (hereafter cited as *FRUS, years*).
3. J. Biehl Del Rio and Gonzalo Fernández R., "The Political Pre-requisites for a Chilean Way," *Government and Opposition* 7: 3 (1972): 308.
4. Harold Eugene Davis, "The Presidency in Chile," *Presidential Studies Quarterly* 15: 4 (1985): 707.
5. Francisco Orrego Vicuña, ed., *Chile: The Balanced View* (Santiago: University of Chile, Institute of International Studies, 1975), 292.
6. In the period surrounding the War of the Pacific, Chile successfully challenged

the United States as the dominant naval power in the South Pacific littoral with its defeats of Peru and Bolivia. American political and commercial dominance of the southern cone was thwarted for several decades and was instead traded between Chile and Argentina. See William F. Sater, *Chile and the United States: Empires in Conflict* (Athens: University of Georgia Press, 1990).

7. Sigmund, *Overthrow of Allende*, 21. Cf. Falcoff, *Modern Chile*, 18.
8. USIB, The Chilean Situation and Prospects," NIE 94-63, October 3, 1963, in *FRUS, 1961–63*, vol. 12, microfiche supplement, doc. 45.
9. Davis, *Last Two Years*, 3.
10. INR, "Salvador Allende, Chilean Presidential Candidate," memorandum, April 24, 1964, in Declassified Documents Reference System, at www.gale.com (hereafter cited as DDRS) (all documents accessed on July 15, 2003, through University of Cambridge Library servers).
11. James D. Theberge, *The Soviet Presence in Latin America* (New York: Crane, Russak, 1974), 51. See also Edward M. Korry, testimony in House Subcommittee on Inter-American Affairs, *The United States and Chile during the Allende Years, 1970–1973: Hearings before the Subcommittee on Inter-American Affairs of the Committee of Foreign Affairs*, 94th Cong., 1st sess., 1975, 11.
12. Eusebio Mujal-León, *The USSR and Latin America: A Developing Relationship* (Boston: Unwin Hyman, 1989), 124–125. See also del Rio and Fernández R., "Political Pre-requisites for a Chilean Way," 316.
13. Julio Faúndez, *Marxism and Democracy in Chile: From 1932 to the Fall of Allende* (New Haven, CT: Yale University Press, 1988), 31, 160–161.
14. Ibid.
15. Sigmund, *Overthrow of Allende*, 17.
16. INR, "Pressures for Change Dominate Chilean Presidential Campaign," memorandum to ARA, May 1, 1964, DDRS.
17. Falcoff, *Modern Chile*, 203.
18. INR, "Salvador Allende."
19. Faúndez, *Marxism and Democracy in Chile*, 109.
20. Falcoff, *Modern Chile*, 14.
21. Walter Howe, dispatch to U.S. State Department, January 8, 1960, in *FRUS, 1958–60*, vol. 5, microfiche supplement, CI-27.
22. Jorgé Alessandri and Dwight Eisenhower, memorandum of conversation, February 29, 1960, in *FRUS, 1958–60*, vol. 5, microfiche supplement, CI-30.
23. Ibid.
24. Ibid.
25. Peter Kornbluh, *Pinochet File*, 4.
26. David Atlee Phillips, *The Night Watch: 20 Years of Peculiar Service* (New York: Atheneum, 1977), ch. 1 passim.
27. John F. Kennedy, "Inaugural Address," in *Inaugural Addresses of the Presidents of the United States: From George Washington to George W. Bush*, 2nd ed. (Washington, DC: GPO, 1989).
28. Alistair Horne, *Small Earthquake in Chile: A Visit to Allende's South America* (London: Macmillan, 1972), 25.
29. William D. Rogers, interview with the author, January 27, 2004.
30. Ibid.
31. Ibid.
32. USIB, "The Chilean Situation and Prospects."

33. Taylor Belcher, Llewellyn Thompson, Ralph W. Richardson, and Paul Carlisle, "Chile," memorandum of conversation, November 14, 1963, in *FRUS, 1961–63*, vol. 12, microfiche supplement, doc. 46.
34. Falcoff, *Modern Chile*, 203.
35. Goldwater, "On 'Covert Actions,'" 86.
36. INR, "Salvador Allende."
37. Goldwater, "On 'Covert Actions,'" 87; Tanya Harmer, "Neutralizing the Threat: Allende's Chile, the United States, and Regional Alignments in Latin America," May 2005, http://www.lse.ac.uk/collections/CWSC/pdf/cambridge_lse_May_2005/Harmer_Paper.doc (accessed August 4, 2005), 7. Che Guevara went to Bolivia in an attempt to foment revolution in continental Latin America, and to prove his theory that a *foco* of armed revolutionaries could spark an otherwise unlikely revolution. While his actions and eventual death occurred in Bolivia, his plan was much bigger, as he had written while still fighting in the Cuban Revolution in the late 1950s: "I've got a plan. If some day I have to carry the revolution to the continent, I will set myself up in the *selva* at the frontier between Bolivia and Brazil. . . . From there it is possible to put pressure on three or four countries and, by taking advantage of the frontiers and the forests, you can work things so as to never be caught." From Jean Larteguy, *The Guerilla* (New York, World Publishing Corp., 1970) p. 19.
38. Davis, *Last Two Years*, 91.
39. Phillips, *Night Watch*, 14–28.
40. U.S. Embassy Santiago, "Assessment Socialist-Communist Candidate Salvador Allende," cable to the U.S. Department of State, April 22, 1964, in *FRUS, 1964–68*, vol. 31, doc. 251.
41. Paul Wimert, interview for the George Washington University National Security Archive, "Backyard," *The Cold War*, CNN, February 21, 1999, http://www.gwu.edu/~nsarchiv/coldwar/interviews/ (accessed August 15, 2006).
42. U.S. Embassy Santiago, "Assessment Socialist-Communist Candidate Salvador Allende."
43. INR, "Salvador Allende."
44. U.S. Embassy Santiago, airgram to U.S. Department of State, April 10, 1964, A-756, Stack 250, Box 2025, Pol 2-1 Joint Weekas Chile, RG 59, NARA.
45. Joaquín Fermandois, *Chile y El Mundo 1970–1973* (Santiago: Ediciones Universidad Católico de Chile, 1985), 262.
46. Haslam, *Nixon Administration and the Death of Allende's Chile*, 158.
47. Ibid., 6.
48. Régis Debray, *The Chilean Revolution: Conversations with Allende* (New York: Pantheon Books, 1971), 118.
49. Robert Hurwitch, letter to McGeorge Bundy, June 19, 1964, in *FRUS, 1964–68*, vol. 31, doc. 259.
50. Ibid.
51. Whelan, *Out of the Ashes*, 294.
52. Gordon Chase, "Chiefs of Mission Conference—Brazil and Chile," memorandum to McGeorge Bundy, March 19, 1964, National Security File (NSF), Country File, Latin America, vol. 1, 11/63–6/64, Lyndon Baines Johnson Presidential Archive, Austin, TX (hereafter cited as LBJPA).
53. Ibid.

54. Christopher Andrew and Vasili Mitrokhin, *The Mitrokhin Archive II: The KGB in the World* (London: Allen Lane, 2005), 69.
55. Ibid., 72, 74.
56. U.S. Embassy Santiago, "Allende's Funding," telegram to Secretary of State and U.S Embassy Ottawa, May 5, 1964, NSF, Country File, Chile, vol. 1, cables 1/64–8/64, doc. 32, LBJPA.
57. Olga Uliánova and Eugenia Fediakova, "Aspects of Financial Aid to Chilean Communism from the USSR Communist Party during the Cold War," *Éstudios Públicos* 72 (Spring 1998): 89.
58. Nikolai Leonov, *Likholetye* (Moscow, Mezhdunarodnye Otnosheniya, 2000), 39. (With thanks to Julie Elkner for translation from Russian.)
59. U.S. Embassy Santiago, "Allende's Funding." See also Phillips, *Night Watch*, 14–28.
60. Leonov, *Likholetye*, 37–40.
61. U.S. Embassy Santiago, "Assessment Socialist-Communist Candidate Salvador Allende."
62. McGeorge Bundy, "Presidential Election in Chile," memorandum to Lyndon B. Johnson, May 13, 1964, NSF, Country File, Chile, vol. 1, 1/64–8/64, Memos to the President, McGeorge Bundy, vol. 4, LBJPA.
63. J. C. King, "Political Action Program in Chile," memorandum to John McCone, January 3, 1964, in *FRUS 1964–68*, vol. 31, doc. 245.
64. Helgerson, *Getting to Know the President*, ch. 3.
65. Ralph Dungan, memorandum to McGeorge Bundy, January 18, 1964, in *FRUS 1964–68*, vol. 31, doc. 246.
66. Edward M. Korry, Joaquín Fermandois, and Arturo Fontaine T., "El Embajador Edward M. Korry en el CEP," *Éstudios Públicos* 72 (Spring 1998): 7.
67. J. C. King, "Political Action Program in Chile."
68. Chief and Deputy Chief, Western Hemisphere Division, and Thomas Mann, "Record of Conversation," memorandum for the record, February 28, 1964, in *FRUS 1964–68*, vol. 31, doc. 247.
69. Ibid. See also U.S. Department of State, INR/IL Historical Files, Special Group Files, Meetings, NARA.
70. Ralph W. Richardson, "Curico By-Election," memorandum to Thomas Mann, March 6, 1964, Santiago Embassy Files: FRC 69 A 6507, 1964, POL 14 Elections (Presidential) 1964, RG 84, NARA.
71. Sigmund, *Overthrow of Allende*, 29.
72. Albert Carter, "ARA-CIA Weekly Meetings, 1964–1965," memorandum to Thomas Hughes, March 26, 1964, in *FRUS 1964–68*, vol. 31, doc. 248.
73. Ralph W. Richardson, letter to Joseph Jova (Santiago DCM), April 3, 1964, Santiago Embassy Files: FRC 69 A 6507, 1964, POL 14 Elections (Presidential) 1964 (1), RG 84, NARA.
74. U.S. Embassy Santiago, "Semi-Annual Politico-Economic Assessment—Chile," airgram to U.S. Department of State, July 16, 1964, A-45, Stack 250, Box 2025, Pol 2-1 Joint Weekas Chile, RG 59, NARA.
75. CIA, "Support for the Chilean Presidential Election of 4 September 1964," memorandum to Special Group, April 1, 1964, in *FRUS 1964–68*, vol. 31, doc. 250.
76. Ibid.
77. Thomas Mann, "Presidential Election in Chile," memorandum to Dean Rusk, May 1, 1964, in *FRUS 1964–68*, vol. 31, doc. 253.

78. CIA, "Support for the Chilean Presidential Election."
79. Ibid.
80. NSC, "Minutes of Special Group Meeting of 2 April 1964," memorandum, April 9, 1964, INR/IL Historical Files, Special Group Files, NARA.
81. Helgerson, *Getting to Know the President*, ch. 3 passim.
82. McGeorge Bundy, memorandum to Lyndon B. Johnson, Memos to the President, McGeorge Bundy, May 13 1964, vol. 4, LBJPA.
83. Helgerson, *Getting to Know the President*, ch. 3.
84. Ibid., ch. 7.
85. Mann, "Presidential Election in Chile."
86. C/WHD, "Request for Approval and Renewal," memorandum to DDP, March 12, 1968, in CIA, "Chile Collection," *Chile Declassification Project*, http://www.foia.state.gov/SearchColls/CIA.asp (accessed July 25, 2005).
87. Eduardo Labarca Goddard, *Chile Invadido: Reportaje a la Intromisión Extranjera* (Santiago: Editora Austral, 1968), 307–317. On top of propaganda, USIS was also distributing bad movies, as one can judge from their film repertoire #286 *Danza Hacia la Libertad* (Dancing Toward Freedom) about two Hungarian ballerinas who bravely flee to West Berlin.
88. Mann, "Presidential Election in Chile."
89. C/WHD, "Request for Renewal of Project," memorandum to DDP, March 20, 1968, in CIA, "Chile Collection."
90. *FRUS 1964–68*, vol. 31, doc. 262 (editorial).
91. C/WHD, "Request for Renewal of Project."
92. *FRUS 1964–68*, vol. 31, doc. 262 (editorial).
93. NSC, "Minutes of Special Group Meeting of 13 May," memorandum for the record, May 14, 1964, NSC, 303 Committee Files, Subject Files, Chile thru 1969, NARA.
94. "Minutes of 303 Committee Meeting 21 July," memorandum for the record, July 21, 1964, NSC, 303 Committee Files, Subject Files, Chile thru 1969, NARA.
95. *FRUS 1964–68*, vol. 31, doc. 246 (editorial).
96. *FRUS 1964–68*, vol. 31, doc. 267 (editorial).
97. Ibid.
98. Charles Cole, "The Presidential Campaign with Two Weeks to Go," airgram to U.S. Department of State, August 21, 1964, NSF, Country File, Chile, vol. 1, cables 1/64–8/64, LBJPA.
99. Jack Devine, interview by the author, March 1, 2004.
100. Charles Cole, "Met Today," telegram to Secretary of State, August 27, 1964, NSF, Country File, Chile, vol. 1, cables 1/64–8/64, LBJPA.
101. Cole, "The Presidential Campaign with Two Weeks to Go." NARA-CP.
102. Ibid.
103. "The Chilean Situation and Prospects," NIE 94-63, October 3, 1963, in *FRUS, 1961–63*, vol. 12, microfiche supplement, doc. 45.
104. McGeorge Bundy, Lawrence O'Brien, and John Reilly, "The Present Political Situation in Chile, 16 June 1964," memorandum to H. H. Humphrey, EX CO 4 Chad, Republic of, Box 21, LBJPA.
105. CIA, "Chilean Election Forecast," memorandum to Department of State/NSC, September 1, 1964, in *FRUS, 1964–68*, vol. 31, doc. 268.
106. Ibid.
107. Gordon Chase, "Chilean Polling," memorandum to McGeorge Bundy, Sep-

tember 4, 1964, NSF, Country File, Latin America vol. 2, 6/64–12/64, LBJPA. See also U.S. Embassy Santiago, telegrams 366–371 to Washington, September 4, 1964, Central Files 1964–66, POL 14 Chile, RG 59, NARA.

108. *FRUS 1964–68*, vol. 31, doc. 269 (editorial).
109. U.S. Embassy Santiago, airgram to the Department of State, September 3, 1964, A-187, Joint Weeka No. 36, Stack 250, Box 2025, Pol 2-1 Joint Weekas Chile, RG 59, NARA.
110. Ibid.
111. U.S. Embassy Santiago, telegram #383 to Department of State, September 8, 1964, Central Files 1964–66, POL 14 Chile, RG 59, NARA.
112. Department of State, INR/IL Historical Files, Chile, 1964–1967, in *FRUS, 1964–68*, vol. 31, doc. 269.
113. Ambassador to Chile, telegram #372 to the Secretary of State, September 5, 1964, Central Files 1964–66, POL 14 Chile, RG 59, NARA.
114. *FRUS, 1964–68*, vol. 31, doc. 269 (editorial).
115. Rogers interview.
116. John. H. Crimmins, interview by the author, March 30, 2004.
117. Labarca, *Chile Invadido*, 24. The original Spanish reads, "Lo cierto es que en la época del gobierno del presidente Frei, Washington se ha valido preferentemente, en su labor corrupta y colonizadora, de personeros democratacristianos."
118. Kaeten Mistry, "The Case for Political Warfare: Strategy, Organization and US Involvement in the 1948 Italian Election," *Cold War History* 6: 3 (August 2006): 301–329.
119. U.S. Embassy Santiago, "President Frei Insisted," cable to Secretary of State, December 21, 1967, Country File, Box 14, Chile, vol. 5, Memos, 8/67–11/68, LBJPA.

CHAPTER 2: SUPPORTING THE MODERATES

1. Walt Rostow, "Ed Korry Reports on Chile," memorandum to Lyndon B. Johnson, January 18, 1968, in *FRUS, 1964–68*, vol. 31, doc. 298. A notation on the memorandum indicates that the president saw it. Original italics.
2. NSC, Memorandum for the record, 32nd SIG Meeting, Memo #57, March 20, 1968, NARA, RG 59, S/S SIG Files, Lot 70, D 263, SIG/RA #34.
3. William V. Broe, "Circumstances Leading Up to CIA Participation in Electoral Operations in Chile," memorandum to Thomas Karamessines, April 26, 1968, in *FRUS, 1964–68*, vol. 31, doc. 304.
4. William M. Leary, *The Central Intelligence Agency: History and Documents* (Tuscaloosa: University of Alabama Press, 1984), 81.
5. COS, "Foll Not to Be Considered," cable to DCI, August 8, 1968, in CIA, "Chile Collection."
6. Edward Korry and Eduardo Frei, "Aboard Presidential Aircraft on Route to Concepcíon," memorandum of conversation, January 3, 1968, DDRS.
7. "Chile," NIE, January 28, 1969, 17, in CIA, "Chile Collection."
8. Directorate of Intelligence, "Chile: A New Opening to the Left?" Special Report Weekly Review, April 12, 1968, DDRS.
9. Miguel Otero, interview by the author, May 12, 2003.
10. COS, "Foll Not to Be Considered."
11. DI, "Chile: A New Opening to the Left?"

12. Board of National Estimates, "Chilean Problems and Frei's Prospects," special memorandum, March 4, 1968, in CIA, "Chile Collection."
13. C/WHD, "Request for Renewal of Project," memorandum to DDP, March 20, 1968, in CIA, "Chile Collection."
14. INR/DDC, "CIA Operations," memorandum to file, INR/DDC Records, August 1, 1968, in State Department, "Chile Collection," *Chile Declassification Project*, http://www.foia.state.gov. Accessed January 15, 2006.
15. DI, "The Popular Front in Chile as a Communist Path to Power," DI special report/weekly review, August 2, 1968, DDRS.
16. COS, "Foll Not to Be Considered."
17. DDP, "Briefing of Mr. Viron Peter Vaky," memorandum for the record, August 6, 1968, in CIA, "Chile Collection."
18. C/WHD, "Progress Report: March 69 Chilean Congressional Election," memorandum to DCI, December 4, 1968, in CIA.
19. Ibid.
20. Ibid.
21. William Broe, "Request Approval of Project," memorandum to DDP, August 13, 1968, in CIA, "Chile Collection."
22. INR/DDC, "ARA/CIA Meeting 24 May 1964," memorandum, May 27, 1968, in State, "Chile Collection."
23. COS, "Foll Not to Be Considered."
24. INR/DDC, "ARA/CIA Meeting 24 May 1964."
25. Ibid.
26. Covey T. Oliver, "Chile: Assistance to Congressional Candidates," memorandum to Charles Bohlen, July 5, 1968, in State.
27. C/WHD, "Ref: Minutes of 303 Committee," memorandum to Director of Office of Planning, Programming, and Budgeting, August 1, 1968, in CIA, "Chile Collection."
28. C/WHD, "Request for Approval of Project," excerpt of 303 Committee approval, memorandum to DDP, July 12, 1968, in CIA, "Chile Collection."
29. Ibid.
30. Oliver, "Chile: Assistance to Congressional Candidates."
31. DDP, "Briefing of Mr. Viron Peter Vaky."
32. INR/DDC, "CIA Operations," memorandum for the record, August 1, 1968, in State, "Chile Collection." The word "perhaps" is a marginal note.
33. Unknown author, "I Realize It Is Late," memorandum to C/WHD, September 17, 1968, in CIA, "Chile Collection."
34. 303 Committee, Excerpt of 303 Committee minutes, memorandum to C/WHD for files, September 3, 1968, in CIA, "Chile Collection."
35. Unknown author, "I Realize It Is Late."
36. COS, "Foll Not to Be Considered."
37. Otero interview.
38. Unknown author, "I Realize It Is Late." Ambassador Korry also mentions that priests were used as couriers in the mission in his interview with CEP: Korry, Fermandois, and Fontaine T., "El Embajador Edward M. Korry en el CEP," 19.
39. Otero interview.
40. Unknown author, "I Realize It Is Late."
41. Unknown author, "State Draft Policy Paper on Chile," memorandum to C/WHD, October 17, 1968, in CIA, "Chile Collection."

42. Ibid.
43. Ibid.
44. C/WHD, "Progress Report."
45. C/WHD, "In Preparation for Amb's Visit," cable to Santiago Station, November 14, 1968, in CIA, "Chile Collection."
46. Santiago Station, "Station Agrees with HQS Briefing," cable to DCI, November 18, 1968, in CIA, "Chile Collection."
47. DDP, "Briefing of Mr. Viron Peter Vaky."
48. DDP, "Visit of Ambassador Edward M. Korry on 20 November 1968," memorandum to DCI, November 19, 1968, in CIA, "Chile Collection." (Filed incorrectly as November 9.)
49. William Trueheart, memorandum to Thomas L. Hughes and George C. Denny, May 27, 1968, in State, "Chile Collection."
50. DDP, "Visit of Ambassador Edward M. Korry."
51. State Department, "Visit of Ambassador Edward M. Korry/ Working Lunch," memorandum for the record, November 22, 1968, in State, "Chile Collection."
52. C/WHD, "Progress Report."
53. DDP, "Visit of Ambassador Edward M. Korry."
54. Korry, Fermandois, and Fontaine T., "El Embajador Edward M. Korry en el CEP," 19.
55. NSC/303 Committee, "Final Report: March 1969 Chilean Congressional Election," memorandum, March 14, 1969, in NSC, "Chile Collection," *Chile Declassification Project*, http://www.foia.state.gov/Search Colls/NSC.asp (accessed July 25, 2005).
56. NSC/303 Committee, "Progress Report: March 1969 Chilean Congressional Election," memorandum, December 5, 1968, in NSC, "Chile Collection."
57. Directorate of Plans, "Briefing Memorandum for Mr. [Deleted]," memorandum, December 17, 1968, in CIA, "Chile Collection."
58. NSC/303 Committee, "Final Report."
59. DDP (WHD?) "Chile: March 1969 Congressional Election," including handwritten "Memo to DCI to Brief Kissinger," memorandum, December 26, 1968, in CIA, "Chile Collection."
60. DDP, "Covert Action Activities to be Covered . . . for Mr. Kissinger," memorandum to C/WHD, December 19, 1968, in CIA, "Chile Collection."
61. COS, "For Reasons Too Complex," dispatch to C/WHD, January 6, 1969, in CIA, "Chile Collection."
62. C/WHD, "Summary of Chilean Congressional Election Operation," memorandum to DDP, March 4, 1969, in CIA, "Chile Collection." The exact date on which three of the candidates for support were dropped is not listed in the material.
63. Acting Chief of WHD, "Termination of Project," memorandum to C/WHD, April 23, 1969, in CIA, "Chile Collection."
64. CIA Headquarters, "In Preparation for Amb's Visit."
65. CIA, "Propaganda Production," memorandum, March 12, 1968, in CIA, "Chile Collection."
66. Santiago Station, "Following Station Analysis," cable to C/WHD, February 11, 1969, in CIA, "Chile Collection."
67. C/WHD, "Request for Approval and Renewal," memorandum to DDP, March 12, 1968, in CIA, "Chile Collection."
68. Ibid.

69. Santiago Station, "Following Station Analysis."
70. DDP, "Project [Deleted]," memorandum, March 12, 1968, in CIA, "Chile Collection."
71. Broe, "Request Approval of Project."
72. Chief of Station, "As Required by the 303 Committee," cable to DDP, August 14, 1968, in CIA.
73. Broe, "Request Approval of Project."
74. Santiago Station, "Station Agrees with HQs Briefing."
75. Santiago Station, "Following Station Analysis."
76. NSC/303 Committee, "Final Report."
77. COS, "Request Amendment," cable to C/WHD, May 31, 1968, in CIA, "Chile Collection."
78. C/WHD, "Amendment to Station Santiago's Project," memorandum to DDP, May 29, 1968, in CIA, "Chile Collection."
79. Unknown Author (Santiago COS?), "FY 1969 Renewal," memorandum to C/WHD, April 22, 1968, in CIA, "Chile Collection."
80. COS Santiago, "Project Approval Notification," C/WHD Authority, August 5, 1968, in CIA, "Chile Collection."
81. Leary, *Central Intelligence Agency*, 82.
82. William V. Broe, "Thematic and Effectiveness Data," memorandum to unknown, May 23, 1968, in CIA, "Chile Collection."
83. Unknown author, "Renewal of Project [deleted] (WH/Chile)," memorandum to unknown, March 3, 1969, in CIA, "Chile Collection."
84. Broe, "Thematic and Effectiveness Data."
85. Otero interview.
86. Santiago Station, "Following Station Analysis."
87. C/WHD, "Request for Approval and Renewal."
88. C/WHD, "Project Renewal for FY 1970," memorandum to DDP, February 20, 1969, in CIA, "Chile Collection."
89. Unknown author, "Renewal of Project [deleted] (WH/Chile)."
90. "The Chilean Congressional Election of 2 March 1969," memorandum for the record, March 4, 1969. This memo has a marginal ink annotation that reads, "Acc@ #980643000012, Safe A-2, Drawer Box 19." See also NSC/303 Committee, "Final Report."
91. Edward M. Korry, cable to DCI, March 7, 1969, in CIA, "Chile Collection."
92. Ibid.
93. NSC/303 Committee, "Final Report."
94. Frank M. Chapin, "Proposed Agenda, Meeting of the 303 Committee", memorandum, April 15, 1969, in NSC, "Chile Collection."
95. Santiago Station, "The Chilean Right," cable to DCI, March 3, 1969, in CIA, "Chile Collection."
96. NSC/303 Committee, "Final Report."
97. Korry, Fermandois, and Fontaine T., "El Embajador Edward M. Korry en el CEP," 19.
98. Ibid., 14. Korry dismissed the figure of $300,000 as the amount spent in Chile and argued that it was significantly less:

    > Now, if you read the Church Committee report, it says that 350,000 dollars was authorized for the elections of '69. So how did a hundred and thirty-five, less than 200,000, get spent? I sent a young officer of

the Political Section of the Embassy . . . to negotiate a new list with the CIA in Washington. The CIA was drawing up the list, and a new set of expenditures, and it was one-third of the 500,000 and one-third of the list.

I have favored the CIA figures as the Agency appears to record expenditures.

99. C/WHD, cable to COS, February 19, 1969, in CIA, "Chile Collection."
100. Unknown author, "I Realize It Is Late."
101. Fermandois, *Chile y El Mundo*, 285.
102. C/WHD, "Summary of Chilean Congressional Election Operation," memorandum to DDP, March 4, 1969, in CIA, "Chile Collection."

CHAPTER 3: LAST-MINUTE SCRAMBLE

1. C. D. Wiggin, "Chile," memorandum to Mr. Timothy Daunt, September 28, 1970, FCO 7/1517, National Archives, Great Britain, Kew, Richmond, Surrey (hereafter cited as TNA).
2. Ted Shackley, *Spymaster: My Life in the CIA*, with Richard A. Finney (Washington, DC: Potomac Books, 2005), 266.
3. Ibid., 109.
4. Henry A. Kissinger, *White House Years* (Boston: Little, Brown, 1979), 660. Christopher Hitchens, "The Case against Henry Kissinger, Part 2: Crimes against Humanity," *Harper's Magazine*, March 2001, 50, is wrong on this point. See also NSC, "National Security Decision Memorandum 40", 17 February 1970, in FRUS, Nixon-Ford, vol. 2, Doc 203.
5. Loch K. Johnson, "On Drawing a Bright Line for Covert Operation," *American Journal of International Law* 86: 2 (April 1992): 286.
6. It is reasonable to assume that the NIE was commissioned specifically by or for the new administration, though there is no direct evidence to confirm this assertion.
7. USIB, Chile," NIE, 17.
8. David Fox Scott, "Valedictory Address," September 12, 1966, FO 371/184703, TNA.
9. Haslam, *Nixon Administration and the Death of Allende's Chile*, 39.
10. USIB, "Chile," NIE, 18.
11. Ibid., 19.
12. DI, "Assessment of the Internal Security Threat in Latin America," intelligence memorandum, October 13, 1969, in CIA.
13. USIB, "Chile," NIE, 15.
14. Ibid., 14.
15. Ibid., 3.
16. Christopher Andrew, *For the President's Eyes Only: Secret Intelligence and the American Presidency from Washington to Bush* (New York: HarperCollins, 1995), 351.
17. Rogers and Maxwell, "Fleeing the Chilean Coup," 165.
18. Andrew, *For the President's Eyes Only*, 351.
19. Helgerson, *Getting to Know the President*, ch. 4.
20. Andrew, *For the President's Eyes Only*, 350.
21. Anthony Summers, *The Arrogance of Power: The Secret World of Richard Nixon* (London: Victor Gollancz, 2000), 330.
22. Helgerson, *Getting to Know the President*, ch. 7.
23. Ibid.

24. Andrew, *For the President's Eyes Only*, 352.
25. Iwan Morgan, *Nixon* (London: Arnold, 2002), 128.
26. Andrew, *For the President's Eyes Only*, 351.
27. Ibid.
28. WHD, cable to Santiago Station, September 23, 1968, in CIA, "Chile Collection."
29. COS, "Thinking Ahead to 1970," dispatch to C/WHD, March 4, 1969, in CIA, "Chile Collection."
30. Ibid.
31. Ibid.
32. NSC, "Proposed Agenda: Meeting of the 303 Committee," memorandum, April 15, 1969, in NSC, "Chile Collection."
33. NSC, "Minutes of the Meeting of the 303 Committee, 15 April 1969," memorandum, April 17, 1969, in NSC, "Chile Collection."
34. Helms, *Look over My Shoulder*, 106, 112.
35. NSC, "Minutes of the Meeting of the 303 Committee 15 April 1969."
36. Harmer, "Neutralizing the Threat," 7.
37. COS, "Political Action—PDC Convention," dispatch to C/WHD, March 11, 1969, in CIA, "Chile Collection."
38. Santiago Station, "We Have Prepared Final Report," cable to WHD, March 17, 1969, in CIA, "Chile Collection."
39. ARA, "The Chilean Vote in Recent Years and Its Meaning for the Candidacy of Former President Jorge Alessandri," memorandum, April 3, 1969, in State, "Chile Collection."
40. COS, "The Chilean Vote," dispatch to C/WHD, May 15, 1969, in CIA, "Chile Collection."
41. Santiago Station, "Sta Has Met with [deleted]," cable to DCI, June 14, 1969, in CIA, "Chile Collection."
42. James R. Gardner, "Santaigo [*sic*] Report of Talk with Ambassador Korry," memorandum to Mr. Tegethoff, July 11, 1969, in State, "Chile Collection."
43. Noam Chomsky, *The Washington Connection and Third World Fascism: The Political Economy of Human Rights* (Boston: South End Press, 1979). See also Smirnow, Gabriel. *The Revolution Disarmed: Chile, 1970–1973.* New York: Monthly Review Press, 1979, and Robinson, William I. *Promoting Polyarchy: Globalization, U.S. Intervention, and Hegemony*. Cambridge: Cambridge University Press, 1996.
44. COS, "Visit of Ambassador Korry to HQ on 20 November 1968," memorandum for the record, November 22, 1968, in CIA, "Chile Collection."
45. COS, "Chilean Vote."
46. WHD, "Discussion of USG Pre-Election Activity," memorandum for the record, January 30, 1970, 4, in CIA, "Chile Collection."
47. Santiago Station, "Station Agrees with HQS Briefing," cable to DCI, November 18, 1968, in CIA, "Chile Collection."
48. James E. Miller, "Taking Off the Gloves: The United States and the Italian Elections of 1948," *Diplomatic History* 7: 1 (1983), 54.
49. COS, "Popular Unity (Att 2: Thinkpiece)," dispatch to C/WHD, August 7, 1969, in CIA, "Chile Collection."
50. WHD, "Discussion of USG Pre-Election Activity," 1.
51. Ibid.
52. James R. Gardner, "Chilean Elections," memorandum to Wymberley Coerr, March 12, 1970, in State, "Chile Collection."

53. WHD, "Chile: Talking Points," memorandum for Secretary of State, January 1, 1970, in CIA, "Chile Collection." "January 1" is penciled in on the memorandum, which also includes some marginal notes discussing its potential dates of origin of the memorandum.
54. Ibid.
55. Viron P. Vaky, interview by the author, February 4, 2004.
56. WHD, "Chile: Talking Points."
57. WHD, "Discussion of USG Pre-Election Activity," 5.
58. Gardner, "Chilean Elections."
59. C/WHD, "Meeting with Ambassador Korry," memorandum for the record, September 19, 1969, in CIA, "Chile Collection."
60. WHD, "Discussion of USG Pre-Election Activity," 5.
61. Santiago Station, "General Augusto (Pinochet) Ugarte," cable to CIA Headquarters, September 23, 1969, in CIA, "Chile Collection."
62. C/WHD, "Background Paper for Meeting with Ambassador Korry," memorandum to DDP, September 17, 1969, in CIA, "Chile Collection."
63. "Discussion of USG Pre-Election Activity."
64. Gardner, "Chilean Elections."
65. Ibid.
66. C/WHD, "Background Paper for Meeting with Ambassador Korry."
67. WHD, "Discussion of USG Pre-Election Activity," 5.
68. Ibid., 4.
69. Santiago Station, "[Deleted] and COS Toured Horizon 18 Dec," cable to DCI, December 18, 1969, in CIA.
70. Shackley, *Spymaster*, 266.
71. 40 Committee, "Political Action Related to the 1970 Chilean Presidential Election," memorandum, March 5, 1970, in CIA, "Chile Collection."
72. Kent Crane, "Elections in Chile," memorandum to Henry A. Kissinger, March 25, 1970, in CIA, "Chile Collection."
73. NSC, "Political Decisions Related to Our Covert Action Involvement," memorandum, August 20, 1970, in NSC, "Chile Collection."
74. Henry Schlaudeman (Santiago DCM), "The Chilean Situation: A Personal Assessment," airgram, A-283, September 1, 1969, in State, "Chile Collection."
75. NSC, "Minutes of the Meeting of the 40 Committee," extract from memorandum for the record, March 30, 1970, in NSC, "Chile Collection."
76. Davis, *Last Two Years*, 5.
77. DDP, "Overview Statements on CIA Involvement in Chile in 1970," memorandum for the record, February 20, 1973, in CIA, "Chile Collection."
78. Andrew and Mitrokhin, *Mitrokhin Archive II*, 72.
79. Harmer, "Neutralizing the Threat," 6.
80. Hersh, *Price of Power*, 263.
81. Hitchens, "Case against Henry Kissinger, Part 1," 53.
82. Edward M. Korry, cable to NSC, June 18, 1970, in NSC, "Chile Collection."
83. Santiago Station, "Believe We Should View," cable to DCI, May 4, 1970, in CIA, "Chile Collection."
84. Viron P. Vaky, memorandum to Henry A. Kissinger, June 26, 1970, in State, "Chile Collection."
85. Wymberley Coerr, "ARA/CIA Weekly Meeting of 20 March," memorandum to Ray S. Cline, March 25, 1970, in CIA, "Chile Collection."

86. Wymberley Coerr, "Ambassador Korry Is Becoming," memorandum to U. Alexis Johnson, June 22, 1970, in CIA, "Chile Collection."
87. Charles Meyer, "40 Committee Has Decided," cable to Edward M. Korry, June 2, 1970, in CIA, "Chile Collection."
88. NSC "Proposed Agenda of 40 Committee meeting of June 27," memorandum, June 29, 1970, in NSC, "Chile Collection."
89. Wymberley Coerr, "Despite the Persuasiveness," memorandum to U. Alexis Johnson, March 25, 1970, in CIA, "Chile Collection."
90. Crimmins interview.
91. Edward M. Korry, "Santiago 02526, Part 1 of 2," cable to Secretary of State, July 6, 1970, in CIA, "Chile Collection."
92. Edward M. Korry, "Santiago 02526, Part 2 of 2," cable to Secretary of State, July 6, 1970, in CIA, "Chile Collection."
93. Senate Select Committee to Study Governmental Operations with Respect to Intelligence Activities, *Staff Report of the Select Committee to Study Governmental Operations with Respect to Intelligence Activities: Covert Action in Chile, 1963–1973*, 94th Cong., 1st sess., 1975, 49 (sect IV, B, 1. a.). (Hereafter cited as Church Committee, *Covert Action in Chile.*)
94. 40 Committee, "Options in Chilean Presidential Election," memorandum, August 31, 1970, in CIA, "Chile Collection."
95. WHD, "Policy Decisions Related to Our Covert Action in the September 1970 Chilean Presidential Election," memorandum, September 13, 1970, in CIA, "Chile Collection."
96. Office of Reports and Estimates, memorandum ORE 47/1, February 16, 1948, DDRS.
97. Secretary of State, "Thanks for Further Amplification," cable to Edward M. Korry, State 107632, July 7, 1970, in CIA, "Chile Collection."
98. 40 Committee, "Options in Chilean Presidential Election."
99. Edward M. Korry, memorandum to John H. Crimmins, August 11, 1970, in State, "Chile Collection."
100. WHD, "Options in Chilean Presidential Election during the Congressional Runoff Phase (5 September–24 October 1970)," memorandum, August 31, 1970, in NSC, "Chile Collection."
101. NSC, National Security Study Memorandum (NSSM) 97, July 24, 1970, Box H-275, NSC Institutional Files, Nixon Presidential Materials, NARA.
102. Viron P. Vaky, "Chile and Phase 2," memorandum to Henry A. Kissinger, August 20, 1970, in CIA, "Chile Collection."
103. "Goldberg's cartoons satirized machines and gadgets, which he saw as excessive. His cartoons combined simple machines and common household items to create complex, wacky, and diabolically logical machines that accomplished mundane and trivial tasks. His inventions became so widely known that Webster's Dictionary added 'rube goldberg' to its listing, defining the term as 'accomplishing by extremely complex, roundabout means what seemingly could be done simply.'" Taken from the website of the Purdue University Rube Goldberg Machine Contest, http://news.uns.purdue.edu/UNS/rube/rube.history.html, November 2003.
104. Vitale, *Para Recuperar La Memoria Histórica*, 184.
105. Korry, cable to Crimmins.
106. Davis, *Last Two Years*, 12.

107. Korry, cable to Crimmins.
108. Charles A. Meyer, "NSSM-97: Extreme Option—Overthrow of Allende," memorandum to U. Alexis Johnson, August 17, 1970, in CIA, "Chile Collection."
109. Henry Hankey, letter to Sir Leslie Monson, April 12, 1972, FCO 7/2212, TNA.
110. Horne, *Small Earthquake in Chile*, 164.
111. Edward M. Korry, "The Communists Take Over Chile," memorandum to State Department, September 12, 1970, in CIA, "Chile Collection."
112. Davis, *Last Two Years*, 6.
113. NSC, "Minutes of the Meeting of the 40 Committee," memorandum, September 8, 1970, in NSC, "Chile Collection."
114. William McAfee, memorandum to U. Alexis Johnson, September 8, 1970, in CIA, "Chile Collection."
115. NSC, "Minutes of the Meeting of the 40 Committee" in NSC, "Chile Collection." See also John H. Crimmins, memorandum to Mr. John Getz (Special Assistant to the Undersecretary of State for Political Affairs), September 14, 1970, in CIA, "Chile Collection," for Kissinger as source of the term "cold-blooded assessment."
116. Edward M. Korry, "Ambassador's Response to State," memorandum to State Department, September 12, 1970, in CIA, "Chile Collection."
117. U. Alexis Johnson, cable to Edward M. Korry, September 15, 1970, in CIA, "Chile Collection."
118. Phillips, *Night Watch*, 221.
119. Edward M. Korry, memorandum to U. Alexis Johnson, September 16, 1970, in State, "Chile Collection."
120. Viron P. Vaky, memorandum to Henry A. Kissinger, September 14, 1970, in NSC, "Chile Collection."
121. NSC, "Review of Political and Military Options in Chilean Electoral Situation," NSC report, September 14, 1970, in NSC, "Chile Collection."
122. Viron P. Vaky, "Korry's Reply to 40 Committee Cable," memorandum to Henry A. Kissinger, September 16, 1970, in NSC, "Chile Collection."
123. Viron P. Vaky, "Chile—40 Committee Meeting (today)," memorandum to Henry A. Kissinger, September 14, 1970, in NSC, "Chile Collection."
124. Viron P. Vaky, "Chile—Our Modus Operandi," memorandum to Henry A. Kissinger, September 14, 1970, in CIA, "Chile Collection."
125. Ibid.
126. DDP, "Overview Statements on CIA Involvement in Chile in 1970," memorandum, February 20, 1973, in CIA, "Chile Collection."
127. "Genesis of Project Fubelt," memorandum for the record, September 16, 1970, in CIA, "Chile Collection." The original document is marked "17 September," but that date is crossed out and "16 September" is written in. The significance or reason for this correction is unknown, although the error may be simply clerical.

CHAPTER 4: THE DANGEROUS SECOND TRACK

1. INR, "The Armed Forces and Police in Chile," research memorandum to Secretary of State, RAR-18, September 3, 1968, DDRS.
2. Hitchens, "Case against Henry Kissinger, Part 1."
3. Hersh, *Price of Power*, 292–293.
4. Kornbluh, *Pinochet File*, xiii.

5. Gabriel Kolko, *Confronting the Third World: United States Foreign Policy, 1945–1980* (New York: Pantheon Books, 1988), 220. See also Hersh, *Price of Power*, 288–290; Hitchens, "Case against Henry Kissinger, Part 1," passim.
6. Kissinger, *White House Years*, ch. 15 and 16.
7. Colby and Forbath, *Honorable Men,* 303.
8. Church Committee, *Alleged Assassination Plots*, 227.
9. Ibid., 228.
10. L. Britt Snider, *Sharing Secrets with Lawmakers: Congress as a User of Intelligence*, (Langley, VA: Center for the Study of Intelligence, 1997), ch. 1.
11. Pape, "Constitutional Covert Actions," 55.
12. WHD, "Genesis of Project Fubelt," memorandum for the record, September 16, 1970, in CIA, "Chile Collection."
13. Santiago Station, "[Deleted] Situation Report #1," memorandum, September 17, 1970, in CIA, "Chile Collection."
14. Phillips, *Night Watch*, 219, 220.
15. Colby and Forbath, *Honorable Men*, 303. See also Snider, *Sharing Secrets with Lawmakers*, ch. 1.
16. Church Committee, *Alleged Assassination Plots*, 228.
17. CIA Headquarters, "As You Will Be Advised," cable to Santiago Station, September 27, 1970, in CIA, "Chile Collection." False-flaggers are used to increase the "plausible deniability" of an operation should it be compromised.
18. Kornbluh, *Pinochet File*, 21.
19. CIA Headquarters, "Highest Levels Here Continue," cable to Santiago Station, October 7, 1970, in CIA, "Chile Collection."
20. Santiago Station, "Effort to Contact and Influence Chilean Military Figures," cable to CIA Headquarters, October 2, 1970, in CIA, "Chile Collection."
21. Vitale, *Para Recuperar La Memoria Histórica*, 181. In Spanish the constitution reads, "La fuerza publica es esencialmente obediente. Ningun cuerpo armado puede deliberer."
22. Santiago Station, "Intelligence," memorandum to CIA Headquarters, September 26, 1970, in CIA, "Chile Collection."
23. Figueroa, *Las Fuerzas Armadas*, 51n. 1.
24. Vitale, *Para Recuperar La Memoria Histórica*, 187. See also Sigmund, *Overthrow of Allende*, 99.
25. Albert L. Michaels, "Background to a Coup: Civil-Military Relations in Twentieth Century Chile and the Overthrow of Salvador Allende" (paper presented at the State University of New York–Buffalo, October 19, 1974), 9.
26. Falcoff, *Modern Chile*, 270.
27. Santiago Station, "Intelligence."
28. DI, intelligence note to file, September 23, 1970, in CIA, "Chile Collection."
29. Edward M. Korry, memorandum to U. Alexis Johnson, October 6, 1970, in State, "Chile Collection."
30. Edward M. Korry, memorandum to John H. Crimmins, August 11, 1970, in State, "Chile Collection."
31. CIA, memorandum for the record, September 23, 1970, in CIA, "Chile Collection."
32. Santiago Station, "Intelligence."
33. WHD, "Track I Propaganda Placements," cable, October 10, 1970, in CIA, "Chile Collection."
34. Hersh, *Price of Power*, 277.

35. Santiago Station, "Situation Report #1," cable, September 17, 1970, CIA, "Chile Collection."
36. Santiago Station, "Ambassador Called in Defense Attache and DCOS," cable to CIA Headquarters, October 8, 1970, in CIA, "Chile Collection."
37. Testimony of Henry Hecksher, in Church Committee, *Alleged Assassination Plots*, 239.
38. Thomas Powers, "Inside the Department of Dirty Tricks," *Atlantic* 244: 2 (August 1979): 48.
39. Santiago Station, "There Is a Possibility That Coup Attempt," cable to CIA Headquarters, September 23, 1970, in CIA, "Chile Collection."
40. Kornbluh, *Pinochet File*, 21.
41. Church Committee, *Alleged Assassination Plots*, 238.
42. DI, "Track II," intelligence note to file, October 10, 1970, in CIA, "Chile Collection."
43. Kornbluh, *Pinochet File*, 20.
44. WHD, "Track II," memorandum, October 7, 1970, in CIA, "Chile Collection."
45. WHD, "Track II," memorandum, October 5, 1970, in CIA, "Chile Collection."
46. Santiago Station, cable to CIA headquarters, October 7, 1970, in CIA, "Chile Collection."
47. DDP, "Long Range Solution," memorandum, October 9, 1970, in CIA, "Chile Collection."
48. William I. Robinson, *Promoting Polyarchy: Globalization, U.S. Intervention, and Hegemony* (Cambridge: Cambridge University Press, 1996), 161. Also Gabriel Smirnow, *The Revolution Disarmed: Chile, 1970–1973*. (New York: Monthly Review Press, 1979), 111.
49. Santiago Station, "It Reported," cable to CIA Headquarters, October 13, 1970, in CIA, "Chile Collection."
50. CIA Headquarters, "Viaux Recontacted ASAP," cable to Santiago Station, October 13, 1970, in CIA, "Chile Collection."
51. Santiago Station, "Arms to Start Uprising," cable to CIA Headquarters, October 6, 1970, in CIA, "Chile Collection." While the words "CIA," "U.S. government," and "Chilean" are all blanked from the document, a reading of the two full pages makes any other insertion inconsistent and unlikely.
52. Santiago Station, "As Dialogue with Viaux Grows," cable to CIA Headquarters, October 13, 1970, in CIA, "Chile Collection."
53. Santiago Station, "In Fast Moving Situation," cable to CIA Headquarters, October 10, 1970, in CIA, "Chile Collection."
54. Santiago Station, "It's Station's Firm Opinion," cable to CIA Headquarters, October 10, 1970, in CIA, "Chile Collection." That this letter referred to the attaché can be determined by comparison of this cable to one cited in Church Committee, *Alleged Assassination Plots*, 55. WHD, "Track II," memorandum, October 12, 1970, in CIA, "Chile Collection."
56. Hersh, *Price of Power*, 286.
57. Santiago Station, "Fact May Not Be Able," cable to CIA Headquarters, October 3, 1970, in CIA, "Chile Collection."
58. CIA Headquarters, "Instructs You Contact Military," cable to Santiago Station, October 7, 1970, in CIA, "Chile Collection."
59. Santiago Station, "Station Has Arrived at Viaux Solution," cable to CIA Headquarters, October 10, 1970, in CIA, "Chile Collection."

60. Santiago Station, "After Debriefing," cable to CIA Headquarters, October 12, 1970, in CIA, "Chile Collection."
61. WHD, "The Coup That Failed," memorandum, October 15, 1970, in CIA, "Chile Collection."
62. Santiago Station, "Situation Report for Military Move," memorandum, October 13, 1970, in CIA, "Chile Collection."
63. NSC, "Minutes of the 40 Committee Meeting, 14 October 1970," memorandum for the record, October 16, 1970, in CIA, "Chile Collection."
64. Henry Kissinger, Thomas Karamessines, and Alexander Haig, "Dr. Kissinger, Mr. Karamessines, Gen. Haig at the White House," memorandum of conversation, October 15, 1970, in NSC, "Chile Collection."
65. Viron P. Vaky, "Chile—Immediate Operational Issues," memorandum for the president, October 18, 1970, in NSC, "Chile Collection."
66. Ibid.
67. Santago Station, "Viaux Group Will Meet," cable to CIA Headquarters, October 14, 1970, in CIA, "Chile Collection."
68. Ibid.
69. Santiago Station, "Summoned Morning," cable to CIA Headquarters, October 16, 1970, in CIA, "Chile Collection."
70. Santiago Station, "Meeting Disaster Concerning Schneider," cable to CIA Headquarters, October 16, 1970, in CIA, "Chile Collection."
71. Santiago Station, "Intelligence Note," memorandum, October 16, 1970, in CIA, "Chile Collection." See also WHD, "Track II," cable to CIA Headquarters, October 14, 1970, in CIA, "Chile Collection."
72. Santiago Station, "Meeting Requested," cable to CIA Headquarters, October 16, 1970, in CIA, "Chile Collection."
73. CIA Headquarters, "Depending How Conversation Goes," cable to Santiago Station, October 18, 1970, in CIA, "Chile Collection."
74. CIA Headquarters, "Realize This Message," cable to Santiago Station, October 19, 1970, in CIA, "Chile Collection."
75. Santiago Station, "Chronology of Events 18 October," cable to CIA Headquarters, October 19, 1970, in CIA, "Chile Collection." Though listed under "chronology of events 12 October," the date of the memorandum is clearly October 18 both in context and when examined with a magnifying glass. See Church Committee, *Alleged Assassination Plots*, 244.
76. Ibid.
77. Santiago Station, "Special Report," memorandum, October 22, 1970, in CIA, "Chile Collection."
78. Santiago Station, "Sent to Visit," cable to CIA Headquarters, October 20, 1970, in CIA, "Chile Collection."
79. CIA Headquarters, "Request Contact General Valenzuela," cable to Santiago Station, October 22, 1970, in CIA, "Chile Collection."
80. Church Committee, *Alleged Assassination Plots*, 245.
81. Horne, *Small Earthquake in Chile*, 115. The last assassination in Chile had been of founding father Diego Portales Palazuelos in 1837.
82. Santiago Station, "Track II," memorandum, October 24, 1970, in CIA, "Chile Collection."
83. Santiago Station, "Special Report," memorandum, October 22, 1970, in CIA, "Chile Collection."

84. Santiago Station, "Intelligence Note," memorandum, October 23, 1970, in CIA, "Chile Collection." See also Santiago Station "Track II," memorandum, October 24, 1970, in CIA, "Chile Collection."
85. Sigmund, *Overthrow of Allende*, 123. See also DI, "Recent Developments in Chile," intelligence memorandum, November 2, 1970, in CIA, "Chile Collection."
86. Haslam, *Nixon Administration and the Death of Allende's Chile*, 69. See also interview 10837 for the George Washington University National Security Archive, "Backyard," *The Cold War*, CNN, February 21, 1999, http://www.gwu.edu/~narchiv/coldwar/interviews (accessed October 17, 2005).
87. Santiago Station, "Supporters of General Viaux," cable to CIA Headquarters, October 22, 1970, in CIA, "Chile Collection."
88. Santiago Station, "Suggested Retired Captain," cable to CIA Headquarters, October 19, 1970, in CIA, "Chile Collection."
89. Santiago Station, "Reflect Realistic Assessment," cable to CIA Headquarters, October 21, 1970, in CIA, "Chile Collection."
90. Santiago Station, "On 2 Nov COS Reviewed," cable to CIA Headquarters, November 3, 1970, in CIA, "Chile Collection."
91. Santiago Station, "Headquarters Will Have Noted," cable to CIA Headquarters, October 22, 1970, in CIA, "Chile Collection."
92. Kornbluh, *Pinochet File*, 33–34.
93. Santiago Station, "Although Security Still Tight," cable to CIA Headquarters, October 29, 1970, in CIA, "Chile Collection."
94. Thomas Karamessines and Henry Kissinger, telephone transcript, August 7, 1975, Kissinger.
95. Wimert interview.
96. Ibid.
97. DDP, "Overview Statements on CIA Involvement in Chile in 1970," memorandum, February 20, 1973, in CIA, "Chile Collection."
98. Brent Scowcroft and Henry Kissinger, telephone transcript, July 19, 1975, Kissinger.
99. Santiago Station, "Review of Significant Developments," cable to CIA Headquarters, October 9, 1970, in CIA, "Chile Collection."
100. Santiago Station, "Track II," memorandum, October 19, 1970, in CIA, "Chile Collection."
101. Santiago Station, "Reports That Meeting of Viaux Group," cable to CIA Headquarters, October 16, 1970, in CIA, "Chile Collection."
102. Wimert interview.
103. H. A. Kissinger to R. M. Nixon, Telcon, October 15, 1970, Kissinger.
104. Church Committee, *Alleged Assassination Plots*, 242.
105. Brent Scowcroft and Henry Kissinger, telephone transcript, June 24, 1975, Kissinger.
106. Brent Scowcroft and Henry Kissinger, telephone transcript, July 19, 1975, Kissinger.
107. Kornbluh, *Pinochet File*, 32.
108. CIA Headquarters, "Agree [deleted] Should Cease," cable to Santiago Station, October 20, 1970, in CIA, "Chile Collection."
108. Santiago Station, "Track II," memorandum, October 19, 1970, in CIA, "Chile Collection."

110. Santiago Station, "Station Making No Attempt," cable CIA Headquarters, October 19, 1970, in CIA, "Chile Collection."
111. Ibid.
112. Vaky interview.
113. Richard Helms, "Delivery of Chile Paper on Track II," memorandum to Henry A. Kissinger, December 2, 1970, in CIA, "Chile Collection."
114. DDP, "Project Termination Approval," cable, May 26, 1971, in CIA, "Chile Collection."
115. CIA Headquarters, "Recognize It Much," cable to Santiago Station, October 19, 1970, in CIA, "Chile Collection." See also CIA Headquarters, "Realize This Message."
116. CIA Headquarters, "Realize This Message."
117. CIA Headquarters, "Recognize It Much."
118. Thomas Karamessines and Henry Kissinger, telephone transcript, August 7, 1975, Kissinger.
119. CIA Headquarters, "Do Not Advise Charge," cable to Santiago Station, October 20, 1970, in CIA, "Chile Collection."
120. Whelan, *Out of the Ashes*, 291.
121. Lawrence Freedman, "Strategic Studies and the Problems of Power," in Lawrence Freedman, Paul Hayes, and Robert O'Neill, eds., *War, Strategy, and International Politics: Essays in Honour of Sir Michael Howard* (Oxford: Clarendon Press, 1992), 291–293.

CHAPTER 5: WATCHING HISTORY UNFOLD

1. Henry A. Kissinger, "NSC Meeting, November 6—Chile," memorandum to Richard Nixon, November 7, 1970, NARA.
2. Canadian Embassy Santiago, "Inauguration of President Allende," telegram to External Affairs Canada, November 3, 1970, FCO 7/1517 Presidential Election in Chile, TNA.
3. Devine interview.
4. Fermandois, *Chile y El Mundo*, 262–263. In Spanish: "pues para exportar la UP, la fórmula chilena, ¡habría que exportar primero la democracia!"
5. John Dinges, *The Condor Years: How Pinochet and His Allies Brought Terrorism to Three Continents* (New York: New Press, 2004), 50–51.
6. Government of Chile, *Report of the Chilean National Commission on Truth and Reconciliation*, English ed. (Notre Dame, IN: University of Notre Dame Press, 1993), part 2, ch. 1.
7. Whelan, *Out of the Ashes*, 307.
8. "*Una necesidad táctica*," said Allende in response to criticism that he had betrayed Marxist principles by signing the Declaration of Constitutional Guarantees in August 1970. Debray, *Chilean Revolution*, 52.
9. Alexander Haig, "Talking Point for the PFIAB Meeting," memorandum to Henry A. Kissinger, December 3, 1970, *FRUS, 1969–76*, vol. 2, "The Intelligence Community and the White House," doc. 218.
10. Theodore Eliot, "NSC Meeting on Chile," memorandum to Henry A. Kissinger, November 3, 1970, in NSC, "Chile Collection."
11. Robert Hurwitch, "NSC Meeting on Chile," memorandum to Secretary of State, November 5, 1970, in CIA, "Chile Collection." The State Department considered options A and B to be essentially identical.

12. NSC, "Options Paper on Chile (NSSM 97)," memorandum, November 3, 1970, in NSC, "Chile Collection."
13. Ibid.
14. H. R. Haldeman, "NSC Meeting," memorandum to Dwight L. Chapin, November 4, 1970, Meetings Box H-029, NSC Institutional "H" Files, Meeting Files, 1969–1974, Nixon Presidential Materials, NARA.
15. Kissinger, "NSC Meeting, November 6—Chile."
16. NSC, "NSC Meeting—Chile (NSSM 97)," memorandum of conversation, November 6, 1970, in CIA, "Chile Collection."
17. Ibid.
18. Ibid.
19. Ibid.
20. Paul Berman, *Terror and Liberalism* (New York: Norton, 2004), 3.
21. Henry A. Kissinger, interview by the author, March 5, 2004.
22. NSC, National Security Decision Memorandum (NSDM)-93, November 9, 1970, in NSC, "Chile Collection."
23. NSC, "Options Paper on Chile (NSSM 97)," memorandum, November 3, 1970, in NSC, "Chile Collection."
24. Guy E. Millard, "Chile," letter to C. D. Wiggin, November 18, 1970, FCO 7/1527, TNA.
25. Hurwitch, "NSC Meeting on Chile."
26. Crimmins interview.
27. NSC, "Options Paper for NSC: Chile," memorandum, November 3, 1970, in NSC, "Chile Collection."
28. Charles Meyer, "Covert Action Program for Chile," memorandum to U. Alexis Johnson, November 18, 1970, in State, "Chile Collection."
29. Sigmund, *Overthrow of Allende*, 149.
30. Ibid, 163.
31. Whelan, *Out of the Ashes*, 418. See also Pierre Kalfon, *Allende: Chile, 1970–1973* (Paris: Atlantica, 1998), 198.
32. Whelan, *Out of the Ashes*, 419.
33. Faúndez, *Marxism and Democracy in Chile*, 237.
34. U.S. Embassy Santiago, "Finale of Aug 21 Violence," cable to Secretary of State, August 22, 1973, in State, "Chile Collection."
35. Faúndez, *Marxism and Democracy in Chile*, 222.
36. Kolko, *Confronting the Third World*, 217.
37. U.S. Embassy Santiago, cable to Secretary of State, February 28, 1972, in State, "Chile Collection."
38. See Ann Helwege, "Three Socialist Experiences in Latin America: Surviving U.S. Economic Pressure," *Bulletin of Latin American Research* 8: 2 (1989): 211–234. See also Morris Morley and Steven Smith, "Imperial 'Reach': U.S. Policy and the CIA in Chile," *Journal of Political and Military Sociology* 5: 2 (1977): 278–309.
39. Haslam, *Nixon Administration and the Death of Allende's Chile*, ch. 4 and ch. 5, passim.
40. World Bank, "Chile and the World Bank," *Inter-American Economic Affairs* 30: 2 (1976): 81–91. See also IBRD, "Notes Relating to Chile's Creditworthiness during the Administration of Presidents Allende and Pinochet," *Inter-American Economic Affairs* 31: 2 (1977): 83–85. These are published versions of text

submitted to separate hearings of the House Appropriations Subcommittee on Foreign Assistance.

41. Church Committee, *Covert Action in Chile*, 29.
42. Whelan, *Out of the Ashes*, 335.
43. Haslam, *Nixon Administration and the Death of Allende's Chile*, 101.
44. Helwege, "Three Socialist Experiences," 220.
45. Peter A. Goldberg, "The Politics of the Allende Overthrow in Chile," *Political Science Quarterly* 90: 1 (1975): 109.
46. Fermandois, *Chile y El Mundo*, 263. In Spanish: "Si Estados Unidos nos cierra sus créditos, buscaremos otras líneas de créditos en otros países donde sea posible . . . no me imagino que Estados Unidos se oponga a que otros países nos presten dinero."
47. Joseph L. Nogee and John W. Sloan, "Allende's Chile and the Soviet Union: A Policy Lesson for Latin American Nations Seeking Autonomy," *Journal of Interamerican Studies and World Affairs* 21: 3 (1979), 349.
48. John H. Crimmins's testimony in House Subcommittee, *United States and Chile*, 69.
49. Davis, *Last Two Years*, 125–127.
50. Crimmins interview.
51. William P. Lineberry, *The United States in World Affairs, 1970* (New York: Simon & Schuster, 1972), 193.
52. Allende, *Chile's Road to Socialism*, 37.
53. Nogee and Sloan, "Allende's Chile and the Soviet Union," 348.
54. Richard M. Nixon, "Second Annual Report to the Congress on United States Foreign Policy," February 25, 1971.
55. Richard Nixon in "Backyard," *The Cold War*, CNN, February 21, 1999, http:// www.cnn.com /SPECIALS/cold.war /episodes/18/script.html (accessed July 12, 2006).
56. Kornbluh, *Pinochet File*, 83.
57. NSC, "Chile: Next Steps," memorandum, November 23, 1971, Box H-052, SRG Meeting, Berlin Negotiations 2-10-71, to SRG Meeting, Pakistan 3-6-71, Nixon Presidential Materials, NARA.
58. Helwege, "Three Socialist Experiences," 222
59. Orrega, *Chile*, 142–145. This is a table of IMF, IDB, and IBRD loans and decisions concerning Chile from 1971 through to 1974.
60. Falcoff, *Modern Chile*, 229.
61. Church Committee, Alleged Assassination Plots, 227.
62. Falcoff, *Modern Chile*, 240.
63. Paul E. Sigmund, "The 'Invisible Blockade' and the Overthrow of Allende," in Orrega, *Chile*, 118. This summarizes the criticism of U.S. military aid to Chile.
64. Church Committee, *Covert Action in Chile*, 41–42.
65. Henry A. Kissinger and U. Alexis Johnson, "Highest Levels Here," cable to Edward M. Korry, October 7, 1970, in State, "Chile Collection."
66. U. Alexis Johnson and Charles Meyer, memorandum to Edward M. Korry, September 23, 1970, in State, "Chile Collection."
67. The air force, notably, was the only Chilean service with a notable American influence. The Chilean navy was a proudly "British" service, and the army had a Prussian influence dating back to the mid-nineteenth century.
68. Edward M. Korry, cable to U. Alexis Johnson, September 16, 1970, in State, "Chile Collection."

69. Viron P. Vaky, "Chile," memorandum to Henry A. Kissinger, October 18, 1970, in NSC, "Chile Collection."
70. Santiago Station, "Strongly Urge That USG," cable to CIA Headquarters, October 22, 1970, in CIA, "Chile Collection."
71. Santiago Station, "There Is More Confidence," cable to CIA Headquarters, November 6, 1970, in CIA, "Chile Collection."
72. Cable, Secretary of State to U.S. Embassy Santiago, "MilGroup and Military Equipment for Chile," December 3, 1970, in State, "Chile Collection."
73. The Church committee report provides slightly different figures: $5.7 million for 1971; $12.3 million for 1972; and, $15 million for 1973. See Church Committee, *Covert Action in Chile*, 39.
74. Charles Meyer, "FMS Credits for Chile," memorandum to Curtis Tarr, February 22, 1973, in State, "Chile Collection."
75. Jorge Edwards, *Persona Non Grata: An Envoy in Castro's Cuba*, (London: Bodley Head, 1976), 118.
76. Carlos Prats Gonzales, *Memorias: Testimonio de Un Soldado* (Santiago: Pehuén Editores Ltda, 1985), 388–390.
77. Fermandois, *Chile y El Mundo*, 91. See also Whelan, *Out of the Ashes*, 389.
78. Ibid.
79. Crimmins interview.
80. WHD, "Covert Action Program for Chile," memorandum, November 17, 1970, in CIA, "Chile Collection."
81. Devine interview.
82. WHD, "Covert Action Program for Chile." See also Santiago Station, "Following Is Covert Action Proposal," cable to CIA Headquarters, January 9, 1971, in CIA, "Chile Collection."
83. Ibid.
84. WHD, "Talking Paper," memorandum, December 7, 1970, in CIA, "Chile Collection." See also ARA, "ARA/CIA Meeting 30 May 73," memorandum, May 31, 1973, in State, "Chile Collection."
85. CIA Headquarters, "Resume of Country Director and INR Comments," cable to Santiago Station, December 13, 1970, in CIA, "Chile Collection."
86. "ARA/CIA Meeting, 30 May 73."
87. Santiago Station, "It Is Station's View," cable to CIA Headquarters, February 8, 1973, in CIA, "Chile Collection."
88. Santiago Station, "In Ref Station Forwarded," cable, January 9, 1971, in CIA, "Chile Collection."
89. Kissinger interview.
90. Devine interview.
91. Arnold Nachmanoff, "Proposals for Covert Support of Chilean Opposition," memorandum to Henry A. Kissinger, January 28, 1971, in NSC, "Chile Collection."
92. WHD, "Request for Approval of Project," memorandum to DDP, February 12, 1971, in CIA, "Chile Collection."
93. Davis, *Last Two Years*, 21.
94. Church Committee, *Covert Action in Chile*, 60.
95. Shackley, *Spymaster*, 269.
96. See Jerry W. Knudson, "Allende to Pinochet: Crucible of the Chilean Press 1970–1984," *Studies in Latin American Popular Culture* 6 (1987): 43–53, for a

review of the history and impact of *El Mercurio*, the world's oldest Spanish language newspaper.

97. Fermandois, *Chile y El Mundo*, 288.
98. Horne, *Small Earthquake in Chile*, 21.
99. Davis, *Last Two Years*, 308.
100. John Crimmins, "Chilean Media under a Marxist Regime," memorandum to the Undersecretary of State for ARA, December 23, 1970, in State, "Chile Collection." See also Faúndez, *Marxism and Democracy in Chile*, 218.
101. David Corn, *Blond Ghost: Ted Shackley and the CIA's Crusades* (New York: Simon & Schuster, 1994), 250.
102. Horne, *Small Earthquake in Chile*, 145.
103. "La doctrina del ejercito," *El Mercurio*, September 24, 1972. See also Haslam, *Nixon Administration and the Death of Allende's Chile*, 138.
104. William J. Jorden, "40 Committee Meeting—Chile," memorandum to Henry A. Kissinger, April 10, 1972, in NSC, "Chile Collection."
105. Church Committee, *Covert Action in Chile*, 60.
106. DDP, "The Agency Covert Action Program in Chile," memorandum, October 3, 1973, in CIA, "Chile Collection." This document is actually undated though it its text corresponds to a report sometime between April and July 1973. Its misfiled date is given.
107. Santiago Station, "On Morning 14 Dec," cable to CIA Headquarters, December 19, 1970, in CIA, "Chile Collection."
108. William McAfee, "Status of Covert Support," memorandum to the Undersecretary of State for ARA, February 1, 1972, in State, "Chile Collection."
109. Charles Meyer, "Status Report on Covert Assistance to Chilean Opposition," memorandum to U. Alexis Johnson, July 5, 1972, in State, "Chile Collection."
110. McAfee, "Status of Covert Support."
111. Charles Meyer, "Sitrep on Covert Assistance to Chilean Opposition," memorandum to U. Alexis Johnson, April 13, 1972, in State, "Chile Collection."
112. Santiago COS[?], "Chile: What Now," memorandum to C/WHD, June 30, 1973, in CIA, "Chile Collection."
113. Santiago Station, "A Massive Demonstration," cable to CIA Headquarters, December 1, 1971. Sigmund cites a low figure of five thousand women. Sigmund, *Overthrow of Allende*, 163.
114. USIB, "Chile: The Alternatives Facing the Allende Regime," NIE 72-342, June 29, 1972, 1, in CIA, "Chile Collection."
115. Charles Meyer and John Crimmins, "As You Know," memorandum to Nathaniel Davis, August 18, 1972, in State, "Chile Collection."
116. Ibid.
117. Shackley, *Spymaster*, 269.
118. Department of State, "Financial Support to the Chilean Private Sector," memorandum to the 40 Committee, August 24, 1972, in NSC, "Chile Collection."
119. Charles Meyer and John Crimmins, "Washington Is at the Point," memorandum to Nathaniel Davis, August 30, 1972, in State, "Chile Collection."
120. Nathaniel Davis, "When I Read," cable to Charles Meyer and John Crimmins, August 31, 1972, in State, "Chile Collection."
121. Unknown Author (WHD?) "Annex to 24 August 1972 Memorandum Entitled 'Financial Support to Chilean Private Sector,'" memorandum to the 40 Committee, September 14, 1972, in NSC, "Chile Collection."

122. Charles Meyer, "Release of Funds to Private Sector," memorandum to U. Alexis Johnson, January 15, 1973, in State, "Chile Collection." See also Haslam, *Nixon Administration and the Death of Allende's Chile*, 150.
123. Charles Meyer, "Covert Aid to Chilean Private Sector," memorandum to U. Alexis Johnson, September 15, 1972, in State, "Chile Collection."
124. Ibid.
125. CIA Headquarters, "Request Approval on Text," cable to Santiago Station, February 21, 1973, in CIA, "Chile Collection." See also Shackley, *Spymaster*, 269.
126. WHD, "Covert Action Options for Chile," memorandum, March 31, 1973, in CIA, "Chile Collection."
127. Santiago COS[?], "Chile: What Now," memorandum to C/WHD, June 30, 1973, in CIA, "Chile Collection."
128. William J. Jorden, "Covert Support for Chilean Private Sector," memorandum to Henry A. Kissinger, August 29, 1973, in NSC, "Chile Collection."
129. DCI, "Have Just Been Advised," cable to Santiago Station, August 21, 1973, in CIA, "Chile Collection."
130. Kolko, *Confronting the Third World*, 221.
131. Vitale, *Para Recuperar La Memoria Histórica*, 222.
132. William Colby, "CIA's Covert Action Program Chile," memorandum to Henry A. Kissinger, September 13, 1973, in CIA, "Chile Collection."
133. Sergio Onofre Jarpa, *Confesiones Politicas*, eds. Patricia Arancibia, Claudia Arancibia, and Isabel de la Maza (Santiago: Tercera-Mandadori, 2002), 174. See also Haslam, *Nixon Administration and the Death of Allende's Chile*, 141.
134. Devine interview.
135. Anonymous U.S. government official, interview by the author, March 2004
136. Haslam, *Nixon Administration and the Death of Allende's Chile*, 140.
137. Anonymous U.S. government official, interview by the author, March 2004.
138. Unknown author, "Policy Objectives for Chile," memorandum to C/WHD, April 17, 1973, in CIA, "Chile Collection."
139. Valenzuela, *Breakdown of Democratic Regimes*, 78.
140. Church Committee, *Covert Action in Chile*, 33.
141. Ibid.
142. COS, cable to C/WHD, November 12, 1971, in CIA, "Chile Collection."
143. C/WHD, cable to COS, December 1, 1971, in CIA, "Chile Collection."
144. Crimmins interview.
145. C/WHD, cable to COS, December 1, 1971, in CIA, "Chile Collection."
146. Church Committee, *Covert Action in Chile*, 37.
147. Devine interview.
148. CIA Headquarters, "While HQs Prepared," cable to Santiago Station, October 23, 1972, in CIA, "Chile Collection."
149. DI, "CIA Bulletin," memorandum, June 30, 1973, in CIA, "Chile Collection."
150. Santiago Station, "The Air Force Did Not," cable to unknown, July 9, 1973, in CIA, "Chile Collection."
151. Haslam, *Nixon Administration and the Death of Allende's Chile*, 181.
152. Santiago Station, "As of 1040 Hours," intelligence report, June 29, 1973, CIA.
153. ARA, "Questions Which May Be Raised Concerning Chile," memorandum, July 1973, in State, "Chile Collection." (Listed as July 1, 1973 in State Department pages.)

154. U.S. Embassy Santiago, "UP Press Ties CIA to Coup Attempt," cable to Secretary of State, July 12, 1973, in State, "Chile Collection."
155. Santiago Station, "Situation Report on Uprising by Military Unit," memo randum, July 25, 1973, in CIA, "Chile Collection."
156. Haslam, *Nixon Administration and the Death of Allende's Chile*, 179–181.
157. Ibid.
158. Cristián Pérez, "Salvadore Allende, Apuntes Sobre Su Dispositivo de Seguridad: El Grupo de Amigos Personales (GAP)," *Éstudios Públicos* 79 (Winter 2000): 51.
159. Onofre, *Confesiones Políticas*, 210.
160. "The Presidential Security Guard," intelligence report, November 1971, in CIA, "Chile Collection."
161. Andrew and Mitrokhin, *Mitrokhin Archive II*, 82.
162. Devine interview.
163. Andrew and Mitrokhin, *Mitrokhin Archive II*, 73.
164. "Close Surveillance," information report, November 16, 1972, in CIA, "Chile Collection."
165. Rogers interview.
166. Crimmins interview.
167. For a better study of Ted Shackley, see Corn, *Blond Ghost*.
168. Shackley, *Spymaster*, 270.
169. Unknown Author, "Dr. Henry A. Kissinger: Biographical Note," memorandum, June 22, 1971, CAB 133/408, TNA.
170. Shackley, *Spymaster*, 270.
171. WHD, "The Agency Covert Action Program in Chile," memorandum, October 3, 1973, in CIA, "Chile Collection." Though undated, this document is filed within the Chile Collection at the date given.
172. Devine interview.
173. Kissinger interview.
174. Devine interview.
175. William Colby, "Proposed Covert Financial Support to Chilean Private Sector," memorandum to Henry A. Kissinger and Jack B. Kubisch, August 25, 1973, in CIA, "Chile Collection."

CHAPTER 6: THE CIA AND ITT

1. NSC, "Minutes of the Meeting of the Special Review Group," memorandum for the record, May 12, 1964, in *FRUS 1964–68*, vol. 31, doc. 257.
2. Jack Anderson, *The Anderson Papers*, with George Clifford (London: Millington, 1974), 112.
3. "ITT: And Now Chile," Editorial, *Washington Post*, March 22, 1972.
4. Senate Foreign Relations Committee, Subcommittee on Multinational Corporations, *The International Telephone and Telegraph Company and Chile, 1970–1971*, 93rd Cong., 1st sess., June 21, 1973.
5. The Church committee's impact from a CIA point of view can be gleaned from former DCI Richard Helms's memoir, Helms, *A Look over My Shoulder*, 404–406, 428–437.
6. Ibid., 437.
7. The precise figures vary. James Whelan reports income of $6.6 billion annually in Whelan, *Out of the Ashes*, 294. *Time* noted revenues of $7.3 billion with similar sized profits for the year 1971. This may be accounted for the fact that

not all published ITT figures took into account the profits of the (280 or so) subsidiaries of its own subsidiaries. See *Time*, "ITT's Big Conglomorate of Troubles," May 1, 1971. Accessed at www.time.com on June 5, 2007.

8. Ibid., 296.
9. Ibid., 297.
10. Kornbluh, *Pinochet File*, 103n. 36.
11. Jack Anderson, "Memos Bare ITT Try for Chile Coup," *Washington Merry-Go-Round* (syndicated column), March 21, 1972.
12. Jack Anderson, "ITT Pledge Millions to Stop Allende," *Washington Merry-Go-Round*, March 22, 1972.
13. Hal Hendrix and Bob Berrellez, "Chile," memorandum to E. J. Gerrity, September 17, 1970. All ITT memos were published in *The ITT Memos, Subversion in Chile: A Case Study of U.S. Corporate Intrigue in the Third World* (London, Spokesman Books, 1972), henceforth ITT.
14. Anderson, "Memos Bare ITT Try."
15. Kornbluh, *Pinochet File*, 102.
16. Corn, *Blond Ghost*, 244–246, 351–352.
17. Senate Committee, *ITT and Chile*.
18. Anderson, "Memos Bare ITT Try."
19. C/WHD to unknown (Station?), "Allende's Campaign Being Funded by USSR through Cuba's Prensa Latina," July 23, 1970, in CIA, "Chile Collection."
20. Crimmins interview.
21. William Broe, memorandum for the record, July 17, 1970, in CIA, "Chile Collection." McCone, as DCI, had previously rejected an ITT approach in 1964.
22. CIA, "Harold D. Geneen—Questions and Answers," memo #1049, undated (July or August 1970?) in CIA, "Chile Collection."
23. William Broe, "We Have Weighed," cable to Santiago Station, August 6, 1970, in CIA, "Chile Collection."
24. Ibid.
25. Ibid.
26. Richard Nixon and Henry Kissinger, telephone transcript, September 12, 1970, Kissinger.
27. E. J. Gerrity, memorandum to Harold Geneen, September 29, 1970, ITT.
28. Ibid.
29. Ibid.
30. Korry, Fermandois, and Fontaine T., "El Embajador Edward M. Korry en el CEP," 24.
31. CIA, "Harold D. Geneen—Questions and Answers."
32. Santiago Station, "Doubt They Can Be Dissuaded," cable to CIA Headquarters, September 10, 1970, in CIA, "Chile Collection."
33. William Broe, memorandum for the record, August 3, 1970, in CIA, "Chile Collection."
34. Santiago Station, "Suggest You Allow," cable to CIA Headquarters, July 18, 1970, in CIA, "Chile Collection." The figure $300,000 is a handwritten marginal note.
35. WHD, "ITT Funding in Chilean 1970 Presidential Election," cable #1061, undated (after April 1972?), in CIA, "Chile Collection."
36. Hal Hendrix and Bob Berrellez, "Chile," memorandum to E. J. Gerrity, September 17, 1970, ITT.

37. Nixon and Kissinger, telephone transcript.
38. William P. Rogers and Henry A. Kissinger, telephone transcript, September 14, 1970, Kissinger.
39. Secretary of State, "Meeting Covered at Length," cable to Edward M. Korry, September 15, 1970, in State, "Chile Collection."
40. Korry, Fermandois, and Fontaine T., "El Embajador Edward M. Korry en el CEP," 25.
41. Hendrix and Berrellez, "Chile."
42. Edward M. Korry, "Significant References to Mr. Korry in ITT Documents," memorandum for the record, September 30, 1970 in State, "Chile Collection." The September 30 date is incorrect; the correct date is likely March 23, 1972, as marginally noted later in the document.
43. Nixon and Kissinger, telephone transcript.
44. Church Committee, *Alleged Assassination Plots*, 227.
45. William Broe, "Genesis of Operation FUBELT," memorandum for the record, September 16, 1970, in CIA, "Chile Collection."
46. John McCone, testimony in Senate Committee, *ITT and Chile*, 130–132.
47. CIA, "ITT Funding in Chilean 1970 Presidential Election."
48. Anonymous government official interview.
49. Hal Hendrix, "Chile," memorandum to E. J. Gerrity, October 16, 1970.
50. Hersh, *Price of Power*, 277.
51. Hendrix, "Chile."
52. Thomas Karamessines (?), "Track II," intelligence note to file, October 10, 1970, in CIA, "Chile Collection."
53. Hendrix, "Chile."
54. Hal Hendrix, "Chile (Bob Berrellez Called This Morning)," memorandum to E. J. Gerrity, October 22, 1970, in ITT.
55. Thomas Karamessines (?), "Track II," memorandum, October 24, 1970, in CIA, "Chile Collection."
56. Frank Church, "Opening Statement," in Senate Committee, *ITT and Chile*, 2.
57. David Boulton, *The Lockheed Papers* (London: J. Cape, 1978), 178.
58. *The Washington Post*, "ITT: And Now Chile."
59. Corn, *Blond Ghost*, 241.
60. Helms, *A Look over My Shoulder*, 413–415, 440–443. The successful prosecution for perjury brought against Richard Helms in 1975, based in part on his testimony to the Senate Subcommittee on Multinational Corporations, was unprecedented and broke new grounds in terms of the balance of power regarding covert operations between the executive and the legislature. Essentially, Helms stated that he lied to the subcommittee because he was bound by an oath to the president not to reveal the operations and that the subcommittee lacked authority of oversight over the CIA. Likewise, Helms claimed that the testimony was in open session and that to have asked for executive session at that point would have been tantamount to answering in the positive.
61. McCone testimony, in Senate Committee, *ITT and Chile*, 103.
62. William Broe, testimony, in Senate Committee, *ITT and Chile*, 250.
63. Charles Meyer, testimony, in Senate Committee, *ITT and Chile*, 399.
64. Falcoff, *Modern Chile*, 210.
65. Broe testimony, in Senate Committee, *ITT and Chile*, 250–251.
66. Bob Berrellez, testimony, in Senate Committee, *ITT and Chile*, 168.

67. William R. Merriam, testimony, in Senate Committee, *ITT and Chile*, 23.
68. Viron P. Vaky, testimony, in Senate Committee, *ITT and Chile*, 436.
69. Fermandois, *Chile y El Mundo*, 265.
70. Falcoff, *Modern Chile*, 132.
71. Unidad Popular, *Programa Básico de Gobierno de la Unidad Popular*, 4th ed. (Santiago: Impresa Horizonte, 1970), 20.
72. Senate Committee, *ITT and Chile*, 2–3.
73. 40 Committee, "Options in Chilean Presidential Election," memorandum, August 31, 1970 in NSC, "Chile Collection."
74. Ibid. and Crimmins interview.
75. Senate Committee, *ITT and Chile*, 2.
76. Bob Berrellez, "Chileans," memorandum to Hal Hendrix, October 22, 1970, in ITT.
77. Anonymous government official interview.
78. C/WHD, "Background Paper for Meeting with Ambassador Korry," memorandum to DDP, September 17, 1969, in CIA, "Chile Collection."
79. Cord Meyer, *Facing Reality: From World Federalism to the CIA* (New York: Harper & Row, 1980), 182.
80. Nixon and Kissinger, telephone transcript.
81. Meyer, *Facing Reality*, 184.
82. Vaky interview.
83. Kissinger interview.
84. Senate Committee, *ITT and Chile*, vol. 2, 1091–1092.
85. Fermandois, *Chile y El Mundo*, 260. The Spanish reads, "La CIA y la integración económica latinoamericana so ahora las armas preferidas."
86. Ibid, 264. The Spanish reads, "Por el contrario, es un ataque siempre oblicuo, subterráneo, sinuoso, pero no por eso menos lesivo para Chile.

CHAPTER 7: THE CAMPAIGN ENDS

1. Salvador Allende, "Ultimas Palabras, 1973," originally aired on Radio Magallanes, September 11, 1973, www.inep.org (accessed August 2006). Translation: "These are my last words: I am certain that my sacrifice will not be in vain; I am certain that, at least, this will be a moral lesson that will punish crime, cowardice and treason."
2. Robinson, *Promoting Polyarchy*, 161–162. See also Robinson, "Capitalist Polyarchy in Latin America," in Michael Cox, G. John Ikenberry, and Takashi Inoguchi, eds., *American Democracy Promotion: Impulses, Strategies, and Impacts* (Oxford: Oxford University Press, 2000), 315. See also James Petras and Morris Morley, *The United States and Chile: Imperialism and the Overthrow of the Allende Government* (New York: Monthly Review Press, 1975), 82.
3. Robinson, *Promoting Polyarchy*, 315.
4. Hitchens, "Case against Henry Kissinger, Part 2," 49.
5. Sigmund, *Overthrow of Allende*, 188.
6. Valenzuela, *Breakdown of Democratic Regimes*, 83.
7. DI, "The Presidential Security Guard," intelligence report, November 1, 1971, in CIA, "Chile Collection."
8. Dinges, *Condor Years*, 50–51.
9. Pérez, "Salvador Allende, Apuntes Sobre Su Dispositivo de Seguridad," 51; Bill Long (former *Miami Herald* reporter in Santiago), telephone interview by the author, February 2, 2007.

10. DI, "CIA Bulletin," memorandum, June 30, 1973, in CIA, "Chile Collection." See also DI, "During the Second Week of August," intelligence report, August 25, 1973, in CIA, "Chile Collection."
11. Horne, *Small Earthquake in Chile*, 139.
12. Santiago Station, "Strike in Chile," cable to C/WHD, August 22, 1973, in CIA, "Chile Collection."
13. Government of Chile, *Report of the Chilean National Commission*, part 2, ch. 1.
14. Otero interview.
15. Long interview.
16. Horne, *Small Earthquake in Chile*, 223.
17. Ambassador D. H. T. Hildyard "Annual Review for Chile 1971", January 12, 1972, FCO 7/2210, TNA.
18. Davis, *Last Two Years*, ch. 8, passim.
19. William Colby, "CIA's Covert Action Program," memorandum to Henry A. Kissinger, September 19, 1973, in CIA, "Chile Collection."
20. Horne, *Small Earthquake in Chile*, 226.
21. Sigmund, *Overthrow of Allende*, 237.
22. Horne, *Small Earthquake in Chile*, 226.
23. Andrew and Mitrokhin, *Mitrokhin Archive II*, 77.
24. Valenzuela, *Breakdown of Democratic Regimes*, 105.
25. Government of Chile, *Report of the Chilean National Commission*, part 1, ch. 2.
26. Dinges, *Condor Years*, 44.
27. Valenzuela, *Breakdown of Democratic Regimes*, 103.
28. Devine interview.
29. Santiago Station, "Situation Report on Abortive Uprising," cable to CIA Headquarters, July 25, 1973, in CIA, "Chile Collection."
30. Mónica González, *Chile La Conjura: Los Mil y un Dias Del Golpe* (Santiago, Ediciones B Grupo Zeta, 2000): 202.
31. Committee of 15, "Memorándum de 1 de Julio de 1973," in González, *Chile la Conjura*: 502–507.
32. Pamela Constable and Arturo Valenzuela, *A Nation of Enemies: Chile under Pinochet* (New York: Norton, 1991), 28.
33. Valenzuela, *Breakdown of Democratic Regimes*, 104.
34. Santiago Military Attaché's Office [MAO], "Events Leading Up to the 11 September Military Coup," intelligence information report, October 29, 1973, in Department of Defense, "Chile Collection," *Chile Declassification Project*, http://www.foia.state.gov/SearchColls/DOD.asp (accessed March 17, 2005).
35. González, *Chile La Conjura,* 255–259.
36. Davis, *Last Two Years*, 165–166.
37. Valenzuela, *Breakdown of Democratic Regimes*, 105.
38. González, *Chile La Conjura*, 279.
39. Sigmund, *Overthrow of Allende*, 239–240.
40. Nathaniel Davis, interview for the George Washington University National Security Archive, "Backyard," *The Cold War*, CNN, February 21, 1999, http://www.gwu.edu/~nsarchiv/coldwar/interviews/ (accessed August 15, 2006).
41. Whelan, *Out of the Ashes*, 470.
42. Ibid, 457. Translation: "Assume control and occupy immediately and effectively municipal and provincial seats of government, provincial offices, and dependencies. . . . Activate security plan immediately."

43. Ibid., 471.
44. Mary Helen Spooner, *Soldiers in a Narrow Land: The Pinochet Regime in Chile* (Berkeley: University of California Press, 1999), 41.
45. Whelan, *Out of the Ashes*, 491.
46. Spooner, *Soldiers in a Narrow Land*, 42.
47. Kornbluh, *Pinochet File*, 113. For a much more authoritative discussion, see Ignacio González Camus, *El Dia En Que Murio Allende* (Santiago: Cesoc, 1988), or Mónica González, *Chile La Conjura*, 368–372. Almost all current sources agree that Allende took his own life with a submachine gun gifted to him by Castro. Some still argue, against evidence, that Allende was murdered by the military, and one DIA source, Chilean colonel Hernan Bejares González, argued that a "fanatical member of GAP" shot Allende in order to martyr him. Santiago MAO "Part II of USDAO/Caracas 7981," cable to Pentagon, September 13, 1973, in Defense, "Chile Collection."
48. Kolko, *Confronting the Third World*, 220.
49. Constable and Valenzuela, *A Nation of Enemies*, 23.
50. Paul Wimert, "Pinochet Ugarte," cable, September 13, 1971, in Defense, "Chile Collection."
51. Santiago Station, "Pinochet at Dinner 5 August 1971," cable to CIA Headquarters, August 6, 1971, in CIA, "Chile Collection."
52. Santiago Station, "August in Talk," cable to DCI, August 31–September 1, 1971, in CIA, "Chile Collection."
53. Santiago Station, "Pinochet at Dinner 5 August 1971."
54. Santiago Station, "Gave Following Impression," cable to CIA Headquarters, September 27, 1972, in CIA, "Chile Collection."
55. COS, "Pinochet, Augusto," intelligence note, June 27, 1972, in CIA, "Chile Collection."
56. Santiago Station, "Pinochet's Changing Attitude," cable to unknown, September 28, 1972, in CIA, "Chile Collection."
57. Kissinger interview.
58. Santiago Station, "Was Sent to the Case Officer," cable to CIA Headquarters, May 2, 1973, in CIA, "Chile Collection."
59. Faúndez, *Marxism and Democracy in Chile*, 245.
60. Santiago Station, "Following the Uncoordinated," cable to unknown, July 7, 1973, in CIA, "Chile Collection."
61. DIA, "Chile: The Resignation," intelligence summary, August 24, 1973, in DOD, "Chile Collection."
62. David Atlee Phillips, "Recent Visit of," memorandum to DDO, August 13, 1973, in CIA, "Chile Collection."
63. Santiago Station, "Situation Report on Abortive Uprising."
64. Santiago MAO, "Chile: Strikes Continue," intelligence summary, August 31, 1973, in Defense, "Chile Collection."
65. Whelan, *Out of the Ashes*, 469.
66. Spooner, *Soldiers in a Narrow Land*, 37.
67. Devine interview.
68. Spooner, *Soldiers in a Narrow Land*, ch. 1 passim.
69. Dinges, *Condor Years*, 44.
70. Santiago Station, "Following Impression," cable to unknown, September 27, 1972, in CIA, "Chile Collection."

71. COS, "U.S. Reaction to Possible Approach by Chilean Coup Plotters," memorandum for the record, October 30, 1970, in CIA, "Chile Collection."
72. Author unknown, "Questions Which May Be Raised Concerning Chile," memorandum, c. July 1973, in CIA, "Chile Collection."
73. COS, "U.S. Reaction to Possible Approach by Chilean Coup Plotters."
74. Santiago COS, "He Described Preliminary," cable to CIA Headquarters, August 25, 1973, in CIA, "Chile Collection."
75. CIA Headquarters, "Agree That Realistically," cable to COS, August 27, 1973, in CIA, "Chile Collection."
76. Devine interview.
77. Kalfon, *Allende*, 239. Kalfon, a French pro-Allende socialist, quotes articles in *Le Monde* predicting a coup starting around August 25, 1973.
78. Davis interview.
79. Santiago MAO, "Chile: Some Disaffected," intelligence summary, May 24, 1973, in Defense, "Chile Collection."
80. COS, "PS Leader Clodomiro Almayda Informed," intelligence report, August 3, 1973, in CIA, "Chile Collection."
81. ARA, "ARA/CIA Meeting," memorandum, September 11, 1970, in State, "Chile Collection."
82. COS, "According to the Navy," intelligence report, September 8, 1973, in CIA, "Chile Collection."
83. Devine interview.
84. COS, "According to the Navy."
85. Devine interview.
86. Ibid.
87. Ibid.
88. COS, "That a Coup Attempt Will Be Initiated," intelligence report, September 10, 1973, in CIA, "Chile Collection."
89. Bonar Sykes, "Chile: Coup," telegram to FCO, September 13, 1973, PRO 7/2411, Internal Political Situation Chile, TNA.
90. COS, "Chile: President Allende," intelligence summary, September 11, 1973, in Defense, "Chile Collection."
91. COS, "That a Coup Attempt Will Be Initiated."
92. Devine interview.
93. William Jorden, "Possible Request for U.S. Government Aid," memorandum to Henry A. Kissinger, September 10, 1970, in NSC, "Chile Collection." This is a telegram that would have gone directly from Santiago to Washington and Langley. The intelligence report in note 65 would have been prepared in Langley from intelligence sent from Santiago the previous day.
94. Santiago Station, "Opposition Parties Are Maintaining," cable to CIA Headquarters, August 24, 1973, in CIA, "Chile Collection."
95. William Colby, "Proposed Covert Financial Support of Chilean Private Sector," memorandum to Henry A. Kissinger, August 25, 1973, in CIA, "Chile Collection."
96. Haslam, *Nixon Administration and the Death of Allende's Chile*, 219.
97. Helms, *A Look over My Shoulder*, 11.
98. Anonymous government officer interview.
99. Kissinger interview.
100. William McAfee, "ARA/CIA Meeting of 7 September," memorandum to James R. Gardner, September 11, 1973, in State, "Chile Collection."

101. Ibid.
102. USIB, "Chile," National Intelligence Estimate, June 14, 1973, in CIA, "Chile Collection."
103. Phillips, *Night Watch*, 238.
104. Hersh, *Price of Power*, 295. Here one reads of the famous arrest lists and "almost daily reports of coups." Reporting the plots, the CIA's function, is imputed by Hersh to directly correlate with their plotting.
105. DI, "Chile," intelligence bulletin, September 13, 1973, in CIA, "Chile Collection."
106. Santiago MAO, "Part I of USDAO/Caracas 7981," cable to Pentagon, September 13, 1973, in Defense, "Chile Collection."
107. William Colby, "CIA's Covert Action Program," memorandum to Henry A. Kissinger, September 19, 1973, in CIA, "Chile Collection."
108. Devine interview.
109. Yuri Pavlov, interview for the George Washington University National Security Archive, "Backyard," *The Cold War*, CNN, February 21, 1999, http://www.gwu.edu/~nsarchiv/coldwar/interviews (accessed August 15, 2006).

CHAPTER 8: CODA

1. Augusto Pinochet, "Discurso de Chacarillas: 9 de Julio de 1977," *Centro de Estudios Bicentenario Chile 1810–2010*, www.bicentenariochile.cl (accessed August 2006). Statement in Spanish: Finalmente, entraremos en la etapa de normalidad o consolidación, donde el poder será ejercido directa y básicamente por la civilidad, reservándose constitucionalmente a las Fuerzas Armadas y de Orden el papel de contribuir a cautelar las bases esenciales de la institucionalidad y la seguridad nacional en sus amplias decisivas proyecciones modernas.
2. Crimmins interview.
3. Kissinger interview.
4. Crimmins interview.
5. Devine interview.
6. DIA, "Chile," intelligence summary, September 25, 1973, in Defense, "Chile Collection."
7. DCI, "The Situation in Chile," briefing note for NSC, September 14, 1973, in CIA, "Chile Collection."
8. Santiago Station, "Following Is Text," cable to CIA Headquarters, September 14, 1973, in CIA, "Chile Collection."
9. U.S. Embassy Santiago, "Chile at Work," cable to Secretary of State, September 20, 1973, in State, "Chile Collection."
10. DIA, "Chile," intelligence summary, October 13, 1973, in Defense, "Chile Collection."
11. "Chile," *Central Intelligence Bulletin*, September 13, 1973, in CIA, "Chile Collection."
12. "Chile," *Central Intelligence Bulletin*, September 18, 1973, in CIA, "Chile Collection."
13. The Rettig Commission produced a thoroughly documented total of just under three thousand deaths for the entire seventeen-year dictatorship (Government of Chile, *Report of the Chilean National Commission*, Appendix II).
14. DIA, "Chile."
15. Santiago Station, "The Junta Believes," cable to CIA Headquarters (?), undated

(September 15–20, 1973[?]), in CIA, "Chile Collection." This document was misfiled under the date September 9, 1973.

16. "Chile, 177," *Central Intelligence Bulletin*, September 27, 1973, in CIA, "Chile Collection."
17. Santiago Station, "Junta Follow-up Activities," cable to CIA Headquarters, September 15, 1973, in CIA, "Chile Collection."
18. Whelan, *Out of the Ashes*, 496.
19. CIA Headquarters, "Consensus Reached," cable to Santiago Station, September 21, 1973, in CIA, "Chile Collection."
20. CIA Headquarters, "Realize Authorised," cable to Santiago Station, September 24, 1973, in CIA, "Chile Collection."
21. Santiago Station, "Ambassador Does Not," cable to DCI, September 28, 1973, in CIA, "Chile Collection."
22. Santiago Station, "Station Plans," cable to CIA Headquarters, October 4, 1973, in CIA, "Chile Collection."
23. Santiago Station, "November 1973," cable to CIA Headquarters, November 12, in CIA, "Chile Collection."
24. Chile Desk, "Project [deleted] Renewal," memorandum to acting C/WHD, November 23, 1973, in CIA, "Chile Collection."
25. CIA Headquarters, "All Political Action," cable to Santiago Station, November 20, 1973, in CIA, "Chile Collection."
26. CIA Headquarters, "Following Are Results," cable to Santiago Station, November 26, 1973, in CIA, "Chile Collection."
27. Ibid.
28. C/WHD, "Amendment for Fiscal Year," memorandum to acting C/WHD, November 28, 1973, in CIA, "Chile Collection."
29. WHD (department unknown), "Amendment No. 1 to Project," memorandum to C/WHD, January 8, 1974, in CIA, "Chile Collection."
30. WHD (department unknown), "[deleted] Project," memorandum to C/WHD, January 9, 1974, in CIA, "Chile Collection."
31. Anonymous government official interview.
32. Santiago Station, "Had Just Left," cable to CIA Headquarters, January 19, 1974, in CIA, "Chile Collection."
33. Government of Chile, *Report of the Chilean National Commission*, part 2, ch. 2.
34. Santiago Station, "Ambassador Popper Will Be," cable to CIA Headquarters, January 23, 1974, in CIA, "Chile Collection."
35. COS Santiago, "Project," March 1, 1974, in CIA, "Chile Collection."
36. Devine interview.
37. Kissinger interview.
38. Ibid.
39. Berman, *Terror and Liberalism*, 178.

CONCLUSION

1. Andrew and Mitrokhin, *Mitrokhin Archive II*, 86–87.
2. Henry A. Kissinger and Richard Nixon, telephone transcript, September 16, 1973, Box 22, Kissinger TELCONS, Nixon Presidential Materials, NARA.
3. Davis, *Last Two Years*, 328.
4. Davis interview.
5. Duanne Clarridge, interview for the George Washington University National

Security Archive, "Backyard," *The Cold War*, CNN, February 21, 1999, http://www.gwu.edu/~narchiv/coldwar/interviews (accessed September 15, 2005).

6. Colin Powell, interview, *Youth Town Hall*, BET, February 20, 2003.
7. Wimert interview.
8. Helms, *A Look over My Shoulder*, 407–408.
9. NSC, National Security Decision Memorandum 40, in *FRUS, 1969–76*, vol. 2, doc. 203.
10. Handel, *Masters of War*, 310.
11. Rogers interview.
12. Handel, *Masters of War*, 310.
13. NSC, "Minutes of the 303 Committee Meeting," memorandum for the record, February 5, 1969, in *FRUS, 1969–76*, vol. 2, doc. 185.
14. Anonymous, letter to the author, April 2006.
15. Pape, "Constitutional Covert Actions," 59.

BIBLIOGRAPHY

UNPUBLISHED SOURCES

Interviews and Transcripts

The following interviews were conducted by the author:

Crimmins, John H. March 30, 2004.
Devine, Jack. March 1, 2004.
Kissinger, Henry A. March 5, 2004.
Long, William. February 2, 2007.
Otero, Miguel. May 12, 2003.
Rogers, William D. January 27, 2004.
Vaky, Viron P. February 4, 2004.

The dates of anonymous or off-the-record interviews are listed in applicable footnotes. At the request of the interviewees, no further information can be given.

Alessandri, Arturo. Interview for the George Washington University National Security Archive. "Backyard." *The Cold War*. CNN, February 21, 1999. http://www.gwu.edu/~nsarchiv/coldwar/interviews. Accessed August 15, 2006.

Claridge, Duane. Interview for the George Washington University National Security Archive. "Backyard." *The Cold War*. CNN, February 21, 1999. http://www.gwu.edu/~nsarchiv/coldwar/interviews. Accessed August 15, 2006.

Davis, Nathaniel. Interview for the George Washington University National Security Archive. "Backyard." *The Cold War*. CNN,

February 21, 1999. http://www.gwu.edu/~nsarchiv/coldwar/ interviews. Accessed August 15, 2006.
Kissinger, Henry A. Telephone transcripts. Transcripts of conversations between Dr. Kissinger and various members of the U.S. government provided by Arnold & Porter LLP, Washington, DC, with the permission of Dr. Kissinger. These have subsequently been released to the public.
Pavlov, Yuri. Interview for the George Washington University National Security Archive. "Backyard." *The Cold War*. CNN, February 21, 1999. http://www.gwu.edu/~nsarchiv/coldwar/interviews. Accessed August 15, 2006.
Wimert, Paul. Interview for the George Washington University National Security Archive. "Backyard." *The Cold War*. CNN, February 21, 1999. http://www.gwu.edu/~nsarchiv/coldwar/interviews. Accessed August 15, 2006.

U.S. & U.K. Government Declassified Documents

CAB 133. National Archives, Great Britain, Kew, Richmond, Surrey.
Central Foreign Policy Files, 1964–1966, Political and Defense. Record Group 59, General Records of the Department of State. U.S. National Archives and Records Administration, College Park, MD.
Central Foreign Policy Files, 1967–1969. Record Group 59, General Records of the Department of State. U.S. National Archives and Records Administration, College Park, MD.
Central Intelligence Agency. "Chile Collection," Tranches 1–3. *Chile Declassification Project*. http://foia.state.gov/SearchColls/CIA.asp.
Department of Defense. "Chile Collection," Tranches 1–3. *Chile Declassification Project*. http://www.foia.state.gov/SearchColls/DOD.asp. Accessed October 2002–August 2006.
EX CO 4 Chad, Republic of, Box 21. Lyndon Baines Johnson Presidential Library, Austin, TX.
FCO 7. National Archives, Great Britain, Kew, Richmond, Surrey.
Foreign Policy Files, Pol Chile, 1976–1982. Record Group 59, General Records of the Department of State. U.S. National Archives and Records Administration, College Park, MD.
Joint SRG-WSAG Meeting File. Nixon Presidential Materials. U.S. National Archives and Records Administration, College Park, MD.
Henry A. Kissinger Telephone Transcripts, Nixon Presidential Materials, U.S. National Archives and Records Administration, College Park, MD.
National Security Council. "Chile Collection," Tranches 2–3. *Chile*

Declassification Project. www.foia.state.gov/SearchColls/NSC.asp. Accessed July 25, 2005.

National Intelligence Estimates. Lyndon Baines Johnson Presidential Library, Austin, TX.

Nixon Daily Diaries. Nixon Presidential Materials. U.S. National Archives and Records Administration, College Park, MD.

NSC Institutional "H" Files, Meeting Files, 1969–1974. Nixon Presidential Materials. U.S. National Archives and Records Administration, College Park, MD.

National Security File, Agency Files and Country Files. Lyndon Baines Johnson Presidential Library, Austin, TX.

National Security File, Country File, Chile, vol. 1, Cables 1/64–8/64. Lyndon Baines Johnson Presidential Library, Austin, TX.

President's Appointment File. Lyndon Baines Johnson Presidential Library, Austin, TX.

State Department. "Chile Collection," Tranches 1–3. *Chile Declassification Project*. www.foia.state.gov. Accessed October 2002 to August 2006.

PUBLISHED SOURCES

U.S. Congressional Reports

U.S. Congress. House. Committee on Internal Security. *The Theory and Practice of Communism: Marxism Imposed on Chile—Allende Regime: Hearings before the Committee on Internal Security*. 93rd Cong., 1st sess., 1974.

U.S. Congress. House. Subcommittee on Inter-American Affairs. *The United States and Chile during the Allende Years, 1970–1973: Hearings before the Subcommittee on Inter-American Affairs of the Committee on Foreign Affairs*. 94th Cong., 1st sess., 1975.

U.S. Congress. Senate. Select Committee to Study Governmental Operations with Respect to Intelligence Activities. *Alledged Assassination Plots Involving Foreign Leaders*. 94th Cong., 1st sess., November 20, 1975, S. Rep. 94–465.

U.S. Congress. Senate. Select Committee to Study Governmental Operations with Respect to Intelligence Activities. *Covert Action in Chile, 1963–1973*. 94th Cong., 1st sess., 1975.

U.S. Congress. Senate. Subcommittee on Multinational Corporations. *The International Telephone and Telegraph Company and Chile, 1970–1971*. 93rd Cong., 1st sess., June 21, 1973.

Other Government Documents

Government of Chile. *Report of the Chilean National Commission on Truth and Reconciliation.* English edition of *Informe de la Comisión Nacional para la Verdad y Reconciliación*, February 1991. Notre Dame, IN: University of Notre Dame Press, 1993.

International Bank of Reconstruction and Development. "Notes Relating to Chile's Creditworthiness during the Administrations of Presidents Allende and Pinochet," *Inter-American Economic Affairs* 31: 2 (1977), 83–85.

John F. Kennedy, "Inaugural Address," in *Inaugural Addresses of the Presidents of the United States: From George Washington to George W. Bush*, 2nd ed. (Washington, DC: GPO, 1989).

Richard M. Nixon, Second Annual Report to the Congress on United States Foreign Policy, February 25, 1971.

Colin Powell, interview, *Youth Town Hall*, Black Entertainment Television, February 20, 2003.

Secretariat General of the Government of Chile. *White Book of the Change of Government in Chile.* Santiago: Government of Chile, 1973.

Unidad Popular. *Programa Básico de Gobierno de la Unidad Popular*, 4th ed. Santiago: Impresa Horizonte, 1970.

U.S. Department of State. *Cuba; American Republics.* Vol. 12 of *Foreign Relations of the United States, 1961–63.* Microfiche supplement. Washington, DC: U.S. GPO, 1998.

U.S. Department of State. *Organization and Management of U.S. Foreign Policy, 1969–72.* Vol. 2 of *Foreign Relations of the United States, 1969–76.* Washington, DC: U.S. GPO, 2006.

U.S. Department of State. *South and Central America; Mexico.* Vol. 31 of *Foreign Relations of the United States, 1964–68.* Washington, DC: U.S. GPO, 2004.

USSR Communist Party Central Committee and USSR Foreign Minister, "Chile en Los Archivos de la URSS (1959–1973)," *Éstudios Públicos* 72 (Spring 1998), 391–475.

Caspar W. Weinberger, "The Uses of Power," remarks presented to the National Press Club, Washington DC, November 28, 1984.

World Bank. "Chile and the World Bank," *Inter-American Economic Affairs* 30: 2 (1976), 81–91.

Memoirs

Allende Gossens, Salvador. *Chile's Road to Socialism.* Baltimore: Penguin Books, 1973.

Almeyda M., Clodimiro. *Reencuento con mi Vida*. Mexico: Universidad de Guadalajara, 1988.

Anderson, Jack. *The Anderson Papers*. With George Clifford. London: Millington, 1974.

Colby, William, and Peter Forbath. *Honorable Men: My Life in the CIA*. New York: Simon & Schuster, 1978.

Corvalán, Luis. *Algo de mi Vida*. Barcelona: Editorial Crítica, 1978.

Davis, Nathaniel. *The Last Two Years of Salvador Allende*. Ithaca, NY: Cornell University Press, 1988.

Debray, Régis. *The Chilean Revolution: Conversations with Allende*. New York: Pantheon Books, 1971.

Edwards, Jorge. *Persona Non Grata: An Envoy in Castro's Cuba*. London: Bodley Head, 1976.

Helms, Richard. *A Look over My Shoulder: A Life in the Central Intelligence Agency*. With William Hood. New York: Random House, 2003.

Kissinger, Henry A. *White House Years*. Boston: Little, Brown, 1979.

———. *Years of Upheaval*. Boston: Little, Brown, 1982.

Leonov, Nikolai. *Likholetye*. Moscow: Mezhdunarodnye Otnosheniya, 2000.

Meyer, Cord. *Facing Reality: From World Federalism to the CIA*. New York: Harper & Row, 1980.

Nixon, Richard M. *RN: The Memoirs of Richard Nixon*. New York: Grosset and Dunlap, 1978.

Onofre Jarpa, Sergio. *Confesiones Políticas*. Edited by Patricia Arancibia, Claudia Arancibia, and Isabel de la Maza. Santiago: Tercera-Mandadori, 2002.

Phillips, David Atlee. *The Night Watch: 20 Years of Peculiar Service*. New York: Atheneum, 1977.

Pinochet Ugarte, Augusto. *The Crucial Day: September 11, 1973*. Santiago: Editorial Renacimiento, 1982.

Prats González, Carlos. *Memorias: Testimonio de Un Soldado*. Santiago: Pehuén Editores Ltda, 1985.

———. *Una Vida Por La Legalidad*. Mexico: Fondo de Cultura Económica, 1976.

Shackley, Ted. *Spymaster: My Life in the CIA*. With Richard A. Finney. Washington, DC: Potomac Books, 2005.

Secondary Works

Andrew, Christopher. *For the President's Eyes Only: Secret Intelligence and the American Presidency from Washington to Bush*. New York: HarperCollins, 1995.

Andrew, Christopher, and Vasili Mitrokhin. *The Mitrokhin Archive II: The KGB in the World*. London: Allen Lane, 2005.

Berman, Paul. *Terror and Liberalism*. New York: Norton, 2004.

Blum, William. *Killing Hope: U.S. Military and CIA Interventions since World War II*. Monroe, ME: Common Courage Press, 1995.

Bobbitt, Philip K. *The Shield of Achilles: War, Peace and the Course of History*. London: Allen Lane, 2002.

Boulton, David. *The Lockheed Papers*. London: J. Cape, 1978.

Camus, Ignacio González. *El Dia En Que Murio Allende*. Santiago: Cesoc, 1988.

Chomsky, Noam. *The Washington Connection and Third World Fascism: The Political Economy of Human Rights*. Boston: South End Press, 1979.

Constable, Pamela, and Arturo Valenzuela. *A Nation of Enemies: Chile under Pinochet*. New York: Norton, 1991.

Corn, David. *Blond Ghost: Ted Shackley and the CIA's Crusades*. New York: Simon & Schuster, 1994.

Cox, Michael, G. John Ikenberry, and Takashi Inoguchi, eds. *American Democracy Promotion: Impulses, Strategies, and Impacts*. Oxford: Oxford University Press, 2000.

Dinges, John. *The Condor Years: How Pinochet and His Allies Brought Terrorism to Three Continents*. New York: New Press, 2004.

Eastman, Jorge Mario. *De Allende y Pinochet al "Milagro" Chileno*. Santafé de Bogotá: Editorial Ariel, 1997.

Falcoff, Mark. *Modern Chile 1970–1989: A Critical History*. London: Transaction Publishers, 1989.

Faúndez, Julio. *Marxism and Democracy in Chile: From 1932 to the Fall of Allende*. New Haven, CT: Yale University Press, 1988.

Fermandois, Joaquín. *Chile y El Mundo 1970–1973*. Santiago: Ediciones Universidad Católico de Chile, 1985.

Figueroa, Andrea Ruiz-Esquide. *Las Fuerzas Armadas Durante Los Gobiernos de Eduardo Frei y Salvador Allende*. Santiago: Centro de Estudios del Desarrollo, 1993.

Garcés, Joan E. *El Estado y los Problemas Tácticos En El Gobierno De Allende*. Madrid: Siglo XXI de España Editores, 1974.

Gil, F. G., and C. J. Parish. *The Chilean Presidential Election of September 4, 1964*. 2 vols. Washington, DC: Institute for the Comparative Study of Political Systems, 1965.

González, Mónica. *Chile La Conjura: Los Mil y Un Dias Del Golpe*. Santiago: Ediciones B Grupo Zeta, 2000.

Handel, Michael. *Masters of War: Classical Strategic Thought*. London: Frank Cass, 1992.

Haslam, Jonathan. *The Nixon Administration and the Death of Allende's Chile: A Case of Assisted Suicide*. New York: Verso, 2005.

Helgerson, John L. *Getting to Know the President: CIA Briefings of Presidential Candidates, 1952–1992*. Washington, DC: Center for the Study of Intelligence, Central Intelligence Agency , 1996.

Hersh, Seymour M. *The Price of Power: Kissinger in the Nixon White House*. New York: Summit Books, 1983.

Hogan, Michael J. *The Ambiguous Legacy: U.S. Foreign Relations in the American Century*. Cambridge: Cambridge University Press, 1999.

Holt, Pat M. *Secret Intelligence and Public Policy: A Dilemma of Democracy*. Washington, DC: Congressional Quarterly, 1995.

Horne, Alistair. *Small Earthquake in Chile: A Visit to Allende's South America*. London: Macmillan, 1972.

Hosmer, Stephen T. *Operations against Enemy Leaders*. Santa Monica, CA: Rand, 2001.

International Telephone and Telegraph Corporation. *Subversion in Chile: A Case Study in U.S. Corporate Intrigue in the Third World*. Nottingham: Bertrand Russell Peace Foundation, 1972.

Kalfon, Pierre. *Allende: Chile, 1970–1973*. Paris: Atlantica, 1998.

Kolko, Gabriel. *Confronting the Third World: United States Foreign Policy, 1945–1980*. New York: Pantheon Books, 1988.

Kornbluh, Peter. *The Pinochet File: A Declassified Dossier on Atrocity and Accountability*. New York: New Press, 2003.

Labarca Goddard, Eduardo. *Chile Invadido: Reportaje a la Intromisión Extranjera*. Santiago: Editora Austral, 1968.

Labin, Suzanne. *Chile: The Crime of Resistance*. Surrey, UK: Foreign Affairs Publishing, 1982.

Larteguy, Jean. *The Guerilla*. New York: World Publishing Company, 1970.

Leary, William M. *The Central Intelligence Agency: History and Documents*. Tuscaloosa: University of Alabama Press, 1984.

Lineberry, William P. *The United States in World Affairs, 1970*. New York: Simon & Schuster, 1972.

Lowenthal, Abraham F., ed. *Exporting Democracy: The United States and Latin America*. Baltimore: Johns Hopkins University Press, 1991.

Lowenthal, Abraham F., and J. Samuel Fitch, eds. *Armies and Politics in Latin America*. New York: Holmes & Meier, 1986.

Miller, Nicola. *Soviet Relations with Latin America, 1959–1987*. Cambridge: Cambridge University Press, 1989.

Morgan, Iwan. *Nixon*. London: Arnold, 2002.

Mujal-León, Eusebio. *The USSR and Latin America: A Developing Relationship*. Boston: Unwin Hyman, 1989.

Orrego Vicuña, Francisco, ed. *Chile: The Balanced View*. Santiago: University of Chile, Institute of International Studies, 1975.

Petras, James and Morris Morley, *The United States and Chile: Imperialism and the Overthrow of the Allende Government*. New York: Monthly Review Press, 1975.

Prados, John. *Lost Crusader: The Secret Wars of CIA Director William Colby*. New York: Oxford University Press, 2003.

Retamal Avila, Julio. *Aylwin: La Palabra de un Democrata*. Santiago de Chile: Editorial Planeta Chilena, 1990.

Robinson, William I. *Promoting Polyarchy: Globalization, U.S. Intervention, and Hegemony*. Cambridge: Cambridge University Press, 1996.

Sater, William F. *Chile and the United States: Empires in Conflict*. Athens: University of Georgia Press, 1990.

Schlesinger, Arthur M. *The Imperial Presidency*. Boston: Houghton Mifflin, 1973.

Schoultz, Lars. *National Security and United States Policy toward Latin America*. Princeton: Princeton University Press, 1987.

Sigmund, Paul. *The Overthrow of Allende and the Politics of Chile 1964–1976*. Pittsburgh: University of Pittsburgh Press, 1977.

Small, Melvin. *The Presidency of Richard Nixon*. Lawrence: University of Kansas Press, 1999.

Smirnow, Gabriel. *The Revolution Disarmed: Chile, 1970–1973*. New York: Monthly Review Press, 1979.

Snider, L. Britt. *Sharing Secrets with Lawmakers: Congress as a User of Intelligence*. Langley, VA: Center for the Study of Intelligence, 1997.

Spooner, Mary Helen. *Soldiers in a Narrow Land: The Pinochet Regime in Chile*. Berkeley: University of California Press, 1999.

Summers, Anthony. *The Arrogance of Power: The Secret World of Richard Nixon*. London: Victor Gollancz, 2000.

Theberge, James D. *The Soviet Presence in Latin America*. New York: Crane, Russak, 1974.

Thomas, Evan. *The Very Best Men: Four Who Dared: The Early Years of the CIA*. New York: Simon & Schuster, 1995.

Tucker, Robert W. *The Purposes of American Power: An Essay on National Security*. New York: Praeger Press, 1981.

Valenzuela, Arturo. *The Breakdown of Democratic Regimes: Chile*. Baltimore: Johns Hopkins University Press, 1978.

Varas, Augusto. *Los Militares En El Poder: Regimen y Gobierno Militar En Chile, 1973–1986*. Santiago de Chile: Pehuen/FLACSO, 1987.

Vitale, Luis, et al. *Para Recuperar La Memoria Histórica: Frei, Allende y Pinochet*. Santiago: Ediciones ChileAmérica-CESOC, 1999.

Warner, Michael, ed. *Central Intelligence: Origin and Evolution*. Washington, DC: U.S. GPO, 2001.

Whelan, James R. *Out of the Ashes: Life, Death and Transfiguration of Democracy in Chile, 1883–1988*. Washington, DC: Regnery Gateway, 1989.

ARTICLES

Anderson, Jack. *The Washington Merry-Go-Round* (syndicated column, U.S.), February–May 1972.

Benjamin, Daniel. "Rendition at Risk," *Slate*, February 5, 2007, at http://www.slate.com, accessed February 5, 2007.

CNN, "Backyard," The Cold War, CNN, February 21, 1999, http://www.cnn.com /SPECIALS/cold.war/episodes/18/script.html (accessed July 12, 2006).

Dahl, Victor C. "The Soviet Bloc Response to the Downfall of Salvador Allende."*Inter-American Economic Affairs* 30: 2 (1976): 30–47.

Davis, Harold Eugene. "The Presidency in Chile." *Presidential Studies Quarterly* 15: 4 (1985): 707–724.

del Rio, J. Biehl, and Gonzalo Fernández R. "The Political Pre-requisites for a Chilean Way." *Government and Opposition* 7: 3 (1972): 305–326.

Fagen, Richard R. "The United States and Chile: Roots and Branches." *Foreign Affairs*, Vol. 53: 2 (January 1975): 297–313.

Falcoff, Mark. "Reviews." *Orbis* 21: 1 (1977): 429–439.

Fediakova, Eugenia, et al. "El General Nikolai Leonov en El CEP." *Éstudios Públicos* 73 (Summer 1999): 1–37.

Fermandois, Joaquín. "Pawn or Player? Chile in the Cold War." *Éstudios Públicos* 72 (Spring 1998): 1–23.

Freedman, Lawrence. "Strategic Studies and the Problems of Power." In Lawrence Freedman, Paul Hayes, and Robert O'Neill, eds. *War, Strategy, and International Politics: Essays in Honour of Sir Michael Howard*. Oxford: Clarendon Press, 1992.

Goldberg, Peter A. "The Politics of the Allende Overthrow in Chile." *Political Science Quarterly* 90: 1 (1975): 93–116.

Goldwater, Barry. "On 'Covert Action in Chile, 1963–1973': A Response to the Church Committee Report." *Inter-American Economic Affairs* 30: 1 (Summer 1976): 85–95.

Grey, Stephen and Don Van Natta. "Thirteen with the CIA Sought by Italy in a Kidnapping," *New York Times*, June 25, 2005.

Harmer, Tanya. "Neutralizing the Threat: Allende's Chile, the United States, and Regional Alignments in Latin America." May 2005. http://www.lse.ac.uk/collections/CWSC/pdf/cambridge_lse_May_2005/Harmer_Paper.doc. Accessed August 4, 2005.

Helwege, Ann. "Three Socialist Experiments in Latin America: Surviving U.S. Economic Pressure." *Bulletin of Latin American Research* 8: 2 (1989): 211–234.

Hersh, Seymour M. "The Coming Wars: What the Pentagon Can Now Do in Secret." *New Yorker*, January 24, 2005, at www.newyorker.com, accessed August 10, 2005.

Hitchens, Christopher. "The Case against Henry Kissinger, Part 1: The Making of a War Criminal." *Harper's Magazine*, February 2001: 33–58.

———. "The Case against Henry Kissinger, Part 2: Crimes against Humanity." *Harper's Magazine*, March 2001: 49–74.

Hudson, Rexford A. "The Role of Constitutional Conflict over Nationalization in the Downfall of Salvador Allende." *Inter-American Economic Affairs* 31: 4 (1978): 63–79.

Johnson, Loch K. "On Drawing a Bright Line for Covert Operation," *American Journal of International Law* 86: 2 (April 1992).

Knudson, Jerry W. "Allende to Pinochet: Crucible of the Chilean Press, 1970–1984." *Studies in Latin American Popular Culture* 6 (1987): 43–53.

Korry, Edward M. "The USA-in-Chile and Chile-in-USA" (also "Los Estados Unidos en Chile y Chile en Estados Unidos"). *Éstudios Públicos* 72 (Spring 1998): 17–74.

Korry, Edward M., Joaquín Fermandois, and Arturo Fontaine Talavera, "El Embajador Edward M. Korry en el CEP," *Éstudios Públicos* 72 (Spring 1998): 75–112.

Leonov, Nikolai. "La Intelligencia Soviética En América Latina Durante La Guerra Fría." *Éstudios Públicos* 73 (Summer 1999): 31–63.

Leonov, Nikolai and Eugenia Fediakova, Joaquín Fermandois, Arturo Fontaine Talavera, David Gallagher, Emilio Meneses, and Olga Uliánova, "El General Nikolai Leonov En El CEP." *Estudios Públicos* 73 (Summer 1999): 65–102.

Maxwell, Kenneth. "The Other 9/11: The United States and Chile, 1973." *Foreign Affairs* 82: 6 (2003): 147–151.

Merom, Gil. "Democracy, Dependency, and Destabilization: The Shaking of the Allende Regime." *Political Science Quarterly* 105: 1 (1990): 75–95.

Michaels, Albert L. "Background to a Coup: Civil-Military Relations in Twentieth Century Chile and the Overthrow of Salvador Allende." Paper presented at the State University of New York–Buffalo, October 19, 1974.

James E. Miller, "Taking Off the Gloves: The United States and the Italian Elections of 1948," *Diplomatic History* 7: 1.

Mistry, Kaeten. "The Case for Political Warfare: Strategy, Organization and US Involvement in the 1948 Italian Election." *Cold War History* 6: 3 (August 2006), 301–329.

Morley, Morris, and Steven Smith. "Imperial 'Reach': U.S. Policy and the CIA in Chile." *Journal of Political and Military Sociology* 5: 2 (1977), 278–309.

Nogee, Joseph L., and John W. Sloan. "Allende's Chile and the Soviet Union: A Policy Lesson for Latin American Nations Seeking Autonomy." *Journal of Interamerican Studies and World Affairs* 21: 3 (1979), 339–368.

Pape, Matthew S. "Constitutional Covert Actions: A Force Multiplier for Pre-emption." *Military Review*, March–April 2004, 52–59.

Pérez, Cristián. "Salvador Allende, Apuntes Sobre Su Dispositivo De Seguridad: El Grupo De Amigos Personales (GAP)." *Éstudios Públicos* 79 (Winter 2000), 31–81.

Pessen, Edward. "Appraising American Cold War Policy by Its Means of Implementation." *Reviews in American History* 18: 4 (1990), 453–469.

Pinochet, Augusto. "Discurso de Chacarillas: 9 de Julio de 1977," *Centro de Estudios Bicentenario Chile 1810–2010*, www.bicentenario chile.cl (accessed August 2006).

Powers, Thomas. "Inside the Department of Dirty Tricks." *Atlantic* 244: 2 (August 1979), 33–64.

Rogers, William D., and Kenneth Maxwell. "Fleeing the Chilean Coup: The Debate over U.S. Complicity." *Foreign Affairs* 83: 1 (2004), 160–165.

Soto, Ángel, and Marco Fernández. "El Pensimiento Político de la Derecha Chilena en los '60: El Partido Nacional." *Bicentenario* 1: 2 (2002), 87–116.

Time, "ITT's Big Conglomorate of Troubles," May 1, 1971. Accessed at www.time.com on June 5, 2007.

Uliánova, Olga. "La Unidad Popular y El Golpe Militar En Chile: Percepciones y Análisis Soviéticos." *Éstudios Públicos* 79 (Winter 2000), 1–89.

Uliánova, Olga, and Eugenia Fediakova. "Aspects of Financial Aid to Chilean Communism from the USSR Communist Party during the Cold War." *Éstudios Públicos* 72 (Spring 1998), 83–171.

Zemelman, H., and Patricio Leon. "Political Opposition to the Government of Allende." *Government and Opposition* 7: 3 (1972), 327–350.

Newspapers

El Mercurio, August 1968–December 1974.

Washington Post, August 1970–December 1974.

New York Times, August 1970–December 1974.

INDEX

ABOUT THE AUTHOR

KRISTIAN GUSTAFSON served as an officer in the Canadian army for six years and later earned his doctorate in history at the University of Cambridge. He was previously a senior lecturer of war studies at the Royal Military Academy Sandhurst in England. He is now a lecturer at Brunel University's Centre for Intelligence and Security Studies in London, and he lives in Reading, England, and Edmonton, Canada.